Birds of the Untamed West:

The History of Birdlife in Nebraska, 1750 to 1875

by

James E. Ducey

Making History
Omaha, Nebraska
2000

BIRDS OF THE UNTAMED WEST: THE HISTORY OF BIRDLIFE IN NEBRASKA, 1750 TO 1875
Copyright ©2000 by James E. Ducey

All rights reserved. No part of this book may be used or reproduced in any manner whatsoever without written permission from the author, except in the case of brief quotations embodied in critical articles or reviews. For reproduction permission or current ordering information, write *Making History*, 2415 North 56th Street, Omaha, Nebraska 68104, or call 402-551-0747.

First printing, 2000.
Cover design, page layout and typesetting by *Making History*.

Front cover: "Sandhill Cranes," by Titian Ramsay Peale *(courtesy American Philosophical Society, Philadelphia, Pennsylvania; B/P31.15d/#88)*.
Back cover: Sioux war club with stone head and eagle feathers *(courtesy Agate Fossil Beds National Monument, Gering, Nebraska)*.

ISBN 0-9631699-5-5 $25.00

TABLE OF CONTENTS

Illustrations vii

Introduction 1

Chapter One: Birds and Nebraska's Native Americans 7
Native Americans and Birds 7; Nebraska Indian Tribes 9; The Winnebago Nation 12; The Omaha Tribe 14; Omaha Pipestems 17; Omaha Sacred Packs of War 20; Omaha War Honor Decorations 21; An Omaha Tribal Game 23; The Ponca Tribe 24; The Otoe and Missouria Tribes 26; The Sioux Tribes 26; Teton Sioux Music 27; Lakota Myth 29; Sioux Artifacts 30; The Pawnee Tribe 33; The Pawnee Use of Birds 33; A Pawnee Spiritual Drum 37; A Sacred Family Bundle 37; The Role of Birds in Pawnee Myths 38; The Pawnee Hako Ceremony 41; Pawnee Pipestems 44; Pawnee Indian Cosmology 45; Arrow-making by the Pawnee 46; Bird Quillwork 47; Birds in the Languages of the Plains Indians 48; Native American Bird Sign Language 55

Chapter Two: Historic Explorations and Accounts of Birdlife in Nebraska 59
Tabeau to the Upper Missouri 63; The Lewis and Clark Expedition 64; The Astor Party of 1810-11 68; Brackenridge's Trip in 1811 68; Stuart's Journey of Discovery 68; The Major Long Expedition 69; The Wilhelm Journey 71; Catlin along the Middle Missouri 72; The Expedition of Prince Maximilian 73; Townsend's Journey across the Rocky Mountains 78; Notes from the Presbyterian Mission 79; Journeys to the Rocky Mountains 79; The Scientific Explorations of Nicollet 80; E. Willard Smith along the Platte River 80; A Tour to the Oregon Territory 81; Frémont in 1842 81; Audubon's Expedition 81; Carleton on an Army Journey 87; The Travels of Father DeSmet 90; The Oregon and Mormon Trails 92; Culbertson's Journey 96; Rudolph Friederich Kurz's Exploration 96; The Warren Expedition 97; The Journal of Mollie Dorsey Sanford 100; Naturalist George Suckley 102; The Fort Laramie

Area 102; A Sand Hills Bone Hunt 103; The Niobrara Expedition of 1873 104; Birds of the Northwest Territory 104; Notes on the Food of Birds of Nebraska 105; Reconnaissance to the Black Hills 106; Miscellaneous Notes from the 1870s 106; Pioneers Settling the Wild Prairie 110

Chapter Three: Bird Habitats from 1750 to 1875 113
The Missouri River 113; Southeast Nebraska 120; The Platte River Valley 120; The Rainwater Basin 121; The Loup Fork 121; The Sand Hills 122; The Niobrara River Valley 124; The Pine Ridge 125; Saline Wetlands 126; The Vegetation of Nebraska circa 1850 126; General Land Office Survey Maps 128

Chapter Four: Birdlife of Historic Nebraska 129
Bird Families 130; Species Analysis 131; Raptors 133; Shore Birds 133; Warblers 134; The Historic Nebraska Bird List 135; The Omaha Tribe 136; The Pawnee Tribe 137; The Sioux Tribes 137; Tabeau on the Upper Missouri 138; The Lewis and Clark Expedition 138; Henry Brackenridge's Expedition 139; The Major Long Expedition 139; The Expedition of Prince Maximilian 139; Townsend across the Rocky Mountains 140; The Audubon Expedition 140; The Warren Expedition 141; Naturalist George Suckley 142; Birds of the Northwest 142; Notes on the Food of Birds of Nebraska 142; Miscellaneous Notes from the 1870s 144; Species by Region 144; The Missouri River Species 145; The Fort Randall Military Reservation Species 146; The Platte River Species 146; The Loup Fork Species 147; Sand Hills Species 148; Pine Ridge Species 150; Birds as Sustenance for Indians 151; Birds as Sustenance at Trading Posts 152

Chapter Five: List of Species 155
Family Gaviidae 156; Family Podicipedidae 156; Family Pelecanidae 156; Family Phalacrocoracidae 157; Family Ardeidae 157; Family Anatidae 159; Family Cathartidae 169; Family Accipitridae 170; Family Falconidae 175; Family Phasianidae 177; Family Rallidae 183; Family Gruidae 184; Family Charadriidae 186;

Family Recurvirostridae 188; Family Scolopacidae 188; Family Laridae 195; Family Columbidae 199; Family Psittacidae 200; Family Cuculidae 202; Family Tytonidae 202; Family Strigidae 202; Family Caprimulgidae 206; Family Apodidae 208; Family Trochilidae 208; Family Alcedinidae 209; Family Picidae 209; Family Tyrannidae 213; Family Alaudidae 216; Family Hirundinidae 216; Family Corvidae 221; Family Paridae 225; Family Sittidae 226; Family Certhiidae 226; Family Troglodytidae 227; Family Muscicapidae 229; Family Mimidae 232; Family Motacillidae 234; Family Bombycillidae 234; Family Laniidae 234; Family Vireonidae 235; Family Emberizidae 236; Family Fringillidae 265

Conclusion 267

Bibliography 269

Index 283

ILLUSTRATIONS

Page	Illustration and Source
8	Historic Nebraska locations
11	Punka Indians Encamped on the Banks of the Missouri, after a painting by Karl Bodmer, *courtesy Joslyn Art Museum, Omaha, Nebraska; gift of the Enron Art Foundation*
16	Omaha dance bustle ornament, *courtesy Nebraska State Historical Society, Lincoln, Nebraska*
24	Hidatsa pit for trapping eagles, *courtesy American Museum of Natural History, Washington, D.C.*
30	Sioux war club with stone head and eagle feathers, *courtesy Agate Fossil Beds National Monument, Gering, Nebraska*
31	Sioux eagle-bone whistle (l.) and Mandan eagle-bone whistle (r.), *courtesy Linden-Museum, Stuttgart, Germany (Inv. no. 12,575, photo by Ursula Didoni)*
32	Oglala Sioux eagle-feather bonnet, *courtesy Linden-Museum*
33	Sioux claw-shaped pipe bowl carved in catlinite, *courtesy Agate Fossil Beds National Monument*
34	Pawnee shield with feathers, *courtesy Department of Library Services, American Museum of Natural History, New York, New York (Neg. no. 31277, photo by R. E. Dahlgren)*
37	Sketch of a Pawnee spiritual drum, *held in The Field Museum of Natural History, Chicago, Illinois*
47	Santee Sioux bird-quill knife case, *courtesy The Field Museum of Natural History*
56	Lakota wooden pipe with Mallard neck feathers, *courtesy Agate Fossil Beds National Monument*
65	Lewis and Clark's map of the Missouri River, August 1804, *courtesy Joslyn Art Museum*
66	Nodaway Island, by Karl Bodmer, *courtesy Joslyn Art Museum; gift of the Enron Art Foundation*
70	Map of Country drained by the Mississippi by Maj. Stephen H. Long, 1823, *courtesy Geography and Map Division, Library of Congress, Washington, D.C.*
72	Canoes Traveling Near Bellevue, by George Catlin, *courtesy National Museum of American Art, Smithsonian Institution, Washington, D.C.*
75	Washinga Sahba's Grave on Blackbird's Hills, after a painting by Karl Bodmer, *courtesy Joslyn Art Museum; gift of the Enron Art Foundation*

84	Mouth of the Big Sioux River, by Karl Bodmer, *courtesy Joslyn Art Museum; gift of the Enron Art Foundation*
94	The Grand Island, as depicted on the Topographical Map of the Road from Missouri to Oregon, by Charles Preuss, 1846, *courtesy Nebraska State Historical Society*
98	Map of Nebraska and Kansas Territories, by Capt. Seth Eastman, 1854, *courtesy National Archives, Washington, D.C.*
107	Nebraska General Land Office Map, 1876, *courtesy the Rare Book Room, Library of Congress*
115	The Missouri below the Mouth of the Platte, by Karl Bodmer, *courtesy Joslyn Art Museum; gift of the Enron Art Foundation*
118	Snags on the Missouri, by Karl Bodmer, *courtesy Joslyn Art Museum; gift of the Enron Art Foundation*
164	Wood-duck at Engineer Cantonment, by Titian Ramsay Peale, *courtesy American Philosophical Society (B/P31.15d/#89)*
197	Least Tern, by Titian Ramsay Peale, *courtesy American Philosophical Society (B/P31.15d/#37)*
205	Burrowing Owl, by Titian Ramsay Peale, *courtesy American Philosophical Society (B/P31.15d/#119)*
219	Cliff Sparrows [Swallows], by Titian Ramsay Peale, *courtesy American Philosophical Society (B/P31.15d/#108)*
222	Magpie, by Titian Ramsay Peale, *courtesy American Philosophical Society (B/P31.15d/#103)*
248	Sparrow at Engineer Cantonment, by Titian Ramsay Peale, *courtesy American Philosophical Society (B/P31.15d/#84)*
251	Grasshopper Sparrow, by John James Audubon, *courtesy New-York Historical Society, New York, New York (1863.17.130)*
256	Chestnut-collared Lark-Bunting [Longspur], by John James Audubon, *courtesy New-York Historical Society (1863.17.394)*
257	Blackbird, by Titian Ramsay Peale, *courtesy American Philosophical Society (B/P31.15d/#95)*
260	Meadow Lark, by John James Audubon, *courtesy New-York Historical Society (1863.17.136)*

INTRODUCTION

The birds of historic Nebraska from 1750 to 1875 lived in a wilderness of prairies, plains, forests, wetlands and rivers. There were Trumpeter Swans in the lakes of the Sand Hills. Carolina Parakeets and Bald Eagles nested along the Missouri River. Colorful and obvious, birds played a large role in and were remembered through Native American tribal myths. Following the first explorations by fur traders after 1700, birds were noted in government and private expedition reports, personal letters, and scientific studies on ethnology and anthropology throughout the period from 1750 to 1875. Other historic notes mention the birds and animals seen in the area by Euro-Americans in summer camps or moving west in wagon trains along the Oregon Trail. Taken together, these oral and written sources reveal the character of the bird life in what would become the state of Nebraska when it was wild and being tamed by settlers.

Native Americans, whether nomadic or settled in scattered villages, were the first to become familiar with the birdlife of the Plains. As the Winged Ones, birds were spiritual creatures who often figured in tribal myths, lore and ceremony of the Omaha, the Pawnee, the Santee and Teton Sioux and other people of the region. These myths and uses of bird material reveal the first knowledge of the birds of modern-day Nebraska. Today a rich variety of records—oral, ceremonial, artifactual and historical—contain information about the relationship between Native Americans and the birds around them. These records tell us that birds were mythologically important for Native Americans who lived in what today is the state of Nebraska, that birds were an important food source for them, that tribal history and life were linked closely to the yearly cycles of migratory and breeding birds, that bird parts and feathers formed a prominent part of ceremonial clothing and objects, such as pipes, and that those objects often were patterned after birds.

The western lands were still wilderness when Native American tribes freely moved around their territories on the Plains. When these people later were moved to reservations, written records were made of oral traditions. These records are very valuable today, for without them and their interpretation, much of the lore surrounding birds would have been lost to scholars and others studying the history of the Native American tribes. More recently, archaeological studies have analyzed relics uncovered at tribal camps and villages and provided more information about the connection between Native Americans and the birds around them.

The Plains that were so well known to the Native Americans were discovered and then invaded by an expanding European population in the 1800s. Beginning in the early 1700s, fur traders used the abundant natural resources of the region. After them, the first Euro-American explorers of the Missouri and Platte rivers studied the area's land features, flora, birds and other animals.

The first known written record of birdlife in the area of the Plains that became Nebraska are the notes of Pierre Tabeâu, who made his journey in 1803. The following year, famed explorers Capt. Meriwether Lewis and Capt. William Clark explored the Nebraska area, which was part of the United States' new Louisiana Purchase.

Different expeditions traveled through the region at least once a decade after Lewis and Clark reported on it, and explorations became more frequent near the middle of the nineteenth century. As they traveled across the area, these explorers—whether U.S. citizens or foreign visitors, government- or privately-sponsored—often compiled species lists, gathered specimens, and noted where a specimen was collected or a particular bird was seen. In general, journeys to new territories did not allow time to linger or make a basic survey of a place, but still most explorers and expeditions made notes and comments on the birds they saw while riding through a region during their season's travels. These records document where various birds were seen and perhaps nested in the summer, well before extensive settlement and development of farms and towns began in the region. Occasionally the explorers recorded more detail on avian life history. The 1819-20 winter stay at the Engineer Cantonment north of present-day Omaha and Dr. Ferdinand V. Hayden's work in the mid-1850s are such exceptions to the general rule.

Both the Native American sources mentioned above and records from the historic period, especially after 1800, provide information which we can compare to recent records. The comparison illuminates how birdlife changed as the land changed from wilderness to farmland, town and city. The material also provides a better understanding of the role bird lore and study played in the early history of Nebraska and in the natural history of the Great Plains. Whatever its source or date, each and every record contributes to a general perspective on birds of Nebraska.

This review of the bird life of Nebraska from 1750 to 1875 relies on material taken from anthropological studies, archaeological digs, expedition reports, personal journals and a variety of other documents.

Several recent studies and written narratives on Great Plains history have helped provide current annotated journals. A number of newly-edited and documented versions of historic journals have been especially helpful. The Lewis and Clark journals recently have been re-edited and republished, incorporating an extensive amount of information that was not available when they first were published (Moulton 1986, 1987). A revised edition of the journals of the German Prince Maximilian of Wied includes many of the detailed and vivid notes he made in 1833 and 1834 (Orr and Porter 1983). The journals of John James Audubon describe the events during the days when he heard and then named the Western Meadowlark, which became the state bird of Nebraska. Other studies also provide source material which allows evaluation of bird sightings within the context of a journey, rather than as an item on an expedition list of natural history material.

Much of the material used here is in the collections of the University of Nebraska libraries in Lincoln, Nebraska. The libraries have many government publications describing Native American lore and history, especially journals from the American Museum of Natural History. The original Maximilian journals and art by Karl Bodmer are in the archives at the Joslyn Art Museum in Omaha, Nebraska. The Nebraska State Historical Society and University of Nebraska-Lincoln also have published several works describing the presence of bird bones in anthropological digs, mostly in the eastern part of the state.

In this study, each bird reference found was reviewed in detail and pertinent information concerning the bird life of the area was extracted. Outmoded bird names given in these sources were compared to publications from the period (e.g., Coues 1874) and other turn-of-the-century sources, and the species then was classified according to current nomenclature. The original source materials then were summarized Particular attention was paid to notes on species occurrence and status in order to present a view of the historic birdlife.

Where appropriate, excerpts from the original sources have been included in this work, and these retain their original spelling punctuation, capitalization and so forth. These extracts focus on the bird notes, but they do not attempt to present the complete tribal tale or the daily events given in the expedition narrative. Since it occasionally was difficult to decide which notes and details were most interesting in the original narratives, the information presented here should be considered an introduction to the rich, vivid and inspiring writings and illustrations on birds in Nebraska. To gain a fuller picture, readers are urged to go to the original sources. They provide an insight and understanding far beyond what a summary work can present.

The sightings noted in the original records have been traced in this study to a specific present-day county, whenever possible. Along the Missouri River, the county of record usually can be determined by using maps of the river. Landmarks, when noted here, are given as a location within political boundaries that were established on the first detailed maps of the Missouri River region (Missouri River Commission 1895). Other sighting locations were found by noting prominent sites on early Plains maps.

This study documents and illustrates the birdlife on the prairie and plains of modern-day Nebraska between 1750 and 1875. Comparing this record to the current condition of birdlife in Nebraska indicates that many changes have taken place in the state's birdlife since 1750. Current information can be found in sources such as my *Nebraska Birds: Breeding Status and Distribution* (Ducey 1988).

Most of the Plains has changed due to human settlement, land changes and other developments during the 120 years since 1875, and this partially is responsible for continuous changes in the birdlife of Nebraska. The habitat for birds will be influenced even more by human impact on the environment in the next hundred years. Obvious changes in distribution, as well as declines and increases in species ranges, have occurred since the sightings of birds made before 1875. Some species have become lost as breeding birds; others have had their ranges reduced. Some birds have become extinct, and other species may be only seasonal migrants, whereas a century and a half ago they nested in the Nebraska region. Others that still return to nest here each year now may have a smaller range of suitable habitat where they can raise young. For woodland species the increase of trees in the region's grassland has provided more nesting areas and resulted in an increased range of distribution.

The primary intent of this work is to provide a single source of historical information on the birdlife of just one portion of the Plains. I hope this goal has been accomplished. However, there likely are some unknown references to Nebraska's historic bird life that I have not seen: a journal or letter from the Oregon Trail may mention ducks or swallows seen somewhere along the trail; Burrowing Owls seen in a prairie dog town may be described in a letter in some document collection. It was not possible to check all sources, but hopefully no source that would add new bird families or species or provide descriptive material on occurrence or status has been left unexamined. Despite many hours spent reviewing available records and checking information, inadvertent mistakes may have been made. Any misleading information or incorrect interpretations are solely the responsibility of the author.

I would like to thank Byron Butler, A. E. "Rick" Wright, Richard C. Rosche and Rushton Cortelyou for their helpful suggestions and comments on various drafts of this book. They helped clarify my interpretations based on the historic bird record. Many other people were helpful during the ten years of research, compilation, analysis and writing needed to prepare this historic record of ornithology in Nebraska. This includes staff at museums in Nebraska, on the East Coast and in Europe as well. The Interlibrary Loan Department at the University of Nebraska's Love Library was essential in obtaining several obscure historic references. Thanks also to the many others who helped in their own ways to assist me in completing this book.

The BirdChat discussion group on the worldwide internet communications network also has been very helpful in keeping me up-to-date on bird taxonomy and provided interesting discussions of bird history. I also feel the need to give a tribute to the lowly photocopier, without which this book would have been nearly impossible to complete.

James E. Ducey
May 2000

CHAPTER ONE:
BIRDS AND NEBRASKA'S NATIVE AMERICANS

A number of Native American tribes lived on the Great Plains in the area of modern-day Nebraska. Prior to contact with Europeans and Euro-Americans, the Omaha, Ponca, Pawnee and Sioux were most prominent, but the Arapaho, Kiowa and Cheyenne occasionally were present. The Omaha, Ponca, Otoe, Pawnee and many Sioux tribes made their home in this area, at least for part of the year, during the period prior to and during historic explorations. After Nebraska Territory was formed in 1854, the Omaha, Ponca, Pawnee, Santee and Teton (Lakota) Sioux, Otoe and Winnebago were settled on reservations in the area that later became the state of Nebraska.

Birds had an important and prominent role in Native American life. These people were as intimately acquainted with birds as they were with many other aspects of their environment, and birds formed a prominent theme in their everyday lives. Birds figured in their survival, since waterfowl and game birds provided a source of food. Tales describing how birds came to earth are part of tribal lore. Birds played a part in many important tribal myths and stories. Bird motifs decorated clothing, housing, and battle gear (e.g., war shields). Personal names often referred to specific birds or bird parts; some tribal clans were named after birds; and birds also played a role in determining and displaying social status. Bird symbolism and body parts were part of many ceremonies, and sometimes birds even played a role in establishing and maintaining relationships between one tribe and another.

Native Americans and Birds

Native Americans knew birds through an intimate awareness of the environment and its changing seasons. Birds were important in the mythology and lore of Native Americans living on the central Plains. This symbolic importance was based on the character of birds flying high in the sky, close to the heavens where tribal gods dwelled. The Winged Ones had the power to bear messages from the heavens, but each bird had a different tribal role. To a tribal member, birds could bring a message for a legend enacted in ceremonies around a campfire. In fact, for the Native Americans of the Plains, the symbolic value of birds was more important than their value as a natural resource.

Birds also had a practical value: local bird life was a resource that helped tribal members survive. Large numbers of birds were

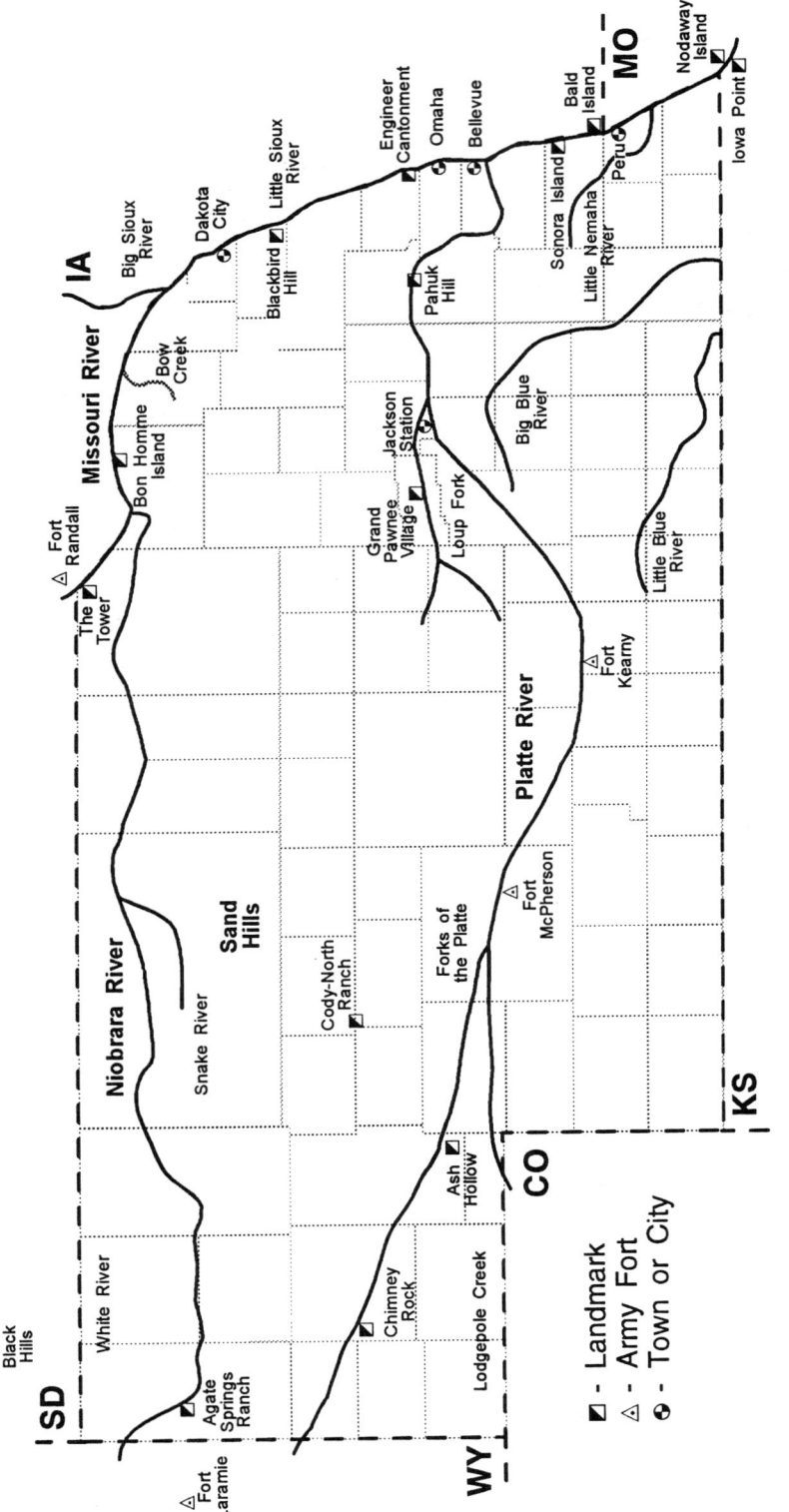

Historic Nebraska locations

hunted as a seasonal source of food. Flights during migrations provided clues to the changing of the seasons. Each season was part of a yearly cycle for birds in the prairie, woodlands, forests, wetlands and other habitats of Nebraska. Flocks of waterfowl heading north meant spring was coming, and the first meadowlark or blackbird meant it would soon be warm. In the fall the migratory flights going south meant the coming of the cold and snow of winter.

Parts of many different birds provided essential items for tribal rituals or ceremonial activities. Many tribal myths had various birds as a central character. A bird provided guidance for making a decision, or the actions of a bird played a vital role in a tribal story that had been passed down through generations. Most available information describes the mythical and ceremonial aspects of various birds. The mythical aspects of birds included roles in tribal societies, mythical tales, ceremonies, sign language and other parts of tribal life. Each of these items are clues to how birds lived with the Plains Indians for centuries prior to visits by the first Euro-American. Native Americans were the first to know and understand bird activity and behavior on the Plains that became Nebraska.

These tribes used wildlife as nourishment for their bodies and for their spirits. Food was a constant concern, and Native Americans went to great lengths to ensure there was enough to eat throughout the year. Hunting parties roamed tribal lands, often hundreds of square miles, hunting for herds of bison, antelope, deer and elk.

Fish, small mammals and birds also were sources of food, but hunting birds was a different matter than pursuing the scattered herds of big game. Birds commonly were used, but not to the extent that bison or other big game animals were. There were no great hunts for birds as there were for the mighty bison. The Missouri River was a primary migration route, and for the tribes living here the seasonal passage of waterfowl provided food. Great flocks gathered only during the spring and fall migration, so the birdlife of the river valley and nearby plains was used whenever it could be gathered. Breeding birds had widely scattered territories during the summer months when they nested. Many of these species were too small for Native Americans to hunt in any number. Larger species, such as waterfowl, prairie chicken, grouse, turkey and other game birds, were taken more often.

Nebraska Indian Tribes

Several Native American tribes lived in the Plains region of the Nebraska Territory (Ludwickson et al. 1987). Their affiliations continually shifted, and tribal village sites moved here and there as lack of resources threatened. By 1750 two tribes predominated in the historic bird record, the Omaha and Pawnee of eastern Nebraska.

When Prince Maximilian of Wied traveled up the Missouri River in 1833, he mentioned that the United States owned the entire right bank from below the Big Sioux River, but it had not taken possession yet. Bellevue, Nebraska, then served as an agency for the Otoe, Omaha and Pawnee living in the areas where the Platte and Niobrara rivers emptied into the Missouri River (Orr and Porter 1983, 369).

The Otoe had territory in southeast Nebraska, south of the Platte and north of the Big Nemaha River, and to the northeast into western Iowa. This tribe was noted in western Iowa as early as 1680 (Chapman 1965). The Nebraska Territory side of the Missouri, from the mouth of the Platte to the Big Nemaha, was the hunting ground of the Otoe (Wilhelm 1928).

To the north of the Otoe, the Iowa lived on the east bank of the Missouri as far north as the Little Sioux River. Their tribal land was a mosaic of tall grass prairie, forests, wooded creeks and streams. After the mid-1870s the Winnebago tribe also lived in the eastern part of the Nebraska Territory along the Missouri River valley.

Omaha tribal land lay along the west bank of the Missouri River, north from the Platte River. One village of earth lodges was built on Bow Creek, which is now called Omaha Creek, in northeast Nebraska. The Lewis and Clark expedition narrative said a Chief Little Bow built a village at that location, and that is where Lewis and Clark found the tribe in 1805. To"wo"to"gatho", the Big Village of the Omaha, was built on Omaha Creek near the present town of Homer. The tribe lived at the Big Village from 1780 to 1840 (O'Shea et al. 1982). Joseph Nicolas Nicollet in 1839 described the village site and its valley as "very beautiful, stirring the imagination and lifting the spirit above the fatigue caused by the slow, monotonous, and difficult progress we are making" (Bray and Bray 1976, 155). Typically the tribe would spend a few months each year in its village raising crops to supplement game and other food sources, such as bison or elk (James 1972).

Other sites were used as settlements by the Omaha during the times of turmoil caused by Euro-American pioneers in the mid-1840s. Villages which lasted only a few years were built on the Elkhorn River, on Papillion Creek west of Bellevue and in Burt County. One of the last tribal settlements of the historic period was in Loup County (Fletcher and La Flesche 1972).

Punka Indians Encamped on the Banks of the Missouri, after a painting by Karl Bodmer

The Ponca land was near the Niobrara River. The Ponca were once a part of the Omaha tribe and had many similar customs. The Ponca started a nomadic lifestyle only after permanent homes had been destroyed by their enemies. Their hunting ground was along the lower Niobrara and the nearby Missouri River.

According to Maj. Gen. Gouverneur Kemble Warren's expedition report of the mid-1850s, the Yankton lived on the east side of the Missouri, along the James and Vermillion rivers, in an area that later became a part of Dakota Territory, and into northwest Iowa (Warren 1875).

The Pawnee lived in the east-central part of what became Nebraska, near the lower portion of the Loup rivers. Their territory included the eastern Sand Hills and grass-covered hills of the lower Loup valley, where the Platte and Loup River were the predominant waterways. Explorers in the region regularly stopped at the Grand Pawnee Village near the Loup Fork.

The Teton or Lakota Sioux lived on the western high plains and ridges of rock and conifer forests in what became the modern state of Nebraska. Lakota territory extended into the Black Hills and west to the foothills of the Rocky Mountains. Part of their hunting lands included the western Sand Hills. The Santee and Yankton Sioux also ranged across the northern part of the present-day state prior to the territorial period.

The Winnebago Nation

The Winnebago Nation originated in the Wisconsin area, east of the Mississippi River. The branches in the Missouri valley were groups that had migrated from South Dakota to make a new home in Nebraska in the mid-1870s. The information specific to the Winnebago is primarily oriented to its woodlands home at the northern lakes. As the Winnebago migrated to the land that would become Nebraska, they carried many of their cultural practices along with them and then adapted them to fit their new environment.

The mythology of the Winnebago explains: "When the Winnebago first originated they were holy and clever. They were equal to spirits" (Radin 1990, 7). One tribal member could "fly like a bird," while another could talk to the trees to find out what it knew of the land. A third could become a buffalo. An owl, and many other animals, were part of the spiritual world of the tribe.

When the eastern Winnebago met the first Frenchmen to visit the area of modern-day Green Bay, Wisconsin, the visitors fired their many guns in welcome. The Winnebago said, "They are thunderbirds" (Radin 1990, 19). This event illustrates the very prominent role of birds, as this great event in their myth and ceremony was associated with a bird the people knew. Circular mounds and effigy mounds of the Wisconsin area on occasion were representations of clan animals. This included several types of effigy mounds with symbology of the goose, raptor and swallow (Radin 1990, 47).

The Winnebago also had a tribal language for birds and bird materials. Their name for bird was *wa-n'i-gi-a*, feather was *wa'-nik-ma'-shu-na*, nest was *o-ma'-na*, and wing was *wa-ni'k-a-hu'-za* (Hayden 1868). The Nebraska branch of the tribe used *wiza'-zek'e* for the name of a bird that appears in a specific month (Radin 1990, 76).

One of the most important of four tribal groups was the Thunderbird Clan. There were a larger variety of names associated with this clan than for others, including:

> *ahugidjinewinga:* young bird that sheds its first feathers as it flaps its wings.
> *ahutco:* blue wing.
> *hiwitcajankega:* fork-tailed hawk.
> *p'etcawinga:* crane woman.
> *rutcgenink'a:* little pigeon.
> *wak'andjaga:* Thunderbird.

These are just a few of the many tribal names that referred to birds or their activities (Radin 1990, 173-177). Related items for this clan include the Feast of the Bird Clan (Radin 1990, 270) and the War Bundle Feast of the Thunderbird Clan (Radin 1990, 379). The Hawk War Bundle associated with the Bundle Feast contained the bodies of an eagle, a hawk, an unidentified bird, a pigeon hawk, and eagle feathers. "The bird bodies were supposed to give the possessor, in times of war, the characteristics of these animals" (Radin 1990, 394).

For the tribe, eagle feathers worn in different manners indicated a coup during a battle. A feather stuck upright on the head was a mark of a first coup. A feather hanging from the head was for a second coup. Birds had other symbology, too. A raven skin hung around a warrior's neck meant that "more than one woman" had been taken in war (Radin 1990, 114). Feather fans were used in the Medicine Dance.

Tribal mythology includes many different references to birds or their roles in a tale. A headdress from about 1850 is made from grouse, crow and magpie feathers and decorated with split bison horns. There are about a dozen black feathers across the front and dozens of grouse feathers on the rest of the headdress (Nebraska State Historical Society collection).

These are a few of the practices that the Nebraska branch of the Winnebago also would have observed. Some species of birds used in ceremonial artifacts may have been less prevalent on the Plains, so other birds may have been used as substitutes. This may have led to a greater variety of species being known to the Winnebago and related tribes.

The Omaha Tribe

By 1800 the Omaha tribe had migrated to the land that would become Nebraska from its original home in the Ohio River valley. The Omaha, with their permanent settlements along the Missouri River, knew best the birds found in the eastern forests, tall grass prairie and marsh or lakes of the Missouri. The myth explaining how the tribe first came to earth shows the importance of birds to Omaha Indian mythology.

> In certain myths that speak of the Creation it is said that human beings were at first without bodies; they dwelt in the upper world, in the air, and the crow was instrumental in helping the people to secure bodies so that they could live on the earth and become as men and women. (Fletcher and La Flesche 1972, 175)

The general Omaha term for birds was *wazhi^n'ga* (Fletcher and La Flesche 1972), and there were many other names these people had for the birds they knew. For the American White Pelican, it was *bthe'xe;* for the American Bittern, the names *mo^n'xata* and *wado^{n}be* were given, since the bird "looks up at the sky" when approached. There were several names for geese and swans; geese were the larger geese, while ducks were the little geese. The Wood Duck was *mi'xa zhi^{n}ga xage egu^n*, or the crying duck, for its call when flying. The Mallard was *pa'hitu* for its prominent green neck. There were two different names for the Blue-winged Teal. Several species of raptors, including hawks, owls and eagles, had tribal names. Other species identified by name were the prairie chicken, the turkey, the bobwhite, the crane and the curlew. Among shore and water birds, the Long-billed Curlew was *ki'kato^{n}ga*, or the big curlew. The Common Snipe was *to^n'i^n*, and the American Woodcock was *pa'xthega* for its freckled head. The Omaha also recognized the Common Nighthawk, Whip-poor-will, Ruby-throated Hummingbird, kingbird, crow, magpie, Blue Jay, wren, blackbird, meadowlark and woodpeckers. The names given by the Omaha to these individual species are listed in the section on tribal names for birds and in the species accounts below.

Additional names for birds in the Omaha tribal language were recorded by Ferdinand Vandeveer Hayden during an 1867 geological survey of Nebraska Territory (Hayden 1868). He included names for the Greater Prairie-Chicken, Northern Bobwhite, goose and Wild Turkey. This list is mostly specific species, and the names also are given in the tribal names for species section and the species accounts below. The account includes the name for goose not given in the study by Fletcher and La Flesche (1972). The names are given in a separate section along with Indian names documented on previous visits to the Nebraska area.

With the origin of the Omaha related to a bird, the crow and other species also had a special role in tribal mythology. Different birds had attributes connected with the feminine or masculine. The swan was connected with women; it was given this association since it provided clothing that gives comfort and it is also a beautiful animal. The left wing of the bird was a symbol of its power.

Native Americans living near the Omaha tribal area also gave spiritual meanings to landmarks based on the birds found at a particular place. In August 1804 Lewis and Clark visited a mound the Indians called Mountain of Little People or Spirits, an elevated part of the grassy plains in what is now northern Cedar County. The expedition narrative describes the birds gathered on this mound:

> Some time before we got to the hill we obsevd. great numbers of Birds hovering about the top of this Mound[.] when I got on the top those birds flw off. I discovered that they wer Ceteching [catching] a kind of flying ant which were in great numbers abought the top of this hill, those insects lit on our hats & necks, Several of them bit me verry Shart [sharp] on the neck, near the top of this nole I observed three holes which I Supposed to be Prarie Wolves or Braroes, which are numerous in those Plains. this hill is about 70 foot high in an emince Prarie or leavel plain[.] from the top I could not observe any woods except in the Missourie Points and a few Scattering trees on the tree Rivers in view. i'e' the Soues River below, the River Jacque above & the one we have crossed[.] from the top of this Mound we observed Several large gangus of Buffalow & Elk feeding[,] upwards of 800 in number[.] (Moulton 1986, 7)

This gathering of birds, likely swallows, shows how the flights of birds took advantage of a rich source of food.

The everyday role of birds is shown in the names given for a tribal clan, also called a gens. Gentes indicated kinship groups that traced their descent in the paternal rather than the maternal line. The most basic family unit had a name that referred to a bird. One of the ten tribal gentes was spoken of as the Eagle Group. Another tribal clan was named "Wajinga-e-ta-je, or those that do not touch any kind of bird, excepting the war eagle" (James 1972, 230).

> The name of this subgenus [Wazhi^n'ga itazhi] is derived from *wazhi^n'ga*, "bird" and; *itazhi*, "do not touch." The rites that once were practiced by the subgenus pertained to the protection of the crops from the depredation of the birds. These rites have long been discussed and are traditional only. It was said that one of the acts was to scatter partially masticated corn over the fields—a symbolic appeal to Wako^n'da to prevent the small birds from attacking the corn and thus depriving the people of food. The rites of this subgenus evidently referred to the period when the people depended more on the cultivation of the maize than they did after they entered the buffalo country.
>
> The tabu was all small birds. Even the boys of this subgenus, in their games, while they would shoot their arrows or strike with sticks at the birds, would never touch one with their hands.
>
> The symbolic cut of the child's hair consisted in the shaving of the head, leaving a fringe of hair around the base of the skull, a short lock in front, and a broad lock behind. The fringe represented the feathered outline of the bird's body, the front lock its head, and the broad lock behind, its tail.
>
> The Wazhi^n'ga itazhi camped next on the left of the Waça'be itazhi. (Fletcher and La Flesche 1972, 160-161)

Another clan, the "Hun-guh ... does not eat white cranes, as the down of that bird is their medicine." The white crane could be the Whooping Crane (James 1972, 230).

Bird skins and feathers played a prominent role in Omaha tribal ceremonies, too. One Omaha tribal dance bustle, decorated mostly with eagle and owl feathers and a few turkey feathers on the top (Nebraska State Historical Society), shows how feathers

Omaha dance bustle ornament

and skins were used for decorative purposes. They also indicated accomplishments made by tribal members.

Among artifacts assembled by Duke Paul Wilhelm of Wurttemberg in 1823 and later placed in the collection at the British Museum is a complete set of a bow with arrows, bow cases and quiver from the Omaha. The arrows are decorated with three feathers, two hawk and one crow. A hide scraper in the collection is from either the Omaha or Otoe and has red- and black-dyed woodpecker scalp feathers as ornaments. Its edge is decorated with a bird's mandible (Gibbs 1982).

Omaha Pipestems

There were peaceful uses for pipes decorated with bird feathers or skins, but it was objects of war that were most lavishly decorated and made with bird parts. Several items of the Omaha tribe illustrate the use of bird material.

> There were . . . two tribal pipes, which were always kept together and were never separated in any ceremonial use. Both had flat stems; one was ornamented with porcupine-quill work, and had fastened on it the head of a pileated woodpecker, with the upper mandible turned back over the crest of the bird. The stem of the other pipe was plain, but had bound in a row along its length seven woodpeckers' heads, the mandibles turned back as just described. (Fletcher and La Flesche 1972, 135)

The Pileated Woodpecker and Ivory-billed Woodpecker were used to ornament the sacred tribal pipes and the Wa'^{n} Pipes (O'Shea et al. 1982). It took many gifts to initiate the Wa'^{n} Ceremony, and the men involved had wealth and high social standing in the tribe. A Hako Ceremony Pipe has the bill of an Ivory-billed Woodpecker on one end. Feathers of the eagle and Great Horned Owl decorate other portions of the pipe (Nebraska State Historical Society collection).

In one ceremony a warrior traded for a skin of the Ivory-billed Woodpecker, which originally would have come from the southeast portion of the United States. The remains of the Ivory-billed Woodpecker were discovered among materials excavated at the Big Village of the Omaha near the present town of Homer, Nebraska (O'Shea et al. 1982). The northern Native Americans would purchase a bill at the cost of two and sometimes three buckskins (O'Shea et al. 1982). Prince Maximilian described how the Mandan of the upper Missouri would trade a quality bison robe, worth six or eight dollars, for the head of a Pileated Woodpecker brought from St. Louis, Missouri.

One pipe contained seven bird heads to symbolize the council of seven chiefs, while another had a single head to represent the unity of authority of the chiefs.

The two objects essential to this [Wa'waⁿ] ceremony were similar to pipestems and ornamented symbolically but they were not attached to bowls and were never used for smoking. Still they partook of the significance of pipes in their sanctity, they were spoken of as pipes, and were held in the greatest reverence. Songs formed an important feature of the ceremony and the singing was always accompanied by rhythmic movements of the pipe bearers and also of the pipes. This movement was spoken of as *nini'ba bazhoⁿ*, "shaking or waving the pipes."

Each stem was of ash; a hole burned through the entire length permitted the passage of the breath. The length was seven stretches between the end of the thumb and the tip of the forefinger. The stem was feathered, like an arrow, from the wing of the golden eagle. Around the mouthpiece was band of iridescent feathers from the neck of the duck; midway the length was a ruff of owl feathers; over the bowl end were stretched the head, neck, and breast of the mallard duck, tied in place by two bands of buckskin painted red, with long flowing ends. Beyond the owl ruff were three streamers of horsehair dyed red, one at the tip of the stem, one at the owl feathers, and one midway between. These hair streamers were bound on by a cord made of the white hair from the breast of the rabbit. From each stem depended a fan-like arrangement of feathers from the tail of the golden eagle, held together and bound to the stem by two buckskin thongs; the end, which hung from the fan-shaped appendage, was tipped with a downy eagle feather. One of these fan-shaped feather arrangements was composed of ten feathers from the tail of a mature golden eagle. These were dark and mottled in appearance and were fastened to the blue stem; this pipe represented the feminine element. The other stem, which was painted green, had its appendage of seven feathers from the tail of the young golden eagle. The lower part of these feathers is white; the tips only are dark. These were the feathers worn by men as a mark of war honors and this pipe symbolized the masculine forces. It is to be noted that among the Omaha, as among the Pawnee, the feathers which were used by the warriors were put on the stem painted green to represent the earth, the feminine element, while those which were from the mature eagle and which stood for the feminine element, were fastened to the stem painted the color of the sky, which represented the masculine element; so that on each pipe the masculine and feminine forces were symbolically united. Near the mouthpiece was tied a woodpecker head, the upper mandible turned back over the red crest and painted blue. The pipes were grasped by the duck's neck, the mouthpiece pointing upward. When they were

> laid down, the stems rested in the crotch of a small stick painted red, which was thrust at the head of a wild-cat skin spread on the ground. This skin served as a mat for the pipes when they were not in use and as a covering when they were being transported. The wild-cat skin was required to have intact the feet and claws, and also the skin of the head. Two gourd rattles, a bladder tobacco pouch to which was tied a braid of sweet grass, a whistle from the wing bone of the eagle, and three downy eagle feathers completed the articles required for use in the ceremony. (Fletcher and La Flesche 1972, 376-377)

According to these studies, the pipe was the most important element for one ceremony. A Native American initiated the ceremony by carrying the pipe, along with many gifts, to the lodge or village of a trade partner. Because of the large quantities of gifts needed, the participants were necessarily men of high social standing.

A tribal tale describes the role of birds in decorating ceremonial pipes. In the "Peace Pipe," an owl called to the tribe, and the leader of the tribe said the bird was sending a message. The sounds of a woodpecker also were heard and incorporated into the tale (Welsch 1981). Later in the tale, an eagle dropped a downy feather where the council sat. This was not the right feather, though. A Bald Eagle and the "spotted eagle" also each dropped a downy feather, but they were not what the council wanted either.

> The eagle with the fantail (imperial eagle, *Aquila heliaca* Savingy) then came, and soared over the people. It dropped a downy feather which stood upright in the center of the cleared space. The leader said, "This is what we want." The feathers of this eagle were those used in making the peace pipes, together with the other birds (the owl and the woodpecker) and the animals, making in all nine kinds of articles. These pipes were to be used in establishing friendly relations with other tribes. (Fletcher and La Flesche 1972, 47)

The role of the birds in the Sing for Someone Ceremony has been thoroughly explained:

> The eagle was the bird of tireless strength. The owl . . . represented night and the woodpecker the day and sun; these birds stood also for death and life respectively. The downy feathers at the end of the thong that bound together the fan-like appendages were sometimes spoken of as symbolizing eggs and again, as the feathers of the young eagle, which fell from the bird when it matured and was able to take its flight. The gourd represented eggs and the reproduction of living forms. (Fletcher and La Flesche 1972, 380)

The prominent eagle figure in the Omaha ceremony was represented by corn in the Pawnee version of the same ceremony. The eagles, hawk, owl and other prominent birds each had a specific role. Different birds had different symbolic roles in different ceremonies, though their actions usually had a consistent theme.

Two Omaha Friendship Pipes in the University of Nebraska State Museum date to about 1900. The role of the pipes and their associated events have been thoroughly described (Fletcher and La Flesche 1972, 376-401). These pipes would have been similar to those used in ceremonies performed years earlier, even prior to 1875. One pipe includes the head of a Mallard and Golden Eagle feathers (Ducey 1992). The bill of a Pileated Woodpecker is on an end of one of the pipes. There are also feathers from the Great Horned Owl and Barred Owl.

Pipestems also were buried with wealthy men, based on the quantity of goods in their graves. Each man had been involved closely with tribal ceremonies using ceremonial pipes decorated with woodpecker heads. Pipes used in tribal ceremonies served, among other functions, to permit peaceful trade and gift exchange to occur among the Plains tribes (O'Shea et al. 1982).

Omaha Sacred Packs of War

Sacred Packs of War were made of skin, frequently of parfleche, and articles could be laid away and kept safely in them. Another name for these packs was "things flayed." This name referred to a pack's contents, which in some cases were the skins of certain birds.

It was the presence of these bird skins, which represented the species and the life embodied in the species, that made the $wai^{n'}$, or pack, $waxu'be$, or sacred.

. . . The pack itself was not sacred, only the contents. The association of birds with the powers of the air is very ancient. Particular birds were thought to be in close relation with the storm and the storm cloud, the abode of Thunder, the god of war. The flight of the birds brought them near the god and they were regarded as his special messengers; moreover, from their vantage point these denizens of the air could observe all that occurred on the earth beneath. When the warrior went forth to battle[,] the birds watched his every act and through them the Thunder became cognizant of all his deeds. The swallows that fly before the coming tempest were regarded as heralds of the approaching god. The hawk and other birds of prey were connected with the destruction caused by the death-dealing storm. The crow and other carrion birds haunted the places where the dead lay and were allied to the devastating forces of the god of war. Upon this ancient belief relative to the connection between the birds of the air and the manifestations of the powers dwelling in the sky (the wind, the thunder, and the lightning) the war rites of the Omaha were built. It was only after the performance of certain ceremonies connected with these packs, wherein were kept the representatives of the birds which could act as officers, so to speak, of the Thunder, that the Omaha warrior could go forth to aggressive warfare with the sanction of the recognized war power of the tribe. (Fletcher and La Flesche 1972, 404)

Omaha War Honor Decorations

Various bird parts were used as war honor decorations, and their features depended on the grade to which a particular warrior was entitled (Fletcher and La Flesche 1972, 438). The grade achieved was based on a warrior's feats in battle. The first grade was conferred for striking an unwounded man and permitted a warrior to wear a white-tipped Golden Eagle tail feather erect in his scalp lock. For the second grade, achieved for being the first to strike a fallen enemy, the eagle tail feather still was worn in the scalp lock, but it projected horizontally from the warrior's head. An eagle feather hung from the scalp lock marked the third-grade honor, awarded for being the second to strike a fallen enemy. Another grade honor was given for taking a scalp, and its regalia was similar to the third. An Omaha man who achieved the first three honors more than once

> became entitled to wear a peculiar and elaborate garment called "the Crow." This was worn at the back, fastened by a belt around the waist; it was made with two long pendants of dressed skin painted red or green, which fell over the legs to the heels. On the skin were fastened rows of eagle feathers arranged to hang freely so as to flutter with the movements of the wearer. An entire eagle skin, with head, beak, and tail, formed the middle ornament; from this rose two arrow shafts tipped with hair dyed red. On the right hip was the tail of a wolf; on the left the entire skin of a crow. This composite decoration illustrated certain beliefs that were fundamental to native beliefs, namely: That man is in vital connection with all forms of life; that he is always in touch with the supernatural, and that the life and the acts of the warrior are under the supervision of Thunder as the god of war. (Fletcher and La Flesche 1972, 441)

The Crow War Ornament and its ritual were devised to preserve a story about a tribal member pondering his future and asking the crow how he would fare in a coming battle against the Pawnee. In a second myth, crows offered to serve as scouts to find enemies of the Omaha, since they eventually would benefit by feeding on the flesh of those left on the field after a battle or a chase (Fletcher and La Flesche 1972, 446).

> "The Crow" decoration is said to symbolize a battlefield after the conflict is over. The fluttering feathers on the pendants represented the dropping of feathers from the birds fighting over the dead bodies. Sometimes the wearer of "the Crow" added to the realism by painting white spots on his back to represent the droppings of the birds as they hovered over the bodies of the slain. (Fletcher and La Flesche 1972, 441)

For the Omaha the feather war bonnet had great importance in tribal affairs and ceremonies. The eagle, a species that provided feathers for these regal bonnets, was associated with war and with the destructive powers of thunder and its attendant storms. This item had special significance.

> There was one ornament which stood for the social relation, the interdependence of men, and which was not directly connected with the supernatural. This was the imposing eagle-feather war bonnet. . . . The right to possess and wear this regalia could be obtained only by the consent of a man's fellow-warriors. To be sure, the person to whom the right was given must have already received, publicly, war honors; but he must also have gained the respect of the leading men of the community. (Fletcher and La Flesche 1972, 446)

The man who wished to have a bonnet would gather the materials, but it was crafted with the assistance of many persons. The man who desired a bonnet held a feast to have his friends recall their coups and other honors in war. Each feather in the crown of Golden Eagle feathers, fastened to stand upright about the wearer's head, stood for a man. Before a feather could be fastened on the bonnet, a man had to count the honors that entitled him to wear the feather and enabled him to prepare it to decorate the war bonnet (Fletcher and La Flesche 1972, 446-447).

Tribal dance also emulated the character of the eagle. In a ceremony with a calumet, the Omaha would "exhibit as much agility as possible in their movements, throwing themselves into a great variety of attitudes imitative of the actions of the war eagle, preserving at the same time a constant waving motion with the calumet in the left hand" (James 1972, 236).

Maximilian observed a tribal ceremony with many references to raptors during his travels up the Missouri River. On May 5, 1833, he witnessed a tribal dance at Jean P. Cabanne's post:

> We were called late yesterday evening to Mr. Cabanné to see a dance of the Omåhås. About 20 of these Indians had gathered before the house in bright moonlight. The main dancer . . . wore on his head a colossal feather headdress . . . made from very long tail feathers and pinions of owls and birds of prey.

> A second one . . . [had] a similar feather headdress on his head. These two men, as well as several younger ones and boys formed a line . . . .
>
> In the middle of it there was one who beat a kind of drum in rather rapid time. . . . The view of this dance was extremely interesting, especially when one thinks of it in connection with this entire, most interesting American evening. The moon appeared full and clear as though it were day on the vast interesting wilderness of the Missouri which we surveyed right and left from this summit. Before us the wild noise and bustle of the grotesquely decorated Indians. On both sides in the forest the loud incessantly and rapidly repeated calls of the whip-poor-whip, so that one could not observe this quite exquisite evening scene without the greatest of interest. (Orr and Porter 1983, 379-380)

Other ceremonial uses of birds besides the eagle include an ash pole more than eight feet long and bent at one end like a shepherd's crook. The staff belonged to the tribal director of the hunt. A swan skin with only the down remaining was cut in strips and wound around the staff. On one side a row of eagle feathers was fastened, and a cluster of Golden Eagle feathers hung at the end of the crook. Crow feathers were placed at the base about ten inches from the bottom of the pole. The ceremonial staff was kept in a buffalo skin cover.

Other myths related tribal tales of birds. The Omaha "Bird Chief Tale" was told by Francis La Flesche (Welsch 1981). This tale describes how a wren was made chief of the other birds. The turkey often was mentioned with the coyote in Omaha tribal myths. The coyote often was considered a trickster, using cunning and deceit for victory over other animals. The Omaha "Coyote and the Turkey's Tale" was an Omaha trickster tale (Welsch 1981).

Myths started in a period far back in the peoples' history. New myths originated when a tribal member had a spiritual event, and others may have survived from very ancient ceremonies.

An Omaha Tribal Game

When food was plentiful, times were settled, and life was good, some of the tribal members played games. In one game, young boys chased small birds from their grassland haunts.

> During the annual buffalo hunt when the tribe remained in a camp for more than a day the boys, ranging from ten to fourteen years of age, would engage in a sport. . . . The boys armed themselves with sticks about a yard long, to which small twigs were attached; then ranging in line through the prairie grass they scared up the little birds. As these rose, the boys threw their sticks into the air and the

fledglings, mistaking them for hawks, tumbled into the grass to hide, only to be caught by the hands of the boys. One lad was chosen to carry the quarry. As soon as a bird was caught, it was killed, scalped, and thrown at the boy appointed to take charge of the game; then it was his duty to run ahead and fall into the grass as if shot. On rising, he took the bird and strung it on his bow string. This little pantomime was enacted with every bird caught. When a number of birds had been captured, the boys retired to a place where they could roast the birds and enjoy a feast. (Fletcher and La Flesche 1972, 364-365)

The Ponca Tribe

The Ponca tribe's territory was around the mouth of the Niobrara River, to the east along the Missouri, and westward. They were first discovered on the Niobrara River in 1789, the same year that George Washington was inaugurated as President (Adams 1977, 15). The Niobrara River was the "River-that-Runs" when the tribe was living just downstream at Bazile Creek in the late 1800s (Howard 1965,

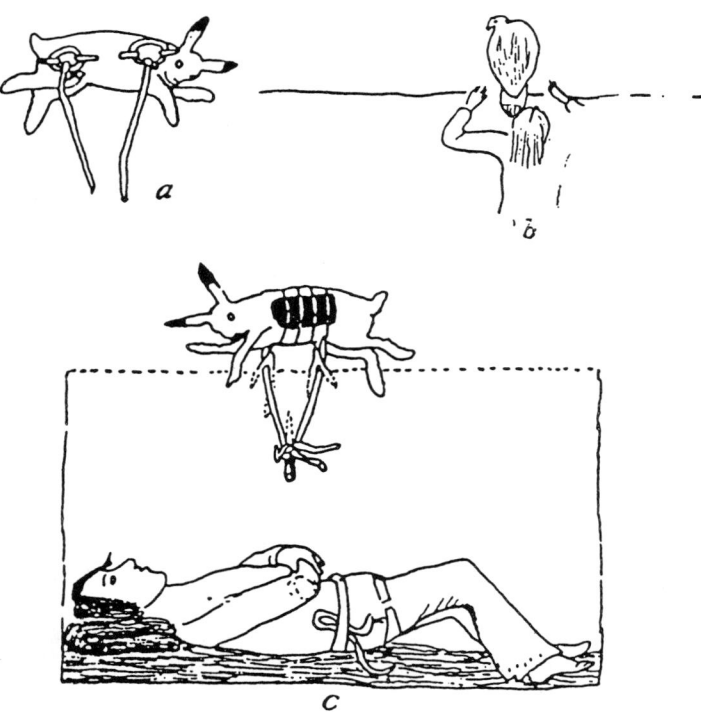

Hidatsa pit for trapping eagles: a) tying thongs to bait, b) taking eagle after capture, and c) eagle hunter inside the pit

24-25). Their tribal lands along the Missouri River therefore experienced a number of visits from people traveling up the river.

Like other tribes of the region, the Ponca incorporated many bird names and bird materials into their culture. February was *Miga-ikiagdegdi-ke-mi*, or the moon when the ducks come back and hide, a sign of approaching spring and summer when the birds would nest. Eagle wing fans were used in ceremonies, along with other eagle feathers. Eagles were trapped in a manner similar to the pit captures by western tribes, such as the Mandan or Hidatsa, shown at left (Howard 1965, 42). Eagles that had just eaten were often heavy from the meal and could be slow to take flight; thus, they could be clubbed by a Native American running to get the bird. The important role the eagle had in the Ponca Sun Dance was indicated by its special prominence on the dance pole. "In the fork of the pole is the nest of the Thunder bird, sometimes spoken of by the Ponca as an eagle, sometimes as a brant or loon. This bird produces rain, thunder, and lightning" (Dorsey in Howard 1965, 75). The nest of a goose possibly could have been used, but the loon would not have nested within the tribal area of the Ponca. It would be more likely that the big stick nests of a Bald Eagle, perhaps a Golden Eagle, would be more suited to being placed on a dance pole. Eagle-bone whistles were used, especially in sacred rituals, and added a musical tone to the events. The Hisada Clan—interpreted as "the stretching of a bird's leg when running"—was said to be "the most important because its members were the tribal rainmakers" (Howard 1965, 90). The purpose of the Sun Dance was to bring rain for the tribe's crops.

Birds also played another prominent role in the Niobrara River area when a boy of the tribe went on a vision quest. If successful in his quest, the boy would return with *xube*, which was the "Ponca term for supernatural power" (Whitman in Howard 1965, 99). "If he were arduous and a bit lucky besides, the spirit of some bird or animal would appear to him and grant him power" (Howard 1965, 99).

Other bird species recognized by the Ponca tribe include the Common Nighthawk, whose call heard by tribal members foretold the coming of a storm. The tribe mistakenly thought these birds lived under a spring, since they had "seen them fly in there" (Howard 1965, 75). Bird skins in ceremonial bundles had scalps attached (Howard 1965, 100). The colorful and prominent Northern Flicker also was important to the tribe (Howard 1965, 123). Some of the material described in this report refers to modern uses of bird material and recognizes species used in historic practices.

The Otoe and Missouria Tribes

The Otoe and Missouria tribes lived in southeast Nebraska, northeast Kansas and northern Missouri, having originally settled in the region prior to 1750. Their villages in Nebraska were primarily along the lower Platte River, the Nemaha River and the Big Blue River (Edmunds 1976). This region was rich prairie land with wood groves along the rivers and streams. Much of the history of these tribes deals with them ceding and selling their tribal lands (Chapman 1965). The first cessions started in the 1830s and continued in the following decades until the tribes moved to a reservation in Oklahoma.

There is one historic reference to the use of bird material by tribal members. When the renowned artist John Treat Irving visited the tribes in 1833 with a party of government officials, he described the greeting they received. He mentioned that an eagle feather plume adorned the scalp lock of these Native Americans (Edmunds 1976, 45). Some of the sketches done by Irving depict the use of feathers as adornment.

The Sioux Tribes

The information available on the birds known to the Sioux tribes mostly is drawn from their tribal language and mythology rather than from accounts of species that may have been present in their territory. The Santee Sioux lived in the Missouri River valley, and the Yankton Sioux had numerous villages north of the Missouri River and east of the Niobrara River in southeast Dakota Territory (Hoover 1988). When this tribe was visited in 1861 by the explorer and artist William de la Montagne Cary, he noted that they "saw a number of crows, hawks & eagles, pet birds hopping around the tipies" (Ladner 1984, 34).

The Teton or Lakota Sioux lived on the western Plains among the pine forests of the Pine Ridge and Black Hills. The desolate Badlands were part of their territory. The lakes and marshes of the Sand Hills were important hunting sites. The region of the western Sioux territory was not visited by Euro-Americans to the same extent as the villages of the tribes in the east along the Missouri River and Platte River. Most of the information on the Sioux and birds is from their language, tribal mythology and other tribal history rather than from specific notes that document the occurrence of a species on a particular date at a specific site.

A note by Edwin James, who saw a Sioux party making a visit to Engineer Cantonment in 1819-20, mentions the skin of the "paroquet," or parakeet, in the hair of one warrior. A number of eagle and owl feathers also were used to decorate their hair (James 1972). Ceremonial burial platforms along the Dismal River, where the Sand Hills Bone Expedition of 1870 collected some Native American skulls, likely would have included items decorated with bird material.

Teton Sioux Music

The ceremonial songs of the Teton or Lakota Sioux included references to the important role of birds. Bird material was used in several ceremonies. Birds also conveyed special messages when they occurred in dreams. The Teton Sioux had the Sing for Someone Ceremony (Densmore 1972), which was very similar to the Pawnee Hako Ceremony. The pipestem used by the Sioux was decorated with tufts of Pileated Woodpecker feathers, with the head of the same species of woodpecker above each tuft. Tail feathers of an eagle also hung from the pipestem. A woodpecker was used to decorate the pipestem because it is "a simple, humble bird, which stays near its nest and is seldom seen. This bird seems to have been considered especially appropriate, because children who underwent this ceremony were more closely guarded and protected than others" (Densmore 1972, 71).

An important article in this tribe's Sun Dance Ceremony was an eagle-bone whistle. The whistle was important for the warrior taking part in the ceremony and

> was hung around his neck by a cord. The whistle was made of the wingbone of an eagle, wound with braiding of porcupine quills and tipped with a downy white eagle feather fastened above the opening so that the breath of the dancer moved the snowy filaments. The mouthpiece was surrounded with fresh sage. The man blew this whistle as he danced. The instrument was decorated by the woman who decorated the Sun-dance pipe. (Densmore 1972, 125)

Bunches of downy white eagle feathers also were placed at the intersections and ends of the lines of the dance enclosure.

Dreams played an important tribal role and were sought by the Sioux. Once a man had a dream, he was obliged to announce it to the tribe. One of the greatest honors was to have a dream of the Thunderbirds. This dream provided a greater obligation to the man than did other dreams of birds or animals. The regard given to the Thunderbird dream was described by one Sioux warrior:

> Dreamers have told us of these great birds in the sky, enwrapped in the clouds. If the bear and other vicious beasts are regarded as dangerous, how much more should we fear the thunderbirds

that cause destruction on the face of the earth. It is said that the thunderbirds once came to the earth in the form of giants. These giants did wonderful things, such as digging the ditches where the rivers run. At last they died of old age, and their spirits went again to the clouds and resumed their form as thunderbirds. While they were on earth, the rain fell without sound of thunder or flash of lightning, but after their return to the sky the lightning came—it is the flash of their eyes, and the thunder is the sound of their terrible song. When they are angry, the lightning strikes a rock or tree as a warning to men. (Densmore 1972, 157-158)

In the "Owl's Hooting Song," the owl had a prominent role, and medicine men considered it to be especially sacred among the birds. The reasons given for this belief were:

> The owl moves at night when men are asleep. The medicine-man gets his power through dreams at night and believes that his dream is clear, like the owl's sight. So he promises that he will never harm an owl. If he did so, his power would leave him. For this reason some medicine-men wear owl feathers. The medicine-man also regards the owl as having very soft, gentle ways, and when he begins to treat sick persons he is supposed to treat them very gently. So in night wisdom and in the manner of carrying itself the owl is greatly respected by the medicine-men of the tribe. (Densmore 1972, 181)

The owl, along with the crow, also was important in the "Dream of the Owl and Crow."

The Crow Owners Society of the Teton Sioux was similar to this society in other Plains Indian tribes. The crow was honored by this society because the warriors wanted their "arrows to fly as swift and straight as the crow" (Densmore 1972, 319) and because the crow was always the first to arrive for the gathering of the animals in the Black Hills. A crow-skin necklace that was carried in a rawhide case was placed around the neck of a warrior before going to war.

In the Grass Dance, an "elk whistle" was made from a tree, frequently ash or box elder. "The open end of the instrument was usually carved to represent the head of a bird" (Densmore 1972, 471). The Grass Dance was a ceremony also practiced by other tribes of the Plains. The participants would dress in ceremonial garb, which included an eagle-feather headdress. While dancing, the Native Americans imitated the action of animals. In the Grass Dance, the men imitated the motions of the eagle and graceful birds (Densmore 1972).

Bird feathers from several different species were employed when making arrows that were used in association with the buffalo hunt, which had its own ceremonial songs. "Some used feathers of the prairie hen, owl, or chicken hawk that were large enough to split, while others used the smaller feathers of the eagle or buzzard" (Densmore 1972, 438). One warrior "considered pelican feathers as best for arrows," so his arrows had one pelican feather with the other two feathers from some other bird (Densmore 1972, 439).

Lakota Myth

Lakota mythology has many references to the role of the bird in Lakota belief and ritual. In the "Creation of the Universe Tale," the mythical being, Maka, made a demand for things to create the world. A portion of this tale says,

> Ksa and Wohpe designed creatures to be clothed with feathers and to have wings. Four kinds they designed, with short beaks not hooked, with short hooked beaks, with long slim beaks, and with flat beaks. Many different creatures of each kind they designed. Wakinyan took eggs of insects and of reptiles, and mingled them. From this mixture he created two of each kind of many kinds of eggs. He took from the ground that with which he created hard shells for the eggs, that the creatures when clothed should be beautiful, Wohpe adorned the eggs with colors. Each kind of egg she colored different from all other kinds. Then the four made nests of twigs and soft grasses, some large, some small, no two nests alike, a nest for each two eggs of a kind. Some nests they placed in trees, some in shrubs, some in grasses, and some on the ground. (Walker 1983, 237)

The entire myth is rich in detail and goes into the events surrounding the mythology of birds when the Lakota world was created.

Other myths have descriptive tales about birds in tribal lore. The eagle is the species mentioned most often; it has the most important spiritual role. "Thunderbird," "war eagle" and other names were given to the regal Golden Eagle. Its feathers graced different types of headdresses used in numerous ceremonies. Other birds repeatedly mentioned in stories were the turkey, prairie chicken and crow. Some species, like the wren, occur to a lesser extent in tribal myths. In one myth the swallow was a messenger for the great mystical Winged One. In the "Stone Boy Story," a Black-capped Chickadee was the messenger (Walker 1983, 93).

The Dakota Sioux were represented by the Santee, who lived in northeast Nebraska near Ponca Creek and the Missouri River. The Santee had the Owl Feather Dance. The dance leader had forty-eight red and black sticks distributed among the tribe. He called together the men who had sticks and a whistle made of a long swan's wing bone, and they gathered where the leader was singing. After giving property to the less fortunate of the tribe, a dance began, and the leader said, "Late in the fall I wish you to find two little birds; kill them and bring them to me. The birds he was referring to were the owl and crow. Sometimes they killed about 150 crows, enough for decorating 48 headdresses" (Wissler 1916, 110).

Sioux Artifacts

The influence of imported materials is seen in some Sioux items collected by James Cook at the Agate Springs Ranch along the western Niobrara River. Cook had treated Chief Red Cloud and his Oglala tribe as friends (Ducey 1986), and the Oglala gave items as presents to Cook in the early 1890s when they came to visit. A collection of about five hundred tribal items was given to preserve the history of the tribe that lived in the Pine Ridge. Cook described these items in his writings from the early 1900s. His manuscripts are part of the James Cook Collection from the Agate Springs Ranch, which was established in 1886 on the western Niobrara, a river that the Sioux called the Mini tanka.

Sioux war club with stone head and eagle feathers

Older items in this collection show some reference to birds typical of the buttes and plains, especially the Golden Eagle. A stone club and a buckskin-head drumstick both have eagle feather ornaments. A ceremonial pipe, carved in catlinite (shown on page 33), has the talons of a hawk grasping the bowl of the pipe. According to Cook, a Council Pipe decorated with eagle feathers was "smoked at Fort Laramie in 1867 when the Black Hills were ceded to the Sioux for as long as the grass grew and water ran" (Cook Collection, Scotts Bluff National Monument). Waterfowl materials decorated the stem of another ceremonial pipe.

Several eagle-feather headdresses are included in the collection. Cook mentioned how the feathers of the Golden Eagle, or Big War Bird, were used to make dance and war bonnets. This eagle was not common enough for each warrior to have a bonnet that used the twelve tail feathers that were most highly prized by the Plains Indians. Based on the features of items in the James Cook Collection, the feathers were attached by rawhide to a buckskin cap.

The small, downy feathers of the eagle also were used for ornamental purposes. These "breath feathers, so called, are from the eagle's breast and can be stirred by the breath. They were greatly valued for ornamentation, and were often dyed with vegetable coloring" (Cook Collection, Scotts Bluff National Monument). The Cook Collection has several items with eagle breath feathers, including ornaments wound with porcupine quills. Bones of the Golden Eagle were used as whistles. These whistles, with eagle feathers bound to them, were used in the Sun Dance by the Oglala bands led by Red Cloud.

The Nebraska State Historical Society's collection of Native American material includes arrows and some shields and clubs with feathers attached. There are several bird-wing fans and eagle-feather headdresses. Most of this material dates from after 1875. Two other items are a dress and a Ghost Dance Shirt decorated with the drawing of a Thunderbird on the front.

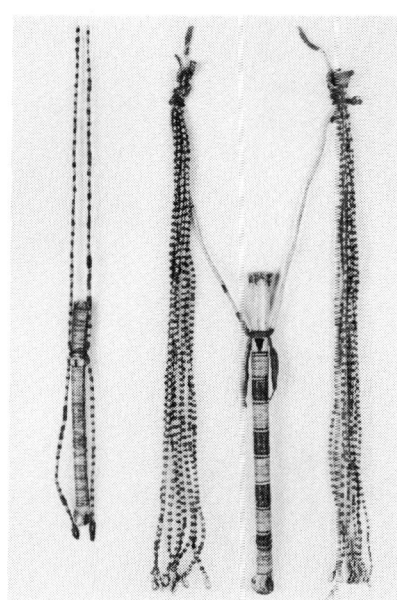

Sioux eagle-bone whistle (l.) and Mandan eagle-bone whistle (r.)

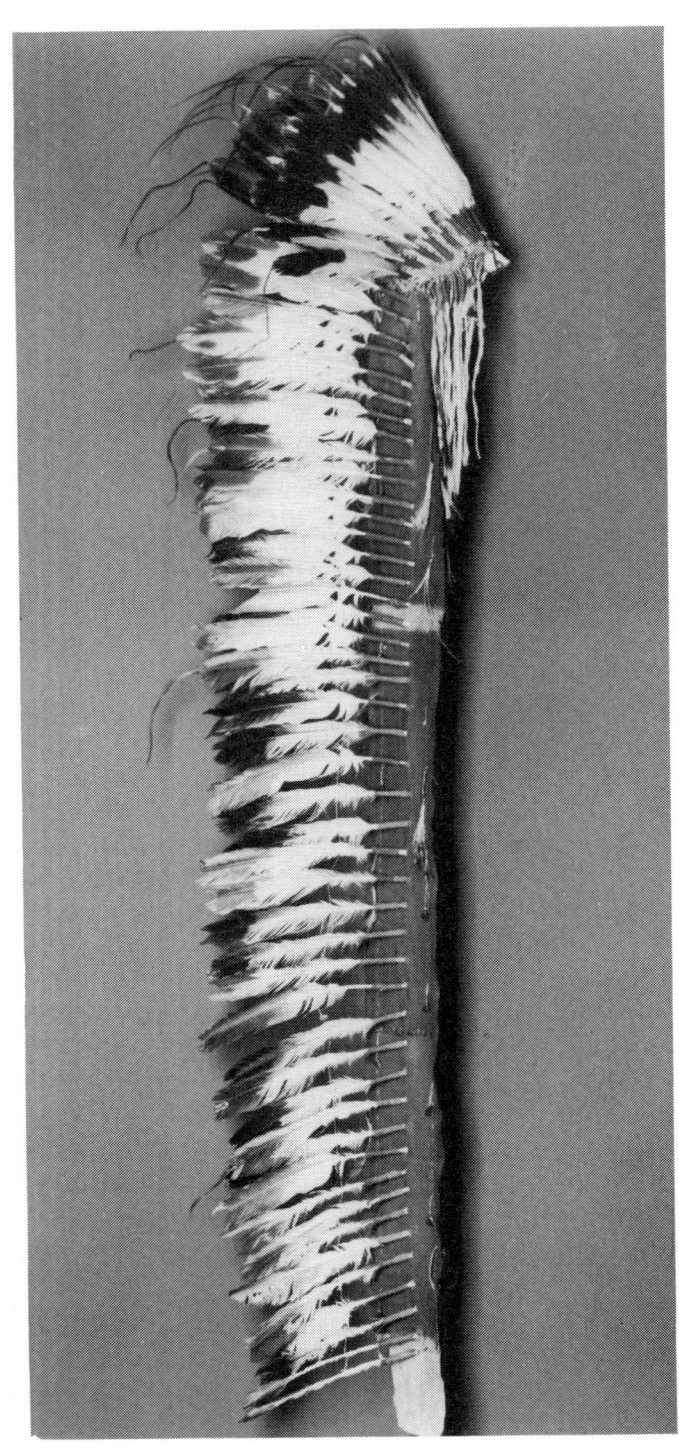

Oglala Sioux eagle-feather bonnet

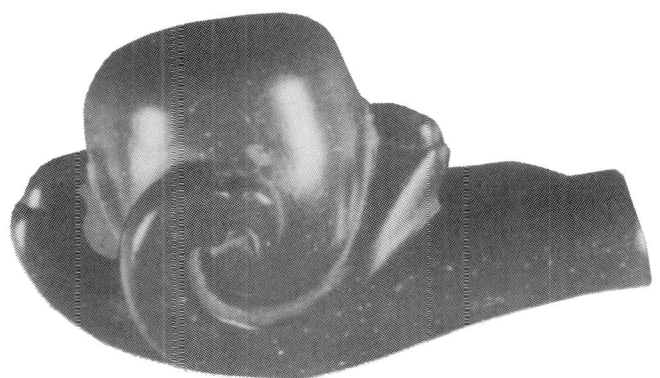

Sioux claw-shaped pipe bowl carved in catlinite

The Pawnee Tribe

The Pawnee lived on the open plains west and south of the Omaha tribe. Villages are known from the lower Loup River and along the Platte River. The Grand Pawnee Village of domed earth lodges was a principal village near the confluence of the Platte and the Loup. Permanent camps often included fields of crops grown to supplement game. Hunting parties chased bison after asking the spirits for a good hunt.

Hayden recorded Pawnee words for birds while doing a geological survey of Nebraska in 1867. Besides specific bird types, there are related words, such as the Pawnee words for all kinds of birds (*li-ka'ts*), beak (*cūsh*), egg (*li-pi'-ku*) and feather (*hit'k*) (Hayden 1868). This list has names for just a few species, such as the Red-headed Woodpecker and Greater Prairie-Chicken, plus blackbird, crow, duck, goose and snipe. Names for specific types of birds are given in the tribal name for species section and the species accounts which follow.

The Pawnee Use of Birds

The missionary John Brown Dunbar noted some interesting items about the role of birds in the tribal life of the Pawnee during the mid-1800s. His years with the tribe, which had its main village along the Loup Fork of the Platte, provided a premier time to note different aspects of the tribe. While observing their habits and customs, Dunbar mentioned that hawks and eagles were included among the animals used to mark a tribal group, such as a sub-band (Dunbar 1880a). Trade with other tribes was used to acquire some items that were in special demand, such as eagle feathers, that came from the Arikara and Mandan to the north and west of the Loup Fork (Dunbar 1880b). The Pawnee traded horses, salt from the plains (perhaps including that from the saline wetlands along Salt Creek south of the Platte), and sometimes corn.

Pitalesharu was the strong leader of the tribe in the 1850s when the "white men" were crowding in on the Pawnee lands. Dunbar said that the chief liked to wear his best clothes and was especially proud of his headdress with many eagle feathers (Dunbar 1880b).

Among Dunbar's few other Pawnee notes on birds, some are about their use as food.

> With regard to meats in general, there was a current saying among them, that the flesh of the carnivorous animals and rapacious birds should not be eaten. The food of the most of these animals was believed to render them unclean. (Dunbar 1880b, 323)

Prairie chickens were readily taken. During the breeding season, these birds and the young of other birds were especially numerous and were used as food. The boys of the tribe were most adept at getting quails and prairie chickens.

> The boys were very expert in capturing prairie chickens and quails. When one of these was started up on the prairie, the exact spot of its lighting was noted. Armed with a withe five feet long, a boy cautiously crept up to within a few feet of the crouching bird, and then darting forward, struck it down with a well-directed blow as it attempted to rise on the wing. (Dunbar 1880b, 334)

Birds had an important role in Pawnee ideology and myths. They linked the sky to the earth and tied the Pawnee people to the gods. Birds figured prominently in ceremonial preparations made for planting corn and for summer hunts. Eagles, owls and woodpeckers were especially notable, particularly in the Hako Ceremony (Fletcher 1904). Most of the information on birds known to the Pawnee is based on their ceremonial and mythical roles. Bird material was used extensively for making pipes and other ceremonial objects. The many bird species of the Loup Fork area, which was the core of their territory, are known and represent many of the common

Pawnee shield with feathers

birds known by the tribe. Some are important characters in the Pawnee myths.

Only a few tribal members had the privilege of using eagle feathers: one or two people could put eagle feathers around a shield, and some men could make themselves a war bonnet with the eagle feathers. The traditional war bonnet of the Plains symbolized a comet to the Pawnee (Weltfish 1977, 376).

Other hunting stories relate how the people called the buffalo or how a coyote scared the buffalo toward a village. They told many coyote stories, for these stories, although not real, would have the effect of bringing them good luck and something to eat. According to Pawnee lore, once upon a time the Coyote People—that is, the coyotes, crows, rabbits, foxes, magpies, hawks, eagles and other animals—went on a buffalo hunt; these birds and animals selected a hawk to look for the buffalo (Dorsey 1906).

Birds were prominent in several tribal ceremonies. In the Great Cleansing Ceremony of the Pawnee, birds represent the waters and animal life that pertained to them, specifically waterfowl, such as swans and loons (Dorsey 1906). According to Duke Paul Wilhelm's journal notes, in 1823 he bartered with the Native Americans for small articles, which he later placed in the collection at the British Museum. Wilhelm obtained items from several tribes, but the few objects he received from Nebraska tribes include a Pawnee shield, shield cover and medallion, all of which contain bird materials.

The roles of several different species have been described as follows for the Pawnee (O'Brien and Post 1988; Weltfish 1977 and other studies):

Eagle: The red eagle (specific species uncertain) is supposed to be the most powerful of all birds. During the Pawnee ceremonial observance of the harvest, eagle feathers in the scalp lock represented Heaven during the creation, and the white downy feathers represented the clouds on which he rode. Eagle feathers had other prominent roles, especially related to the eagle-feather headdress.

Hawk: Sometimes spoken of as the messenger of the Morning-Star in a Pawnee ceremony, its skin was generally found in bundles, especially in the warrior bundles.

Owl: The role of these species varied (O'Brien and Post 1988, 491). The owl symbolizes the four powers in the west, who never sleep; owls are referred to in other places as the four assistants of the Evening Star (the Wind, Clouds, Lightning and Thunder). The owl is the leading medicine man among the birds. "Owl feathers and skins were worn by priests and doctors. The owl is a messenger; he teaches individuals how to worship" (Murie in O'Brien and Post 1988, 491). The owl is the chief of night and has the power to help and protect people at night.

Kingfisher: In a story about the poor boy Small and Pa-hu-ka along the eastern Platte River, the kingfisher points out that, since he is always along the edge of the creek, he can go into the water and escape, and the boy will be unable to kill him if the bird is unwilling (Weltfish 1977, 334). The habits of this bird describe the hunting methods of the Belted Kingfisher at Pahuk Hill.

Blue Jay: The Blue Jay was "the carrier of prayers and sacrifices to the sky; the messenger between man and Tirawahat. Its skin and feathers were tied to a red pipe devoted to the sun or a black pipe devoted to the moon" (O'Brien and Post 1988, 491).

Magpie: The Pawnee believed magpies were the most successful birds in finding food and generally associated them in their minds with the near presence of the buffalo. In the story about the Pawnee tribal site at Pahuk, the magpie is the errand bird of the medicine lodge of the island. The boy Small follows the magpie, which leads him to the animal lodge Pahuk. In a tree at the doorway sit all sorts of birds—particularly black, bald and spotted eagles, and also chicken hawks.

Woodpecker: Woodpeckers were supposed to interpret the wishes of Tirawa through their ability to understand the voice of the Thunders. The use of their skins, in the form of a cap, was confined to the sons of chiefs, who thus gave evidence that they were under the protection of Tirawa. They likewise wore leggings with scalps to show that they were guarded by the gods of the earth. Murie noted that the woodpecker has the special protection of Tirawahat and the Thunders because this bird cries out fearlessly during storms and builds its nest in decaying trees. The woodpecker is Chief of Trees and can protect the Pawnee from harm brought by storms and lightning. The woodpecker is the protector of the life of the people (O'Brien and Post 1988). Red-headed Woodpeckers and woodpeckers in general were considered important by the Pawnee.

Bluebird: The bluebird was regarded as the messenger or errand boy between Tirawa and the people. It was positioned on the pipe so that it carried not only the sacrifice but also the prayers of the Pawnee to Tirawa.

Quail: Studies based on earth lodge excavations in Kansas indicate that the Northern Bobwhite had an important role in Pawnee ceremonies (O'Brien and Post 1988). Four sets of quail wings were found in a pit containing ceremonial items. One study suggests the quail nest may have been a model for the earth lodge. Other correlations between Pawnee tribal life and the life history of the quail also are suggested. A drawing in this paper shows how the hairstyle and facial paint of a young warrior were vaguely similar to the head patterns of the quail. The authors concluded that the Bobwhite Quail provided an obvious pattern after which the Pawnee could fashion themselves. This proposition has been questioned by another researcher, who stated that it is not supported by available evidence (Roper 1994).

The quail could have had a lesser role when the tribe lived in Nebraska. This bird was noted primarily along the Missouri River, an area claimed by other tribes. The Pawnee in the Nebraska area were known to have used alternate birds for ceremonies: the turkey replaced the brown eagle (likely the Golden Eagle), and the woodpecker replaced the turkey (Fletcher 1904).

The roles of other bird species varied. The meadowlark is often spoken of as the messenger or errand boy of the Evening Star (O'Brien and Post 1988, 491). The duck is the Chief of Water, who knows the trackless paths of the sky, water and streams of the Earth. The wren "is an element of humility revealing that all Pawnee, however small and insignificant, can be cheerful and happy" (O'Brien and Post 1988, 491).

A Pawnee Spiritual Drum

A spiritual drum of the Pawnee (sketched below) shows the great importance that birds had in tribal lore. A warrior seeking a message received the vision that was permanently recorded on a ceremonial drum. The drum shows how the message was received from the spirits, vividly depicting swallows racing with the Thunderbird in a storm. The drum had great mystical power (Chamberlain 1982).

Pawnee spiritual drum

A Sacred Family Bundle

In 1873 about four hundred Pawnee on a hunt were attacked by one hundred Sioux along Frenchman's Creek, west of the Pawnee Loup Fork village. Most of the Pawnee were killed, but one child escaped with a Pawnee Sacred Family Bundle. This bundle was recovered and found to have an important role in tribal heritage. It contained several bird items among its contents, each of which had a prominent role in a ceremony (Good 1989). Material among the sacred items of the bundle includes wing and tail feathers, eight bird skulls and a portion of a Bald Eagle leg. Each bird is wrapped in a leather pouch (Good 1989, 17), and the bird skins typically are stuffed with tobacco. Species identified include a Merlin, three Swainson's Hawks and three Northern Harriers.

The Role of Birds in Pawnee Myths

Birds played a very prominent role in the myths of the Pawnee. When a warrior received a spiritual message, it often was a bird that carried the message. Since birds were an obvious part of the Plains environment, the person seeking a message would see a bird and make it part of the message and its myth. This is apparent in many myths of the tribes that lived in the Nebraska region, especially the Pawnee.

The majestic eagle is the main avian character in the story of the Pawnee Thunderbird Ceremony, although crane feathers from a medicine man are important as well. According to Mouth-Waving-in-Water (Kitkehahki), during the ceremony a dead warrior's hair was covered with soft, downy feathers, and a long, downy feather was stuck through his scalp lock (Dorsey 1906). The ceremony also is known as the Elk Medicine Ceremony, because of the great feather appendages placed on the bird standing on the altar and which bear a superficial resemblance to the antlers of the elk. This ceremony was not held after the Pawnee were forced to settle on a reservation.

The eagle had an important place in the "Sun Dance Myth" told by Cheyenne, Chief of the Skidi band of Pawnee. The recorded version of the tale is considered only a fragment of the tale of the origin of the Sun Dance among the Skidi (Dorsey 1906). This tale is of an eagle who takes a poor boy of the Pawnee village to a ceremony and teaches him to dance and to learn the Eagle Dance rites. Swans provide a message, and owls sing. When the young man starts the dance, he has visions so that he clearly knows the rites he is to perform. After the first dance, the boy knows the ceremony and gives many Sun Dances during the following summers.

The Great Cleansing Ceremony was another Pawnee ceremony in which bird feathers had a prominent role. The bottom of a pit representing the Garden of the Evening Star was covered with soft, downy feathers (Weltfish 1977).

Two symbolic eagle-feather pipes were used during the ceremonial observance of the harvest. The calumet, for peace and trade with another tribe, carried an ear of sacred corn representing the universe. It was painted blue around its bottom half and had four blue lines leading up toward the point representing the cardinal directions, or pathways, of prayer to Heaven. On the point of the corn was a single white feather representing Heaven (Weltfish 1977, 254).

In the second part of this ceremony, a chief performed a ritual representing the essential nature of the world. Four warriors took positions at the cardinal places. Each was dressed in full regalia, wearing an otter fur collar, a sacred ear of corn on the left shoulder, and a hawk skin on the right shoulder. On the head, each wore a ball of white down feathers, and an eagle feather was placed transversely in the scalp lock. Each element of the costume had symbolic meaning—the otter collar, awakening of life in the spring; the ear of corn, Mother Corn guiding them over the world; the hawk, strength and fierceness; the eagle feathers in the scalp-lock, Heaven during the creation; the white downy feathers, the clouds on which he rode. Each man's face was painted with red streaks along the sides and a birdfoot on the forehead, representing the Bird's Foot Constellation (Weltfish 1977, 260).

In the Big Doctor Ceremony, there were four or five bird doctors. One of them was dressed in feathers with a whistle in his mouth. All imitated birds and then went back into the lodge. They circled around, and the crowd stood around them at a little distance; some people were on the top of the earth lodge (Weltfish 1977, 298).

Pahuk Hill is a ceremonial place of the Pawnee that overlooks the lower Platte in current Saunders County, Nebraska. One day Small, a poor boy, is lying at the edge of the bluff at Pahuk Hill, under a tree with his bow and arrows, hoping to catch some birds to eat. The myth says:

> Right on the sheer bluff of the high bank was a cedar tree. This is the doorway to the animal lodge of Pahaku. Sitting on the tree are all sorts of birds—particularly eagles—black, bald, spotted and also the chicken hawk. (Weltfish 1977, 332-333)

The errand men for the animal lodge at Pahuk Hill were the duck, or *kiwakski*, and a bluish bird with a wide stripe around its neck, or *kiskatararaxka*. The habits of a bird called "striped neck" are similar to the hunting methods used by a Belted Kingfisher.

When shown the site in 1876, Luther Hedden North provided additional information regarding Pahuk Hill, the "place where the *nah-hoo-kach* (spirit animals) live" (North 1961, 198-199). The Pawnee said they had followed a "little bird which acted as guide" to the underwater entrance of the spirit house (North 1961, 199). The leader of the lodge animals "was a great beaver, and there were elk and deer, antelope, foxes, coyotes, big wolves and birds, such as swans, sand hill cranes, wild geese and many other animals and birds" (North 1961, 199).

The "Animal's War Party" was a story told to show how the rabbit, turtle and spider-woman make a charge against the warriors, who are the hawks (Dorsey 1906). The hawks were known among the Indians as warriors, and they kill the rabbit, turtle and spider-woman. The story means to show that the warriors always should imitate the hawk instead of the rabbit, turtle or spider-woman.

The "Turkey Ritual Tale" is similar to many others in which the buffalo voluntarily offers itself to the people for food. Besides the references in the tale which afford explanations of certain rites, the story is interesting because it teaches the young men that a prophet is without honor in his own country (Dorsey 1906). In other words, to obtain the favor of the young women, the young men must go off into the enemy's country and perform deeds of valor. The paints referred to in the tale are supposed to be those found in the colors of the turkey's coat.

Besides adult ceremonies, tribal lore helped teach manners to children. The "Poor Boy Who Turned into an Eagle" is a Pawnee myth that illustrates the moral that children, especially brothers and sisters, should not quarrel among themselves. The tale also refers to the sacrifice by the Skidi Pawnee of a maiden in the Morning Star Ceremony (Dorsey 1906).

In the Pawnee "Coyote and Prairie Chicken Tale," each animal has its own song. The story was told by Young-Bull, an eight-year-old Skidi Pawnee boy (Dorsey 1906). His mother, Woman-Newly-Made-Chief, was the daughter of the great medicine man, Scabby-Bull. She had many stories about the different animals that she told her son. This story was told to the children to teach them that stones, poison-ivy, berries, etc., are poisonous for people but not for prairie chickens. The tale says how the coyote sang about the poison-ivy berries and juniper berries. The prairie chicken could eat these with no harm. The "Coyote and Prairie Chicken Tale" also was told to teach the children always to be on the lookout, so they would not be frightened by prairie chickens flying up in front of them (Dorsey 1906).

The "Coyote and the Turkeys Roll Down the Hill Myth" taught the children that when they grow up and hunt for game and kill, they always should be sure to keep watch over it and preserve it (Dorsey 1906). In this tale, the coyote tricks the turkeys by first letting them roll him down the hill in a sack. The coyote then gives the turkeys their turn to roll down the hill, but instead he catches most of the flock of sixty turkeys in the sack. When he leaves, however, they all escape.

The "Coyote and the Dancing Turkeys Story" was told by White-Eagle (Dorsey 1906). The story was told to the children so that they might imitate the dancing of the turkeys and dance this dance while playing at night. Other tales with Turkey and Coyote included those for making the young children brave when they became warriors. The "Coyote Shows Turkey the Scalp-Offering Ceremony Story" was told to the children so that when they grew up they would want to take scalps and make scalp-sacrifices to the gods in the heavens (Dorsey 1906).

The rabbit also knew a bird that lived in the eastern forests and woodlands. The "How Rabbit Captured the Turkeys Myth" (Welsch 1981) is about a young man in search of food. The tale uses the events of the hunt to explain why turkeys have red eyes.

The Pawnee Hako Ceremony

A seasonal celebration that made prominent use of bird material and bird lore was the Hako Ceremony. It was named for the two feathered stems, which were waved to the rhythm of the songs (Fletcher 1904). This ceremony was performed by two separate tribal groups, which represented the Father and the Children.

The Hako Ceremony lasted five days, with some ceremonies taking place during the night. The ceremony took place "in the spring when the birds are mating, or in the summer when the birds are nesting and caring for their young, or in the fall when the birds are flocking" (Fletcher 1904, 24). The idea and teaching of the Hako are laid out throughout the ceremony. It refers many times to using a bird nest as a symbol for the home of young children. The children of the tribe were blessed ceremonially throughout the ritual. The report by Alice Fletcher describes each item and its preparation, ceremonies and incidental rituals.

The purpose of the ceremony was to bring the promise of children, which ensured a long life of plenty. It also was meant to affect the social relations of the participants of the ceremony by establishing a bond between two distinct groups of persons, belonging to different clans, gentes, or tribes, to ensure friendship and peace between them (Fletcher 1904, 280). There were many rituals of the ceremony that formed an unbroken sequence from the beginning of the rites to their end. There were twenty different rituals involving many different objects decorated with bird items:

The objects peculiar to this ceremony were two feathered stems about a meter in length, made of ash wood. They were rounded and smoothed, and the pith was burned out to leave an opening for the breath to pass, as through a pipestem. One of these stems was named *Raha'katittu*, from *ra*, the, this one; *ha=hak*, a part of the word *hakkow*, breathing mouth of wood, the *k* being dropped for euphony . . . ; *katit*, dark, brown, or black; *tu=ruru*, moving, the change of the *r* to *t* being for euphony. The translation of the whole word would be, the breathing mouth of wood with the dark moving feathers. The other stem was named *Rahak'takaru*, from *ra*, the, this one; *hak*, from *hakkow*, breathing mouth of wood; *taka*, white; *ru*, from *ruru*, moving or swaying. The translation of the whole word would be, the breathing mouth of wood with the white moving or waving feathers. . . .

The feathered stem *Raha'katittu* . . . was painted blue to symbolize the sky, the abode of Tira'wahut, the circle of the lesser powers. A long straight groove running its length was painted red, the symbol of life. The red groove was the path along which the spirits of the various birds traveled on their way to bring help.

Three split feathers from an eagle's wing were fastened to the stem as to an arrow, to give sure flight to the symbol-freighted stem. On it was tied the fan-shaped pendant of ten feathers from the mature brown or golden eagle. This eagle was called *Kawas* in the Hako ceremony. It represented the mother and led in certain of the rites. It is this feathered stem that was carried by the Ku'rahus. This eagle is consecrated to the powers; it soars near their abode and is a medium of communications between them and man.

The woodpecker's head was fastened near the mouthpiece end of the feathered stem, the upper mandible turned back over the red crest and painted blue. This treatment of the upper mandible had a double significance. The red crest, which rises when the bird is angry, was here held down; it must not rise. The blue paint represented the clear, cloudless sky. The woodpecker has the favor of the storm gods and can avert from man the disaster of tempest and of lightning. The owl feathers were tied near the middle of the feathered stem. This bird has power to help and protect during the night. Soft blue feathers were fastened around the mouthpiece end. These blue feathers symbolized the clear sky, and it is this end which was always upward toward the abode of the powers.

The other end of the stem was thrust through the breast, neck, and mandibles of the duck. It was by this end that the feathered stem was held. The duck is familiar with the pathless air and water and is

> also home on the land, knowing its streams and springs. It is the unerring guide. . . .
>
> The other feathered stem, *Rahak'takaru* . . . , differed from the first feathered stem already described in two particulars, namely, it was painted green, to symbolize the earth, and the fan-shaped pendant was made of seven tail feathers from the white eagle (the young brown or golden eagle . . .). This eagle was not consecrated. It represented the male, the father, the warrior, and the defender. This feathered stem was carried by the Ku'rahus's assistant, and it was never allowed to be next to the Children; its place was always on the outside. There, it was explained, it could do no harm, could rouse no contention, but would serve to protect and defend. (Fletcher 1904, 19-21)

Fletcher also explained, "All the birds on the stems are leaders: the eagle is chief of the day; the owl is chief of the night; the woodpecker is chief of the trees; the duck is chief of the water" (Fletcher 1904, 40).

The feathered stems were treated with the utmost respect. The pipestems never were placed on the ground or on a seat, but were laid carefully on the skin of a wildcat (Fletcher 1904, 19-23) or another special item. The pipestems were preserved intact and passed from warrior to warrior and sometimes were freshened and repaired by their owners.

The feathered stems were pointed in the primary directions during the Consecrating the Lodge portion of the ceremony:

> The eagle soars in the skies and can communicate with the powers that are above; so the eagle represents these powers. As we stand facing the east the white-eagle feathered stem, on the right, toward the south, represents brightness, the light, the day, the sun, and it is the male. It is for defense and is carried on the side farthest from the people. The brown-eagle feathered stem, *Kawas*, is to the left, toward the north; it represents darkness, the night, the moon, and is the female. *Kawas* is carried nearest the people. (Fletcher 1904, 99)

The celebrants would be swaying while this stanza was being sung. Before being laid down, the feathered stems would be carried around the lodge four times and waved over the heads of the people, while being moved to represent the eagle hovering over her nest and then alighting on her young. The songs and movements were a prayer for the gift of children and for a true and strong bond between the Father and Children.

Other items associated with the two feather pipestems included an ear of corn; two sticks from a plum tree; a wildcat skin; a shell; two wooden bowls; a braid of buffalo hair; a braid of sweet grass; blue, green and red clay; and the fat from a deer or buffalo.

Each object used in this ceremony had its own significance and meaning. The participants wore certain attire and sang songs to the powers during the ceremony, their chanting accompanied by drums. The lyrics of songs included a thanks or welcome for the return of the parent. The eagle wings would be fanned to represent the flight of the birds. Warriors and others of the tribes had their roles.

There was a part named "Songs of the Birds" that took place on the third day:

> The songs about the birds begin with the egg, so the song of the bird's nest where the eggs are lying is the first to be sung. Then comes the song about the wren, the smallest of birds. After that we sing about the birds that are with the *Hako,* from the smallest to the largest.
>
> These songs are to teach the people to care for their children, even before they are born. They also teach the people to be happy and thankful. They also explain how the birds came to be upon the feathered stems and why they are able to help the people. (Fletcher 1904, 168)

Other songs for this ceremony were the "Song of the Bird's Nest," the "Song of the Wren," the "Song of the Woodpecker and Turkey," the "Song of the Duck" and the "Song of the Owl." The songs were meant to instruct the people in their parental duties. By following these teachings, the people would receive the gifts of the Hako. For each song there is a detailed explanation of the symbolism of the lyrics (Fletcher 1904).

Pawnee Pipestems

The "Origin of the Pawnee Pipe Stick Ceremony" was told by Cheyenne-Chief, whose father Pipe-Chief was one of the leading Skidi Pawnee holy men and chiefs (Dorsey 1906). This tale relates to the origin of one of the most interesting Skidi Pawnee ceremonies, the Pipe-Stick or Calumet.

Ceremonial pipestems were decorated with eagle feathers and other ceremonial material. One pipestem had the feathers of the brown eagle, likely the Golden Eagle,

> signifying 'night,' 'female,' 'fruitfulness' and known as *ra-hak-katitu*, 'one-mouth-black'; and the other with feathers of the white eagle, signifying 'day,' 'male,' 'defense,' 'war' and called *ra-hak-takaru*, 'one-mouth-white.' At various stages in the ceremony these were waved about so that they symbolized the flight of the eagles. (Weltfish 1977, 392)

Pawnee Indian Cosmology

The Plains Indians used the stars to help guide their lives. The positions of constellations told the tribal elders the time to plant corn in the spring and the time to have a harvest ceremony in the fall. Tribal cosmology is described in the most detail for the Skidi Pawnee, who lived along the Platte and Loup rivers (Chamberlain 1982).

The Pawnee believed the Morning Star was the great power on the east side of the Milky Way galaxy. The hawk—representing the bird that killed with its wings as the Morning Star did with his club—was his symbol, and red was his color (Murie 1981, 38). The Morning Star played an important role in the Pawnee Captive Girl Sacrifice, where a young virgin captured from another tribe was offered to tribal deities. This ceremony made use of the Morning Star Bundle, which contained an otter skin collar, Mother Corn, a hawk skin, an extra pipe, some soft down feathers and a wildcat skin with its legs filled with native tobacco and paints (Weltfish 1977, 107).

The Bird's Foot Constellation apparently was an important symbol that sometimes was painted on the faces of warriors (Chamberlain 1963, 110, 116, 429, in Murie 1981). During face-painting, a warrior

> takes red ointment and with his fingers makes two straight marks down the right side . . . [;] then he makes a picture of the bird's foot upon his forehead. That bird's foot is not intended for a real bird's foot; it is the bird's claw picture in the Milky Way in the heavens. (Chamberlain 1963, 114 in Murie 1981, 64-65)

The Turkey's Foot Constellation painted on the forehead was a part of the symbolic face-painting used as a mark of office among the Pawnee (Dorsey and Murie 1940, 112, in Chamberlain 1982). Although it sometimes is called a "turkey's foot" in the literature, it is apparent that the Bird's Foot Constellation was associated with the Morning Star, the protector of warriors (Chamberlain 1982).

For the Pawnee the summer season began when two small, twinkling stars, the Swimming Ducks, appeared in the sky (Murie 1981, 40-41, 53). The Swimming Ducks rise in the eastern sky during the spring and disappear in the fall.

> All the Pawnee ceremonies end in the month of October, for all the animals are hibernating and the birds have gone south. Even the stars have changed their places. The two shining stars known as the duck stars have disappeared. These stars may be seen southeast of the Milky Way. The snake head has disappeared; only his body can be seen southeast of the Milky Way. . . . In the month of January the animals begin to stir. . . . The two duck stars again appear in the

> heavens; the snake stars are out in full. The birds begin to migrate north. It is now time for ceremonies. . . . The birds are now flying north. The two duck stars are now in the pond. The water animals, by their powerful breath, have broken the ice. . . . Brother medicine men, the two duck stars in the heavens are now swimming in the pond. . . . (Chamberlain 1982, 118 in Murie 1981, 201-203)

The description of the Thunder Ritual of the Skidi says that the time for the Evening Star Bundle Ceremony was fixed approximately by the appearance of the Swimming Ducks on the northeastern horizon. The Pawnee began this ritual with

> the Evening Star bundle lying open before them. The sacred objects were spread out on the skin of a tawny yellow calf representing the herds of buffalo. Two sacred ears of corn represented their staple food, two owlskins the watchfulness of the chiefs, hawkskins the ferocity of the warriors, flint for fire and sweet grass for incense. . . . (Weltfish 1977, 80)

The pair of stars, Lambda and Upsilon Scorpii (the end of the tail of the Scorpion), are a very reasonable choice for the Swimming Ducks (Chamberlain 1982). At latitude 41° north, these stars rise in the south-southeast and reach an altitude of about 10° one hour before sunrise by mid-February. They reach altitude 12° one hour before sunrise in early April. In the springtime, they indeed appear to fly across the south, as if to suggest to the wild ducks that it is time to migrate northward. About mid-August, they culminate one hour after sunset. The two stars are gone from the sky by November.

Arrow-making by the Pawnee

Arrows typically were made of dogwood shafts, and warriors gathered their own feathers. The distinctive character of the shaft was confined to the makers, not the owners. Turkey feathers were used for the most part, since they tore straight, but, if these were not available, hawk or goose feathers were substituted (Weltfish 1977, 138-139). Once the wood shaft was finished, the feathers were attached to the blunt end. While splitting the feather, the maker chewed some sinew to make it soft enough to use to bind three splints of feathers to the arrow. The feathered end of the arrow then was smeared with a gummy paste of boiled hide, after which the feathers were bent onto the stick, pasted down and tied in place with wet sinew at their lower ends. After straightening, downy feathers were fastened on at the lower ends of the feathers that already were attached (Weltfish 1977, 391).

Bird Quillwork

Besides serving as ornamental decorations, the quill of the feather also was used to sew designs onto objects, even though bird quills split and break when flattened for sewing. There are not many items that display this type of quillwork from Plains Indians, but one Santee knife case (shown below) does have the lower portion covered by long quills. Bird quills were used to a small extent, either independent of or in connection with porcupine quills (Orchard 1984, 6-8).

> Bird-quills are also easy to use, generally readily available and easier to dye than porcupine quills. Because of their length, bird quills are better suited than porcupine quills for use on items such as pipe stems, awl cases, whistles and bows.
>
> There appear to be two major areas—the Fort Berthold and Santee Sioux areas—where bird quills were used to cover large decorative fields. . . . (Feder 1987, 56)

An additional study indicates how bird quills were used in tribal artifacts.

> A split bird-quill is frequently found where an edging has been made, . . . or surrounding a pattern that has not been worked out to the edge. In such cases the bird-quill has been used as a filler, that is, the porcupine-quills are wrapped around the bird-quill and then sewed to the leather. . . . In some instances, however, a strip of leather or cord has been used for the same purpose, perhaps because the bird-quill was too stiff to produce the soft, graceful curves obtainable with other materials.
>
> . . . There are two objectionable features in the use of bird-quills, namely (1) the uneven, ragged appearance of the edges, due to splitting, . . . mars the neatness that is so characteristic of the work in which quills of the porcupine are used; (2) they do not make a clean, sharp fold where they are turned under the stitches, hence the edges of the patterns are uneven and the whole presents the appearance of an inexpert piece of work, and to the stiffness may be due the absence of any form of decoration other than geometrical. (Orchard 1984, 8)

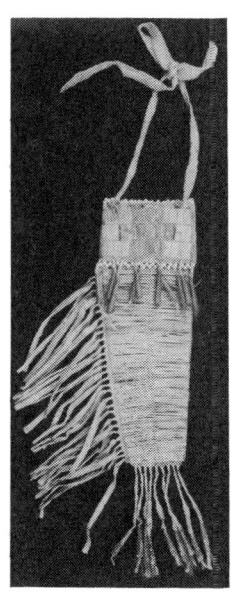

Santee Sioux bird-quill knife case

Quills from the crow, raven and other black birds were used to provide the color black, a color unavailable in natural dyes (Feder 1987). Many other quills present on objects are a dull blue-green color. A pair of Yankton leggings from around 1820 has strips of bird quills along the fringe. Duke Paul Wilhelm, who traveled through eastern Nebraska, collected a Sioux eagle-bone whistle wrapped with green bird quills (Feder 1987).

Birds in the Languages of the Plains Indians

The important role of birds in the lives of Plains Indians also is shown by the variety of oral- and sign-language names. The first pertinent dictionary published was prepared in the 1850s by Stephen Return Riggs for the Sioux, primarily the Santee Sioux (Riggs 1968), and a revised edition was published in the 1880s. This dictionary provides a very comprehensive treatment that includes words and statements, many of which pertain to birds. One entry for "to sing in praise of" describes a derived term, *zitkadan pa ado-wan,* which means to sing praises of the honorable deeds of another person while holding several woodpecker heads (Riggs 1968, 9). The term *zithatanka en ahiyahe* means a flock of birds landing in a field (Riggs 1968, 14). The term *a-ho-ton* is a verb for "to cry out for," as in a young bird crying out for food (Riggs 1968, 16). There are many other references to birds in this dictionary, but the items included here are terms specifically for birds. An example of a term not included here is *wa-ka'-hun-ta,* which is for "*to make rough,* as the birds do by tearing open the husks of corn" (Riggs 1968, 506).

Another extensive study on the spoken names for birds was made in the 1850s by Ferdinand V. Hayden, who thoroughly described them in a report prepared after the Warren Expedition (Hayden 1863b). The sign language used to describe birds also is known for tribes of the western Plains—the Pawnee, Sioux and Crow (Clark 1885). Tribal language for the Omaha has been described well (Fletcher and La Flesche 1972). Spoken legends and tribal sign languages included names for familiar species, giving additional insight into which species were known and most familiar to Native Americans in Nebraska.

The tribal names given in the species accounts are repeated here to provide an overall summary of material from the reference sources. Each word is attributed to a specific tribe. Additional information given for the tribal bird name that is taken directly from the source material is included in parentheses below, while any editorial comments are enclosed within square brackets.

Beak: Otoe—*pa-thūh'.* Pawnee—*ćōs; cūsh.* Dakota Sioux—*i-ksu'.*
Bird: Omaha—*wa-żing'-a.* Otoe—*wa-yeng'-e.* Pawnee—*li-kūts'-ki; kit-o-ka'-ru* (all kinds of birds); *li-kū'ts.* Sioux—*zit-ka'-la.*

Winnebago—*wa-n'i-gi-a*. Dakota Sioux—*ćaŋ-śiŋ-ća-hpu* for a small species of bird; *ćan-śke-du-ta* for the red bird; *taku kiŋye ćiŋ* (birds); *śin-yan'-ta-ka-dan* (a small bird which frequents the rice lakes); *śke-du'-ta* (a small red bird); *śuŋk-ta'-wa-na-piŋ-na* (the name of a small bird); *wa-hu'-pa-ko-za* (wing-flappers, i.e., fowls); *wa-kiŋ'-yaŋ-na* (birds, fowl); *wa-kiŋ'-yaŋ-pi* (those that fly, birds); *zi-tka'* for birds of all kinds; *zi-tka'-ćaŋ-hpaŋ-na* for a small bird with a large bill; *zi-tka'-daŋ*, a generic name for small birds; *zi-tka'-sdi-daŋ*, a kind of bird; *zuŋ-ziŋ'-ća*, which is the yellow-hammer, a kind of bird [likely a woodpecker].

Bittern, American: Omaha—*mo^n'xata, wado^{n}be* (looks up at the sky).

Blackbird: Omaha—*mo^{n}gthi'xta*. Pawnee—*li-kū't-ska-ti*. Dakota Sioux—*wa-hpa'-ho-ta* (a species of blackbird).

Blackbird, Common: Dakota Sioux—*wa-hpa'-taŋ-ka; zi-tka'-taŋ-ka* [This may also refer to the Red-winged Blackbird.].

Blackbird, Red-winged: Dakota Sioux—*wa'-mdo-śa* (a species of blackbird with red on its wings).

Bluebird, Eastern: Omaha—*wazhi^n'tu*.

Bobwhite, Northern [partridge]: Omaha—*u-shi-wa'-re; u'shiwathe* (one who fools people) [spelled as *u-she-w'a-the* (Hayden 1868, 408)]. Otoe—*to'-shra-eng-a*. Pawnee—*ōt-kis'-is; āt-kās*.

Bunting, Lark: Dakota Sioux—*wa'-mdo-ska* (a species of blackbird with white on its wings; the *wapagića*).

Chickadee, Black-capped: Dakota Sioux—*wi'-yu-śkiŋ-śkiŋ-na* ("the chickadeedee," the black-capped titmouse).

Cormorant, Double-crested: Dakota Sioux—*huŋ'-tka*.

Cowbird, Brown-headed: Dakota Sioux—*wa-hpa'-ho-ta* (a brown bird that follows cattle, the cow-bird).

Crane: Omaha—*pe'to^n*. Dakota Sioux—*pe-haŋ'* (the crane of several species).

Crane, Sandhill: Dakota Sioux—*pe-haŋ'-gi-daŋ* (the gray or sandhill crane).

Crane, Whooping: Dakota Sioux—*pe-haŋ'-saŋ* (the large white crane).

Crow: Omaha—*ka'xe*. Pawnee—*ka'-ka*. Dakota Sioux—*uŋ-ći'-śi-ća-daŋ*.

Curlew: Omaha—*ki'ko^{n}çi*. Dakota Sioux—*ri-'ća-ni-će-taŋ-ka* (a species of curlew).

Curlew, Long-billed: Omaha—*ki'kato^{n}ga* (big curlew). Dakota Sioux—*pa-su'-ś'ko-pa* (the prairie curlew).

Dove: Omaha—*thi'ta.*
Dove, Mourning: Omaha—*thitato^{n}ga* (big dove). Dakota Sioux—*tin'-wa-ki-ye-daŋ* (the house-pigeon and the turtle dove).
Duck: Omaha—*nih'-a-shing'-a; mi'xazhi^{n}ga* (little goose). Pawnee—*ki'-waks; ki'-sat; ki'-i-nuks.* Dakota Sioux—*ma-ga-si-ća ću'-kcaŋ* for a kind of duck; *ću-kćaŋ'-pa-ġi* for a duck about the size of a Mallard, with a gray head and white breast; *ću-kćaŋ'-pa-sa-pa* for a species of duck with a black head and neck; *ću-kćaŋ'-taŋ-ka* for the large species of duck which they called *ću'-kćaŋ; ho'-ta-daŋ* (a small sharp-billed duck); *ma-ġa'-ksi-ća* (duck, ducks, the generic name); *pa-su'-mda-ś'ka* (a broad-billed duck); *ś'do-ka'* (a kind of spotted duck); *ś'u-pe'-ć'o-wo-ź'u* (a species of duck so called because its entrails are always full).
Duck, Wood: Omaha—*mi'xa zhi^{n}ga xage egu^n* (the crying duck). Dakota Sioux—*s'ki-s'ka'.*

Eagle: Omaha—*xitha'.* Otoe—*hra.* Pawnee—*lih'-ta-kats; li-ta'-kuts.* Winnebago—*tcaxce'p.* Dakota Sioux—*ćaŋ-śka'-waŋ-mdi-waŋ* for a species of kite or eagle; *hu-ya'* for the common eagle; *huya ćiŋća* for a young eagle; *waŋ-mdi'* (the royal or war-eagle).
Eagle, Bald: Omaha—*paçu^n'* (whitish head); *xitha'gthezhe* (spotted eagle). Dakota Sioux—*a-nog'-pa-ska* (white-headed eagle).
Eagle, Golden: Omaha—*Xitha' çka* (white eagle). Pawnee—*wam-bi-li'* (the bird that sails). Sioux—*wam-bi-li'* (the bird that sails).
Egg: Omaha—*wet-a'.*

Feather: Otoe—*mēh'-e; mi-ah'e.* Pawnee—*hi'-tu; hit'k.* Winnebago—*wa'-nik-ma'-shu-na; tcaxce'p mącū'* (eagle feathers). Dakota Sioux—*śuŋ* (the large feathers of birds' wings); *wa-će'-hiŋ* (the long, slender feathers growing near the tail of an eagle); *wi'-ya-ka* (a quill, a feather of the wing or tail of geese).
Fledgling: Dakota Sioux—*uŋ-źiŋ'-ća* (a bird before the tail has grown).
Flicker, Northern: Omaha—*tho^n'çiga.*

Goldeneye, Common: Dakota Sioux—*na-wa'-te-ska-daŋ* (a kind of small duck with a white spot on each side of the head).
Goose: Omaha—*mih'-e; mih-a-hi'* (goose-hair or feathers); *m'i-ha.* Otoe—*meh'-e; meh'-shing-a* (little goose); *meh-ath'-ka-han'-ye* (a swan, white goose). Pawnee—*kat-o'-rūt.* Loup Pawnee—*ko-hat'; kat-o-rūt'-a-ka; ka-to-ni-ta-ka* (white goose). Dakota Sioux—*ma-ġa'* (a goose, geese).

Goose, Canada: Omaha—*mi'xa toⁿga* (big goose). Dakota Sioux—*maġa'-śa-pa* (the common wild goose).
Goose, Snow: Omaha—*kiçnuⁿ'*. Dakota Sioux—*ma-ġa'-paŋ-paŋ-na; ma-ġa'-śe-kśe-ća-daŋ* (both the brant).
Grouse, Ruffed [yellow wood bird or pine pheasant; the mountain pheasant is the Ruffed Grouse]: Sioux—*wa-zi'-shi-o.* Dakota Sioux—*zi'-ća-ti-hda-bu-daŋ* (the drumming partridge).
Grouse, Sharp-tailed: Sioux—*shi-o'-ći-ka'-la.*
Gull: Omaha—*ne'tha.* Dakota Sioux—*wi-ća'-taŋ-ktaŋ-ka; wi-ća'-taŋ-ktaŋ-ka-daŋ.*

Harrier, Northern: Dakota Sioux—*pte-ġo'-pe-ća* (a kind of hawk, so called because it frequents marshes).
Hawk: Otoe—*hre'-ta.* Pawnee—*pi-a'k-i; ki-ta'-wi-kūts* (a kind of hawk). Winnebago—*k'eredju̧'sep.* Dakota Sioux—*ćaŋ-śka'* (a species of hawk); *će-taŋ'* for the chicken hawk [Cooper's Hawk] or the Pigeon Hawk [Sharp-shinned Hawk]; *u-pi'-zi-ća* (a yellow-tailed hawk) [possibly the Red-tailed Hawk, since the Omaha tribal name refers to the bird with a yellow tail].
Hawk, Red-shouldered: Omaha—*gthoⁿshka'.*
Hawk, Red-tailed: Omaha—*iⁿ'beçiga* (yellow tail).
Hawk, Sharp-shinned: Winnebago—*k'irik'īri'sgera* (Pigeon Hawk).
Heron: Dakota Sioux—*ho-k'a'; ho-k'a'-ġi-ća* (a small kind of heron).
Heron, Great Blue: Dakota Sioux—*ho-k'a'-to* (the blue heron).
Hummingbird: Omaha—*wati'ninika wazhiⁿga* (butterfly bird) [probably the Ruby-throated Hummingbird].

Jay, Blue: Omaha—*iⁿchoⁿg'agiuduⁿ* (fond of mice). Dakota Sioux—*zi-tka'-to; te-te'-ni-ća.*
Jay, Pinyon: Sioux—*zit-ka'-to* (bluebird; also called the Maximilian's jay in historic nomenclature).
Junco, Dark-eyed: Sioux—*pa-ća-shi'-wa-ta.*

Kestrel, American: Omaha—*gthedoⁿ.*
Kingbird, Eastern: Omaha—*wati'duka.*
Kingfisher, Belted: Omaha—*noⁿxi'de shkuniⁿ.* Dakota Sioux—*ku-śde'-ća.*
Kite: Dakota Sioux—*ua-ni'-ya-ka-taŋ-ka* (the hen hawk, a species of kite).

Lark, Horned: Omaha—*ma'çi çka.*
Loon, Common: Dakota Sioux—*huŋ'-tka.*

Magpie, Black-billed: Sioux—*ūnk-ći'-ki-ća*. Dakota Sioux—*un-kće'-ki-ha; zi-tka'-wa-kaŋ-taŋ-haŋ*.
Mallard: Omaha—*pa'hitu* (green neck). Dakota Sioux—*pa-ġoŋ'-ta*.
Meadowlark: Omaha—*ta'tithiⁿge*. Dakota Sioux—*śdo'-śdo-daŋ*.
Merganser: Sioux—*pa'-pe-sto-la* ("sharp-nose" or fish-duck) [likely the Common Merganser].

Nest: Dakota Sioux—*ho-hpi'; wa-ho'-hpi*.
Nighthawk, Common: Omaha—*te'ubixoⁿ* (the buffalo inflator). Dakota Sioux—*pi'-śko*.

Owl: Omaha—*pa'nuhu*. Otoe—*mam'-po-ke*. Pawnee—*pa-ho'-du*. Dakota Sioux—*hiŋ-haŋ'; hiŋ-haŋ'-ći-ka-la* for a small species of owl; *hiŋ-haŋ'-ka-ġa* and *hiŋ-yaŋ'-ka-ġa* for an owl; *hiŋ-haŋ'-saŋ* for the gray owl; *hiŋ-haŋ'-sa-pa* for the black owl; *hiŋ-haŋ'-śa* for the red owl.
Owl, Barred: Omaha—*wapu'gahahada*.
Owl, Burrowing: Sioux—*i-ha'-mi-ko-ti-la* (the owl that lives with the prairie dogs).
Owl, Great Horned: Omaha—*pa'nuhu hetoⁿ egoⁿ* (owl having horns). Dakota Sioux—*hiŋ-haŋ'-he-toŋ-na* for the horned owl, probably *Strix bubo=Bubo virginianus*.
Owl, Snowy: Omaha—*iⁿ'chuⁿçuⁿ* (snow white). Dakota Sioux—*hiŋ-haŋ'-śka* (white owl).

Partridge or pheasant: Pawnee—*āt-kās*. Dakota Sioux—*zi'-ća*.
Pelican, American White: Omaha—*Bthe'xe*. Dakota Sioux—*mde'-ġa*.
Pheasant: Dakota Sioux—*ti-ća'-bu-dan*.
Pigeon: Dakota Sioux—*wa-ki'-ye-daŋ*.
Pigeon [Passenger Pigeon]: Otoe—*pu-će'-eng-e*. Dakota Sioux—*wa-kiŋ'-ye-la* (the pigeon, a dove).
Plover: Pawnee—*ūt*.
Poorwill, Common: Sioux—*źo'-a-to-pi* (so named from its note).
Prairie-Chicken, Greater: Omaha—*shu*. Pawnee—*pūks* and *u'-ut*. Dakota Sioux—*śi'-yo*.

Raven, Common: Dakota Sioux—*kaŋ-ġi'*.
Robin, American: Dakota Sioux—*śi-śo'-ka*.
Rosy-Finch, Gray-crowned: Sioux—*wa-zi-zit'-ka-la* (yellowstone bird: the bird that lives among the yellow ferruginous sandstones).

Screech-Owl, Eastern: Omaha—*ne' thazhibe.* Dakota Sioux—*po-po'-tka; po-po'-tka-daŋ.*
Snipe, Common: Omaha—*toⁿ'iⁿ.* Otoe—*wi-tūh'-e.* Pawnee—*paks-ki'-ra-rūts.*
Stilt, Black-necked[?]: Dakota Sioux—*si-yu'-kaŋ-śa-śa-daŋ* (a bird having slender reddish legs); *pe-han'-ka-dan* (a small, slender bird which frequents the water) [The stilt is a small, slender bird that occurs in marshes, and its red legs are a characteristic identification feature.].
Swallow: Omaha—*nishku'shku.* Dakota Sioux—*i-ća'-pśiŋ-pśiŋ-ća* (a species of swallow); *i-ća'-pśiŋ-pśiŋ-ća-daŋ* (the common swallow).
Swallow, Barn: Dakota Sioux—*u-pi'-źa-ta* (the fork-tailed swallow).
Swallow-tailed Kite, American: Omaha—*iⁿ'be zhoⁿka* (forked tail).
Swan: Dakota Sioux—*ma-ġa'-ska; ma-ġa'-taŋ-ka* (the swan, swans).

Teal: Dakota Sioux—*śi-ya'-ka* (There are five additional terms for teal.).
Teal, Blue-winged: Omaha—*a'hiⁿ hide tu* (blue wing); *mi'xc wagthoⁿxe* (betrayer duck, so called because it betrayed the water monster in the myth of Ha'xegi). Sioux—*ho-pa-wa'-to-to* (blue wings).
Thrush: Omaha—*taçka'çka.* Dakota Sioux—*wa-ġi'-yo-ġi* (There are two birds bearing this name, one of which probably is a species of thrush.).
Towhee, Rufous-sided: Sioux—*ćāŋ-o-hu'-ya* ("wood-color" or *chewink*).
Turkey, Wild: Omaha—*çiçi'ka,* spelled *zi-z'i-ka* by Hayden. Otoe—*ye-ih-hun-chy.* Dakota Sioux—*wa-gle'-kśuŋ; zi'-ća-taŋ-ka.*

Vulture, Turkey: Omaha—*he'ga.*

Warbler, Yellow, or American Goldfinch[?]: Dakota Sioux—*wa-źuŋ'-tka; wa-źuŋ'-tka-daŋ* (the name of a small yellow bird).
Waterfowl: Dakota Sioux—*mah-ćiŋ'-ća* (the young of geese and ducks); *maġaksića-agli-wi* (the moon when the ducks come back, April); *maġaokada-wi* (the moon when the geese lay eggs, April); *waśuŋpa-wi* (the moon when geese shed their feathers, July).
Whip-poor-will: Omaha—*ha'kugthi.*
Wing: Omaha—*a'n-he.* Pawnee—*a'-hu.* Winnebago—*wa-ni'k-a-hu'-za.*
Woodcock, American: Omaha—*pa'xthega* (freckled head). Otoe—*thka'-ge.* Pawnee—*kau'-pat.*
Woodpecker: Otoe—*to'-kre-kre'-the.*

Woodpecker, Hairy: Omaha—*zhoⁿ'panini*.
Woodpecker, Pileated: Omaha—*wazhiⁿ'gapa* (bird head).
Woodpecker, Red-headed: Omaha—*tu'cka; mu'xpa.* Pawnee—*ka'-put.* Dakota Sioux—*wa-hnuŋ'-ka*.
Wren: Omaha—*kixaxaja* (laughing bird). Dakota Sioux—*pte-ġaŋ'-ni-ća-daŋ*.

Bird species were prominent in the language of the Omaha. Many of the terms in this dictionary are general words, such as beak, bird, duck, feather, goose, owl and plover. The species these Native Americans noted most were waterfowl, especially ducks (which could have been any of several species). Other notable and typical birds are the American Swallow-tailed Kite, Canada Goose, Red-shouldered Hawk, Northern Bobwhite and Wood Duck. The Omaha word for the American Bittern, with its head-to-the-sky response to an intruder, perfectly describes the behavior of this marsh bird. The American White Pelican, Belted Kingfisher and gulls are other typical birds of the Missouri River. Forest birds are represented by the Barred Owl, Pileated Woodpecker and Red-headed Woodpecker. Species identified in their language are typical birds of the Missouri valley and the Omaha tribal area of eastern Nebraska.

Other species familiar to the Omaha and Pawnee also are typical species of the prairies and woods of eastern Nebraska. The Greater Prairie-Chicken, found on the prairie, was an important part of life for both tribes. The Common Snipe would have occurred along the Missouri River and Platte River within the territory of these tribes. The well-known Northern Bobwhite is in the historic language of both tribes. The Pawnee language referred to the blackbird, the crow, the plover and the hawk.

The Otoe also recognized several woodland species, such as woodpeckers, that were not known to tribes farther west on the Great Plains. The languages of these tribes were less specific, using generic terms rather than the species identification practiced by the Omaha.

The Sioux language was especially rich with terms identifying different types of birds and their features. There were many terms for birds, and the beak and different types of feathers are identified. The Sioux were very aware of the breeding season, having a name for the April moon based on when the geese lay their eggs. Terms for nest, young waterfowl and fledgling are included in the tribal dictionary. A name for the July moon was based on the geese losing their feathers while undergoing the summer molt.

Some species were noted only for the Dakota Sioux, including the Lark Bunting, Black-capped Chickadee, Double-crested Cormorant, Sandhill Crane, Whooping Crane, Great Blue Heron, American Robin and Barn Swallow. These are very characteristic birds of the plains and the woods along the rivers. Species that would be somewhat more typical of the habitats of the eastern tribes of the Sioux include the Common Loon and Common Goldeneye. Species noted only in the Hayden report—Pinyon Jay, Dark-eyed Junco, Common Poorwill, Rufous-sided Towhee and Gray-crowned Rosy-Finch—are western species; this may indicate these birds were more familiar to Sioux in the western part of their vast territory, for example the Lakota Sioux of the Black Hills region. Though the Gray-crowned Rosy-Finch specifically was known, there was no mention of the vocal Rock Wren, which occurs in similar habitat. The wren of the "rice lakes" was familiar to tribal members. The modern dictionary of the Lakota language has additional terms for bird types and species (Karol and Rozman 1974).

Native American Bird Sign Language

Descriptions of tribal sign language provide additional history about birds known to the Pawnee of eastern Nebraska and the Sioux and Crow of the western Plains (Clark 1885). The information presented here is quoted verbatim as it is given in W. P. Clark's *The Indian Sign Language*.

> Bird. Conception: Wings. Bring the hands, palm outwards, fingers extended and touching above, to right and left in front of shoulders, hands same height; move them simultaneously to front and downwards, repeating motions, imitating the motion of wings; care must be taken to imitate closely. The wings of small birds move rapidly; those of large ones slowly. Some peculiarity may have to be noted,—the manner of flying or soaring, its habits, and even its tone of voice. A goose would be known by indicating the long, slow motion of its wings and the triangular figure taken by these birds in their flight to the South or distant North, and perhaps indicating the noise made by them. . . .
>
> Deaf-mutes hold right hand, back up, near mouth, thumb and index extended and touching at tips, other fingers closed; thumb and index represent the bill of the bird. . . .
>
> Black. The sign for *color* with many tribes is used for *black*, but the more safe way is to point to something black in color. . . .
>
> Crow. Make sign for *bird* and for *black*. . . .

Duck. The usual signs are for *bird* and *water*. Sometimes the gestures for flat bill, the color of legs, shape of feet, manner of flying are made, and the quack! quack! sounds imitated. Portions of the skin of the head and neck are used to decorate the medicine-pipes of the Indians, not only on account of the beauty of the feathers, but also from the important and sacred part assigned this bird in many of their myths of creation.

Deaf-mutes make their sign for *bird*, and imitate with both hands the waddling motion of the bird in walking. . . .

Lakota wooden pipe with Mallard neck feathers

Eagle. Conception: Wings and black tips of tail-feathers. Make sign for *bird;* then hold extended left hand horizontally, back up, in front of left breast, fingers pointing to front and right; lay the lower edge of extended and vertical right hand, back to right and outwards, fingers pointing to left and front, on back of left, about on knuckles; move the right hand outwards and to the right, then make sign for *black;* this represents the black ends of the tail-feathers, and sometimes the sign for *tail* is made before this sign.

The bald-headed eagle is represented by signs for *bird* and bald head. . . .

The tail-feathers from the "chief of all birds," as they call the golden eagle, are highly prized, and are the chief and talismanic decoration of war-bonnets. These feathers are fastened in the hair, and also in the manes of their war-ponies. Some tribes only allow a man who has killed some one in a fight to wear a feather of this kind on the head; *i.e.,* stuck in the scalp-lock. Should two or three be worn there, they indicate the number of people killed by the wearer. Some Indians claim that this bird was created and given them by God for its beauty, for decorating themselves, and as a special charm in battle. The Indians, as did the ancients, regard the golden eagle as an emblem of strength and courage. "Its extraordinary powers of vision, the great height to which it soars in the sky, the wild grandeur of the scenery amidst which it chiefly loves to make its abode, and its longevity, have concurred to recommend it to their poetic regard, inspired them with hope and confidence of success and victory." (*See War-bonnet.*)

The wings of the bald-headed eagle are prized for fans, and the large bones of eagles' and hawks' wings are used for whistles. (*See Whistles.*)

Deaf-mutes make their sign for *bird,* and then indicate a crooked bill, or beak. . . .

Hawk. Make sign for *bird;* then hold the partially-compressed right hand in front of and little higher than right shoulder; move it to front and downwards, finishing on a slight upward curve, imitating the manner in which a hawk "dives" through the air after smaller birds, swooping down after its prey. . . .

Night. Conception: Earth covered over. Bring extended hands, backs up, well out in front of body, fingers pointing to front, right hand very little higher than left, hands about height of breast and several inches apart; move the right hand to left, left to right, turning hands sightly by wrist action, so that fingers of right hand point to left and front, left hand to right and front, terminating movement when wrists are crossed. . . .

Owl. Conception: Big eyes. Make sign for *bird;* then bring the curved index and thumbs of both hands over and around the eyes, other fingers closed. Sometimes the extended index fingers are held up alongside of temple to denote the horns, and I have also seen the sign for *night,* and the hooting of the owl imitated.

Deaf-mutes use the same sign. . . .

Turkey. Conception: Beard. Make sign for *bird,* and then hold compressed right hand under chin, close to breast, fingers pointing downwards; shake the hand slightly, which is held loosely at wrist. Sometimes only index of right hand is extended.

Deaf-mutes hold right index on bridge of nose, to denote the wattle of the turkey-gobbler. . . .

War-bonnet. Carry the extended hands from front to rear, parallel and close to sides of head, fingers pointing upwards, tips little higher than top of head, palms of hands towards head; then sweep the right hand from the crown of the head well down to rear of body. Sometimes the sign for tail-feather of the golden eagle is added. . . .

The usual explanation for its use is that it makes a man as brave as the birds from which the feathers are taken, carries fear to the hearts of the enemy, and is handsome. (*See Eagle.*) . . .

Water. Conception: Drinking out of palm of hand. Hold partially-compressed right hand, back down, in front of, close to, and little above mouth, fingers pointing to left and upwards; move the hand downwards, turning palm towards mouth.

Deaf-mutes make their sign for the letter W, holding tip of index against lips, and moving hand out two or three inches, repeating motion. . . .

Woodpecker. Make sign for *bird;* then hold left forearm about vertical, in front of left shoulder, left hand extended, back to left; bring partially-compressed right hand, and place palm against left forearm on right side near elbow, fingers pointing upwards (direction of forearm); move the hand with a jerk or jump to left side of forearm, and a little higher up, then again to right side, imitating the peculiar manner of hopping on the surface of a tree of this bird; then lower the left hand, and tap the palm several times with the tip of curved index of right hand, others and thumb closed.

The first time I saw this sign made was in conversation with an Indian who claimed to be a medicine-man of high degree, and he informed me he had learned a wonderful remedy for a special disease from the whisperings of this bird at night. His gestures were graceful, and the peculiar habit of the birds so clearly imitated that I recognized and understood the sign instantly.

Deaf-mutes indicate in the same manner. (Clark 1885, 67, 138, 157-158, 209, 271, 275, 384, 397-398, 399, 408)

Other sources contain additional material on the tribal languages of Plains Indians. Tomkins' *Indian Sign Language* is similar to the above source for the historic period and lists words in general use, synonyms, a history of tribal sign language and the use of smoke for signals (Tomkins 1969).

CHAPTER TWO:
HISTORIC EXPLORATIONS AND ACCOUNTS
OF BIRDLIFE IN NEBRASKA

The first explorations in the Great Plains of the trans-Mississippi West occurred decades prior to 1750. These expeditions discovered rich natural resources in the area, but they did not take any notes on its birdlife. The French voyageurs probably were aware of birds, but their concern was establishing a fur trade, not making notes on animal life.

In 1703 the explorer Louis Armand de Lom d'Arce, Baron de Lahontan, traveled up a "sluggish stream" named the "Long River" (now known as the Missouri River), which is a tributary of the Mississippi River (Phillips 1961). Other French voyageurs and explorers ascended the Missouri River including journeys in 1708 and 1712, trying to find a route to the Pacific Ocean. The 1712 account mentions the Nebraska or Platte River and the Native American tribes in the area west of the Missouri (Phillips 1961, 487). Pelts were exchanged with the tribes, which may have been either the Omaha or the Pawnee. Visits prior to 1750 also established trade with the Sioux. The French traded for bison and beaver pelts and other rich furs at posts north and east towards the Great Lakes (Kay 1979). Native Americans most often took big game, which were important for subsistence, and species whose behavior made them easier to kill. Tribes would travel long distances to reach productive hunting grounds, since different species were abundant in certain habitats.

Birds generally had no practical connection with the fur trade (Chittenden 1986, 824). Hunters had little use for the swan, eagle, crane, hawk, raven and magpie as food, since elk or bison would provide more meat. Birds were used for decorative or ceremonial purposes, and the large and colorful skins of rare birds were traded on an occasional basis.

One exception was the skin of swans. During the latter part of the 1700s and the first half of the 1800s, numerous swan skins were shipped by fur traders such as the Northwest Company, American Fur Company and Hudson's Bay Company from North America to London, England (Hanson 1977). The American Fur Company shipped thirty from the Western Outfit in 1830, eight from the Upper Missouri Outfit in 1838 and sixty-eight from the Northern Outfit in 1840. Some of these birds could have originated in the Nebraska area, although birds nesting in regions such as the Sand Hills would have been affected less due to the remote character of the region. The Hudson's Bay Company gathered greater numbers of skins. Its annual reports show 2,576 were shipped in 1844, 2,453 in 1845 and 1,922 in 1846 (Hanson 1977). "The commercial importance of swan feathers stemmed from the use of the down for powder puffs, the small feathers for dress trimmings and quills for pens" (Hanson 1977, 46). In some years as many as ten thousand skins were exported. Apparently most of the skins were from the Trumpeter Swan. John James Audubon was said to have preferred the use of swan quills over steel pens. With increased settlement and a decline in swan numbers, fewer birds were shot and fewer skins exported.

The first Spanish exploration of what became Nebraska was in 1720, when Lt. Col. Pedro de Villasur came from Mexico through Kansas, crossed the Arkansas River, and continued north to the Platte River. A Spanish mural depicts a battle which took place either at the Loup Fork or, more likely, at the forks of the Platte River (Brandon 1990, 166-173). The mural shows feathers hanging from the bows of the warriors and many arrows with feather vanes, though there are no feathers tied in the hair (as is typical of many portraits of area Native Americans, such as the Pawnee). If the warriors depicted actually were from Nebraska, this mural is possibly the first historic record of tribal use of bird material in the area.

In 1739 French fur traders Paul Mallet and Pierre Mallet went up the Missouri as far as the village of the Pawnee, located in what now would be Dakota County. They named the Platte, spelling it "Plate." The Mallet brothers did not keep any notes on the area's natural history, however.

The rich history of the Great Plains that includes Nebraska has been well studied (Adams 1977). Great explorers and large expeditions traversed the territory and studied its occupants, wildlife and features of the land. Euro-American pioneers battled the harsh elements to create homes. The taming of the Great Plains brought many changes in its environment, including the wildlife and birds (Dodge 1989). During this exploration and early settlement of the Plains, many records of the birdlife of the "Wild West" were penned.

Some of the first note fragments on the landscape were made by James Mackay in his journal about the Sand Hills in 1795. He described the region as "deserts of drifting sand," without any trees, water or animals (Twedt and Wolfe 1976, 198). Although there was supposedly no water, marshes were mentioned, some of which had wild rice. Mackay went through Cherry County across Gordon Creek and the Snake River before reaching the Niobrara, followed it to the

Missouri and then downriver. No bird history notes are available from the expedition.

From 1750 to 1875, expedition narratives, naturalists' notes and journals of pioneers provide information on birds of the region. The rigors of constant travel and more demanding obligations allowed little time for natural history studies, as expeditions constantly moved toward their destinations. On occasion a few days of delay provided a chance to better study a particular site—for instance, a serious mechanical problem would stop steamboat travel along the Missouri River—but typically the naturalists exploring the uncharted Nebraska Territory had just a few hours to chase birds or to collect plants.

There are many records of explorations in Nebraska Territory before the state was established. Pierre Tabeau journeyed to the Upper Missouri from 1803 through 1805. From 1804 to 1806, Lewis and Clark charted the land in the Louisiana Territory that recently had been bought from the French by the United States government.

Several sources include information from the Missouri River around 1820. The journal of surgeon John Gale, from the 1818-20 Missouri Expedition led by Col. Henry Atkinson, notes several species along the Missouri in September and October 1819 (Nichols 1969). Gale spent the winter of 1819-20 at Cantonment Missouri, the same winter Thomas Say spent with the Long Expedition, headed by Maj. Stephen Harriman Long (Thwaites 1905). The botanist, geologist and surgeon for Long's expedition was Edwin James. Members of this party also traveled to the Pawnee village near the Loup, crossing the Elkhorn (called *Wa-ta-tung-ya* by the Otoe) on their journey (James 1972, 282).

The first German to visit the Nebraska region was Duke Paul Wilhelm in 1823. He made some of the first records of animals other than those along the Missouri River. Wilhelm crossed the Elkhorn River and continued to the mouth of the Niobrara River.

In the early 1830s, the stylistic passages George Catlin wrote in his journal describe the wild landscapes he saw as he journeyed down the Missouri River. About the same time, notes taken by Prince Maximilian of Wied, kept in a journal separate from his daily journal, provide exceptionally vivid views of the flora and fauna of the wild Missouri River valley during 1833 and 1834. He described the many songbirds in the forest and commented on a new prairie lark heard on the prairie. The Linden-Museum in Stuttgart, Germany, has many items, such as shields and feather headdresses, collected by Prince Maximilian of Wied in 1833 and 1834. Some of the shields are adorned with eagle feathers. Although the material is from many different tribes, some items were made by the Omaha, Otoe and Pawnee in the Nebraska region.

The famed naturalist John James Audubon, accompanied by another skilled naturalist, Edward Harris, went up the Missouri River in 1843, taking notes and gathering material to illustrate Audubon's work on the quadrupeds of America. His many notes on birdlife include the first record of the Western Meadowlark, now the Nebraska state bird (Audubon 1960; McDermott 1951).

Europeans and Euro-Americans made many journeys along the Missouri River before they visited the Platte. Some useful notes are in material written about 1835 at a Presbyterian mission near the Grand Village of the Pawnee (Dunbar 1915). Most records from the Platte valley part of the region date from the 1840s and 1850s, during the mass movement of pioneers traveling to the western United States along the Oregon Trail.

Army troops and pioneers in their covered wagons slowly traveled across the open plains on the Oregon Trail. The rigors and duties of the journey meant little time was available to note animal life. If wildlife was noted, it was usually because it was being shot for food. Still, some people mentioned local birds in their notes and letters.

Army Lt. James Henry Carleton traveled from eastern Kansas, along the Blue River, and westward along the Platte in the 1840s. Another journey along the same route was made in 1843 by explorers heading for the West Coast (Johnson and Winter 1932). Rudolph Friederich Kurz continued the legacy of visits by earlier German naturalists when he explored along the Missouri River in 1851 and 1852 (Kurz 1970).

The first European explorers on the Great Plains journeyed through land peopled by Native Americans but claimed by European governments. The first trappers and traders visited for only short periods of time to harvest furs or to sell goods. After the Louisiana Purchase added millions of acres that the United States government owned but knew little about, expeditions were sent to explore the new territory. Early travelers explored an uncharted wilderness, but, once the travel routes were established, naturalists and other explorers followed. Most of the early historical accounts deal with the Missouri River region, due to the easier journey using steamboats on the river. The Missouri River and the Oregon Trail along the Platte River were major routes used to explore the Great Plains region that became Nebraska.

Government expeditions and naturalists first explored the wilderness of the Platte and Missouri rivers. Military men had less concern for natural history, since their objectives were to describe the location and size of tribes and determine the general features of the land for others who were to follow. Naturalists would walk or ride across the country, making notes in their journals and often collecting plant and animal specimens for museums in the eastern United States and Europe.

French explorers from the lake country to the north first started to explore the Plains region around 1675. By 1714 French traders and trappers had traveled nearly one thousand miles up the Missouri River to establish the claim for France (Swenk 1935). In 1739 the Mallet brothers went up the Missouri as far as the village of the Pawnee, located in modern Dakota County. Fragments of information in the natural history notes made by James Mackay in 1795 tell of the Sand Hills (Twedt and Wolfe 1976), but there is no mention of birds in this material.

At the turn of the nineteenth century, the Louisiana Territory west of the Mississippi had been explored little and remained an uncharted wilderness to Europeans and Euro-Americans. In 1803, just before the French sold the land to the United States, a journey along the Missouri River marked the first of many explorations of the land, its people and its wildlife. This expedition opened a route to be followed by many naturalists and explorers in subsequent decades.

Europeans influenced the handcrafted goods made by tribes living on the Plains in several ways. First, when Europeans introduced new materials such as cloth, metals, bright paint pigments, dyed wool yarns, mirrors, hawk bells, brass tacks and glass beads (Feder 1986). Native Americans adapted the new materials to their old methods. This resulted in goods that were more colorful but unchanged in form. For example, native-dyed buckskin material was replaced by black cloth; porcupine quills were replaced by glass trade beads and silk ribbon. The use of foreign materials also changed the appearance of artifacts that used bird items.

> One indirect impact of European contact on Native American art was the extinction of certain species of wild birds and land animals whose images had been used symbolically and physically in the making of sacred implements and clothing. After the extinction of the ivory-billed woodpecker and the Plains grizzly bear, artists often attempted to bleach or paint the body parts of related species in imitation of the animals favored by their forefathers. (Feder 1986, 99)

The loss of certain prominent species, such as the American Swallow-tailed Kite, Bald Eagle and others, required that items from different species had to be used.

Tabeau to the Upper Missouri

Although Pierre Tabeau first journeyed up the Missouri River in 1775, only brief notes are available from that trip (Abel 1939). A fur trader with a party led by Regis Loisel that explored the Missouri to evaluate the trading potential of the area's Native Americans, Tabeau left St. Louis on June 22, 1803, for his second trip up the Missouri and returned on May 20, 1805 (Abel 1939). Tabeau went to Isle of Cedar, where the fort, made of juniper, included the house of Loisel, the expedition's sponsor. Part of Tabeau's return trip was made with the Lewis and Clark Expedition. His notes mention the features of the river, the vegetation on its banks, and daily events and also contain brief notes on birdlife and a brief description of how tribes of the western Plains hunted eagles in the fall. No specific localities were given, but the notes are for the river region in general.

The Lewis and Clark Expedition

In 1803 the Louisiana Purchase added the Missouri River territory to the United States. For only pennies per acre, the wilderness of the Plains was bought from the French and became United States government land. President Thomas Jefferson ordered an expedition to visit the newly-acquired territory. Capt. Meriwether Lewis, Jefferson's private secretary, was selected to lead the group. His chosen assistant was Lt. William Clark. The expedition started upriver from St. Louis on May 14, 1804. The party consisted of forty men traveling in a fifty-five-foot keelboat and two smaller navigation boats called "pirogues." Two horses traveled along the river bank at the same time.

They reached the land now called Nebraska on July 11, 1804, when they camped across from the mouth of the Nemaha River. Three months were spent moving along the eastern boundary of the territory that became Nebraska's state line. Journal entries of both men are available (Moulton 1986, 1987), and these narratives support documents from other expedition sources. Extensive footnotes provide current information and facts about events that occurred after this expedition narrative.

The site records for the Nebraska region begin when the expedition reached the area of Nodaway Island on July 8, 1804. For the species accounts, some bird identifications were based on the habits of the bird mentioned. For example, the journal entry that reads, "a number of Burds Nests in the holes & crevises of this rock which Continus 2 miles," refers to the Cliff Swallow (Moulton 1987, 383). The identification is based on the text, as well as on the presence of a rock bluff along the river. These rock bluffs were prominent features, and their association with nesting Cliff Swallows is noted in many of the historic references. Great numbers of young geese were seen along the

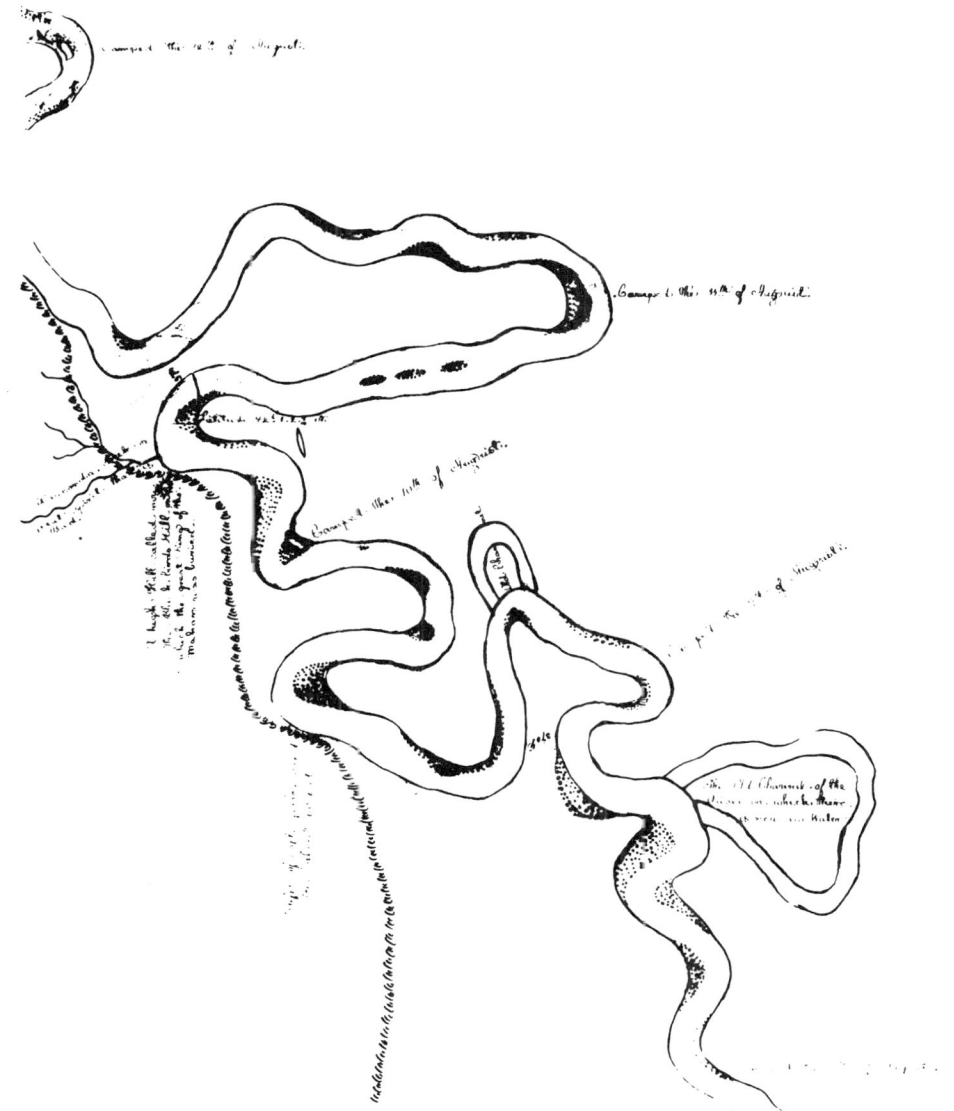

Lewis and Clark's map of the Missouri River, August 1804

Nodaway Island, by Karl Bodmer

Missouri in the southeast area of Nebraska. Grouse, likely Greater Prairie-Chickens, were noted in Sarpy County. The Lewis and Clark notes have a lengthy description of Great Egrets collected in the area of the Council Bluff.

The Least Tern was identified and is the subject of a lengthy account. While in the area of modern Burt County during August, Lewis killed two birds and mentioned terns being more common here than on the portion of the river already traveled. Several young terns were caught, and the journal entry mentions the habit of the birds to "squeak" as they fly. Most of the notes on this bird are descriptions of its physical size, coloration and behavior. On August 8, while just south of the village of the Omaha, Lewis noted:

> [W]e had seen but a few aquatic fowls of any kind on the river since we commenced our journey up the Missouri, a few geese accompanied by their young, the wood duck which is common to every part of this country & crains of several kinds which will be described in their respective places. (Moulton 1987, 459-460)

The "crains" could refer to the Sandhill Crane, egrets or herons. On the same day, Lewis' journal narrative has information about the great number of pelicans seen. A few days later, Clark wrote of ducks and different kinds of plovers on ponds as well as on the river.

Near the mouth of the Vermillion River, Clark noted a great number of birds hovering about the top of a mound. The birds flew off when he approached. Swallows, either Bank Swallows or Northern Rough-winged Swallows, hovered in vast numbers there. He noted prairie larks (meadowlarks) on the grassy hills at this mound. The Red-winged Blackbird and House Wren were among the many birds noted on the plains. A type of bittern, which could have been an American Bittern, was collected. The expedition stayed in this area for several days due to a steamboat equipment failure. There are few other notes for the remainder of their Nebraska trip. Pertinent journal information for the trip upriver ends on September 8, when turkeys were seen in the western part of the Fort Randall Military Reservation.

The trip downriver, from August 29 to September 11, 1806, went much faster, as the boat swiftly floated on the river current. The expedition did not linger, but quickly returned to St. Louis and continued back to the cities of the east. They made few notes on birdlife.

The Astor Party of 1810-11

John Jacob Astor of New York organized the American Fur Company, and its partners traveled to the West Coast. The Astor Party spent a winter at the mouth of the Nodaway River, just south of the present Nebraska boundary. Although the party started up the river in April 1811, they left the state near the end of May without recording any bird notes.

Brackenridge's Trip in 1811

The Henry Marie Brackenridge Expedition left St. Louis in early spring 1811 and moved quickly upriver to catch the Astor Party. The parties traveled together to provide a larger force of men. Henry Brackenridge went through Nebraska from May 4 to May 28, 1811 (Brackenridge 1976). This group included Manuel Lisa, who was hired by Englishman John Bradbury to collect natural history specimens, and Thomas Nuttall, who had been hired to collect plants. Lisa had convinced Brackenridge to accompany him on the Missouri River trip.

The narrative mentions bison, antelope, plant types, land features and other natural history items. The only birds recorded were pigeons and wild ducks killed at Sonora Island in northeast Nemaha County. A flock of turkeys also was seen. On May 7, 1811, while a steamboat mast was being made from a fallen oak, Brackenridge hiked into the hills along the river and noted: "On my return to the boat, killed some pigeons [maybe Passenger Pigeons] and wild ducks, and saw a flock of turkies" (Brackenridge 1976, 76) in the vicinity of the Isle à Beau Soleil. Sun Island and Sonora Island were names given to the same island.

Stuart's Journey of Discovery

Although Robert Stuart was born in Scotland, he lived in the wilds of the West Coast of America. In 1812 he was working for John Jacob Astor's Pacific Fur Company at Fort Astoria, and in June he left with dispatches to deliver to Astor in New York (Stuart 1953). Stuart and his men followed the Columbia and Snake rivers, crossed the Rocky Mountains, and then went down the Platte River. The route they discovered and recorded established a path that many pioneers followed in later decades when they traveled west to the unsettled land of the coast.

Stuart's party reached the North Platte River region of modern Nebraska the day before Christmas 1812. They spent a week in this area building canoes because this was where the first suitable trees were present. As the weather warmed in March, Stuart noted the first birds in his journal. He wrote that the first wild goose made its appearance; it was shot and cooked for dinner (Stuart 1935, 211-212). A couple of weeks later, another "fat goose" was killed.

As they floated eastward, the few notes on birds continued. Several miles west of the confluence of the North and South Platte rivers, where Lake McConaughy now is located, Stuart observed,

> ... Some distance above and below last nights station is an extensive swamp, the residence of immense numbers of Geese & Brants; a few Swans and an endless variety of Ducks; and during [the latter part of] this days march we found many similar places all well stocked with Wild Fowl. (Stuart 1953, 145)

Later the same day (March 27, 1813), Stuart killed three swans and a goose with a single shot from his gun. "Prairie hens" also were present, leading Stuart to remark that the Missouri River bottoms must not be far, since these birds were known not to occur very far westward on the Plains.

Elsewhere along the Platte River, other birds were sighted, including geese and swans. Curlews and "field" larks were present near the "Grand Isle" of the central Platte. The party left the Nebraska area on April 22, 1813. The only other comment Stuart made about birds was how plentiful turkeys were along the Missouri River below the mouth of the Platte River.

The Major Long Expedition

Following the report of Lewis and Clark, the government was concerned with western expansion and the defense of the frontier, and a major effort went into the building of forts. In 1819 and 1820 Maj. Stephen H. Long led one of two expeditions sent upriver to establish these posts. Major Long was part of the Army Topographic Engineers, which was responsible for exploring the western Plains, including a large area of modern-day Nebraska. The government records include observations made by Thomas Say, the zoologist in charge of natural history. There is more than one source containing information from the Long Expedition (Thwaites 1905; James 1972; Benson 1988).

Long's party visited Fort Leavenworth, in modern-day Kansas, traveled northward up the Missouri River, and established a winter

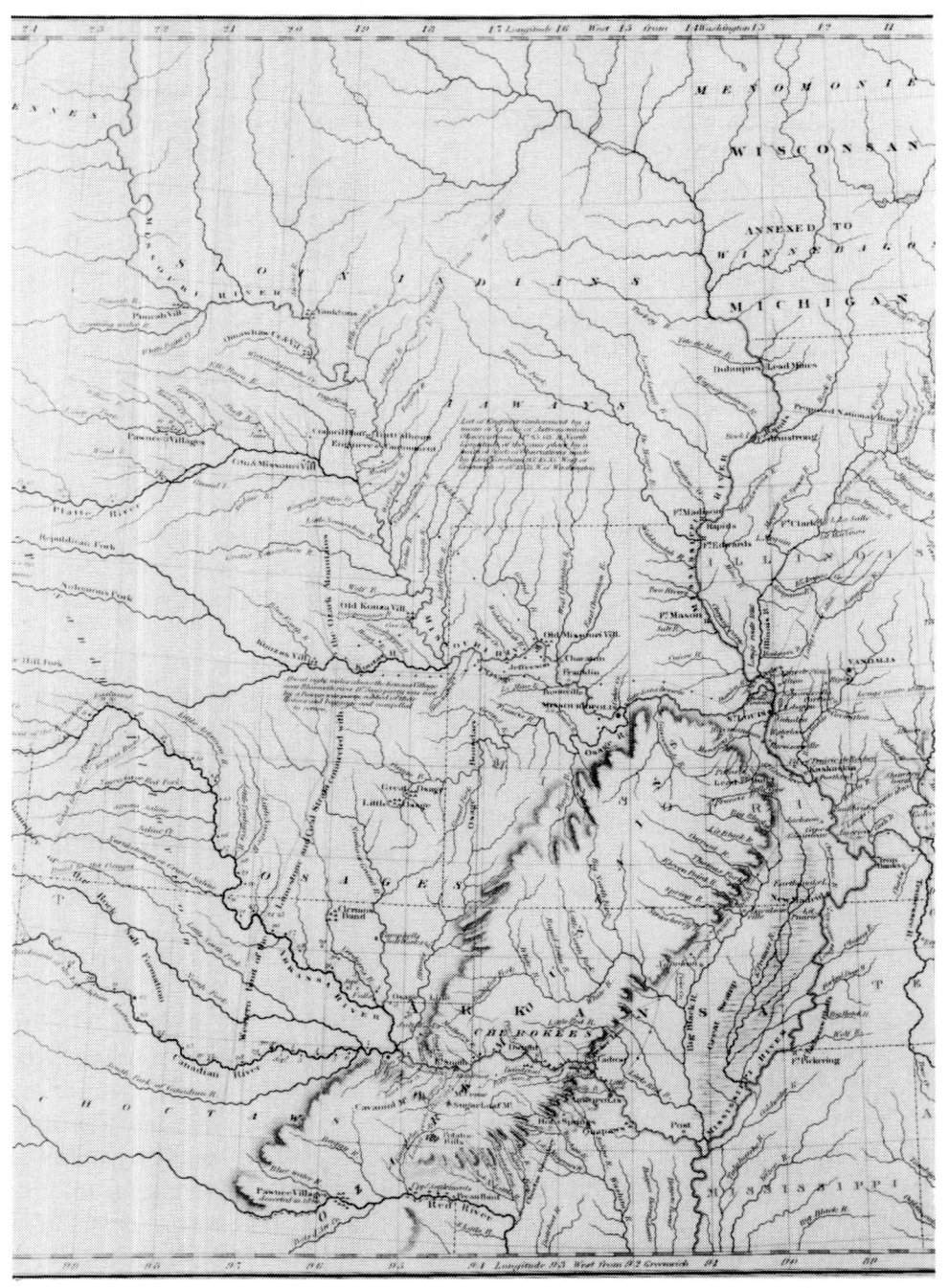

Map of Country drained by the Mississippi, by Maj. Stephen H. Long, 1823

camp in fall 1819. Known as Engineer Cantonment, Long's government camp was situated on the Missouri River, five miles below Lewis and Clark's Council Bluff. With a limestone cliff three hundred feet high providing shelter from the northerly winter winds, the cantonment served as winter quarters for Long's government party in the very southeast corner of what is now Washington County, Nebraska. One of the more prominent landmarks in the immediate vicinity of the cantonment was the trading post, Fort Lisa. After Long headed westward in the spring of 1820, Fort Atkinson was built on a site just east of the present town of Fort Calhoun.

Observations were made in this area from September 19, 1819, until June 6, 1820. They provide excellent information about the birdlife of a specific localized area, since they contain records from different seasons. The list, which includes spring arrival dates, is from a catalog of the names of animals observed at the cantonment (Thwaites 1905, Appendix A). During the summer the expedition headed west through the Plains, which Major Long labeled the "Great American Desert," but just a few bird sightings were made away from the Missouri River.

Several species seen in the area were illustrated by the artist-naturalist Titian Ramsay Peale. He painted a watercolor of the Sandhill Crane in 1820 (Benson 1988). The Scarlet Tanager, Black-billed Magpie, Yellow-headed Blackbird and Wood Duck also were captured in watercolor at Engineer Cantonment in 1820. Pencil sketches depict other animals, such as the bison, seen elsewhere during the Long Expedition.

The Wilhelm Journey

The German naturalist Duke Paul Wilhelm was in his mid-twenties when he embarked on a three-year journey through North America (Wilhelm 1928). This young man had been studying natural history for several years prior to his visit to the area of modern-day Nebraska from July to September 1823. The expedition used the Missouri River as a travel route until it reached Fort Atkinson. Wilhelm then went northwest along the Elkhorn to the mouth of the Niobrara. After several weeks in South Dakota, he boated down the Missouri and returned to St. Louis.

Sightings for the Missouri River area are included in the notes made by Wilhelm prior to reaching Fort Atkinson and again upon reaching the river near the Niobrara, although notes on the species seen are fragmentary. One of the more notable observations was of the Least Tern at the mouth of the Platte. Wilhelm's party gave good location data for the Missouri River, where many of the prominent landmarks were named. Other useful sightings were made in Knox County, where the Niobrara River was a notable landmark.

Catlin along the Middle Missouri

George Catlin traveled among the Native American tribes of the Plains from 1832 to 1839. His writings describe the wild lands and the

*Canoes Traveling Near Bellevue,
by George Catlin*

events he experienced, his paintings of the Native Americans, and views of the wild landscape (Catlin 1965). In one of his letters, Catlin described a voyage made from the upper Missouri region downriver to the Cantonment Leavenworth in Kansas. This journey, which Catlin said was the most delightful of his whole tour, was a float trip down through the middle Missouri River region. His notes include many vivid descriptions of the landscape. He took only a few notes on the birdlife, but he did mention the "sportsman's fever was roused and satisfied; the swan, ducks, geese, and pelicans . . . were *'stretched'* by our rifles . . ." (Catlin 1965, 3). There is no mention of specific species. Although the quick trip downriver meant Catlin wrote only brief passages, his art work captures several views of the rolling hills and open expanses of northeast Nebraska along the Missouri River.

The Expedition of Prince Maximilian

On April 26, 1833, an expedition led by Prince Maximilian of Wied, Germany, reached the western Plains that were to become Nebraska and remained there until May 13, 1833. The two-week return voyage the following year lasted from May 5 to May 18, 1834 (Orr and Porter 1983). During the trip, artist Karl Bodmer recorded the land, people and nature the party saw in exquisite watercolor paintings and other sketches. David Dreidoppel was the expedition's taxidermist and skilled huntsman.

Prince Maximilian visited a wilderness of splendid forest and endless prairie and penned some of the most thorough natural history observations of the Missouri River region made during the period of early exploration. He kept a personal notebook giving each day's events, as well as a record of natural history observations (Orr and Porter 1983). Maximilian also made drawings and sketches in the margins of his journals.

During the expedition, the men explored the river valley and nearby uplands, collecting plant and animal specimens and observing the features of the land. In his journals the prince described in detail the character of the Missouri valley. The notes made by this naturalist provide a written record of the vegetation and the habitat provided for birds. The plant species, the birds seen and their habitat during this historic period can be understood better through his notes.

The journal entries for the Nebraska region begin just to the south of its present boundary, when, steaming against the swollen current of the Missouri River, the *Yellowstone* passed the large and beautiful Nodaway Island. Prince Maximilian sat on deck, watching the land and writing observations in his journals. Nearby, Karl Bodmer sketched scenes of the wilderness. The narrative mentions that off to the left was a Bald Eagle nest in the tall timber. On the northern shore of the channel were remnants of huts built by the Iowa Indians. The steamboat chugged up the river, passing other rivers, streams, islands, sloughs, swamps, lakes and forests. As the crews struggled to move the boat off a sandbar where it had run aground, the party saw many familiar birds, including a Rufous-sided Towhee farther upriver.

Two flocks of pelicans flew overhead and Turkey Vultures floated above the hills. Canada Geese nested along the river bank.

After lunch on May 2, the boat reached Weeping Water Creek. On an island to the right was a bank with a great many snags with Wood Ducks sitting on them. Approaching the Platte, Maximilian noted that its water could be distinguished from the Missouri,

> since it is clear and blue. It ran separately to the bank lying to our left, actually the right one, of the river. A mile farther the Platte water is nearly covered with white foam bubbles because this river has grown, and in this way we also got more water. (Orr and Porter 1983, 367)

Maximilian's party spent a pleasant evening on the balcony of Cabanne's home at Cabanne's post near the Council Bluff, and Maximilian wrote about the splendid Missouri shining in the still evening air. Frogs were croaking, and the Whip-poor-will called incessantly as a full moon rose up over the eastern horizon (Orr and Porter 1983, 379). The next night, on May 5, 1833, the expedition enjoyed twenty Native Americans dancing and singing under a full moon that, along with the loud and repeated calls of the Whip-poor-will, created a musical chorus in the Missouri River wilderness. The main dancer wore a headdress made of feathers from owls and other birds of prey.

Maximilian said in his notes that north of the Council Bluff the prairie was monotonous in its sameness. The description given for an area seen during the day on May 6 does not, however, match this expressed mood. The prince observed wild geese swimming in the snag-filled river. Farther on, to his right, was a beautiful forest, heavily shaded, its floor covered with dense undergrowth. He also noticed that the wild grapevines had started to bloom (Orr and Porter 1983, 384).

Later in the day, a stop was made for wood. Many trees were quickly felled, thanks to forty or fifty men swinging their axes. While the crew worked, the naturalists visited a nearby prairie that had Monarch butterflies flying about. The prince also noted the Eastern Kingbird and Scarlet Tanager in the woods, and ducks and geese were abundant. Sandpipers foraged on the sandbars.

On May 7, 1833, Prince Maximilian had been gone from his home in Neuwied, Germany, for a year. The morning brought excellent weather. Prairie, river bank willows, sandbars and wooded gullies lined the banks of the river. On a steep, yellow limestone bluff along the river, countless swallows were nesting and flying about like a swarm of bees. On the left was a green chain of hills he called the Blackbird Hills. Maximilian wrote that the most powerful chief of the

Washinga Sahba's Grave on Blackbird's Hills, after a painting by Karl Bodmer

Missouri region, the Omaha Chief Blackbird, was buried sitting on a live mule in a grave on the summit. In this region were the first notes describing how the conifers and broad-leaved trees grew mixed in the woods. The first signs of beaver were seen on a creek along the river.

North of Blackbird Hill, the boat stopped for the night on a sandbar next to the forest. The crew cut wood and started a great fire on the beach. Fireflies flew in every direction in the forest. Calls of the Whippoor-will echoed unceasingly. Bodmer returned late and almost had lost his way while following a Wild Turkey. Along the river's edge were tracks of wolves and elk, the prince said.

Prairie chickens and antelope lived on the open grasslands of what was to become northeast Nebraska. On the river shore were steep chalk bluffs, which on Lewis and Clark's maps are called the Calumet Bluffs. After an hour the boat reached the White Bear Bluffs, where Bodmer sketched the landscape. Dreidoppel encountered the Greater Prairie-Chicken, the Long-billed Curlew and an Upland Sandpiper. Maximilian observed in his entry for May 11, 1833:

> The prairie next to us was wet, and puddles and mud holes stood on it
> . . . .
>
> ... We made excursions into these prairies and found a few kinds of plants with long turnip-like roots.... The great yellow-breasted lark ... was scattered individually everywhere in the prairie. (Orr and Porter 1983, 403-404)

A day later he remarked how everywhere he saw

> the beautiful, cheerful region; the beautiful broad river in the brightest gleam of the sun; the one steamboat riding at anchor; one group of men on shore and a steamboat in motion; a large keelboat in the river—everywhere this isolated wilderness [was] full of life. On the shore one could see the novel-looking Indians covered in their buffalo hides.... (Orr and Porter 1983, 407)

Passenger Pigeons were seen flying about in the forest near the mouth of the Niobrara, or L'Eau qui Court, as it was identified by the French. After passing the Ponca Creek a few miles farther, there were numerous prairie dog towns with rattlesnakes living in the holes. Along the river was a chain of bluffs with swallow nests clinging to the cliffs. Though the naturalists noted juniper, dogwood, elm, wild grape, the edible wild turnip and several other types of plants in the prairie and woods, only a few birds, such as the Mourning Dove, were sighted. Burrowing Owls might have been expected in the prairie dog town.

Maximilian's expedition left the Nebraska region in mid-May. The journey continued onward to the upper Missouri, and the group spent the winter in Mandan territory at Fort Clark in present-day North Dakota. The return voyage downriver started in May 1834. On his return the prince continued his daily habit of making extensive notes on the wild features of the land, its flora and fauna in his diary. The trip downriver took less time than when going upstream.

Despite the hurry, Maximilian found a splendid number of items for his natural history log near the James River on May 7, 1833. He observed numerous swallows, warblers, swallow-tailed kites, butterflies and dragonflies. At the camp that night, the night birds were heard.

> At dusk a number of Whip-poor-wills . . . arrived which deafened our ears with their calling and flew about the fire within 3 paces. A couple of them were killed. They often sat themselves on the branches of trees. . . . Today we had heard the first Whip-poor-wills; from here on down they are common and we often heard calling. (Orr and Porter 1983, 422)

The region was rich in bird life. Species noted include the Purple Martin, Red-winged Blackbird, House Wren, herons, ducks, sparrows and thrushes. Spring migration was underway, and birds moving north, as well as those that had returned for the summer, could be seen.

Dreidoppel shot a specimen of a tern on May 11, 1834. On the same spring day, south of Blackbird Hill, Maximilian commented,

> In the dense willow bushes . . . were very many interesting birds, the rust-red thrush, the many-voiced *Icteria viridis* [Yellow-breasted Chat] with its splendid lemon-yellow throat, the lovely *Muscicapa ruticilla* [American Redstart], *Sylvia aestiva* [Yellow Warbler], and others. We saw extraordinarily many wood ducks (*Canard branchu*), above the tall forest hovered the lovely white *Falco furcatus* [American Swallow-tailed Kite] in pairs. . . (Orr and Porter 1983, 427)

On May 12, a few miles upriver from the Bellevue outpost, Prince Maximilian went on an excursion after lunch. His notes read:

> The surrounding hills and forests now were resplendent in the most luxuriant foliage. Blackbirds, the fire-colored and black Baltimore bird [oriole], *Muscicapa ruticilla* [redstart], *Sylvia aestiva* [Yellow Warbler] . . . were frequent. *Turdus migratorius* [robins], *Columba carolinensis* [doves], *Picus pubescens* [woodpeckers], . . . *Fring.[illa] erythrophth.* [towhee] and several other finches animated a lovely, gently ascending side valley, through which the Omahas have a path upwards towards their villages. (Orr and Porter 1983, 429)

The kite was seen along the river twice during the trip downriver. Moving quickly, the steamboat soon passed Bellevue, where many birds, including cuckoos, doves, the Yellow Warbler and Rufous-sided Towhee, were present. Farther south, Maximilian wrote of a primeval forest with many kinds of birds. On the afternoon of May 14, 1834, the first Carolina Parakeets were seen in the area that was to become Nemaha

County. Here the hunters along on the expedition sought Wild Turkeys but did not get any, the prince said.

Continuing downriver, the expedition soon reached the end of its journey through the Nebraska region. Maximilian was able to see two now extinct species, the Passenger Pigeon and the Carolina Parakeet, during some of his daily hikes.

All in all, the notes in Maximilian's diary provide details of the natural character of the land and its people over 150 years ago. His diary and the sketches and paintings by Bodmer provide a vivid reminder of the ancient wilderness of the Missouri River. Settlements at this time were limited to scattered forts and a few trading posts, such as the one located at the present site of Bellevue.

Townsend's Journey across the Rocky Mountains

John Kirk Townsend was a trained ornithologist on an expedition to Oregon in 1834 (Townsend 1978). The party left Independence, Missouri, in late April and reached the Nebraska region in early May. Moving westward along the Platte River portion of the Oregon Trail, the party took great interest in birds, but their narrative lacks details. The journal refers just to general species; localities are not mentioned regularly. In southeast Nebraska, Townsend observed:

> The little streams in this part of the country are fringed with a thick growth of pretty trees and bushes, and the buds are now swelling, and the leaves expanding, to 'welcome back the spring.' The birds, too, sing joyously amongst them, grosbeaks, thrushes, and buntings, a merry and musical band. I am particularly fond of sallying out early in the morning, and strolling around the camp. (Townsend 1978, 40)

The expedition narrative mentions the Sandhill Crane and the Long-billed Curlew seen near Fort Kearny. Birds are said to be abundant in the Ash Hollow area—a considerable variety, the trip narrative notes—but no species are mentioned. On some occasions Townsend could not investigate sites where birds were abundant because the expedition was ready to continue west.

As the men traveled along the Platte River, Townsend mentioned seeing species he thought were new to science. He collected and described more than thirty recently-discovered and newly-described species in his second report to the Philadelphia Academy of Sciences (Townsend 1837, 1839). His expedition list mentions the Lark Bunting and Chestnut-collared Longspur from along the Platte, but the reports are mostly a list of species with descriptions not very useful for locating Nebraska species. His records of the Lark Bunting and

Chestnut-collared Longspur from western Nebraska are the first known of these species.

Notes from the Presbyterian Mission

As a minister of the Presbyterian Church, John Dunbar spent a few years around 1835 or 1836 in the area of the Grand Pawnee Village near the Loup Fork. Most of his notes were based on letters he wrote, and they contain a few descriptions of the area, such as the following:

> I have passed up the Platte, the winter past, about 300 m. [miles] from its mouth. have seen but little timber, & that scattering on the banks & Ilands [islands] of the Platte & small creeks. The waters of the Platte are shoal [shallow]. . . . Between the Platte & the Loupfork, there are frequent hills of sand, some of them are high & steep. (Dunbar 1915, 699)

Dunbar wrote on March 20, 1835, that

> the spring birds sing finely. The sand banks of the Platte are covered with multitudes of wild geese, ducks, and other water fowl, that quackle, and croak with all their wonted hoarseness. (Dunbar 1915, 612)

Samuel Allis was another Presbyterian minister who came to Nebraska at the same time as Dunbar, but Allis apparently moved to different sites more often than his colleague. The two men exchanged letters that sometimes mention birds. Letters from Allis (Allis 1887) also are included in the Dunbar material.

Journeys to the Rocky Mountains

Two journeys made to the Rocky Mountains in the 1830s have left us brief notes regarding birdlife along the wagon trail. In 1834 William Marshall Anderson traveled along the Platte River west to the mountains (Morgan and Harris 1967). This journey was made from March to September in the company of trappers who left from Independence, Missouri, to visit the annual fur trade rendezvous. These men from fur companies, along with United States Army personnel, were opening the West for the many settlers. During the journey, Anderson witnessed the founding of a trading post by William L. Sublette, who led the party. The site became Fort Laramie. Most of Anderson's information on birdlife is found in a diary and a narrative published in 1871 in an Ohio newspaper.

A few notes were taken on the birds seen along the western Platte. Two interesting notations tell of a hawk's nest on a Native American burial platform near Scotts Bluff. A flock of pelicans along the Missouri River is mentioned on the return trip in September. There are more descriptions of the land and its features.

In 1839 Frederick Adolph Wislizenus, a German M.D., traveled along the Platte River (Wislizenus 1912). Although he left few notes regarding birds, he did write about several species while in the Big Bend Area of the central Platte River. The travel account reads:

> Many water birds were also about. The birds we had seen hitherto consisted chiefly of prairie chicken, lark, snipe, and a small kind of starling that was continuously swarming around us, and was so tame that it would at times sit on our pack animals while on the march. Here we got sight chiefly of water birds, such as ducks, geese, cranes, pelicans, gulls, and some very large kinds of snipe. (Wislizenus 1912, 43)

Only a few of these birds can be identified to specific species: the lark is likely the meadowlark; the starling is probably some type of blackbird, presumably the Brown-headed Cowbird, which would have been numerous around animal herds. Additional bird notes are limited to the Burrowing Owl seen in the area of Scotts Bluff.

The Scientific Explorations of Nicollet

French astronomer Joseph Nicollet came to North America with the intent of studying physical geography. By the time he reached this region on April 21, 1839, on the steamboat *Antelope,* he was making numerous notes on the geology of the Plains. Nicollet noted the prominent rock outcrops along the Missouri at several sites, including two which had nests of swallows (likely Cliff Swallows) built on the exposed limestone cliffs. These were the only birds recorded. On May 11, 1839, the group continued to the north and east of the Nebraska area (Bray and Bray 1976).

E. Willard Smith along the Platte River

These records from the fur-trading period on the Plains comprise the first and only complete record of a journey to trading posts and forts from St. Louis west to the Rocky Mountains and then eastward along the Platte River (Hafen and Hafen 1955, 152). A twenty-three-year-old college engineering graduate turned journalist, Smith headed west in August 1839 to Fort Davy Crockett, a favorite trappers' rendezvous spot in a valley of the Green River in northwest Colorado. He spent the winter on the Continental Divide after his party was forced to leave the vicinity of the fort due to hostilities with the Sioux. After spending weeks along the South Platte River, at the end of April 1840, Smith's party used a mackinaw boat made of hand-sawn timbers to float down the Platte with the hides that had been taken during the winter hunting. They reached the mouth of the Platte in the latter part of June. Although Smith noted Indian activity, bison and the general environment, he took no notes of birds that were seen along either the Platte or the Missouri River on the way to St. Louis, where they arrived July 3, 1840.

A Tour to the Oregon Territory

A band of emigrants was organized in 1841 at Weston, Missouri, to head for the Oregon Territory. Included in this party of about seventy people was sixty-three-year-old Rev. Joseph Williams, who was on the first of his three trips to the West Coast (Hafen and Hafen 1955, 199). Williams' group reached Nebraska at the end of May, entered the state along the Blue River, then headed to Fort Kearny and west along the Platte. Although Reverend Williams did not make any notes of birds, he mentioned features of the landscape, flat-bottomed boats loaded with robes and skins floating down the river, and events that occurred as his party traveled west. Prominent game animals he discussed were bison, elk and prairie wolves.

Frémont in 1842

John C. Frémont, of the United States Army Topographic Engineers, went overland from Kansas along the Blue River to the Platte River and then followed the great Platte River Road west. His September 1842 trip downriver along the Platte included a stop at the Loup Fork. Although Frémont took more notes on species of plants he observed, his only reference to birdlife is one about the turkey along the upper reaches of the Big Blue River, somewhat south of Fairbury, Nebraska (Frémont 1956).

Audubon's Expedition

In 1843 John James Audubon observed wildlife along the Missouri River from St. Louis to the mouth of the Yellowstone River at Fort Union. The summer journey was a chance for the naturalist and his companions to visit the untamed western frontier. Audubon had been studying birds and other wildlife for nearly forty years and intimately knew the variations in plumage, the differences in song and the other descriptive details needed to identify bird species properly.

He had studied avifauna throughout the great forests of the East, the Gulf Coast, along a few Midwest rivers and across the Atlantic in England, but he had not yet taken a trip west of the Mississippi River to the prairies and plains of the West and the rugged foothills of the Rocky Mountains. The bird skins collected in the West by ornithologists such as John Kirk Townsend in the late 1830s undoubtedly got Audubon excited about searching for new species. His journey along the Missouri River was to provide numerous observations of new landscapes and native flora and fauna.

The party that left St. Louis in April 1843 included not only Audubon but also two other naturalists. Edward Harris, Audubon's close personal friend since 1824, was an ardent benefactor of the study of birds. John R. Bell was a taxidermist from New York. They traveled on the steamboat *Omega* with a crew who gathered wood, hunted game and took care of other chores needed to make the voyage a success. Audubon's notes (Audubon 1960) and the notes of Harris (McDermott 1951) both provide birdlife information. In addition to their field notes, the naturalists kept records by shooting uncommon birds or trapping mammals and preparing these specimens for museum collections.

Their journal entries contain few references to landmarks, but many notes on birds. Records start on May 6, 1843, the day after their visit to St. Joseph, Missouri, about forty-five river miles south of the Nebraska border. Within days the expedition reached present-day Nebraska. They spent just two weeks in this region of the middle Missouri River. Another few days in late September and early October were spent along this stretch during the return trip.

While the *Omega* moved up river, the spring migration brought birds to their northern breeding grounds. This seasonal movement provided an even greater diversity of birds to be seen and added to the species list. Great flocks of waterfowl, which included swans, Sandhill Cranes and shore birds, flew overhead or were seen resting on the open water and mid-river sandbars. In the woods, the vibrant colors of warblers were seen flashing through the trees. Each day the naturalists took almost continual notes on the different types of avifauna they encountered. One of the more exciting events occurred on May 6, 1843, when Harris shot one of the new finches that could not be identified. For the next several days, similar birds were shot and compared to species with which the three naturalists were familiar. Eventually they discovered that this finch had not been described in any previous ornithological literature. Audubon was "truly proud to name it *Fringilla Harrisii* [Harris' Sparrow], in honor of one of the best friends I have in this world" (Audubon 1960, 499).

There was not always the excitement of identifying a new species, but there were opportunities each day to add to the list of birdlife present along the Missouri River. Audubon noted the large nests of Bald Eagles in cottonwoods along the river. Wild Turkeys were plentiful, and when shot they provided meat for an evening meal. Perhaps one of the more colorful birds observed was the Carolina Parakeet. The "paroquet," as it also was called, was said to be as plentiful as the turkey at two or three woodland to forest areas. As the expedition moved along the river, the list of birds grew.

Audubon's notes refer to prairies covering thousands of acres. He noted that members of the Iowa tribe killed Wild Turkeys, geese and crows for food. On May 9 he wrote at Bellevue,

> We have seen a Fish Hawk, Savannah Finch, Green-backed Swallows, Rough-winged Swallows, Martins, Parrakeets, Black-headed Gulls, Blackbirds, and Cow-birds; I will repeat that the woods are fairly alive with House Wrens. Blue herons, Emberiza pallida—Clay-colored Bunting of Swainson—Henslow's Bunting, crow blackbirds. . . . (Audubon 1960, 477)

The next day, while visiting a military camp near the abandoned Fort Atkinson, Audubon recorded seeing a Yellow-headed Blackbird, a completely new and different type of blackbird:

> . . . I heard the note of a bird new to me, and as it proceeded from a tree above our heads, I looked up and saw the first Yellow-headed Troupial alive that ever came across my own migrations. The captain thought me probably crazy . . . for I suddenly started, shot at the bird, and killed it. Afterwards I shot three more at one shot, but only one female amid hundreds of these Yellow-headed Blackbirds. They are quite abundant here, feeding on the surplus grain that drops from the horses' troughs; they walked under, and around the horses, with as much confidence as if anywhere else. When they rose, they generally flew to the very tops of the tallest trees, and there, swelling their throats, partially spreading their wings and tail, they issue their croaking note, which is a compound, not to be mistaken, between that of the Crow Blackbird and that of the Red-winged Starling. After I had fired at them twice they became quite shy, and all of them flew off to the prairies. (Audubon 1960, 480)

Harris also wrote in his journal about their visit to the camp. His notes mention that the magpie was present in the winter season and easily was caught in snares. There were two tame ones caught during the last winter at the camp. Audubon noted that the magpies had been caught with nooses and were being held captive in a cage.

Mouth of the Big Sioux River, by Karl Bodmer

Just a few days later, John Bell shot a small vireo in the area of what is now Dixon County. The bird was named Bell's Vireo in recognition of the man who first scientifically identified it.

On Monday, May 15, the day's events along the river west of the Big Sioux River are described in Audubon's journal.

> This morning the gale kept up, and as we had nothing better to do, it was proposed that we should walk across the bottom lands, and attempt to go to the prairies, distant about two and a half miles. This was accordingly done; Bell, Harris, Mr. La Barge—the first pilot—a mulatto hunter named Michaux, and I, started at nine. We first crossed through tangled brush-wood, and high-grown rushes for a few hundreds of yards, and soon perceived that here, as well as all along the Missouri and Mississippi, the land is highest nearest the shore, and falls off the farther one goes inland. Thus we soon came to mud, and from mud to muddy water, as *pure* as it runs in the Missouri itself; at every step which we took we raised several pounds of mud on our boots. Friend Harris very wisely returned, but the remainder of us proceeded through thick and thin until we came in sight of the prairies. But, alas! between us and them there existed a regular line of willows—and who ever saw willows grow far from water? Here we were of course stopped, and after attempting in many places to cross the water that divided us from the dry land, we were forced back, and had to return as best we could. We were mud up to the very middle, the perspiration ran down us, and at one time I was nearly exhausted; which proves to me pretty clearly that I am no longer as young, or as active, as I was some thirty years ago. When we reached the boat I was glad of it. We washed, changed our clothes, dined, and felt much refreshed. During our excursion out, Bell saw a Virginian Rail, and our sense of smell brought us to a dead Elk, putrid, and largely consumed by Wolves, whose tracks were very numerous about it. After dinner we went to the heronry that Harris had seen yesterday afternoon; for we had moved only one mile above the place of our wooding before we were again forced on shore. Here we killed four fine individuals, all on the wing, and some capital shots they were . . . . (Audubon 1960, 492-493)

Harris wrote about his outing on the same day in his notes of May 15:

> After dinner walked down the river to the Heronry which I discovered yesterday, we shot four of them and a Raven which came to feast on their eggs when they found the herons absent. The trappers who are very much in our way on our shooting excursions had been shooting all the morning at them and had only killed one. (McDermott 1951, 65)

He mentioned finding fresh eggs—"one in full order, ripe, and well colored and conditioned" (Audubon 1960, 493)—in the heronry. A raven was seen eating eggs in a nest. Beneath the trees the young that had died and fallen from the twenty to thirty stick-nests were known to later provide food for roving wolves. This find of the Audubon party is the only record of a heron colony from the historic period.

Audubon wrote about the land along the bluffs on the west, or Nebraska, side of the Vermillion River that

> the immense flat prairie on the east side of the river looked not unlike a lake of great expanse, and immediately beneath us the last freshet had left upwards of perhaps two or three hundred acres covered by water, with numbers of fowl on it. . . . From the tops of the hills we saw only a continual succession of other lakes. . . . (Audubon 1960, 497)

The lakes were created by flood water flows from the river channel. Canada Geese, a marsh hawk, gulls and terns were a few of the water birds seen along this stretch of the river. The flood plain meadow described would have been a haven for birds.

A few days later, on Monday, May 22, Audubon recorded, "We have not seen Parrakeets or Squirrels for several days; Partridges have also deserted us, as well as Rabbits; we have seen Barn Swallows, but no more Rough-winged" swallows (Audubon 1960, 507). Although there were no new birds, an important event for the bird history of Nebraska occurred in the following days.

Near the current state line of northern Nebraska, Audubon commented that "we saw Meadow Larks whose songs and single notes are quite different from those of the Eastern States; we have not yet been able to kill one to decide if new or not" (Audubon 1960, 506). On the Fort Randall Military Reservation near Fort Randall (which was one mile north of the Nebraska boundary in what is now South Dakota), Harris wrote about the bird with a new song, "We have seen a Meadowlark to-day which must prove a new one, its note is so entirely different from ours" (McDermott 1951, 69). These are Harris' first notations of the "Missouri Meadow Lark," which Audubon illustrated and eventually was designated the Western Meadowlark. Additional notes were made on the prairie lark: "Bell and Sprague saw several Meadow-larks, which I trust will prove new, as these birds have quite different notes and songs from those of our eastern birds" (Audubon 1960, 509).

Harris also was excited about the new birds and wrote on May 24 that they shot specimens of the red-shafted woodpecker, Say's flycatcher, Arkansas kingbird and lark finch, as well as

> several of the new Meadow Larks, for new I will insist it is, notwithstanding that we cannot from the books establish any specific difference, yet it is utterly impossible that the same bird in different parts of the world can have notes so totally different. (McDermott 1951, 70)

Earlier expeditions, both Lewis and Clark's and Maximilian's, had noted a difference in the song of this prairie bird, but they did not recognize it as a new species, perhaps because the similarities in plumage made them think it was the Eastern Meadowlark with an odd song. Today the Western Meadowlark is the official state bird of Nebraska.

The natural-history observations of Audubon's expedition continued as the group made its way upriver to Fort Union in Montana and then began the trip downriver in September. Moving downriver took much less time, and the journal entries for this period are shorter and less frequent than the May notes. Notable journal entries mostly refer to hunting Wild Turkeys, but ducks and geese were seen during a peak in the number of birds that were part of the waterfowl migrations along the river:

Sunday, October 1. . . . Bell killed a hen, and Harris two young birds; these will keep us going some days. . . .

Monday, [October] *2d.* . . . we found a fair camping-place and made our supper from excellent young Geese.

Tuesday, [October] *3d.* . . . Killed two Mallards; the Geese and Ducks are abundant beyond description. . . . (Audubon 1960, 170-171)

The Audubon party left the area of Nebraska on October 7, 1843, after six months along the Missouri River. The Harris journal does not mention any birds for the trip downriver through Nebraska.

Newly-identified bird species and additional personal sightings were included in illustrations and descriptions compiled for a revision of *Birds of America*, published in 1844. The mammal records provided new observations which were included in the magnificent work on the *Quadrupeds of America*. Although Audubon had pursued birds throughout the colonial and frontier states of America, the trip along the Missouri River provided new and exciting views of birds. He added new species to his personal list and continued to use his skills as a master of ornithology to name new species that other observers had missed.

Carleton on an Army Journey

The first military expeditions by Meriwether Lewis and William Clark, Maj. Stephen H. Long and John C. Frémont discovered travel routes for other military wagon trains to follow. Settlers heading for the West Coast moved along the same routes. Most military men did not take time to study natural history; they traveled whenever possible, and little time was spent on anything other than getting to the next point in a journey. Their notes have few references to specific landmarks, since they were following a wilderness trail, not a travel route, and natural-history notes often were very limited. When bird notes were made, there was little information, if any, given on the precise locality where birds were seen. Notes generally concerned the military affairs needed to lead the wagon train.

This was the type of 1844 army expedition that included Lt. (later Maj. Gen.) James Henry Carleton. His notes started as the wagon train left Fort Leavenworth, Kansas, to go to the Grand Pawnee Village on the Loup (Carleton 1983). They reached a fork of the Blue River, probably in the Jefferson County area, after leaving the headwaters of the Nemaha River on August 19, 1844. Carleton described the setting thus:

> It is well timbered, and has a wide intervale which is exceedingly rich, from getting all the wash from the uplands. It is singular that *so far* we have seen but a very few birds. The groves of the prairies being, generally, vocal with their sweet songs—we have been struck with the silence which seems to pervade all the woods upon this route. The only birds we have seen being paroquets, grouse (*one* grouse; it being the half a brace killed in a chapter or two back, by the Nimrod of the command), partridges, black-birds, prairie-hawks, whip-'o'wills, larks [meadowlarks], plovers and swallows—and a very few of them. (Carleton 1983, 34)

A brief note while along the Blue River mentions the association between prairie dog towns and the small owl living in the burrows. The Burrowing Owl would have been resident in the many prairie dog towns across the Plains in this area.

The military dragoon moved across the land, following the trail through the prairies and fording the rivers and streams in its path. One August day, moving along south of the Platte near the Loup Fork, a great number of Sandhill Cranes were seen: "These birds are very large, and as an article of food are said to be very delicious. They have a very loud and peculiarly discordant note" (Carleton 1983, 59-60).

At the Grand Pawnee Village, Carleton noted that on the lodge walls, among other decorations, were medicine birds or stuffed bird skins which were kept as amulets (Carleton 1983, 67). The party also visited the other Pawnee village to the north, where, Carleton noted, "The Loup Fork of the Nebraska is a very beautiful river—it is about six or seven hundred yards wide, and runs with a very swift current" (Carleton 1983, 95). He also observed that, in the village during ceremonies, tribal chiefs wore "caps made of war-eagle feathers, which gave a splendid contour to their heads" (Carleton 1983, 102).

Eventually, starting in early September, the party continued from the Loup eastward to the Council Bluff. They made some notes on flora, especially flowers, along the way. Carleton mentioned the Elkhorn River with its scattered groves of trees and butterflies in the valley of the Papillion Creek. The expedition then traveled overland to the eastern side of the Missouri, south to Kansas and back to Fort Leavenworth.

In 1845 Carleton made a second journey along the Blue River to the Platte, westward to the North Platte, then to the South Pass of the Rocky Mountains. From here they went along the Plains east of the mountains and returned to Fort Leavenworth through central Kansas. This dragoon expedition was under the command of Col. Stephen Watts Kearny. During the overland trip to the Blue River from near the headwaters of the Nemaha on May 19, the narrative recorded: "Early in the forenoon they attempted to get up an excitement at an unfortunate curlew that was too low spirited to fly" (Carleton 1983 177). This site was a few miles from the 1844 trail.

Carleton noted on May 27, while leaving the valley of the Little Blue and heading towards the Platte River,

> We also saw considerable game. Spanish curlews (*sickle-bills*) upland plover, grouse, and ducks were scared up at almost every rod and antelopes were seen from time to time, but not near enough to be taken. Our hunters rode at some distance from us upon the flanks of the columns, and enjoyed fine sport in keeping up a sort of running fire at the birds; some of which it is thought were seriously wounded; especially a few kildees; for they would only fly a short distance at a time—and then hobble along the ground as if every leg and wing had been broken. However, whenever the sportsmen dismounted to pick them up, they seemed suddenly to recover strength enough to fly away, and that, too, with wonderful alacrity. (Carleton 1983, 194)

This is the typical response of a Killdeer trying to lure an intruder away from its nest or young birds.

Carleton noted that, near the forks of the Nebraska (Platte) River, the rugged gorges were filled with a growth of juniper; wooded river islands consisted mostly of cottonwood, a few hackberry, and now and then an ash. Farther west the landscape was mostly prairie-like. A limestone bluff was seen for the duration of an afternoon's travel while in the rugged country near Ash Hollow. On June 8 Carleton wrote about the many Turkey Vultures on the ridge and peaks of the buttes. Often "great numbers" of vultures were seen in roosts. Hundreds of nests in "colonies on the bluffs" were probably breeding sites of Cliff Swallows. Purple Martins were observed to nest in crevices and holes. The next day, at hills farther west along the Platte

River, there was an occasional growth of junipers and a few cottonwoods on the river bank. Some men climbed a tree and captured a young Bald Eagle. The nearly-fledged eaglet was in a nest among the branches of the tree.

> At last . . . one man took hold of one of its wings, and another of the other, and stretching them apart, they ran for the wagons with the eagle between them. But he punished them severely on the way, by turning up first to the one on his right and fixing the sharp claws of both feet into his leg, and then serving the one upon his left in the same manner. The old eagles came around and filled the air with shrieks at the loss of their off-spring; but they did not attempt a rescue. It is the intention of the officers to take this belligerent captive 'to the states' if possible—and he has been provided with a perch upon one of the howitzers. If any one approaches him he shows his game blood at once, and immediately commences bristling up for a fight; but if he sees in his neighborhood a fine piece of meat or fish, he is quite conciliating until he gets hold of it, but after that it is quite as well to keep out of his reach. (Carleton 1983, 230)

Later that same day, an unusual shore bird was collected in the wetlands along the North Platte. The journal entry reads:

> A curlew was shot by one of the gentlemen to-day, which belonged to a species different from any we had ever seen before. It was quite as large as the Spanish curlew, or sickle-bill, but had a brown head—white body—black wings, and blue legs [an American Avocet]. Capt. Eustis prepared it with a view of sending it to the National Institute. Although it has probably been described, it must be quite rare, and will therefore be interesting. (Carleton 1983, 231)

The military expedition stopped near a temporary Sioux village in the vicinity of Chimney Rock. When members of the tribe came to visit, they had decorative "feathers, hawk's bells" and other items on their garments (Carleton 1983, 240).

Farther west the river narrowed and had a few groves of cottonwood and willow. The bluffs along the river decreased in height. The party camped just west of "Fort Platte," better known as Fort Laramie. This ends the travel notes made by Carleton that are from Nebraska, since the expedition did not go through the state on its return to the East.

The Travels of Father DeSmet

Fr. Pierre-Jean DeSmet, a member of the Society of Jesus, spent many decades traveling throughout the West. Wherever he went, his religious tasks included baptizing Native Americans and caring for the sick. In the Nebraska region, he visited along the Missouri River and, in the western and central part of the state, along the North Platte River and the Platte River Road route used by wagon trains heading west to California. Among DeSmet's journals occasional bird references can be found.

While traveling down the Missouri River to St. Louis in November 1846, in the Fort Vermillion area, two Canadians traded several turkeys to DeSmet's party for coffee and sugar. The turkeys were said to be scarce in that area of the country.

In 1851 Father DeSmet returned to visit the Sioux in the White River/Badlands area. The vast prairie dog towns were of special interest. The Badlands had towns which covered areas several square miles in extent. In addition to his notes on the behavior of the prairie dogs, DeSmet entered a note saying, "A kind of small owl . . . [was] commonly found at the entrance" to the prairie dog burrows (Chittenden and Richardson 1905, 623). This was undoubtedly the Burrowing Owl.

Later in the year, Father DeSmet was at a Great Council of Indians at the mouth of the Horse River, about thirty-five miles down the Platte River from Fort Laramie. While there, hunters killed a number of animals between August 1 and September 9, 1851. In addition to deer, antelope, bison, bears, Rocky Mountain sheep and other assorted animals, thirteen ducks, eighteen heath cocks and sixteen pheasants were taken (Chittenden and Richardson 1905). The heath cocks were likely some type of grouse, and the pheasants may have been Sharp-tailed Grouse, since there were no "true" pheasants (i.e., Ring-necked Pheasant) present at the time.

Continuing downriver, Father DeSmet commented on the character of the Platte from Ash Hollow to Fort Kearny, especially noting that woodlands were rare along the river. He made additional comments in October about the country between the Missouri River and Big Blue River, where there were

> forests of oak and nut trees of all varieties, with maple and cottonwood and a variety of trees found in the east. The hillsides in several places abound in fine springs of water surrounded by beautiful groves . . . [;] the prairies on all sides, surrounded by forests which protect the watercourses, present to the sight an ocean of verdure adorned with flowers, agitated by the wind and perfuming the air with a thousand odors. (Chittenden and Richardson 1905, 689)

In September 1859 DeSmet and his party of three oarsmen and a pilot made a quick journey down the Missouri River to St. Louis from Fort Benton. A steamboat at Omaha replaced the little skiff. The few notes from this journey mention the abundance of game. The rivers along the route provided

> excellent fish, water-fowl, ducks, geese and swans; the forests and plains gave us fruits and roots. We never wanted for game: we found everywhere either immense herds of buffalo, or deer, antelope, mountain sheep or bighorn, pheasants, wild turkeys and partridges. (Chittenden and Richardson 1905, 775)

The partridge was likely the Northern Bobwhite. The abundance of other birds may have been due to flocks of migratory waterfowl occurring along the river.

The Oregon and Mormon Trails

Wagon trails along the Platte River were the road west for pioneers heading to the coast. They wound their way along the Oregon Trail, which followed the south side of the Platte near Fort Kearny, or along the Mormon Trail, which originated at Kanesville, Iowa (known today as Council Bluffs), and followed the north side of the Platte. Each summer for many years during the 1840s and 1850s, covered wagon trains followed the ruts gouged in the soil of the prairie.

Some journals did not contain any notes of the birds along these routes. One such example is the journal of Elisha Douglass Perkins in the spring and summer of 1849 (Clark 1967). Two Mormon handcart caravans heading west in July and August 1856 did not enter any notes of birds in one journal from the trip (Hafen and Hafen 1960).

Others did make a few notes about birdlife in their letters and journals. Some wrote of swallows nesting on the cliffs at Ash Hollow. They mentioned occasionally eating birds for breakfast or dinner. A letter written while traveling in a wagon train about seventy-five miles east of the forks of the Platte describes a typical use of birds as food: they ate curlew, snipe, plover and duck for supper (Morgan 1963). This was something different than the meat, crackers and biscuits that were generally eaten for breakfast as well as supper. A "brace of ducks" provided the table fare for an expedition crossing southeast Nebraska from the Missouri River and along the Oregon Trail to Fort Kearny (Delano 1936, 10).

Samuel Hancock, a member of another wagon train headed for Oregon in 1845, stopped overnight along the central Platte near an Indian camp. The Indians soon visited, bringing along prairie dogs and screech owls. The journal says: "Doubtless these are considered delicacies among them, but fortunately we had plenty of food more familiar and palatable to us, and we declined partaking in these rare dishes, though they were strongly recommended to us" (Hancock 1927, 7). Although wild fowl and game were a good source of fresh meat, they most often were a supplement to the emigrants' pantry of food, which typically consisted of bread, beans and other essentials (Williams 1993).

Johann Heinrich Lienhard's notes from a July 26 to September 8, 1846, journey mention only "cranes" (likely Great Blue Herons) in the Grand Island area of the central Platte, probably in July or August, during the breeding season. The only other birds mentioned are the owls living in prairie dog towns near the confluence of the North Platte and South Platte rivers (Lienhard 1961).

An 1849 report of the march of a regiment of mounted riflemen to Oregon mentions a hawk that was shot in June along the Platte River. The bird "measured four feet ten inches from the tip of one wing to the other, and was quite remarkable in other respects" (Cross 1967, 25).

Additional bird notes from 1849 are included in the diary of twenty-six-year-old Peter Decker, who was heading west to the gold mines of California (Decker 1966). Upon his arrival at St. Joseph, Missouri, he wrote a letter to his sisters back in Columbus, Ohio, and in it mentioned the many kinds of birds in the trees near his camp (Decker 1966, 14-15). His notes on birds continued during the journey west on the Oregon Trail with the Columbus California Industrial Company. Traveling along the Nemaha River in early May, Decker recorded, "Prairie hens are scarce, Snipes we have shot a few of, Black birds are in great numbers on the prairies & along wooded ravines everything is musical with their noise & that of other birds" (Decker 1966, 66). Prairie hens, snipe and also plover were noted in an entry a few days later on May 8, 1849, when the caravan was in the vicinity of the current Nebraska state line. The journal entry for this date also observes: "Here is a peculiar bird of the black bird species & [it] associates with the many flocks on the prairie. Its neck, breast & lower part of wings are of beautiful yellow & other part black" (Decker 1966, 68). Except for the yellow on the wings, these details match the characteristics of the Yellow-headed Blackbird. The morning after Decker reached the Platte River, he noted that, "as the sun rises beautifully[,] birds hold a jubilee" (Decker 1966, 73). These same species, as well as the mockingbird, geese and ducks, also are mentioned in Decker's later diary entries.

A wagon train moving along the Little Nemaha River towards Fort Kearny around the same time noted that only a few plovers were seen since leaving the Missouri River (Delano 1936). Ducks were

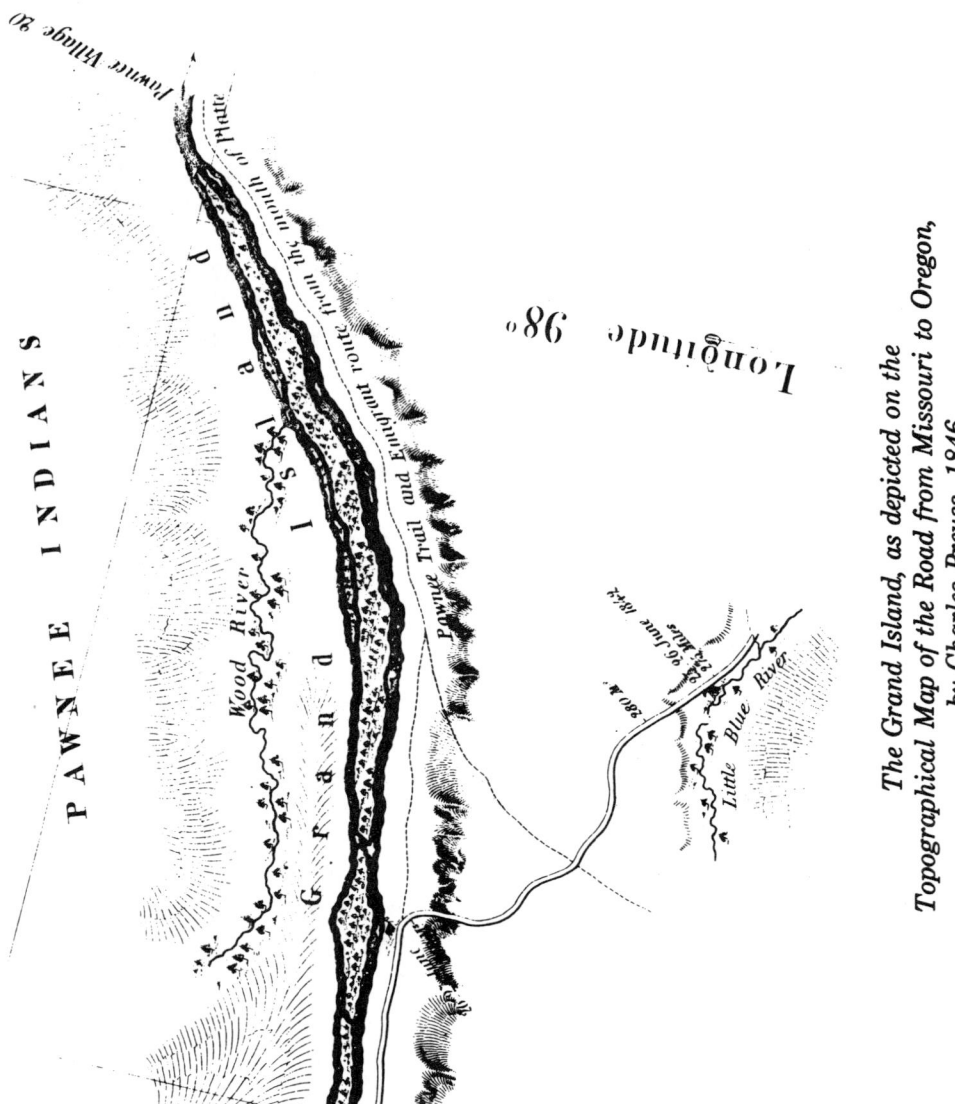

The Grand Island, as depicted on the
Topographical Map of the Road from Missouri to Oregon,
by Charles Preuss, 1846

numerous on the Little Nemaha a few days later at a spot where the party camped. In 1850 William H. Kilgore mentioned the owls in a prairie dog town at the east end of the Grand Island, seven miles from Fort Kearny (Muench 1949).

There are some good notes on birds and the general environment of the Platte River from travelers heading west in 1852 (Eaton 1974). Although they may be simple comments, they help portray these people's perceptions of the birdlife. On one occasion near the eastern Platte on the Mormon Trail, two Native American chiefs approached the wagon train and asked payment for the grass that the cattle were eating. A duck and a snipe were among the items they were given in payment (Eaton 1974, 78). Farther west along the same trail on the north side of the Platte, "prairie hens, ducks, snipe plenty—killed 12 snipes" was included in an entry for May 23, 1852 (Eaton 1974, 84). Farther west ducks and wild geese were seen.

Other notes discuss the meat value of birds shot along the Oregon Trail in the central Platte region. One journal mentions snipe and ducks (Eaton 1974, 90). An entry in another journal written while near the intersection of the Oregon Trail and the South Fork of the Platte River lists several types of game: "Abundance of game abounds along the Platte[,] such as elk, antelope, deer, grey & prairie wolves, panthers, buffalo, prairie dogs, cranes, wild geese, ducks, &c" (Eaton 1974, 97).

Farther west on the Oregon Trail, Ash Hollow in June impressed the emigrant John Hawkins Clark enough for him to write about his pleasurable stop there on the journey west. He mused,

> [N]othing we have yet seen can exceed the beauty of Ash Hollow. It was a lovely morning as we entered it; birds were singing joyously amid the branches of beautiful trees; flowers were everywhere blooming, making fragrant the air we breathed; women and children were gathering wild roses and singing some sweet song which put us in mind of other times and other localities. There were many camps in this valley; the shade of the green trees was truly inviting, and a stream of clear, cold water and plenty of wood made it a desirable place for a few day's rest. (Eaton 1974, 101)

This entry continued, describing the abrupt bluff in the Platte valley and the birds, undoubtedly Cliff Swallows, that were nesting on the cliffs.

Birds were a source of entertainment along the central Platte, according to notes made during a mule-train trip to the West Coast in 1862.

> For amusements at this camp, there being usually a dearth as well as an indisposition to search for diversion, most of the party

indulged in shooting at some small birds, about the size of wrens; the birds were not injured. (Hewitt 1906, 107-108)

In his 1852-54 journal, William H. Woodhams only referred to one or two bird species for the Platte River area (Martin 1974). Other bird notes often are limited to a sentence about the habits of the Burrowing Owl (Johnson and Winter 1932). The 1864 diary of Kate Dunlap, for example, notes only the Burrowing Owls living in prairie dog towns along the central Platte River (Dunlap 1969). Other letters, like those of Jonathan Blanchard in 1864, mention one or two species (Keller 1982).

Culbertson's Journey

Thaddeus Ainsworth Culbertson, an East Coast naturalist on an expedition partly sponsored by the Smithsonian Institution, left St. Louis on March 21, 1850, and went overland along the Iowa side of the Missouri River. The party continued north along the Vermillion River, then boarded the steamboat *El Paso* to quickly return downriver in July (McDermott 1952). Culbertson collected numerous natural history materials, including fossils, animal skins and plant specimens. His main interest was geology; thus, his journal contains many comments on the character of the land but only a few notes on birds of specific localities. Culbertson's complete list of species of the Missouri River from Fort Leavenworth to the Fort Union area is not useful for bird identifications, since the locality of a sighting is not given. The only notes used in this review are of the magpie seen near the mouth of the Nishnabotna River, the Canvasback shot near the mouth of the Vermillion River, and Cliff Swallows on the Missouri River near the Niobrara River (McDermott 1952). After passing the mouth of the Niobrara, Culbertson noted that the limestone cliffs were used as nesting sites, probably by swallows—likely the Cliff Swallows that previous visitors had noted and described.

Rudolph Friederich Kurz's Exploration

The German traveler Rudolph Friederich Kurz was in the United States from 1846 to 1852. He spent a year or so (about the same amount of time as Prince Maximilian of Wied) exploring the Missouri River region. Kurz first reached the Nebraska area while going upriver in May 1851. Most of his notes, including a description of warriors hiding in pits to capture eagles, are from the Fort Union area. Kurz's records include line drawings of animals, people, items around the fort, and the landscapes seen near the fort and along the Missouri River, but the only birds noted in the Nebraska region are three species seen on the downriver trip in June 1852.

The Warren Expedition

During a mid-1850s reconnaissance for a travel route to the Black Hills, the Warren Expedition explored the Nebraska and Dakota territories. The main responsibility of this three-year effort was to assess potential trails for horse-drawn wagons and to determine the best route to western outposts from a Missouri River depot. Wagon trains of supplies from Missouri River steamboats were to supply government posts, such as Fort Laramie, and the northern Great Plains in general. Gouverneur Kemble Warren's party, including the naturalist Ferdinand V. Hayden, left St. Louis and took the *Genoa* as far as Fort Pierre.

The men recorded natural history features, made sketches of river features seen from the boat, and paid particular attention to the factors influencing river navigation. Their report is a summary of the region, but unfortunately it does not give specific localities where birds were observed (Hayden 1863a; Warren 1875). After the expedition was completed, Hayden prepared a catalogue of collections in geology and natural history. The catalogue includes geology, paleontology, fish, reptiles, mammals, birds and plants. Each category contains notes on the general distribution, site of occurrence and status of large and small mammals and bird and flora specimens collected in the central and western Missouri River valley areas (Hayden 1863a).

In the expedition report, Warren described the western prairies of Nebraska as an "irreclaimable desert, with only a little wood and cultivable land" (Warren 1875, 28). A section about the lakes in the Sand Hills mentions "water . . . impregnated with salts and unfit to drink" (Warren 1875, 26). Other lakes elsewhere did have water suitable for life, however (Warren 1875, 26). The Loup Fork, in the eastern hills, is described as being similar to the lower reaches of the Elkhorn River. The source of the Loup Fork is said to be similar to the western Niobrara River. The Snake River, in the northern Sand Hills, flows through a rugged and narrow pine-covered valley. The Dismal River is called the "Sand Hill Fork" (Warren 1875).

During each of three years, they visited a different portion of this vast region. In 1855 the expedition moved along the Missouri from Fort Leavenworth to Fort Pierre, south to Fort Kearny, west along the Platte to Fort Laramie, back to Fort Pierre, then on to the mouth of the Big Sioux. In 1856 they covered the area from Fort Pierre to Fort

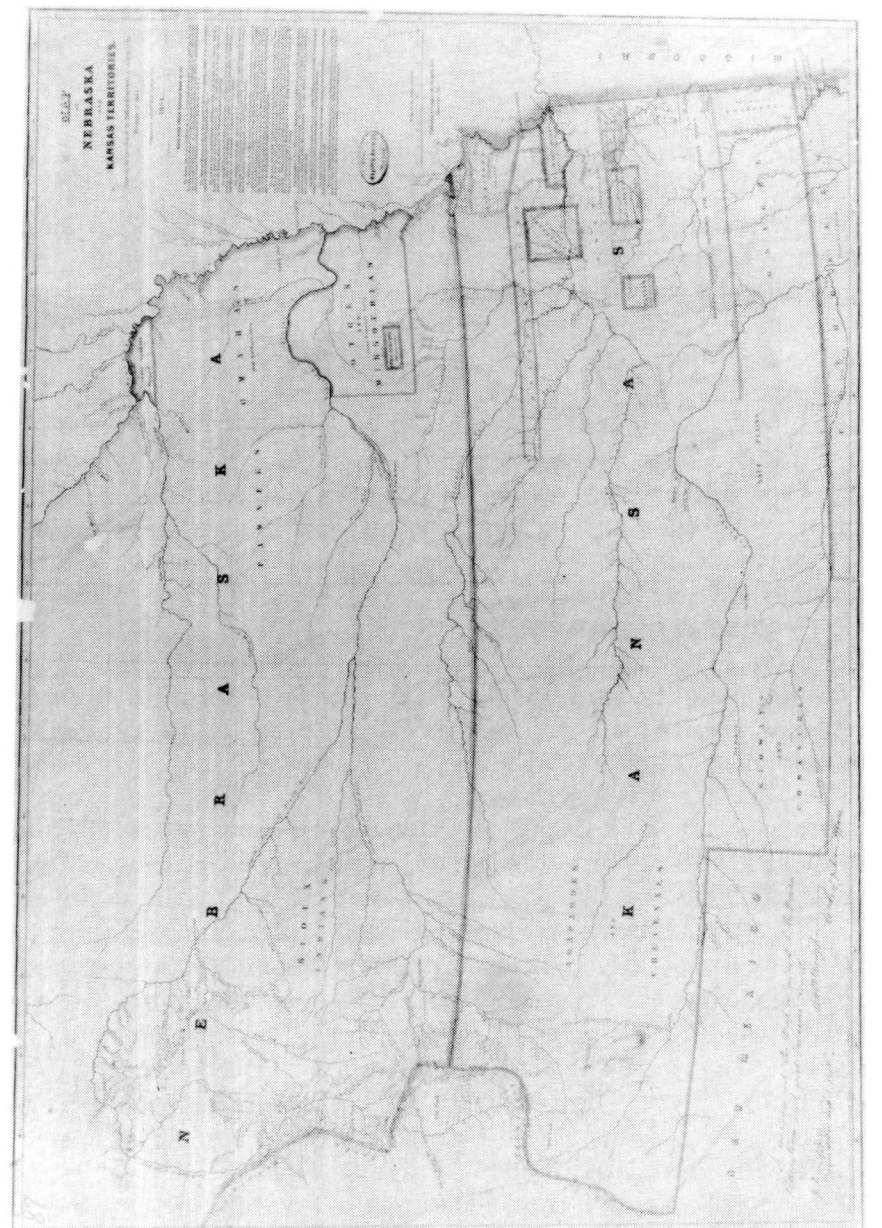

Map of Nebraska and Kansas Territories, by Capt. Seth Eastman, 1854

Union to the region of what is now western North Dakota and Montana. They spent most of the 1857 season in the Nebraska region, and a good portion of two of the three summers was spent exploring the modern state of Nebraska. During summer 1857, two parties of the expedition met at the mouth of the Loup River and continued westward. They traveled from the headwaters of the Middle Loup River north and west through southwest Cherry County, then north through eastern Sheridan County to the Niobrara River. They continued to Fort Laramie, went through the Black Hills, and returned to Fort Pierre. A steamboat was used to return to St. Louis.

The marshes of extreme northwest Missouri and the Big Nemaha River area along the Missouri River formed the southernmost point of the bird records included for the Nebraska region. Fort Randall, just north of what became the northern Nebraska state line, was located on a prominent plateau, which overlooked the Missouri River. The two localities provide the first and last points of reference for the historic bird records of the Missouri River region of Nebraska.

Rather than being a simple list, the notes from the Warren Expedition contain details about a bird's status, including relative abundance and distribution along the river. Records taken from this account include those for the Fort Randall, South Platte and Big Nemaha river areas, which are not specifically within the present-day boundaries of Nebraska. However, these locations are in close proximity to modern Nebraska, so they are included here to provide more information pertinent to the Nebraska area. In some cases there may have been inadvertent omissions if the name of a historic locality was uncertain or considered outside the area of Nebraska. Examples are Fort Lookout, the Medicine Bow area, Fort Union and Fort Pierre. Some localities are in Nebraska but have a Kansas Territory site listed. For example, the Platte River and Fort Randall are given a locality of Kansas Territory in several instances. Both are in the Nebraska Territory, based on the site names given for other specimens and known geographic information.

The species list in the Warren Expedition narrative gives only a very general statement of observations during the expedition. The localities specify larger regions such as western North America, the Black Hills, the Missouri River and the high central Plains. A notation such as "westward to the Loup Fork of the Platte," given for the location of a Henslow's Sparrow, is a definite exception.

More detailed information on bird occurrence from this expedition is available in other reports. The summary prepared by noted ornithologist Spencer Fullerton Baird (Baird et al. 1860) identifies bird skins and notes the dates and localities where the specimens were collected. Baird included many of the Warren Expedition's observations and prepared a summary of the field records of the United States Army Topographic Engineers while he was Assistant Secretary of the Smithsonian Institution. John Cassin of Philadelphia and George Newbold Lawrence of New York helped compile the reference to birds of North America north of Mexico (Baird et al. 1860). It reviews many specimens collected by several United States Army expeditions, including Warren's, Lieutenant F. T. Bryan's and others. Baird used Bryan's journal of his travels along the wagon road from Fort Riley, Kansas, to Bridger's Pass, Utah, as a source. Other works he published are general in scope and repeat the location records. References other than his *A History of North American Birds* (Baird 1874) and *The Birds of North America* (Baird et al. 1860) do not contain any additional useful records.

The Baird work is a good overall reference for explorations during the mid-1800s and an example of the species taxonomy current in the 1850s. Baird listed specimens collected by the War Department expeditions that were deposited in the Smithsonian Museum. Most of the specimens are from Bald Island, from Fort Kearny, and from areas along the Missouri River, the mouth of the Vermillion River, the Niobrara River, the Platte River, the Loup Fork, the Platte Forks, and the North and South Platte rivers. Pole Creek is included, since Lodgepole Creek is in the southern part of the Nebraska Panhandle. The North Platte collection, dated August 20, 1857, is similar to the date for specimens collected at Scotts Bluff. These reports also include records for specimens collected by Audubon during his travels in the west. *Birds of the Northwest* (Coues 1874) lists more specific sites to document where specimens had been collected.

Baird cited examples of naturalists who were medical doctors on the Army expeditions: Ferdinand Hayden was with the Warren expedition; James Graham Cooper accompanied the 1857 W. M. F. Magraw party to Fort Kearny and the Rockies; W. A. Hammond, who was in the Black Hills about the same time as the Warren party, also collected on Kansas and Nebraska trips, and his notes are included in the important Pacific railroad reports (see Baird et al. 1860).

The Journal of Mollie Dorsey Sanford

Mary E. "Mollie" Dorsey (later Sanford) came with her family to Nebraska Territory, arriving at Nebraska City on April 10, 1857. She was eighteen and recorded events and her thoughts in her journal

(Sanford 1959). The family lived in a log-house town for a period. One of the first entries describes the setting of the family cabin:

> Our cabin is near the banks of the creek, where a grove of tall, naked trees stretch their branches towards the sky. Perhaps, when clothed in their summer foliage and the birds singing 'mid their boughs, they may suggest more of the beautiful than now. (Sanford 1959, 14)

On June 5 the family moved to its homestead on the Nemaha River, about fourteen miles from town. Although her journal entry recording their arrival at their new home in early morning does not mention specific birds, it vividly portrays the scene:

> The sunrise was glorious! the trees full of singing birds, ringing out a welcome. Soft zephers floated o'er us, bright flowers gave out their perfume, and all nature was glad. Father had named the place 'Hazel Dell,' and we christened it by singing that sweet song. And such a chorus as went up from those lumbering wagons! Birds stopped their carols to listen, and festive chipmunks flew from their hiding places, bewildered with the noise. And when we reached the cabin joyful hurrahs! resounded long and loud. (Sanford 1959, 32)

Later in the summer, the journal mentions one night she heard "Ter hoo! Ter hoo" outside her window. At first she thought it was her grandfather arriving, but then discovered it to be the "night owl's screech" (Sanford 1959, 47). On October 5 the journal entry speaks of the "golden autumn days" and how soon "the bright birds that have cheered us with their melody will seek more genial climes" (Sanford 1959, 56). The term "bright birds" is repeated in an entry from September 1858, when Dorsey took her composition book out to the prairie. Part of the day's entry read:

> I laid me down by the fragrant hay, and looking up through the crimson and golden foliage of the grand forest trees, I could see patches of the blue sky, and watch the feathery clouds drift and float away, until they seemed throngs of white-robed angels soaring up into the golden portals of heaven. Bright birds twittered above me. (Sanford 1959, 79)

After Dorsey's marriage on February 16, 1860, to "By" (her name for Byron N. Sanford), the newlyweds headed west to Denver on the Oregon Trail on April 12, 1860. They departed from the family home at Hazel Dell. During their journey, the only bird notation Sanford made in her diary is a reference to mud hens, an alternate name for coots, shot by hunters in the vicinity of Fort Kearny.

Naturalist George Suckley

George Suckley, physician, professional naturalist and one of the ornithologists of the United States Army Medical Corps, traveled with an Army expedition from Fort Leavenworth west along the Platte River in 1859 (Beidleman 1956). The Pacific railroad reports volume published by Spencer F. Baird in 1860 was the field guide used for the trip (Hume 1942).

Suckley noted summer birds, their nests and eggs in his journal. Some of the nesting birds at the Little Blue River area, west and north of Rock Creek Station in Jefferson County, included the Brown Thrasher, the Gray Catbird and the Western Meadowlark. Several egg sets from the Fort Kearny area, including those of the Mourning Dove and Common Nighthawk, were sent to Baird at the Smithsonian Institution. The stomachs of four Burrowing Owls taken near the fort included grasshopper and beetle fragments and the forefoot of a small rodent.

The Fort Laramie Area

Fort Laramie was situated along the North Platte River about twenty-five miles west of today's Nebraska-Wyoming state line. Some of the birds that were sighted there also would have occurred along the North Platte River of western Nebraska. Notes on birds in the region of Fort Laramie were kept by Col. Caspar Wever Collins, who was stationed at the fort for several years, and he described area birdlife in letters to his relatives. In November 1863 Collins received a letter from the Smithsonian Institution asking him to collect eggs of birds at Laramie Peak and to the west. This request also asked for skins of certain birds (Spring 1927).

In a letter dated September 21, 1862, Collins wrote about the birdlife at Fort Laramie, Nebraska Territory. Specific species noted include several grouse about the fort: the Sharp-tailed Grouse was present at the fort and to the east; the Sage Grouse was typical of the plains west of the fort, and many were shot by hunters. A portion of the letter describes other birds:

> Geese are plenty, although I have never killed any yet. Ducks of a great many different kinds are also abundant on the creeks, ponds, sloughs, etc. My father and I killed fourteen as we were going along the road before we got to our noon camp. Among the kinds found are mallard, wood duck, widgeon [wigeon], green- and blue-winged teal, a brown duck called summer duck, and a fine large kind that I am sure is not found with us, called the Pacific canvasback. The green-winged

> teal are found mostly in marshes, from whence they spring up to be shot, like snipe. Curlew, plovers, sandpipers and our kind of snipe are also plenty. . . . There is one kind of curlew about the size of a pheasant and the color of a woodcock, that is the best of the tribe. (Spring 1927, 138)

In another letter, dated December 15, 1862, there are additional references to birdlife in the Fort Laramie area. Species mentioned include the prairie chicken and Blue Grouse. Ducks, both Mallard and Canvasback, and geese were present despite the December date (Spring 1927). Collins also wrote again about snipes, plovers, curlews and sandpipers.

A Sand Hills Bone Hunt

An expedition of Yale University students led by Yale professor Othniel Charles Marsh, who held the first chair of paleontology ever established in the United States, traveled from Omaha west to Fort McPherson, then north into the Sand Hills in July 1870. For two weeks the party of more than ten men, including George Bird Grinnell, traveled by horseback through the Sand Hills area north of North Platte (McIntosh 1988). The prominent regions visited were the headwaters area of the South Loup River, Cody Lake (now called Jefford Lake on United States Geological Survey topographic maps), the Dismal River valley, and north of Birdwood Creek in the Schick Lake and Diamond Bar Lake area. Unfortunately the published account of the expedition does not contain any notes on birds in Nebraska (Grinnell 1923b).

One of the expedition's members, John G. Mitchell, later recalled Grinnell

> following a creek, jump-hunting ducks for the evening meal. Suddenly he beholds this funeral scaffold made of willows, the corpse elevated on a litter. It is the custom of the Sioux to bury their warriors in the sky. This warrior could not be long dead, for there is no rust on the scalping knife beside him. The long black hair on the skull appears shiny and fresh. And what is *this*! A barn swallow? Two barn swallows skimming the sky to dive beneath the scaffold's litter. The swallows are robbing the warrior's grave to build their nest. It is a terrible thing to look so closely, but what else can he do? The swallows are *scalping* this fallen warrior. They are lining their nest with the warrior's hair. (Mitchell 1987, 101)

Many other typical summer birds in the Sand Hills lake and grassland region would have been seen and enjoyed by members of the expedition.

The Niobrara Expedition of 1873

Thomas G. Maghee was the physician with the Niobrara Expedition led by Yale professor Othniel Marsh in 1873. From mid-June to mid-July, they went from Fort McPherson to explore the Sand Hills region, then looked for fossil remains along the Niobrara River. They traveled north through McPherson and Grant counties, into western Cherry County, down the Niobrara River eastward to Valentine, then south to North Platte (Lindsay 1929).

Although Maghee's notes are usually about the party's health, there are a few notes on animals and landscape. On June 21 in eastern Grant County, he found "several valleys[,] some of which were swampy, all of them full of lakes" (Lindsay 1929, 255). In the northwest corner of the county, "Upton" or "Upson" Lake had "40 or 60 islands containing swan ducks & Mosquitoes" (Lindsay 1929, 257). To the north in southern Cherry County at "Raymond Lake," he saw several "wild swan," likely Trumpeter Swans. These are the only references to birds in the Sand Hills along their route.

Birds of the Northwest Territory

Elliott Coues compiled a summary of the birds of "the Northwest," a territory that encompassed the region drained by the Missouri River and its tributaries in the western United States (Coues 1874). This detailed work includes material on species nomenclature, where specimens had been collected by expeditions of the United States Army Topographic Engineers, and natural history notes for each species. In some cases there are general descriptions of a species' status at the time. For example, Ferdinand Hayden reported the Warbling Vireo to be abundant along the wooded bottoms of the Missouri River. Specimen records for the Nebraska area include those from the Missouri River region, from along the Platte River, and a limited number from the Loup River.

Coues repeated the localities of observations made during the Warren Expedition, including Hayden's collections. The species accounts also provide information on general distribution based on Coues' sightings. New information, including many records for the Fort Randall area of the Missouri River, also is presented. This fort was located along the river in Todd County, South Dakota, just a mile north of Nebraska, according to Missouri River Commission maps. The Fort Randall Military Reservation continued to the west several miles and into Gregory County, South Dakota.

In his summary, Coues mentioned the typical winter birds of the area, especially of the river bottoms. There were some Sharp-tailed Grouse, Greater Prairie-Chickens, Horned Larks, American Tree Sparrows, Tufted Titmice, Hairy Woodpeckers, hawks, owls, quails, crows, magpies, snow-birds, longspurs, and shrikes (Coues 1874).

Notes on the Food of Birds of Nebraska

Samuel Aughey sent records of observations he made in the 1860s and 1870s to the United States Entomological Commission (Aughey 1878). His notes detail how the birds preyed on the swarms of locusts which devastated crops in newly-settled areas of Nebraska. Most of the records relate to the Missouri River region, especially in northeast and southeast Nebraska. Since Aughey was interested primarily in birds eating the locusts that plagued crops in the summer, he usually noted species from spring through fall.

Based on studies of "economic ornithology," Aughey's accounts list the species, provide a brief summary of status, then list the number of birds whose stomachs were checked to determine the number of locusts ingested. Specimens also were received from local residents. Notes on birds observed eating locusts also are included, even when no specimen was available, as is additional information on other stomach contents (such as insects, seeds, grains and other food). In addition, the water wren and the Traill's Flycatcher (the Willow Flycatcher, which is among the hard-to-identify flycatchers) are included on Aughey's species list because of expected behavior, although no specimens were received and no birds were observed. The report adds numerous records for species not reported by any other historic accounts; however, species that could not be identified based on the common or scientific names given in Aughey's report are not used in this review.

Aughey's list of birds suffers from many shortcomings (Sharpe 1993). Aughey was an entomology professor who lacked the knowledge needed to identify some species; other species likely were misidentified; and others may have been added to his species list based on their being mentioned in other reference books. His notes list a "Mountain Bluebird," which could have been a Western Bluebird, which has not been documented in Nebraska. Examples of other probable misidentifications include the Great Black-backed Gull, Pomarine Jaeger and Virginia's Warbler. There are other questionable records included in Aughey's species accounts that are not accepted as valid records of Nebraska ornithology. Still his many records for common species, especially summer nesting birds, are important contributions that provide useful records of occurrence.

Reconnaissance to the Black Hills

A journey to the Black Hills in July and August 1874 was led by William Ludlow, the chief engineer of the Department of Dakota within the United States Army Engineer Department. During the trip, George Bird Grinnell kept notes on the fauna. A detailed summary of Grinnell's observations is included in the expedition report (Ludlow 1875). Species occurrences are not included in the species summary. The bird report is an important part of Plains ornithology, which indicates some species that may have occurred in similar habitats in the Pine Ridge of Nebraska, a region whose birdlife was unrecorded prior to 1875.

The Black Hills formed part of the Dakota Territory north of Nebraska in 1875, and the expedition report includes a realistic scale map of the Black Hills during the summer visit. While conditions on the Plains were hot and dry, the Black Hills were cooler, with clear, cold, running springs and streams providing water. Ludlow stated that the vegetation there was much more lush and fresh than that on the Plains. The forested hills and rocky buttes have habitats similar to those of the Pine Ridge, and species seen on this expedition indicate some of the species expected in the region.

Miscellaneous Notes from the 1870s

Citations from the publication *Forest and Stream* contain useful ornithological information about the 1870s and 1880s. There are pertinent notes for birds from hunting expeditions in the east prior to 1875 (Coveter 1876; Grinnell 1873; Phillips 1876) and some sightings from the western Sand Hills (Grinnell 1877). Some information concerns wild lands near the first cities in eastern Nebraska (Phillips 1876).

George Bird Grinnell recognized the central Platte River as a haven for wildlife. One of his articles, mostly about big game like bison, elk, deer and antelope, also mentions game birds (Grinnell 1873). The Greater Prairie-Chicken, Sharp-tailed Grouse and Upland Plover were game birds of the open prairie, and the Northern Bobwhite was said to occur along the river bottoms in eastern Nebraska.

Nebraska's abundant game prompted a second hunting trip for Grinnell in 1877, this time to the Sand Hills of the Cody-North Ranch

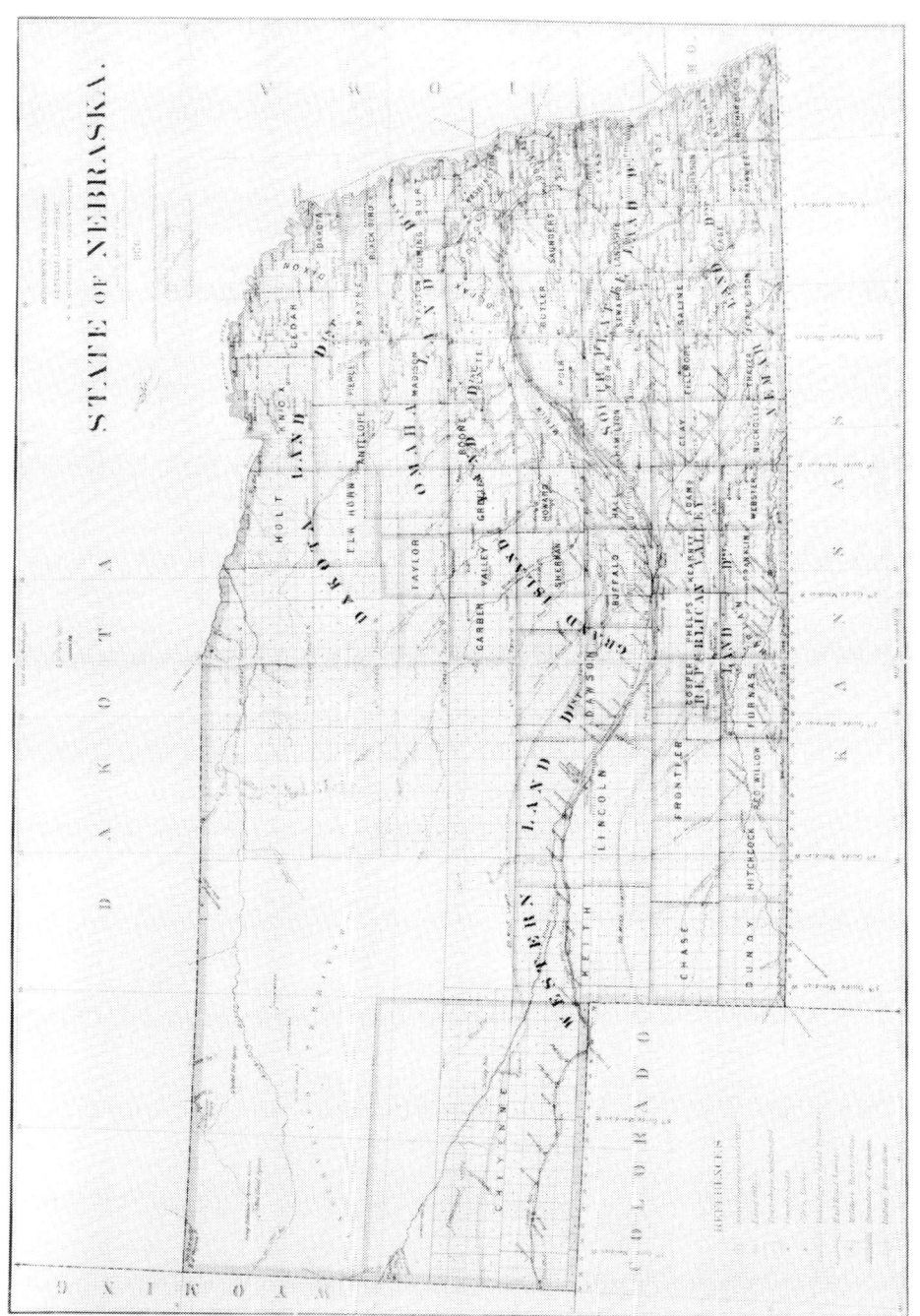

Nebraska General Land Office Map, 1876

and its headquarters in the southwest corner of Hooker County (North 1961). There Grinnell wrote that he was hosted by a prominent cattle king. In 1877 William Cody and the North brothers started this ranch on the Dismal River, about sixty-five miles northwest of North Platte (Aeschbacher 1946). Cattle ranged about the hills like buffalo once had, but the only reminder of the once vast buffalo herds were bones "thickly strewn along the margin of the lake" that Grinnell visited (Grinnell 1877). Based on his description and the location of the ranch, the lake was likely in southeast Grant County. The presence of numerous waterfowl, such as ducks and geese and numerous breeding Trumpeter Swans, which use an extensive marsh for nesting, would require a larger lake similar to those present in this region.

The abundant game was described by Luther Hedden North, who recorded that this region of the Sand Hills had many prairie chickens and that the lakes to the west of the headwaters "of the Dismal River were alive with wild fowl; [sic] swans, sand hill cranes, geese and ducks by the millions" (North 1961, 239). North wrote several paragraphs about the nest of a Trumpeter Swan on a muskrat house in a lake west of the head of the south Dismal River (North 1961). He provided food to the bird and cared for its nest, and the young became so tame they would follow a boat around the lake. The young grew, and one day, while most of the men were gone from the ranch, a hand from another ranch and a Cody-North ranch hand clipped the wings of the young birds so they could not fly. Unable to migrate before the arrival of winter, the young birds were caught and eaten by coyotes. Later their remains were found scattered in the hills.

At a campsite west of the headwaters of the Dismal River in early September, Grinnell noted,

> On . . . [the river's] surface can be seen at any hour of the day thousands of ducks and geese, and tens of thousands of waders. The most abundant ducks which we see are the smaller broadbills (*Fuligula affinus)* [Lesser Scaup] and the blue-winged teal (*Q. dincora*), though mallards, black ducks [American Black Duck] and gadwalls are numerous. Flocks of geese alight on the lake every day, and to my surprise I learned that two pairs of swans (*Cygnus Americanus*) bred on its shores during the past summer. (Grinnell 1877, 152)

Waders to which Grinnell referred included the Killdeer, Baird's Sandpipers, snipes, many avocets, the "oxeyes" (Semipalmated Sandpiper or Least Sandpiper) and "hundreds" of phalaropes.

Several bird specimens were collected from this region in September 1878: seven specimens of the Rusty Blackbird, Common Grackle and McCown's Longspur were collected in the locale of the Dismal River. These specimens are included in the collection of the Birdcraft Museum operated by the Connecticut Audubon Society in Fairfield, Connecticut.

Two reports by agents of the Union Pacific Railroad in the 1870s describe the abundance of game at Jackson Station, in the Platte valley about one hundred miles west of Omaha (Coveter 1876), and along the Missouri River at Gilmore in Sarpy County (Phillips 1876). Jackson Station was a mile north of the Platte, three miles south of the Loup Fork and about eight miles from the confluence of the two rivers, in modern Platte County. The area had "a range of hills . . . cut up by numerous ravines and basins, and extending many miles to the southwest, affording good shelter for wolves, which are very numerous, antelopes and deer" (Coveter 1876, 27). Other notes mention the birds that could be readily hunted nearby, perhaps using the railroad as handy transportation.

> The Platte[,] being wide and shallow[,] seems to be a favorite place of resort for water fowl which feed in the fields and rest on the sand bars, which form a large portion of the stream. There was no day during the winter of '75-6 that good shooting could not be had within 1 1/2 miles of the railroad depot. Geese, ducks, swan, crane, etc [were among the birds hunted]. (Coveter 1876, 27)

Other game birds mentioned are Northern Bobwhites, whose population was said to have been "nearly all killed by the severe winter of '74-5" (Coveter 1876, 27), and prairie chickens, noted as being numerous in the region.

A report from along the Missouri River in eastern Nebraska lists the many different game birds present for the sportsman from there westward to the Rocky Mountains. Geese, ducks, swans, grouse, snipes, plovers, curlews, sandpipers, turkeys and big game are all listed. The minimal notes on each group give the species present and comment that Common Snipe were plentiful and afforded great sport hunting. The American Woodcock could be found among the willows on the banks of the Missouri River. Other hunters' notes state that the Eskimo Curlew, once thought to be extinct, visited the region in large numbers and that a great variety of sandpipers was present in the state as quarry for hunters (Phillips 1876).

Once portions of Nebraska were settled and began to develop, the type of bird studies undertaken changed. By this time a bird watcher no longer had to travel great distances as part of territorial explorations, but could spend time becoming familiar with a certain tract of nearby land. Instead of making brief notes during a journey, people kept records for the places where they lived. More information was gathered on the birdlife of a particular area instead of a larger region. One of the areas studied was the southeast part of the state, along the Missouri River near Peru (Taylor and Van Vleet 1888a, 1888b, 1889). These and other studies describe the state's historic birdlife and indicate some of the changes as farms, settlements and small towns developed. Additional published notes for the historic period are available for the eastern part of Nebraska (Kline 1883). Other material with information for the Nebraska region was reviewed, but most have few, if any, useful records (e.g., Ludlow 1875; Boller 1972).

Papers on birds along the Missouri River and elsewhere in the eastern part of the state in the 1860s and 1870s start the modern era of bird records and ornithology journals for the Nebraska region (Wolcott 1902). Myron Harmon Swenk compiled the first review of historic material on Nebraska birds. He published a series of papers on explorations and their bird-sightings in Nebraska (Swenk 1933, 1934b, 1935, 1937). His topics included the roles animals played in Native American life and myth.

Pioneers Settling the Wild Prairie

As Euro-American pioneers settled and established homes in the eastern part of the state, they had a profound influence on its birdlife. Birds were hunted and killed without any regard for season. Prairie was turned by the plow, and this brought about slow but certain changes in habitat.

A. J. Leach, who became a Nebraska resident in 1867, hunted and took notes on wildlife about 1870, primarily in Antelope County but also in nearby Wheeler and Garfield counties (Leach 1916). This early resident recorded "great changes" that occurred to resident and migratory birds as a result of settlement during the years he lived in Antelope County. He was observant enough to note that some species were no longer present; others had diminished in number; others had increased in number; and new bird species had entered the region since he arrived. Birds that had been present in the "early days" but were rarely seen by 1870 were the "wild turkey, the raven, the magpie and the curlew." Wild geese, brants, wild ducks, prairie chickens and Sharp-tailed Grouse "diminished in number." The vulture and plover, which were once common, became rare (Leach 1916, 87). Other birds became more prevalent as the available habitat changed. Species Leach noted include

> blackbirds, robins, bluebirds, blue-jays, brown thrushes and quails. Among those that have about held their own are the meadow larks, turtle doves, cat birds, swallows, martins, night hawks, kingfishers, kingbirds, song sparrows, bobolinks, yellow-hammers [flickers], woodpeckers, the hairy, the downey and the red heads, and the Baltimore orioles. (Leach 1916, 87-88)

Woodland species that became common as woody habitat increased were the Wood Thrush, Rose-breasted Grosbeak, the "peewee" and the Orchard Oriole.

Other early pioneers also noted the abundance of wildlife when the state was being settled. There are some especially nice notes made by settlers in Custer County (Purcell 1936). Their records mention the wild game they hunted and ate. Although these people did not have an extensive awareness of the birdlife, they did mention many different bird types. One pioneer noted that about 1879 "myriads" of geese were present along Victoria Creek. Lots of grouse and prairie chickens meant meat was "no problem" to another settler. In some cases, without the plentiful supply of these birds, families would have gone hungry. On occasion a swan may have been shot. On another occasion a mother shot some prairie chickens for her family; thus, they had sufficient food until their father returned from town with other food (Chrisman in Purcell 1936, 148).

Birds were not seen always at the end of a gun barrel. They were often part of a pleasant day. One pioneer child recalled the croaking frogs, quacking ducks, booming prairie chickens and abundant prairie flowers of summer mornings (Cannon in Purcell 1936, 86).

The memoirs of Berna Hunter Chrisman refer to a bird "paradise" in Custer County, where her family moved in the 1880s. A young child fascinated by the wilds, Chrisman recalled,

> The Cedar Canyon was a regular paradise for birds, and we saw many varieties, bluejays, orioles, red-headed woodpeckers, catbirds, thrushes, mocking birds, the woods rang with their songs in

> summer. Hoot owls, hawks and screech owls were plentiful and so were buzzards. A large tree near our door had a wren's nest in it and we often saw bullsnakes climb this tree and get the eggs or the young birds. We children threw clods at the snakes until they came down and crawled away. (Chrisman in Purcell 1936, 144)

Being a young child, this observer likely did not know the specific names for birds that she came to know by name as she grew older.

The Greater Prairie-Chicken was especially notable in pioneer history. The prairie chicken provided meat for many early settlers in eastern Nebraska (Purcell 1936; McDermott 1939; Skinner 1980). The planting of crops such as corn helped the birds thrive, since it provided a source of food that had not been present when there was just grassland. In the late 1870s, one woman carried a gun with her when she herded cattle and shot all the birds her family could eat (McDermott 1939, 129). Some prairie chickens were caught with traps made

> from strips of wood fitted together with notches, to form a figure 4. An ear of corn was slipped over the sharpened end of the horizontal stick, over which a box was balanced. When the bird pecked the corn[,] the stick and the box fell, and the bird was held captive. (Skinner 1980, 252)

Vast numbers of prairie chickens were killed during the early settlement period of the state, including the years after 1875 and into the 1880s. One pioneer in Custer County noted how "as many as one hundred" were killed in a single day (Purcell 1936, 166). Another hunter killed many dozens of prairie chickens a week (Lowder in Purcell 1936, 173-174). Only the enactment of game laws changed the practice of killing birds during any time of the year, reduced the numbers of game birds killed, and afforded some protection to birdlife.

CHAPTER THREE:
BIRD HABITATS FROM 1750 TO 1875

Before 1875 modern-day Nebraska was wilderness and included a great diversity of natural habitats for birds. Many of the expeditions and journeys that took place during the historic period left records describing the typical plants and vegetation of the state's different regions. These descriptions start with the early explorations along the Missouri River.

The Missouri River

There are many notes from the well-traveled Missouri River. On July 12, 1804, William Clark wrote from a site with Native American mounds in the southeast corner of present-day Richardson County,

> ... I had an extensive view of the Serounding Plains, which afforded one of the most pleasing prospects I ever beheld, under me a Butiful River [the Nemaha] of Clear water of about 80 yards wide Meandering thro: a leavel and extensive Meadow, as far as I could See, the [view of the] prospect Much enlivened by the fine Trees & S[h]rubs . . . bordering the bank of the river, and the Creeks & runs falling into it,—. The bottom land is covered with Grass of about 4½ feet high and appears as leavel as a Smo[o]th Surfice . . . [; the upper land] is also covered with Grass and rich weeds & flours, interspersed with Copses of the Osage Plumb. [The flood-plain prairie would have included prairie cordgrass, slough grass and big bluestem.] on the riseing lands, Small groves of trees are Seen, with a numbers of Grapes and a Wild Cherry resembling the Common Wild Cherry, only larger and grows on a Small bush on the tops of those hills in every derection. (Moulton 1987, 369-370)

Along the Missouri River in present-day eastern Otoe County, Clark remarked that there was not much timber. Woodlands occurred on islands in the river and along the creeks and rivers, and the typical trees were cottonwood, mulberry, elm and sycamore.

Other notes describe the character of the river. In northeast Otoe he wrote that near the mouth of the "great River Plate [Platte] the Sand bars [are] much more numerous[,] and the quick or moving Sands" are worse than below the Platte (Moulton 1987, 396).

On July 30 Clark commented that a

> ... Prarie [near the historic Council Bluff] is Covered with grass about 10 or 12 Inch high, (Land rich) rises about ½ a mile back Something higher and is a Plain as fur as Can be Seen, under those high Lands

next the river is butifull Bottom interspersed with Groves of timber, the River may be Seen for a great Distance both above & below meandering thro: the plains between two ranges of High land..., each bend of the river forming a point which Contains tall timber, principally Willow[,] Cotton wood[,] some Mulberry[,] elm[,] Sycamore & ash. (Moulton 1987, 428)

In 1811 Henry Brackenridge also described the Missouri River near the mouth of the Platte:

At the mouth of this river there is so great a number of bars and small islands, that its entrance is scarcely perceptible. It enters by a number of channels or mouths: the color of its waters is the same with that of the Missouri. The country hereabouts, is entirely open, excepting in some spots along the river, where there are groves of cotton-wood, and on the hills a few scattered dwarf oaks. (Brackenridge 1976, 78)

Brackenridge noted how the vegetative character of the Missouri valley changed. Near the Omaha Indian village in present-day Thurston County, he wrote:

The scenery now undergoes an entire change; forests are seen no more; the wooded portions of the river are composed of small cotton-wood trees, whose slender and delicate growth have a much more beautiful appearance than the huge giants on the lower part of the river. (Brackenridge 1976, 91-92)

The prairie here had a great variety of beautiful flowers and served as a pasture for bison in an immense herd that was moving along the river. The sound of their hoofbeats, even at the distance of two miles, resembled the rumbling of distant thunder.

The country around Engineer Cantonment had all the habitat diversity of the wilderness found along the Missouri River. The forested valleys along the Missouri near the mouth of the Platte were interspersed with wide prairie meadows (James 1972). Maps of this historic region show rugged bluffs, earthen banks, open-water lakes and cutoff channels, flood plain and upland forest, wetland meadows, emergent marsh, upland prairie, many mid-channel sandbars, and sandbar areas overgrown with willows (Missouri River Commission 1895). Each of these habitat types could have been visited by a member of the government party preparing those maps, and the birds that were present could have been included in the final expedition bird list.

Prince Maximilian of Wied made detailed notes of the vegetation at several places along the Missouri River. Notes of the habitat at Cow Island, Sonora Island, tributary rivers and Blackbird Hill describe specific plant associations and the birds present. Along the river the features changed from savannah, prairie, forest islands and sandbars

The Missouri below the Mouth of the Platte, by Karl Bodmer

that could be noted from the boat or seen during brief forays along the riverbank. One area had a mixture of prairie, grassland savannahs, forest, river sandbars, islands and wetland meadows and marsh. Another site changed from forest to savannah, sometimes sandbars, then prairie, willows and cottonwoods. Rock bluffs were noted often.

Near the Council Bluff, Maximilian observed that the landscape became smoother and flatter. Sometimes there was a forest; other times the woods were more open, with only a few isolated trees. Other areas were vast expanses of prairie. Other types of riverine habitat had cottonwoods and willow growth (Orr and Porter 1983).

Traveling along the river, expedition crews had to deal constantly with navigation obstacles present in the channel. The untamed Missouri meandered at will in countless bends curving across the flood plain. The channel was choked with numerous sandbars, jagged tree snags and large islands covered with dense forest growths of massive cottonwoods. Wetlands, such as oxbow lakes, cattail marshes and prairie meadows, were predominant on the lowland plains along the river. The entire valley of the Missouri was a pristine environment of forest, prairie and wetlands.

George Catlin described the setting near Blackbird Hill in present-day Thurston County after he climbed the bluff several times:

> ... I sat and contemplated the solitude and stillness of this tenanted mound; and beheld from its top, the windings infinite of the Missouri, and its thousand hills and domes of green, vanishing into blue in distance, when nought but the soft-breathing winds were heard, to break the stillness and quietude of the scene. Where not the chirping of bird or sound of cricket, nor soaring eagle's scream, were interposed 'tween God and man; nor aught to check man's whole surrender of his soul to his Creator. I could not *hunt* upon this ground, but I roamed from hill-top to hill-top, and culled wild flowers, and looked into the valley below me, both up the river and down, and contemplated the thousand hills and dales that are now carpeted with green.... (Catlin 1965, 4-5)

The northern portion of the Missouri held other paradises as well. During a delay at the Vermillion River after a boiler of the steamboat *Omega* burned out on May 17, 1843, Audubon wrote about the wetlands and small lakes along the river that were filled with birds (Audubon 1960, 497).

The Warren Expedition narrative describes several features of the Missouri River. The river was generally uniform in width—about one-third to one-half mile when its banks were full. Numerous dry sandbars were present in mid-channel when the water was low. Bluffs of the river valley were covered with trees to the mouth of the Platte. Above this point, woodland was confined to sheltered tributaries and ravines on the upland and lowlands along the channel. Above the James River, the flood plain was limited to a narrow valley less than one and one-half miles wide. Downstream it was several miles from bluff to bluff, including some points that were nearly fifteen miles apart. The river was considered to be excellent for navigation, if the many snags dangerous to steamboat navigation were removed.

Along the Missouri in southern Nebraska, the Big Nemaha River drained into the Missouri in what is now Richardson County. The region had rugged bluffs, flood-plain forest and sandbars. Across the river in the state of Missouri, flood-plain forest and meadows were extensive.

Bald Island lay in the same general vicinity, northwest of Peru on the modern-day Otoe County line. This locality also was known as McKissock Island. The island was several square miles in size and contained habitat such as flood-plain willow forest, channel cutoffs and a large upland grassland known as Lone Tree Prairie.

Warren noted in the 1850s that Bon Homme Island was a wooded island in the narrow river valley near the Santee Indian settlement. That expedition investigated the entire course of Ponca Creek, which empties into the Missouri just downriver from rugged bluffs a few miles west of the Niobrara River.

Deciduous flood-plain forests grew along the Missouri River and its tributaries in the east. Cottonwood, bur oak, elms and willows along the lower Platte River occurred to a greater extent within the river valley and along the uplands bordering the river (Rothenberger 1989). Small groves and isolated trees were found to a limited extent in the tall grass prairie. Prairie fires were a predominant force in controlling tree growth and survival.

Warren remarked that "along the banks of the Missouri the bluffs are generally clothed with various species of trees as far up as the mouth of the Platte; above this point the timber is generally confined to the ravines and bottom lands" (Warren 1875, 36). Tree snags were a common feature of the river channel. According to Hayden,

> The river bottoms, which are quite extensive, . . . sustain a luxuriant vegetation, while the broad upland prairies, clothed with grass and flowers of great variety and beauty, meet the eyes of the traveller on every side. (Hayden 1863a, 5)

One example would be Weeping Water Bottom. Hayden mentioned that the river bottom south of Decatur on the Nebraska side of the river

Snags on the Missouri, by Karl Bodmer

exhibited an occasional small grove of cottonwoods. From Council Bluffs to Sioux City, he found the Iowa side "covered in many places with heavy bodies of timber, chiefly cottonwood, with a mingling to some extent of ash, elm, black walnut, &c" (Hayden 1863a, 8).

Three tributaries east of the Missouri are mentioned in Coues' listing of expedition bird specimens. Each of these rivers became a part of southeast Dakota Territory. The Big Sioux River emptied into the Missouri at Sioux City. The channel meandered along the bluffs of Iowa through a Missouri flood-plain nearly ten miles wide. Before settlement and cultivation, this lowland probably was a vast meadow-prairie with more woodland along the river and on the upland along the Nebraska side of the Missouri channel. The Vermillion River flowed through upland prairie, with only a few miles through forest and grassland along the Missouri. The James River was just below Yankton in the Dakota Territory at a site of extensive flood-plain forest, lowland meadow and grassland suitable for cultivation. On the south side of the river, a steep valley wall probably provided cover for growth by some type of woodland plants. Farther west was the Tower, a prominent landmark on the Nebraska side of the river. The flood plain at this point was less than one and one-half miles wide and contained wetland meadow, groves of cottonwoods and a river with channels around and through numerous sandbars.

Landscape features of the Missouri River valley just after 1875 are indicated on the maps prepared by the Army Topographic Engineers (Missouri River Commission 1895). These detailed maps show general land features, including towns, landmarks, numerous lakes and wetlands. There were several prominent lakes on both sides of the channel north of the Platte and many islands within the river channel that looped across the flood plain. Open areas of prairie within the loops of the river and larger prairie areas also are noted on the maps. Examples of flood-plain prairies include Lone Tree Prairie. Few other prairies were given names, even though they were typical features of the river valley. Trees designate woodlands on the maps. Sites near Bellevue and Brownville were extensively forested. Other sites had flood-plain forest, wooded swamps and a few lakes and cutoffs among the trees. Near Blair much of the lowland was forested in a twenty-five-mile stretch of the river. Some area maps show sites, such as that near the Niobrara River, where the water scoured the channel at the base of the bluffs. The rocky cliffs were excellent nesting habitat for some birds, especially Cliff Swallows. Earthen banks would be used by nesting swallows, like the Northern Rough-winged Swallow, and Belted Kingfishers.

Southeast Nebraska

There are few notes on the wild habitats in southeast Nebraska from the historic period. Lt. John Charles Frémont's description of the Little Blue River area mentions well-timbered ravines and a wooded stream with a sandy channel (Frémont 1956). Another traveler noted a stream fringed by willow and cottonwood with frequent groves of oak: "Between the upper reaches of the Little Blue and the Platte the timber had gradually thinned out until nothing was found but a few cottonwoods and willows" (Ghent 1929, 129). Hayden observed that the area between the Platte River and Bellevue was mostly prairie. Timber was noted only along the small tributary creeks of the Platte.

The Platte River Valley

Descriptions of the Platte River valley were not recorded until the period of the Platte River Road, when Army expeditions and Euro-American pioneers wrote about the landscape seen while heading west on the Oregon Trail. The first notations about the area were made by Frémont in 1842 on the Platte near the head of Grand Island. He noted that the timber (cottonwood, elm and hackberry) was limited mostly to islands in the river channel and along the bank (Frémont 1956, 26).

Frémont also described the Platte River forks in Lincoln County on July 2, 1842. Between the forks was a prairie that stretched from their confluence for eighteen miles westward to the hills; there the prairie expanded to five and one-half miles in width. It was thickly covered with grass, and a few scattered cottonwoods and willows grew along the banks (Frémont 1956, 30).

A drawing of the historic Grand Island area of the Platte is included in a history of Fort Kearny written by William Willman in 1930. There, several water channels with trees bordered the main channel. The next channel north also was wooded. An area map included by Willman describes a strip of well-wooded area that extended about a half-mile from the north shore of the river; the map indicates this was about the only woodland in the area (Willman 1930).

In the western part of Nebraska, near the present-day state boundary, the Platte River valley was described by Kurz from a bluff overlooking the valley in 1852. For Kurz the broad valley and river with numerous islands covered with green willows contrasted pleasantly with the gray color of the river (Cole 1902, 180).

The Platte was a broad, grass-covered valley, according to the Warren Expedition report. Juniper grew westward from the confluence of the North and South Platte rivers (Warren 1875). The Platte River had a broad grass-covered valley with a flood plain four to eight miles wide. Cottonwood could be found from the mouth as far west as Fort Kearny, but it became more scarce to the west of the fort. The waters of the Platte were shallow, except during the spring rise, and many sandbars were present. Along the lower Platte, Hayden noted the adjoining uplands held timber consisting of ash, elm, oak, maple and other species. The bottoms of the river were mostly cottonwood woodland (Hayden 1863a).

There was much less timber along the western Platte River and its forks. In the 1840s the land near the junction of the North and South Platte rivers was described as follows:

> To the forks of the Platte the valley of that river extends from three to five miles on each side, being enclosed by steep sandy bluffs, from the summits of which the prairies stretch away in broad undulating expanse to the north and south. The "bottom," as it is termed, is but thinly covered with timber, the cottonwoods being scattered only here and there; but some of the islands in the broad bed of the stream are well wooded, which leads to the inference that the trees on the banks have been felled by Indians who formerly frequented this river as a chosen hunting-ground. (Ruxton 1951, 65-66)

The Rainwater Basin

Another area of extensive wetlands existed in the south-central part of the state, where rainwater basins provided marsh habitat. Shallow to deep water marshes were common. Carleton described one basin along the forks of the Little Blue River: "We at one time (about mid-day) came to a sort of shallow basin, which contained a little stagnant water that was standing" among the marsh plants (Carleton 1983, 48). There are no other known accounts of this region dating from the 1750 to 1875 period, primarily because the early expeditions traveled along the rivers away from the uplands where there were wetland basins. The only portion of the Oregon Trail that passed within several miles of basins was in southeast Clay County and northern Nuckolls County (Franzwa 1982, 69); however, the pioneers likely were not aware of the extensive marshes just a few miles to their north.

The Loup Fork

In the 1820s the Loup Fork already was a notable landmark, probably because of the nearby Grand Pawnee Village. The Platte to the south was described as having a sand bottom with many sandbars, and the flood plain was said to run from two to ten miles wide (James 1972, 305). Beyond the river valley were the plains.

The troop led by Carleton in 1842 reached the Nebraska River (now called the Platte) near the mouth of the Loup Fork at the end of August. From a river overlook, Carleton remarked:

> The bed of the river is but one wide expanse of quicksand, which is formed in bars, and these are continually changing and driving about. On account of the great breadth of the river, the channels are innumerable, but are usually only a foot or so deeper than the surrounding water. The river is filled with beautiful islands. They are all well wooded, but only here and there is there any timber growing upon the main banks. Sometimes we found the channels between some of the islands and shore, entirely dry; presenting to the eye a wide extent of sand, which, as the wind swept over it, was blown about in clouds, as one sometimes may have noticed it upon the barren coast of the ocean. The bottom lands are what would be called high river prairie. . . . (Carleton 1983, 58)

Gouverneur Warren wrote that the valley of the Loup Fork was well wooded up as far as the old Pawnee villages. The Dismal was said to be similar, according to the Warren Expedition report (Warren 1875, 43), while the Elkhorn was noted by Warren to have a broad, fertile and well-wooded valley. This would have been along the eastern part of the river.

The Sand Hills

The unique Sand Hills, with prairie, wetlands and natural shallow-water lakes, comprised about one-fifth of the central and north-central portion of Nebraska. The Sand Hills would have been a vast grassland, but when James Mackay wrote about the Sand Hills in 1795, he described the region as deserts of drifting sand, although he included some references to marshes (Twedt and Wolfe 1976, 198). His description suggests drier conditions that would have produced less grass cover on the hills and fewer lakes and marshes.

Drier conditions also are suggested by remarks Warren made in the 1850s, when he called the area a desert. Despite this attribution his expedition narrative mentions wetlands: "About the sources of the Loup Fork [were] many . . . lakes . . ." (Warren 1875, 26). According to Hayden, who visited the Sand Hills during the Warren Expedition, the area was

> composed of loose sand which has been thrown up into hills and ridges fifty to two hundred feet in height. . . . Though totally unfit for agricultural purposes, this tract of country cannot be said to be

> destitute of vegetation. In the valleys and depressions among the hills are many fine spots of grass, and sometimes the hills are covered with varieties of grass adapted to so meager a soil. . . . On the head of the Loup Fork, and between that stream and the Niobrara at various localities, are numerous saline and fresh-water lakes. The fresh-water lakes contain a great profusion of various species of water-plants and their peculiar animal life. . . . (Hayden 1863b, 367)

Hayden described the lakes as "a resort for myriads of water birds, ducks, geese, gulls, &c" (Hayden 1863a, 13).

Early expeditions to the southwest Sand Hills noted and named several lakes in the area near the headwaters of the South Loup River, south of the Dismal River branches and near Birdwood Creek (McIntosh 1988). Lake Cody was named in recognition of William "Buffalo Bill" Cody; a lake to the east was called Mud Lake. An alkaline lake farther west was dry when the men on a Sand Hills bone hunt visited on July 26, 1870. The next day the same group labelled another lake Schick Lake. The Dismal River valley was narrow with steep walls providing shelter for ash, cottonwood, juniper and pine trees. The notes of the expedition refer to marching "over the burned prairie that stretched as far as the eye could reach . . ." (McIntosh 1988, 87). There were only isolated clumps of grass remaining after the land along the Dismal was burned by a party of Native Americans, which the men on the expedition believed was trying to "harass" them.

In 1873 Thomas G. Maghee described the general features of the Sand Hills. Besides referring to several lakes, in late June he observed a large valley with a good growth of grass. Otherwise, Maghee related that most of the Grant County area was barren sand hills (Lindsay 1929, 255). Several valleys were swampy and full of lakes, his narrative relates. A "well-watered" valley with a lake and pond and several other lakes was present northwest of the headwaters of Kaskopa Creek (Goose Creek) (Lindsay 1929, 262).

George Bird Grinnell published an article about the Sand Hills that describes the area when it was first being utilized as an open range for cattle:

> Imagine if you can, a strip of territory one hundred miles wide and four hundred in length covered by a mass of sand so soft and yielding that a horse's hoof at each step sinks two or three inches into the ground, and so fine and light that it is carried hither and thither in clouds by the winds that blow almost without ceasing. A little vegetation clothes the hillsides, but it is very sparse and there are wide spaces of bare sand between each tuft of grass or weeds. A few streams are scattered at wide intervals through the region and flow into the North Platte River, or the Loup Fork; and it is only along

these streams that the rich dark green of living grass and shrubs appear to relieve the everlasting monotony of the gray sandhills with their scanty covering of subdued brown. (Grinnell 1877, 152)

General Land Office Survey maps from the period around 1875 show some of the lakes present in some areas. In the central Sand Hills, in the lake district that eventually became Valentine National Wildlife Refuge in the 1930s, many of the lakes currently present are shown on the survey maps. Big Alkali Lake measures about 460 acres in size. Other open-water lakes noted on the maps are Clear Lake, Whitewater Lake, Red Deer Lake, North Marsh Lake, Dad's Lake and Middle Marsh Lake. South Marsh Lake is shown as a pond surrounded by marsh vegetation. Trout Lake, Hackberry Lake and Watt's Lake are shown as marsh, rather than as open-water lakes.

In the eastern Sand Hills, several lakes identified on the maps are still present, such as Wolf Lake, Pony Lake and Frazier Lake. Dora Lake, shown as a pond surrounded by marsh, was described as a shallow lake liable to dry up. Neither Otter Lake nor Snipe Lake are depicted on the map, although both are within section lines. Other survey maps from the region show current lakes, such as Moon Lake and Ender's Lake in Brown County, as marshes. Whitewater Lake in McPherson County is shown as a dry valley. In eastern Grant County, some of the expected lakes, such as Moran Lake, Anderson Lake, Negro Lake, Round Lake, Big Buckboard Lake, Claw Hammer Lake and others now present on section lines, are not shown. Some of the lakes in the area that became Crescent Lake National Wildlife Refuge are shown on the land survey maps.

The extent of water present would have influenced the occurrence of wetlands, marshes and sub-irrigated meadows. Drier conditions would have meant fewer lakes and marshes, since groundwater levels would have been lower, while higher water levels would have provided more wet places.

The Niobrara River Valley

In this period the western Niobrara River valley would have been predominantly grasslands, though limited woody growth of willows could have been present. Along the central Niobrara River were pine forests, and the valley and its side canyons would have had a good growth of woody plants. Farther east along the river were some areas with extensive growths of cottonwood forest on the flood plain. Some lakes in the valley provided marsh and open water habitat. Grasslands would have been typical of the uplands next to the river valley.

The Warren Expedition report talks about the changes in vegetation along the Niobrara. The Niobrara was remarkable for its narrow, rugged valley. In the west the valley was predominantly grassland. Some pine trees started to occur in the central stretch of the river, where the canyons became deeper, with cottonwood, elm and ash along the river (Warren 1875, 40). For about 180 miles to the east, the river ran in a valley between rocky buttes, and there was a "luxuriant" growth of grass in the small tributaries. Along the eastern Niobrara, the flood plain consisted of grassy meadows with cottonwood, oak, walnut and ash timber. The Niobrara River at its mouth was wider than the Missouri. The tributaries flowing from the south were abundant with pine, beautiful oak groves with "gushing springs," and deep valleys with abundant oak, ash and pine (Warren 1875, 40). The wider eastern river valley had a greater variety of trees. Maghee wrote about its large pines and junipers while moving eastward down the Niobrara valley through Cherry County in 1873, noting one river bottom of about six hundred acres (Lindsay 1929).

The Pine Ridge

The Pine Ridge includes pine forest on the buttes and grasslands on the flatlands and in the valleys. Deciduous woods grow along the water courses. Similar pine forests occur in the Wildcat Hills along the North Platte River.

Several studies of the region's avifauna were made around 1900 (Cary 1902; Carriker 1902). According to Melbourne Armstrong Carriker, Jr.,

> The face of the [Pine Ridge] plateau . . . , which ranges from three to five hundred feet, is cut into an endless series of deep, precipitous cañons, some of which are short, while others extend back into the plateau for miles, with many twistings and side branches. . . . The upper portion of the cañon walls is invariably composed of "rim rock" rising sheer from ten to even a hundred and fifty feet in height in some places. From the base of this "rim rock" there is a steep slope of earth and rocks to the usually narrow bottom, along which there is to be found in most cases a little streamlet of clear cold water. The slopes are covered with a more or less dense growth of pines (*Pinus ponderosa*) ranging from a few feet to sixty and seventy feet in height, while the rich soil along the banks of the brooks is thickly overgrown with black birch, quaking aspen, and willow, with an occasional elm and box elder. The innumerable little streams issuing from the cañons flow out into the valley where they eventually join, to form the stream known as Hat Creek. There is always a thick

growth of trees and shrubs along the banks of these valley streams, but it is generally more bushy than in the cañons. (Carriker 1902, 76)

The Badlands, an area which is mostly barren rock with only limited plant growth along the water courses, offers an additional habitat in the Pine Ridge area. There is also a small amount of sagebrush plains in the extreme northwest part of the state and elsewhere in the Panhandle.

Saline Wetlands

Before 1875 Nebraska's saline wetlands habitat was limited to eastern Nebraska along Salt Creek and its tributaries near Lancaster (which later was renamed Lincoln). After a survey of the area in 1867, Ferdinand Hayden wrote in his legal description that

> there was a great salt basin near the town of Lancaster, covering 400 acres, another of 200 acres between Oak creek and Salt creek and a third of like extent, called Kenosha basin, on the Little Salt, besides numerous small basins on Middle creek. (Hayden in Morton 1907, 277)

Salt springs are noted on the first plat maps for land in the Lincoln area. The saline wetlands offered a variety of habitats, including open mud flats, flats with saline plants, wetland meadow, marsh, open water, woods and prairie. Sheltered draws in the uplands would have had woods in the uplands. In 1862 salt works at the historic Salt Basin had ten furnaces operating. Extracting salt was the first use of saline wetlands, and salt was taken from the water in the area through the 1880s. Many saline flats west of Lincoln eventually were destroyed by the railroad tracks and switching facilities of the Burlington Northern Railroad, but the worst impact on the state's saline wetlands came from the continual construction and development of Lincoln.

The Vegetation of Nebraska circa 1850

A map of the native vegetation of Nebraska defines the habitats of the state during the historic period and lists specific plants that were characteristic. The summary here is based on the map prepared for the 1850 period (Kaul and Rolfsmeier 1993).

Rocky Mountain Forest: Found in the Pine Ridge and Wildcat Hills areas, this habitat offered ponderosa pine, with shrubs and herbs typical of the mountains.

Eastern Deciduous Forest: This habitat offered several species of oak with other trees, such as basswood, elm, redbud and pawpaw. It occurred along the Missouri, Niobrara, Blue and Nemaha rivers in southeast Nebraska.

Both Rocky Mountain forest and Eastern deciduous forest habitats were found along the central Niobrara River. A variety of grassland types also were present along the river valley. This area also was recognized for its spring-branch canyons.

Flood-plain Prairie and Forest: Containing canary grass, cordgrass, cottonwood and willow, this habitat existed mostly along portions of the Missouri north of the Platte and along the central and eastern Platte. Some flood-plain forest could have been found along the lower Niobrara River.

Tallgrass Bluestem Prairie: This type of prairie occurred in the entire eastern third of Nebraska. It exhibited bluestem grasses, switchgrass and Indian grass, along with a rich variety of forbs and other plants. Trees and shrubs are now more numerous on these prairies due to a lack of prairie fires.

Mixed Prairie: Bluestem grasses, grama grasses and buffalo grasses characterized this prairie habitat, which occurred north and south of the Platte River in central Nebraska.

Shortgrass Prairie: Found mostly in Nebraska's Panhandle region, shortgrass prairies consisted of blue grama grass and buffalo grass.

Sandsage Prairie: Bluestem grasses, sandsage and sandreed grass formed this type of habitat, which was limited to southwestern Nebraska.

Sand Hills Prairie: This habitat was characterized by bluestem grasses in the meadows and sandreed grass, needlegrass and yucca on the dry uplands. Marshes in the area were dense with aquatic meadows, marsh and lakes.

Dakota Prairie: Limited to the northwest corner of Nebraska, these prairies exhibited western wheatgrass, threadleaf sage and needlegrass.

Kansas Mixed Prairie: Bluestem grasses, grama grasses, and many other grasses and forbs made up Kansas Mixed Prairie habitat, which was found along the southern boundary of Nebraska Territory.

Eastern Saline Wetlands: The small areas of Eastern Saline Wetlands habitats present near Lincoln are included on this map.

Woodland habitat was influenced largely by prairie fires, which also would have burned large tracts of grassland. Whether started by lightning or by humans, fires limited the encroachment of trees into prairie along wooded streams and rivers and effectively maintained the grassy character of the open plains.

Natural forces, such as grazing wild animals, also would have affected Nebraska's natural habitats. Near the end of the period, the removal of herbivores, such as the bison and elk, meant a more extensive growth of grass in areas where these animals once grazed. During and after Euro-American settlement, cattle became the dominant herbivore on grasslands, and cattle and other livestock replaced the wild herbivores.

Although farmers plowed fields in the native prairie in eastern Nebraska by 1875, agriculture was a recent intrusion and not the primary land use. The development of farms and ranches methodically changed the diverse natural settings in eastern Nebraska to a typical monoculture of crops and agricultural land, but wildlands continued to exist in the western half of the state.

General Land Office Survey Maps

The maps defined the township, range and sections of land in Nebraska and also contain much information on general land features and characteristics, which can be used to establish the pre-settlement conditions of the land (Galatowitsch 1990). They often note specific information on lakes in regions such as the Sand Hills and woodland in the eastern part of the state. The lower Platte River area was surveyed from 1855 to 1857, for example, and maps prepared during the survey indicate the extent and types of trees (Rothenberger 1989). Documenting the occurrence of specific land features, where noted, can indicate the habitat historically available for birds.

CHAPTER FOUR:
BIRDLIFE OF HISTORIC NEBRASKA

Although Native Americans had observed birds in present-day Nebraska for many "moons" of their tribal histories, the first explorers from the eastern United States started the organized field work necessary to identify scientifically many of the species along the rivers and on the plains of Nebraska. These observers relied on personal knowledge and previous experience, since there were no field guides for classification, or often they collected species and sent them to museums for identification. Several specimens collected in Nebraska provided the basis for the first descriptions of new species (American Ornithologists' Union 1983). For example, the Western Meadowlark was present in Nebraska, but it had not been listed separately from the Eastern Meadowlark until John Audubon noted the differences between the two types of birds in 1843. On the same journey, Edward Harris also identified new species from the Missouri River region. This period in ornithological history was exciting because of the identification of bird species previously unknown to science and also because of the creation of new bird distribution records, which led to a better understanding of the natural history of birds.

Many naturalists endured the hardships of travel to remote and unexplored places in order to view birds, and often their expedition narratives provide rich views of historic places with abundant birdlife. The variety of historic references available from the period before 1875, especially between 1820 and 1860, shows the interest in exploring the uncharted territory owned by the United States. For Euro-American explorers this was new land with new natural-history discoveries to be made.

Most of the birds noted between 1750 to 1875 were breeding-season residents present when most exploratory travels occurred, that is, during the summer months. Other birds were not noted, since explorers avoided the harsh winter months. The only early winter records come from Omaha tribal lore and from the Long Expedition's winter at Engineer Cantonment. Most Army expeditions did not travel on the Plains between late fall and early spring, when other typical birds could have been seen and perhaps collected.

Many of the species not noted have subtle characteristics that are used to distinguish them from very similar birds. Different types of shore birds, gulls, flycatchers, sparrows and warblers are difficult to identify in the field. Observers often collected skins in order to identify birds, but plumage alone may not be sufficient to identify a species.

There were no field guides to use to note the markings needed for field identification, and viewing lenses were primitive tools at that time. Conditions were often harsh, and watching birds probably held low priority when compared to hunting an evening's meal. Despite the difficulties and hardships of the travels that yielded bird records, each published record helps build a composite view of the historic avifauna.

Bird Families

Based on current avian nomenclature (American Ornithologists' Union 1983, 1985, 1987, 1989, 1991; DeBenedictis 1993), forty-two bird families were noted for the period between 1750 and 1875 in the territory that became Nebraska. Samuel Aughey recorded the most birds in Nebraska, many of them at the end of the historic period. Gouverneur Warren's Expedition and Ferdinand Hayden's reports also record many historic avifauna. Much of the avifauna reported from the period is based on these records.

Aughey's report lists thirty-eight families, primarily from the eastern part of the state. There are 250 species from Nebraska in his account (Sharpe 1993). The Barn Owl (Family Tytonidae) was reported only in the study of the Rocky Mountain locust. The highest numbers in specific families were reported for waterfowl (Anatidae), raptors (Accipitridae), shore birds (Scolopacidae), gulls and terns (Laridae), owls (Strigidae), flycatchers (Tyrannidae), thrushes (Muscicapidae) and songbirds (Emberizidae). This report does not include any reference to the parrots which had become extinct in Nebraska by Aughey's time.

The Hayden records include thirty-four of the forty-two families observed in the period. Each plover (Family Charadriidae) was reported. The Warren report lists fifteen of the sixteen species of shore birds (Family Scolopacidae) and eight of the nine flycatcher (Family Tyrannidae) species seen during 1750 to 1875.

Those reports with more than two-thirds of the families represented during 1750 to 1875 are Say's at Engineer Cantonment, Warren's, Hayden's, Coues' and Aughey's reports. Other sources (such as Prince Maximilian's journal, the Baird survey and Suckley's work in southern Nebraska) have from eleven to twenty-one families represented. George Grinnell noted species in only six bird families, which was the lowest number of represented families.

In the raptor and waterfowl families, no single report includes most of the species. Except for the Aughey list and the Engineer Cantonment bird list, only about one-third of the noted hawks and eagles (Family Accipitridae) were reported. Only Aughey's and the Warren and Hayden notes include more than one-third of the recorded swans and ducks (Family Anatidae). The others note about one-third or less of the species in this family. Other families—owls (Family Strigidae), flycatchers (Family Tyrannidae), swallows (Family Hirundinidae) and corvids (Family Corvidae)—generally are included in higher numbers in reports.

The availability of records from several sources provides a composite view of the remaining families, without relying on any prominent source. Each report typically notes several of the five to ten species within a family, although Audubon and Harris did not report any owls or the Belted Kingfisher (Family Alcedinidae).

Families reported in only two or three reports include loons (Family Gaviidae), grebes (Family Podicipedidae), cormorants (Family Phalacrocoracidae), cuckoos (Family Cuculidae), Barn Owls (Family Tytonidae), swifts (Family Apodidae), creepers (Family Certhiidae), pipits (Family Motacillidae) and waxwings (Family Bombycillidae). Several families were mentioned only in a single report. The Common Loon was reported based only on the Omaha knowing the bird.

The modern avifauna includes several families that were not recorded historically. These include Family Anhingidae (the anhinga), Family Ciconiidae (storks), Family Threskiornithidae (ibises), Family Alcidae (murrelets), Family Cinclidae (the dipper) and Family Ptilogonatidae (the phainopepla). These birds are considered accidental and typically are seen only a few times in a decade. Others have undergone a recent change in distribution that has brought the species to Nebraska.

Species Analysis

There were about 274 species noted in records available for the period from 1750 to 1875. This number depends upon including some records from the period that some ornithologists do not accept. If they are not included, the actual number of noted species is reduced.

The highest number recorded is 245 species (89% of the 274), which occurs in Aughey's economic ornithology reports. The Hayden material, which includes the Warren report, has 155 species (57% of the 274). Other high numbers of species are mentioned in Coues' survey (93 species—34%) and in the notes from Engineer Cantonment (89 species—32%). Four other reports contain from 84 of the total species (31% in Audubon and Harris) to 62 of the total species (23% in Prince Maximilian). The other sources note less than 25% of the overall species given in the species accounts. The number of species noted ranges from the mid-fifties by Baird to seventeen by Grinnell in the 1870s.

More than twenty common species were mentioned in more than six of the ten expeditions or reports. Only ten reports are considered here, since others typically were based on just a few sightings. The ten reports are the Omaha tribe notes, Lewis and Clark, Engineer Cantonment, Prince Maximilian, Audubon and Harris, the Warren Expedition, Baird's summary, and the notes by Suckley, Coues and Grinnell.

By comparing the species lists from these sources, the species most often reported can be identified. The twenty-two species most frequently noted by a majority of the ten reports are:

Canada Goose	Wood Duck
Mallard	Blue-winged Teal
Turkey Vulture	Bald Eagle
Greater Prairie-Chicken	Wild Turkey
Northern Bobwhite	Mourning Dove
Common Nighthawk	Whip-poor-will
Red-headed Woodpecker	Horned Lark
Cliff Swallow	American Crow
Common Raven	House Wren
American Robin	Yellow-breasted Chat
Red-winged Blackbird	Western Meadowlark

Waterfowl, raptors, game birds and other obvious species are mentioned most often. The nighthawk and Whip-poor-will are the prominent night birds. The most common prairie birds are the Horned Lark, prairie chicken and meadowlark.

Other species noted in greater numbers (six of the ten reports) are the Great Blue Heron, American Kestrel, Killdeer, American Avocet, Long-billed Curlew, Passenger Pigeon, Barred Owl, Red-bellied Woodpecker, Northern Flicker, Eastern Kingbird, Eastern Bluebird and Rufous-sided Towhee. Most of these birds were observed in Nebraska's eastern forests or along the Missouri River. The Brown-headed Cowbird was noted predominantly in association with animal herds, including those that were part of wagon trains along the Platte River.

The typical summer-breeding avifauna were the Horned Lark, Lark Sparrow, Lark Bunting, meadowlarks and a variety of other grassland species. The large prairie dog towns scattered across the Plains were a haven for the Burrowing Owl. Each of the other wildlife habitats was home to different birds.

Raptors

The Bald Eagle was included in more reports than any other raptor. The Turkey Vulture and American Kestrel also were reported often; both would have been common along the Missouri River. The Northern Harrier was a common summer resident in wetland regions and probably common as well during migration. The American Swallow-tailed Kite was noted numerous times along the Missouri River. The Osprey was seen fewer times in the same region, possibly indicating there were a few breeding pairs. The Red-tailed Hawk was prevalent in wooded areas and would have been reported more often, since most travels were made where there was wood available. The Swainson's Hawk is a bird of the open prairie. Another hawk seen on the open plains was the Ferruginous Hawk, for which there are no indications of its historic breeding range. The few notes concerning the Rough-legged Hawk are a direct result of a few journeys made in the late-fall to early-spring period, when the birds would have been present.

Among the falcons the Prairie Falcon was limited to areas with suitable nesting cliffs, especially the western part of the state. The Peregrine Falcon was probably a seasonal visitor.

The Burrowing Owl was the most noted owl because of its association with prairie dog towns. Also common were the Great Horned Owl and Eastern Screech-Owl, despite the few records for the latter species. Long-eared Owls likely occurred to a greater extent than the available records indicate. Short-eared Owls were uncommon in wet prairie areas, though the many wet meadows along the Missouri and Platte and in the Sand Hills would have provided suitable habitat. Snowy Owls would have been irregular winter visitors, but few records occur, since there were few people keeping notes during the winter season.

Shore Birds

There was extensive shore bird habitat throughout the area of modern Nebraska prior to 1875. The Missouri River had large areas of open-water channels, and the Platte was miles wide in places, with shallow water and sandbars that would have been prime shore bird habitat. The Sand Hills and extensive wetland regions offered additional suitable habitat.

The largest number of shore bird types was noted by Aughey, who listed twenty-six species. Hayden mentioned twenty species. The Coues summary notes eleven, the next highest number. Most of the reports mention from three to seven species. The Omaha tribal information, Lewis and Clark's journals, and Suckley's report contain the fewest species (one to three) of shore birds.

The plovers noted most frequently were the Killdeer and Mountain Plover. Abundant Killdeer were present throughout the state. On the western Plains, the heavily-grazed prairies could have supported a larger number of Mountain Plovers than occur in modern times. The shorter vegetation present during dry periods may be the reason for the sightings of this species in eastern Nebraska.

The American Avocet and Long-billed Curlew also were noted in several of the historic accounts. Avocets were sighted along the Missouri River and in the Sand Hills. It would have been an abundant breeding bird in areas of the Sand Hills, where suitable open-shore habitat existed, but this area was not visited by expeditions or naturalists. Long-billed Curlews probably also were present across Nebraska in suitable grassland habitats.

The Upland Sandpiper probably was most common in the eastern prairies, westward along the Platte and into the Sand Hills. The American Avocet and Long-billed Curlew could have been expected eastward to the Missouri River, but they would have been less common there than in western Nebraska. The Spotted Sandpiper was present throughout the state, but, since this bird is not seen readily, it would have been noted to a lesser extent.

The Common Snipe was prevalent in suitable wetland meadows, and the American Woodcock was a common shore bird of the river forests. The Wilson's Phalarope likely nested in the Sand Hills, although there are no specific references to breeding activity.

Several of the shore birds noted were typical migrants. Both species of yellowlegs would have been especially abundant. Large flocks of migratory Eskimo Curlews gathered on the prairies, especially in central Nebraska. Unfortunately their large numbers and the birds' hesitation to fly from hunters meant many birds were shot for market. Birds spoiled and were wasted when many were killed at once. Smaller shore birds, the peeps or sandpipers, would have moved through in flocks, but their small size meant they were noted less often, and their occurrence remains undocumented.

Warblers

Thirty-five warbler species were noted by these expeditions or explorations. Aughey noted thirty-four of them due to his efforts to look for birds in the woodlands and forests of eastern Nebraska. His repeated efforts and his visits in different seasons meant more of these harder-to-see species were noted. Fifteen species are reported only once, fourteen of them by Aughey. Hayden listed eleven, eight of which were seen at Engineer Cantonment. Prince Maximilian, Audubon and Coues reported either five or six species.

The Yellow-breasted Chat, included in more of the reports, was first noted at Engineer Cantonment, and it appears in subsequent reports from the Missouri River region. This was the most prominent summer resident among the warblers. Several reports note the Yellow Warbler, another common nesting bird in woodlands near water. Other prominent Missouri River warblers reported a few times were the American Redstart, Ovenbird and Northern Waterthrush. Each of these, along with the Northern Parula and Prothonotary Warbler, were breeding-season residents in the forests and wet places of the river valleys. The Common Yellowthroat, another small bird, occurred in wetlands throughout the state, even though it rarely was reported.

Typical migratory species included the Magnolia Warbler, Yellow-rumped Warbler and Blackpoll Warbler. Other warblers were reported only a few times, which indicates either they occurred to a lesser extent or they simply were not seen.

The Historic Nebraska Bird List

Several species first were described scientifically from specimens taken in the territory that became Nebraska. These include the Long-billed Dowitcher from the Council Bluff; the Lark Bunting from the Platte River forks; the Lark Bunting at Ash Hollow; the Orange-crowned Warbler from the Council Bluff; the Chestnut-collared Longspur from the western Nebraska plains; and the Yellow-headed Blackbird from the Pawnee villages along the Loup River near Fullerton (American Ornithologists' Union 1983). The Harris' Sparrow and Western Meadowlark were recognized first in Nebraska, although they were named from specimens from another state.

The historic species list for Nebraska does not include all the birds present from 1750 to 1875. Some species had not been described scientifically during many of the trips prior to about 1835, and some of these species were seen and recorded in Nebraska only after 1875. Examples of some historic species and when they officially were described include:

Redhead (1838)	Common Poorwill (1844)
White-throated Swift (1853)	Western Wood-Pewee (1859)
Least Flycatcher (1843)	Brown Creeper (1838)

Gray-cheeked Thrush (1848)   MacGillivray's Warbler (1838)
Clay-colored Sparrow (1832)   Harris' Sparrow (1840)
McCown's Longspur (1851)   Brewer's Blackbird (1829)
Cassin's Finch (1854)

The current list of Nebraska birds includes more than 405 species (Bray et al. 1986). Additional species have been added to the state bird list in recent years, when avian taxonomy was revised once again. The current Nebraska species list includes all confirmed and recognized state records, including more than 120 years of records since 1875.

The Omaha Tribe

The Omaha tribe knew many birds in the historic Nebraska Territory. Their knowledge preceded any records made by explorations and expeditions from the eastern United States. Their bird lore was retained in tribal history and passed from generation to generation.

There were about forty species known to the Omaha tribe. The groups with the higher number of species noted are waterfowl, upland game birds and raptors. They recognized several corvids and woodpeckers, perhaps because these groups often were mentioned in Omaha tribal myths. Many other birds, especially those common where the tribe lived, were described through language and lore. The Omaha recognized that habitat and behavior were different for some birds and assigned them tribal names based on these characteristics.

The Omaha did not note different species among songbirds, including warblers and sparrows. Only the meadowlark is represented from the Family Emberizidae. These smaller, less conspicuous birds occurred in the areas where the Omaha lived, but their recognition would have required noting slight differences in plumage.

Bird remains were found in human burials at the Omaha Indian village near the present town of Homer (O'Shea et al. 1982). Species found were the Common Loon, Mallard, Bald Eagle, Pileated Woodpecker, Ivory-billed Woodpecker and Common Raven.

The Omaha used material from several other birds in their artifacts. Items collected around the turn of the century have entire skins, heads, feathers or other parts of ten different species (Ducey 1992). A friendship pipe has an eagle, an owl and a woodpecker represented. Martins were designated "birds of war." Similar use of bird material would have occurred during the period from 1750 to 1875.

The Pawnee Tribe

Several species of birds were important to the Pawnee. Besides their prominent use of eagles, owls and woodpeckers in ceremonies, Blue Jays, ducks and wrens also were used. Species associated with Pawnee tribal lore include eagles, hawks, owls, ducks, loons, geese, swans, cranes, crows, ravens, blackbirds, magpies, turkeys, prairie chickens, snowbirds, woodpeckers, swallows, kingfishers, mockingbirds, snipes, larks, orioles and quails (Dorsey 1906). Wrens, bluebirds or Blue Jays, which were prominent in earlier tribal lore, are not mentioned in works published in the latter 1800s (O'Brien and Post 1988, 499). Cormorant skins were valued so highly by the Pawnee in Nebraska that they supposedly would trade a lodge for a single skin (Dunbar 1915, 708).

The Sioux Tribes

Most species known to the Sioux were species typical of the western Nebraska region. As already noted, the western Sioux had general terms in their language for birds, such as bird and duck. Some of the specific birds with which the Sioux were familiar include the Golden Eagle, Ruffed Grouse, Sharp-tailed Grouse, Pinyon Jay, Dark-eyed Junco, Burrowing Owl, Common Poorwill, Gray-crowned Rosy-Finch, Rufous-sided Towhee, Blue-winged Teal, mergansers and magpie. These birds are characteristic of the plains where the Sioux lived in the Nebraska region. The Golden Eagle nested on the buttes of the Pine Ridge or in trees along the rivers where sheer cliff faces were not present. The rocky setting of the Badlands and the buttes of the Pine Ridge and Black Hills provided homes to the Gray-crowned Rosy-Finch, Common Poorwill and magpie. The Dark-eyed Junco and Pinyon Jay were very typical of the pine forests of the Black Hills area. Wetland species included the Blue-winged Teal and mergansers, all typical of small ponds and marshes. The woods of the Pine Ridge, Black Hills and Niobrara River valley would have contained breeding Rufous-sided Towhees, and the males' colorful song would have been heard readily by the Sioux. Other species typical of the north lake country of present-day Minnesota and Wisconsin were familiar to other eastern Sioux people.

The use of bird material on Sioux objects with great ceremonial significance shows that birds played an important role in their tribal lore and mythology. Several ceremonial pipestems and eagle-bone whistles were adorned with feathers, and other artifacts also illustrate the important role of birds to this tribe. Birds were important characters in dreams and myths as well. Consider the importance of the different birds in the Lakota "Creation of the Universe Tale."

Tabeau on the Upper Missouri

The explorer Pierre Tabeau's journal contains several passages with notes on the birdlife seen during his travels through the modern state of Nebraska. In his travels between 1803 and 1805, Tabeau mentioned that Wild Turkey hens were common on the flood plain of the Missouri from the Platte south to the Osage River in Kansas. Turkeys seldom were seen above the Rive qui Court (Niobrara River). Plovers were abundant in autumn, and Greater Prairie-Chickens or grouse (which Tabeau calls pheasants) likely were abundant throughout the year. According to Tabeau,

> Aquatic birds, not finding food upon the banks of the Missouri, never linger there and, except the bustards and ducks which rest on the marshes, they very rarely fly along them. Small birds cannot be numerous in the desert places so little adapted to attract the nightingale [Whip-poor-will?], the goldfinch, and the many kinds that throng the groves of the Ilinois [sic]. The plovers [Upland Plovers] in the autumn and the spring and the pheasants [Greater Prairie-Chickens?] in every season are abundant. Turkey-hens are seldom seen above the River Qui Court. The hawk, the merlin, the crow, the owl, and others similar are very common. (Abel 1939, 88)

The journal mentions magpies and the problems they caused for Native Americans because the birds fed on the raw flesh of their horse's saddle sores. Tabeau also commented about the way in which these tribes prized the Golden Eagle.

The Lewis and Clark Expedition

During the entire time the Lewis and Clark party spent in the Nebraska region, they recorded twenty species of birds among the natural-history features noted during their visit. Some of these birds are not specifically identified in the source material, so their designation to a species is based on the general description. Examples include the Wood Duck (ducks), Red-tailed Hawk (hawk), American Golden-Plover (plover), Piping Plover (small kildee), Bank Swallow (swallows), the meadowlark and bunting (a black bird).

Henry Brackenridge's Expedition

In 1811 Brackenridge noted Turkey Vultures, prairie hens, turkeys and pigeons (Swenk 1937). Other species of the period were noted by John Astor of the American Fur Company as he moved down the Platte to the Missouri River on his return east in 1813. Robert Stuart's narrative notes a few species of birds seen in late spring (Stuart 1935). Some of the birds are identified using common names, but others are identified with such general terms (*wildfowl*, for example) that their specific species cannot be determined. Species observed during this expedition include swans, ducks, prairie chickens, the Long-billed Curlew and meadowlarks along the Platte River.

The Major Long Expedition

The expedition led by Maj. Stephen Long recorded one of the highest species numbers—eighty-nine species. The only sightings of the Northern Saw-whet Owl and Blue-winged Warbler in modern-day Nebraska before 1875 were made while this party camped at Engineer Cantonment. Both breeding-season residents and migratory birds are included in this expedition's list, so it represents what could be considered the typical birds of the Missouri River environs at the time.

Type specimens for the Yellow-headed Blackbird and Burrowing Owl were collected by Thomas Say near the Pawnee villages on the Platte River near the lower Loup (Swenk 1933). Both specimens were taken while going to the Pawnee village along the lower Loup. The Burrowing Owl was taken at one of the many prairie dog towns east of the mouth of the Loup. These species are not included in the list for the Cantonment.

Yellow-headed Blackbirds were collected along the Platte near the Pawnee village. As the expedition continued up the Platte to the eastern slope of the Rocky Mountains, they noted at one site many species of birds, including Carolina Parakeets, Bald Eagles and swans (James 1972, 430). The party returned east along the Arkansas River in modern Kansas and made several observations of birds there.

The Expedition of Prince Maximilian

Sixty species were noted by Prince Maximilian of Wied on his expedition in the territory of Nebraska. With birds and prominent flora described in vivid detail for places such as Bellevue and along the river in northeast Nebraska, Maximilian's notes contain some of the best early information on species and their general habitat. His diaries also contain bird notes and describe the many different lands of the wild Missouri valley. Wild river, forest and prairie formed daily backdrops against which the breeding birds sang and flashed their vibrant colors in the sunlight. Many birds typical of a day on the Missouri River are recorded in the May 1834 notes Maximilian made for the Richardson County area. These include the:

House Wren	swallow
Red-headed Woodpecker	Northern Flicker
Red-bellied Woodpecker	Mourning Dove
Yellow-breasted Chat	Common Yellowthroat
Great Crested Flycatcher	Northern Cardinal
Northern Oriole	

Other birds noted include nesting Bald Eagles and breeding waterfowl like Canada Geese and Wood Ducks. Maximilian's list includes about forty songbirds. His notes also present good species lists in other areas. Species noted only by the naturalists on the Maximilian Expedition were the Common Tern and Winter Wren.

The diaries of Prince Maximilian have more detail on birds and their habitats than any other early source of material for the Missouri River. His notes, collected over a two-year period, surpass those of Audubon, who hurried through the region in a few months.

Townsend across the Rocky Mountains

John Kirk Townsend was a zoologist from an Eastern college who came to visit the Platte River country. He saw many species in the Nebraska area, but only five specifically are mentioned in his daily journal. Species new to science include the Lark Bunting he collected at Ash Hollow and the Chestnut-collared Longspur he took along the Platte River. Other new species are described from farther west in the High Plains and Rocky Mountains (Townsend 1837, 1839). Skins of the new species Townsend collected were used by Audubon to illustrate his work on the birds of America.

The Audubon Expedition

John James Audubon and Edward Harris observed many bird species during the months they traveled along the Missouri River in present-day Nebraska. The two men and their traveling companions noted eighty-four species during their journey. The smaller songbirds are more common on their list, but herons and other water birds, raptors and large shore birds also are recorded. Species noted only by this expedition were the Yellow-crowned Night-Heron, Virginia Rail, godwit, Franklin's Gull and Cedar Waxwing.

Several new species described by Audubon's party include the Sprague's Pipit, Bell's Vireo, Baird's Sparrow and Western Meadowlark. These species would have been present when Townsend made his studies, but Audubon detected the more subtle differences needed to distinguish these species. He also was much more aware of the songs of the birds. The Western Meadowlark had been noticed by other explorers for several decades before Audubon identified it as a new species. The Bell's Vireo is another example. The Virginia Rail also would have been obvious in the marshes and lakes along the river to those who knew and recognized its voice.

Harris collected 159 specimens that were packed for transport to the East after the party returned to St. Louis. Thirteen Carolina Parakeets in the collection were seen on the lower portion of the Missouri at Bald Island near Nebraska City. Other species observed were mostly songbirds, warblers, sparrows and blackbirds. A few of the species seen were shot for scientific preservation. Harris took about three hundred individual birds for his private collection, and Audubon took a share of skins to use as models for sketches and paintings and as sources of information for his writings. Harris' journal holds a list of the number of each species collected during their passage along the river. The largest numbers are for the Carolina Parakeet, Clay-colored Sparrow, Lark Sparrow and Rufous-sided Towhee.

The Warren Expedition

The Warren Expedition's bird list contains about 120 species, lists the species seen, and indicates the number of each that was collected. Species noted include several shore birds, warblers and sparrows. Birds that would have occurred during the different seasons of the year, except winter, also were observed. Examples include twelve Carolina Parakeets, five Piping Plovers, one Trumpeter Swan and three Least Terns.

Although the bird records are attributed to the Warren Expedition, Ferdinand Hayden did most of the work gathering the information, and the bird list was prepared by him. Another report he wrote on the birdlife of the area provides a good review of birds in the Nebraska territory during the mid-1850s (Hayden 1863a). About 155 species can be found in Hayden's work from the Warren Expedition and other studies.

Naturalist George Suckley

Twenty-three bird species were seen by George Suckley during his travels in the northwest Kansas and Nebraska areas of the Platte River Road in 1859. Most were nesting songbirds, such as the Gray Catbird, Brown Thrasher, Rufous-sided Towhee, Blue Jay, Western Meadowlark and others. He observed water birds, such as nesting Blue-winged Teals and Hooded Mergansers, along the Blue River, recorded two Bald Eagles in the Ash Hollow area, and noted a Least Tern on the North Platte River. Some of his specimens were sent to the Smithsonian Institution, where Suckley was in contact with Baird.

Birds of the Northwest

The survey by Elliott Coues includes many records from the Army expeditions. Often his only notes for a species are from a prior source, but Coues also made his own observations and listed them in his survey for the region. Several species given in Coues' report had not been noted by earlier studies: previous visitors had not mentioned the Cinnamon Teal, Canvasback, Bufflehead, American Pipit, Nashville Warbler, Prothonotary Warbler, Fox Sparrow, Snow Bunting or Cassin's Finch. Several of these species likely were present throughout the period but simply were not noticed or recorded by earlier observers. The waterfowl were typical in the wetlands of the west, although the teal would have occurred in lesser numbers. Some of the species, like the warblers given only in this report, were seasonal migrants in the woodlands along the Missouri River.

Notes on the Food of Birds of Nebraska

Samuel Aughey traveled mostly around the eastern part of present-day Nebraska during his economic ornithology work for the University of Nebraska. His field studies took him through recently-settled areas where locusts were affecting the new crop fields; in fact, most of the species he listed are specimens that were dissected to determine the number of locusts in their stomachs. Repeat visits and observations Aughey made through the year provide better information on bird species occurrence than that previously available

His notes of species seen and specimens studied add one family and more than forty species to the historic Nebraska bird list. Having a bird in hand was useful to Aughey in identifying most species except meadowlarks and flycatchers, which are most readily identified by their song. His accounts list the Eastern Meadowlark but do not include any information for the Western Meadowlark, which he incorrectly referred to as a variety; thus, his records cannot be separated according to species.

Some of Aughey's new listings are obvious species, such as the Redhead, Herring Gull, Forster's Tern and Barn Owl. Many of the other species are songbirds, such as the Bohemian Waxwing and Summer Tanager, that would be expected in eastern Nebraska. The seasonal occurrence of some warblers and shore birds meant that Aughey's notes from different occasions added species to the Nebraska bird list.

The status of species in this account are based solely on Aughey's observations for the sites he visited; therefore, his assessment may not reflect the status for a larger region. Aughey commented that there were comparatively few Blue Jays, although notes from another observer said they were abundant in a specific county. Similarly, Aughey said the Killdeer was sparingly present, but accounts by Hayden and Coues show it probably was common or abundant.

Some Aughey records are questionable, including the Hermit Thrush, the Rock Wren nesting near Lincoln, the nesting Nashville Warbler, nesting Prairie Warbler, nesting Mourning Warbler, nesting Philadelphia Warbler, summer records of the Yellow-bellied Sapsucker and the occurrence of the Arctic Tern (Sharpe 1993). Other occurrence dates of species fall outside the typical range of dates recorded by other observers. References to some species, such as the Chimney Swift, Long-eared Owl, Snowy Owl and Black Tern eating insects, are also erroneous (Sharpe 1993). Other records that are doubtful for eastern Nebraska include the Pygmy Nuthatch, Violet-green Swallow, Black-headed Grosbeak and Gray-crowned Rosy-Finch.

Aughey may have misidentified other species as well, since he was not familiar enough with some birds and did not know the field marks needed to make a proper identification. For example, he incorrectly noted a species occurrence for the Virginia's Warbler, Pomarine Jaeger and Great Black-backed Gull; he concluded that the American Tree Sparrow bred in the area based on a June specimen from Dixon County, but the species did not nest in this region; and he also stated that the White-crowned Sparrow and Harris' Sparrow bred in the area, although their breeding ranges are far north of Nebraska. The young of the Solitary Sandpiper supposedly were seen in Dakota County during August, and Aughey suggested they bred there occasionally, but the bird was only a migrant through Nebraska.

Miscellaneous Notes from the 1870s

Nebraska became a state in 1867, and most of its eastern part had been divided into counties by 1875. The University of Nebraska had been established in Lincoln, bringing scientists that would study natural history. Bird enthusiasts pursued birds in their local haunts around the state. Reports of birds seen on trips were published in ornithology journals. New railroads provided easy means of travel to newly-established towns and outposts on the frontier. This ready access brought visitors who were interested in hunting game animals and birds, and most of the notes from this period stem from hunting trips.

George Grinnell's notes, for example, are based on what could be considered hunting trips to the central Platte River and Sand Hills in the 1870s. Typical game birds Grinnell hunted along the central Platte were the Greater Prairie-Chicken and Sharp-tailed Grouse. Upland Plovers were also targets of the hunters' guns. In the Sand Hills, Grinnell may have sighted the fewest number of species in comparison, but his notes form some of the first for several species in the region. His note of the Barn Swallow nesting on a ceremonial burial platform, cited previously, is especially interesting.

Other species also were shot by hunters brought in by the railroads. Along the eastern Platte at Jackson Station, swans (likely Trumpeter Swans) and cranes (likely Sandhill Cranes) were mentioned, along with the obligatory ducks and geese. Other reports add plovers, curlews and sandpipers to the list of birds pursued by hunters. The large numbers of Eskimo Curlews (or "Prairie Pigeons," as they also were called) were another favorite target (Swenk 1915). Sometimes hunters from Omaha would shoot a wagonload of birds; when they were especially numerous, piles of dead curlews would be left to rot on the prairie. The decade from 1870 to 1880 marked the start of the decline in the great flocks of these birds (Swenk 1915, 37).

Species by Region

The compiled reports provide the records needed to build a composite list of species for a specific region. This type of information is available mostly for the Missouri River and the central Platte and somewhat in the Sand Hills. In some cases, such as Ash Hollow, a site-specific list can be prepared from separate observations.

The Missouri River Species

Historic Missouri River birdlife was studied by many naturalists on several expeditions. In fact most records prior to 1850 pertain to the Missouri River. Species that occurred historically but are now extinct throughout their entire ranges are the Carolina Parakeet and Passenger Pigeon, both of which nested along the Missouri.

Forests along this river sported nesting Bald Eagles, American Swallow-tailed Kites and many other species requiring forest tracts of oak and cottonwood. Many less common species, such as the Blue-Winged Warbler and Northern Waterthrush, probably were present, even though there are few records before 1875. Woody places would have been home to the Northern Flicker, Eastern Kingbird, Eastern Bluebird and orioles. The Yellow Warbler, Red-winged Blackbird and Yellow-headed Blackbird would have been common in wetland habitat. Cliff Swallows were abundant; nesting on the rock bluffs along the banks of the Missouri, they were one of the area's most obvious species. Extensive colonies of Bank Swallows probably meant the birds dove around steamboats as they passed the earthen banks cut by the river.

Large flocks of waterfowl moved north or south with the changing of the seasons. The Missouri River was a prime habitat for these birds; its shallow water and sand bars were used by migratory waterfowl, water birds and shore birds.

Species that had nested along the Missouri River but suffered a decline in range from 1750 to 1875 included the Canada Goose and Wood Duck. The Canada Goose often was sighted, but it eventually was extirpated. The Wood Duck had a similar experience; it declined as the river was altered and developed as the human population increased. The Ruffed Grouse was noted along the Missouri, where it currently does not occur, and the Greater Prairie-Chicken had a much more extensive range due to broad grasslands throughout the Nebraska region. The Wild Turkey was common in the woods along the larger rivers, but human encroachment and loss of habitat meant the species was eradicated from its historic breeding range. The Northern Bobwhite would have been a common game bird. Other changes in the birdlife of the Missouri River region can be observed when historic records are compared to those of the recent period (Haecker and Moser 1941).

The Fort Randall Military Reservation Species

This reservation included many square miles of area that extended from the Tower, which is in Nebraska, north and west for nearly thirty miles along the twisting Missouri River. Fort Randall was located on a prominent point along Garden Creek, according to the maps published by the Missouri River Commission. There were several wooded islands and grass meadows along the river channel, which in some places cut along rock cliffs.

The three prominent sources of bird information for this site are sightings made by Audubon and Harris in 1843, reports of the Warren Expedition in 1856, and notes made by Coues during his extended stay in the early 1870s. There are more than forty species noted. The notes made by Audubon record the species present in May and include the Turkey Vulture, American Kestrel, Sharp-tailed Grouse, Blue Grosbeak, Lazuli Bunting, Lark Sparrow and swallows—all typical summer-breeding birds. It was here that Audubon and Harris collected their specimens of the Western Meadowlark.

The Warren Expedition's sightings of birds, such as the Prairie Falcon, Brewer's Blackbird and Common Raven, were made in October and, thus, give some indication of fall birds.

Coues noted several winter species, such as the Snowy Owl, Northern Shrike, American Tree Sparrow, Harris' Sparrow and Snow Bunting, that other observers were not present to see. The arrival of Snow Geese was noted in late March or early April. Other important notes document abundant migrating American Golden-Plovers and Eskimo Curlews. His records of some summer birds contribute to the list of nearly twenty species that would have been expected to nest in the area.

The Platte River Species

Few records of any particular prominence exist for central Nebraska; most of those that include the Platte River valley date from after the start of the Platte River Road of the Oregon Trail. Some pioneers made a few notes, and a few are found in records of Army escorts. There is no mention of large flocks of migratory birds, such as the Sandhill Cranes that gather in large numbers during spring migrations in modern times. Typical birds sighted along the central Platte were the Burrowing Owl, Upland Sandpiper, Common Nighthawk, Grasshopper Sparrow and Western Meadowlark.

At least twice a Bald Eagle was seen nesting farther west near Ash Hollow. Another species in this area of the eastern North Platte River was the Cliff Swallow. Other area species included the Mourning Dove, American Robin, Vesper Sparrow, Lark Bunting and Western Meadowlark.

The Loup Fork Species

More than fifty species were noted in the Loup Fork area near the confluence of the Loup River and the Platte River in eastern Nebraska. Some of the first notes were made in 1813, but most of the notes were Hayden's, especially during the years of the Warren Expedition. Grinnell also recorded a few observations there in 1873.

The Piping Plover (which Hayden said occurred only on the Platte River) was seen with the Least Tern on the Loup Fork near the Platte. The Marbled Godwit notably was observed in a flood-plain meadow on the lower Platte River near the Loup. If this is an accurate sighting of the Long Expedition, it is the only confirmed historic record of the bird breeding in Nebraska. Other birds of wetland meadow habitat sighted in the Loup Fork area include the Common Snipe, Sedge Wren, Bobolink and Eastern Meadowlark.

The Loup Fork was one of the prominent areas for noting birds during the historic period. Birds sighted in the Pawnee tribal area included the Bald Eagle, Northern Harrier, Swainson's Hawk, Merlin and Burrowing Owl. Other species, such as hawks, eagles, prairie chickens, bobwhite quails, snipes, owls, crows and blackbirds, have Pawnee names and may have been known from the area near the village. Geese and ducks were noted, but no species were identified at the Grand Pawnee Village.

Species noted in the Loup Fork area during the mid-1850s were the:

Bald Eagle	Northern Harrier
Swainson's Hawk	Merlin
Sage Grouse	Greater Prairie-Chicken
Sharp-tailed Grouse	Wild Turkey
Northern Bobwhite	American Coot
Piping Plover	Killdeer
Mountain Plover	Spotted Sandpiper
Upland Sandpiper	Long-billed Curlew
Marbled Godwit	Semipalmated Sandpiper
Least Sandpiper	Common Snipe
American Woodcock	Least Tern

Black Tern
Burrowing Owl
Northern Flicker
Western Kingbird
Sedge Wren
Brown Thrasher
Common Yellowthroat
Blue Grosbeak
Vesper Sparrow
Lark Bunting
Henslow's Sparrow
Bobolink
Eastern Meadowlark
Brown-headed Cowbird
Northern Oriole

Black-billed Cuckoo
Common Nighthawk
Western Wood-Pewee
House Wren
Eastern Bluebird
Yellow Warbler
Yellow-breasted Chat
Dickcissel
Lark Sparrow
Savannah Sparrow
Song Sparrow
Red-winged Blackbird
Western Meadowlark
Orchard Oriole

This area of the state had a very diverse avifauna. Several raptors and game birds were seen, and Hayden noted several shore and water birds like the Long-billed Curlew, Least Tern, Black Tern and sandpipers. The Henslow's Sparrow was a noteworthy sighting, since, at the time, it was the westernmost record of this species.

Several birds indicate other habitat types as well. The Yellow Warbler sighting indicates woody habitat at a wetland; shrub habitat is documented by the presence of the Black-billed Cuckoo, Brown Thrasher and Yellow-breasted Chat; woodland habitat is indicated by the Northern Flicker and Northern Oriole. The Common Nighthawk, Lark Sparrow, Lark Bunting, Grasshopper Sparrow and Western Meadowlark use upland grasslands as nesting habitat. Some of the few historic records for the Sage Grouse and Mountain Plover come from this area; since both are more typical of drier habitats, such as the dry plains in the western part of Nebraska, these records are doubtful ones.

Sand Hills Species

The Sand Hills were not well surveyed, even though the Warren and Marsh parties traveled through the area; however, later notes associated with the first ranches in the southern part of the hills provide additional clues to help illustrate the region's birdlife. The Warren Expedition referred to nearly thirty species during its initial and later visits. Three songbird species were noted during Marsh's 1870 bone hunt. Wetlands birds also were observed during the 1873

Niobrara Expedition (of which George Grinnell was a member) and during Grinnell's 1877 hunting visit. The notes made by Luther North vividly portray his interest in the young of the Trumpeter Swan and Sandhill Crane when ranching came to the region.

Despite the "Great American Desert" description given by Long, the area's wetland habitats included subirrigated meadows, shoreline, vegetated marsh and open water. These Sand Hills lakes, marshes and wetland meadows would have been home to many species besides the wetland birds historically seen in the region. All but a few species recorded for the Sand Hills occur in wetland habitats, including the American Bittern, six species of waterfowl, shore birds and marsh songbirds. Species noted in the Sand Hills region were the:

American Bittern	Trumpeter Swan
Canada Goose	American Black Duck
Mallard	Blue-winged Teal
Gadwall	Lesser Scaup
Sandhill Crane	Killdeer
American Avocet	Solitary Sandpiper
Baird's Sandpiper	Common Snipe
Wilson's Phalarope	Barn Swallow
Marsh Wren	Lark Sparrow
McCown's Longspur	Red-winged Blackbird
Rusty Blackbird	

The historic bird list has the Gadwall and Lesser Scaup only in the western Sand Hills during the period. The few upland species seen were the Barn Swallow, Lark Sparrow, McCown's Longspur and Rusty Blackbird. Each of these species still occurs in the region, although its status may have changed since 1875 due to changes in habitat conditions.

Warren noted one especially prominent summer resident of the Sand Hills: he referred to Sandhill Cranes in August 1857. Based on additional records from the region, he may have sighted breeding birds. There were other records of this crane in the Sand Hills region. Hayden said it was not rare, especially in this area. A young bird was adopted and raised at one of the first Sand Hills ranches, and the bird continued to nest in the region after 1875 (Bruner 1902).

The extensive number of other birds that probably inhabited the lakes and wetlands of this region was not documented in this period due to a limited amount of field work by early explorers. Many types of waterfowl, phalaropes, curlews, other shore and water birds, the Bobolink and other songbirds could have been expected in suitable places.

Additional species were sighted along the Snake River, which in its lower reaches has wooded habitat more typical of the Niobrara valley. This is reflected in the Lewis' Woodpecker, Mountain Bluebird and Western Tanager that were noted. These three species occur in the pine habitat along the lower Snake and Niobrara. The Eared Grebe and American Pipit also were observed along the Snake River.

Pine Ridge Species

There are no historic sightings of the birds of the Nebraska Pine Ridge. Although the region was home to the Sioux, most sightings for similar habitat are from the Black Hills. Only the Warren Expedition noted the Prairie Falcon, a typical butte-country bird. Surprisingly there are no notations of this bird along the North Platte River, for example, near Scotts Bluff, where falcons would have been expected.

Some of the species that would have been seen in the Pine Ridge are noted in the Black Hills region to the north. This pine forest would have been similar to the forest in the Pine Ridge and Wildcat Hills in the Nebraska area. Some of the species seen there also could have occurred among the buttes and grasslands of the Panhandle or elsewhere in Nebraska. The Long-eared Owl was sighted in the Rocky Mountain forest of the Black Hills; the Common Nighthawk was noted on the plains; and the Northern Flicker was observed in wooded areas. In 1874 William Ludlow reported hearing meadowlarks constantly during the day throughout his Black Hills journey (Ludlow 1875). The Western Wood-Pewee also was seen in the Black Hills. Western Kingbirds and Horned Larks were common on the Dakota plains. Purple Martins were shot for naturalists' skin collections. Cliff Swallows nested on rocky buttes along the rivers. The Loggerhead Shrike, Solitary Vireo, crow, raven and several songbirds are species that could have been expected on the historic Nebraska bird list.

While on a journey with Gen. George Armstrong Custer in the Black Hills, George Bird Grinnell noted the Lewis' Woodpecker, which prefers burned pine forest habitat (Ludlow 1875). This party also saw the Violet-green Swallow and Gray Jay among the forested hills, and several Western Tanagers were seen each day on the expedition. The Ruffed Grouse, Sharp-tailed Grouse, Dark-eyed Junco and Evening Grosbeak also were known to nest in the Black Hills (Coues 1874).

Birds as Sustenance for Indians

The Omaha material is the only source from this area and period that specifically refers to birds the tribe used as food. Species eaten include waterfowl, game birds and some songbirds (Fletcher and La Flesche 1972), specifically:

swan	Snow Goose
Wood Duck	Mallard
Blue-winged Teal	Greater Prairie-Chicken
Wild Turkey	Northern Bobwhite
crane	Long-billed Curlew
Common Snipe	American Woodcock
Mourning Dove	Horned Lark
American Robin	blackbird
meadowlark	

Most of these species are larger birds. Small songbirds would have been eaten less often, likely when harsh conditions limited the available food resources.

However, material from other studies provides information that indicates when birds were used as food. Archaeological digs at Native American camps and villages along the Missouri River have found bird material. The camp at the Walker Gilmore Site, about one-quarter mile from the Missouri River along Sterns Creek in modern Nebraska, dates to the Woodland period (Haas 1983). Several hearths and trash-filled pits were excavated, and the remains of several bird species were identified, including many game birds like geese, ducks and grouse (Falk and Angus 1983). Aquatic birds predominate, with upland game birds (turkeys, grouse and bobwhites) comprising the majority of the remainder. Material that had been burned (in a camp fire, for example) came from geese, ducks, herons, cranes, turkeys, grouse, bobwhites and crows. Cut-marks occur on bones of Canada Geese and Wild Turkeys (Haas 1983). Although this material dates from before 1750, it indicates Native American use of birds as food.

Although information about the Ponca tribe is mostly ceremonial, a small amount of ethnographic material was found concerning Native Americans hunting birds. One report says waterfowl hunting did not seem to have been an important Ponca activity, even though birds were hunted to some extent. According to one observer, birds usually were stalked by individual hunters (Howard 1965). The area at the mouth of the Niobrara River was known as a good place to shoot geese, ducks and grouse.

Birds as Sustenance at Trading Posts

Archaeological studies at Fontenelle's trading post, at the Bellevue Agency, at Cabanne's post north of Omaha, and at Fort Atkinson document vertebrate faunal remains at sites along the Missouri River (Bozell et al. 1990). Fontenelle's post at Bellevue was active from 1822 to 1842, and Cabanne's was active from 1822 to 1839. Hunting and eating wild game was a primary component of the subsistence pattern at these trading posts (Bozell et al. 1990, 12). Birds typically were used as a supplemental part of the local diet. Seasonal exploitation is suggested for most of the waterfowl noted at both sites, and avian remains are abundant at both. Modifications to the bones include charring, cut-marks made by human implements or tools, and holes made by the teeth of gnawing carnivores or the impact of buckshot.

The remains of about twenty-two species or bird types from thirteen taxonomic groups compose over twenty percent of the material at Bellevue. Waterfowl comprise more than seventy percent of the material sample. Species represented by the remains are:

swan	Snow Goose
Canada Goose	duck
Wood Duck	Mallard
teal	Northern Shoveler
Lesser Scaup/Ring-necked Duck	American Goldeneye
Bufflehead	Common Merganser
Red-tailed Hawk	grouse/domestic chicken
Wild Turkey	American Coot
Sandhill Crane	Passenger Pigeon
American Crow	meadowlark

Mallards, teals and various other ducks comprise the largest percentage of the remains. The species remains noted in the lowest amount are the Bufflehead, Common Merganser, Red-tailed Hawk, American Coot and meadowlark. The three water birds are noted to have a poor palatability, which may explain their occurrence in lesser numbers.

The remains of about twelve species or bird types from seven taxa contribute over forty percent of the material at Cabanne's post. Waterfowl comprise about fifty-eight percent of the bird species (Bozell et al. 1990, 36). Species represented by the remains are the Snow Goose, Canada Goose, Wood Duck, Mallard, Wild Turkey, Killdeer, ducks, teal, grouse/prairie chicken, domestic chicken, plover or turnstone, and sandpiper. The teal and Wood Duck comprise the largest percentage of the remains. The species remains noted in the lowest amount are the Canada Goose, Snow Goose, Mallard, ducks, and sandpipers.

Aquatic, riparian, grassland, and forest or forest-edge are the habitats represented by the birds identified from the animal remains at these posts. The largest number of Bellevue animals comes from riparian and forest-plant communities (Bozell et al. 1990, 97). At Cabanne's post animals of forest and riparian habitats were used most extensively.

Vertebrate remains from Fort Atkinson, which was occupied from 1820 to 1827, indicate the species used there (Mundell 1979). The greatest number of bone specimens are from Passenger Pigeons, teal, an unidentified duck, and geese. Additional species noted from this site are Bufflehead, Wild Turkey, teal, grouse, chicken and crane. Most of these species would have inhabited riparian habitats along the river. The Wild Turkey, grouse and prairie chicken are the only upland species represented.

CHAPTER FIVE:
LIST OF SPECIES

In this chapter, specific information on the species of birds mentioned in the literature reviewed above is presented. Historic records for each bird are listed by date of sighting (when known) and location (as best can be determined). The location of the sighting may be either a specific place or just a general reference for the Nebraska territory.

Included with the species account are tribal names and common names used in the historic material (1750 to 1875). The status of the species from 1750 to 1875 also is suggested. Where insufficient information is available for analysis, no status is given. Sightings are listed in chronological order within each particular bird's account.

As for geographic location, many of the edited journal narratives have footnotes that give the specific site or landmark where the sighting occurred. When the location was not specified in the report, it is plotted here as best as possible, using historic or modern maps. The Lewis and Clark Expedition made the first maps of the Missouri River (Moulton 1986, 1987), and other useful historic Missouri River maps identify prominent river features (Missouri River Commission 1895). The Oregon Trail also has been mapped to a specific route (Franzwa 1982). When no particular location was noted for a sighting, however, just the general location is listed here.

Where possible, the county where the bird was sighted is included with the species record below. The county name is printed in capital letters, when the county could be determined. A question mark included with a location means the site is likely the locality or political area of the sighting, although there was not sufficient information to confirm it. For sightings on or across the Nebraska border, the two-letter state code is given, when the state could be determined. Semi-colons separate a string of sightings or comments from the same bibliographical source, while periods separate sightings from different sources.

Within each bird's account, the apparent status and other notes are used to illustrate the status of the species between 1750 and 1875. This material is a summary of the notes reviewed. Any notes on occurrence that are included with a record below typically have been taken from the noted reference source. When a naturalist's observation is found in a work published by another author, the material below indicates both the naturalist and the author who quoted that naturalist. Any additional comment or clarifying information that is not taken from the original sources is enclosed in square brackets.

Taxonomy follows the main list for North America as defined by the American Ornithologists' Union (1983, 1985, 1987, 1989, 1991; DeBenedictis 1993). Common names used in the species accounts are accompanied by current scientific names and a listing-order based on the current avian taxonomy presented in the most recent report on North American birds.

Family Gaviidae

Common Loon. *Gavia immer.*
Tribal name: Dakota Sioux—*huŋ'-tka.*
The Common Loon was found in material excavated at the site of the Big Village of the Omaha, near the present site of Homer, DAKOTA (O'Shea et al. 1982).

Family Podicipedidae

Eared Grebe. *Podiceps nigricollis.*
Apparent status: This grebe was a regular migrant along the Missouri and Platte rivers and at other Nebraska wetlands and probably was a summer resident in the Sand Hills.
On 17 September 1856, Snake River, CHERRY (Warren in Baird et al. 1860). North Platte River (Coues 1874). Rather abundant, especially on the Platte and Missouri rivers; specimen received September 1874 from Columbus, PLATTE; specimen from the Missouri River near Bellevue, SARPY (Aughey 1878).

Family Pelecanidae

American White Pelican. *Pelecanus erythrorhynchos.*
Tribal names: Omaha—*bthe'xe;* Dakota Sioux—*mde'-ġa.*
Apparent status: The many records for the Missouri River indicate pelicans were common migrants. The single Platte River record indicates migrants also occurred along this river.
Present in the Omaha tribal area, THURSTON (Fletcher and La Flesche 1972). Killed on 6 August 1804, eastern BURT, where they were catching fish in the river; 8 August 1804, over 100 gathered in an area covering several acres on the upper end of an island, just north of Little Sioux River, BURT (Lewis and Clark in Moulton 1986 and Moulton 1987). On 21 September 1819, on the Missouri River, OTOE (Nichols 1969). On 28 April 1833, flock of about 100 flying north, and 29 April 1833, flock of 200 flew by, Good Sun [Sonora?] Island area,

northeast NEMAHA; 6 May 1834, Niobrara River area, KNOX; 10 May 1834, THURSTON; 11 May 1834, northeast WASHINGTON; 12 May 1834, central WASHINGTON; 14 May 1834, Little Nemaha River area, NEMAHA (Maximilian in Orr and Porter 1983). In May 1834 in the Big Bend area of the central Platte River (Wislizenus 1912). Large flock on 13 September 1834 at Bellevue, SARPY (Morgan and Harris 1967, 213). On 7 May 1843, NEMAHA/OTOE; 9 May 1843, SARPY; 11 May 1843, WASHINGTON; 24 September 1843, Niobrara River area, KNOX; 26 September 1843, James River, CEDAR; 3 October 1843, Little Sioux River, BURT; 6 October 1843, Platte River, CASS (Audubon 1960). Frequently seen during migration; two May 1872, May 1873, and two May 1875, LANCASTER (Aughey 1878).

Family Phalacrocoracidae

Double-crested Cormorant. *Phalacrocorax auritus.*
Tribal name: Dakota Sioux—*huŋ'-tka.*
Common name: shag.

Apparent status: Cormorants were regular migrants along the Missouri, possibly remaining to breed in this region. There are no reports of nesting, but this bird likely nested in western Nebraska.

Potential breeder about 1820 in the Engineer Cantonment area, WASHINGTON (Thwaites 1905). On 8 May 1834, opposite mouth of the Vermillion River, DIXON (Maximilian in Orr and Porter 1983). Said to breed along the Missouri River (Coues 1874).

Family Ardeidae

American Bittern. *Botaurus lentiginosus.*
Tribal names: Omaha—*moⁿ'xata, wadoⁿbe* (looks up at the sky).
Common names: Indian hen, bittern, stake-driver (Baird et al. 1860).

Apparent status: The marshes of the state would have been prime breeding habitat. They probably nested along the Missouri River and in the Sand Hills. Although there are no records, breeding birds probably also were found in the Rainwater Basin, where suitable habitat would have been available.

Present in the Omaha tribal area, THURSTON (Fletcher and La Flesche 1972). Found as high as the entrance of the Sioux River, DAKOTA (Lewis and Clark in Swenk 1935). May 1856, mouth of the Vermillion River, DIXON (Warren in Baird et al. 1860); 15 July 1856, forks of the Platte, LINCOLN (Bryan in Baird et al. 1860); 11 August 1857, western Sand Hills (Warren in Baird et al. 1860); 20 August 1857, north fork of the Platte River (Magraw in Baird et al. 1860); Platte River (Warren in Baird et al. 1860). Not uncommon where marshes or lakes are found in the West (Hayden 1863a). Occasional; specimen received September 1873 from Grand Island, HALL (Aughey 1878).

Great Blue Heron. *Ardea herodias.*
Tribal name: Dakota Sioux—*ho-k'a'-to.*
Common name: great blue crane.

Apparent status: Great Blue Herons were known to nest from the Missouri River to northwest Nebraska. They would have occurred along the Missouri wherever there was suitable habitat. Heronries also would have been found along the Platte and other rivers where trees for nesting were present. The lack of suitable trees elsewhere in the state would have limited their occurrence during the breeding season.

On 11 August 1804, above Blackbird Hill, THURSTON, and opposite Yankton, CEDAR (Lewis and Clark in Swenk 1935). Potential breeder about 1820 in the Engineer Cantonment area, WASHINGTON (Thwaites 1905). On 9 May 1834, DIXON (Maximilian in Orr and Porter 1983). On 18 May 1834, along the central Platte River, likely BUFFALO (Townsend 1978). On 9 May 1843, at Bellevue, SARPY; 14 May, nesting colony of 20-30 nests, northwest DAKOTA (Audubon 1960, McDermott 1951). In summer of 1846, a number of "cranes" [probably the Great Blue Heron] on the central Platte River, likely near the Grand Island, HALL or BUFFALO (Lienhard 1961, 42). May 1856, near Big Sioux River, DAKOTA (Warren in Baird et al. 1860). Generally distributed throughout the West, along the watercourses (Hayden 1863a). A young heron, or "crane" as it was called, was brought to the party on 17 June 1871 along Thompson Creek, FRANKLIN (Green 1954). Occasional; August 1871 south of Dakota City, DAKOTA (Aughey 1878).

Great Egret. *Casmerodius albus.*
Common names: great white egret, white heron.

Collected on 2 August 1804 in the Council Bluff area, WASHINGTON (Lewis and Clark in Swenk 1935). [The Council Bluff was a landmark on the Nebraska side of the river, near Engineer Cantonment and Fort Atkinson.] May 1873 on the Nemaha River, RICHARDSON (Aughey 1878).

Snowy Egret. *Egretta thula.*
Common names: little white egret, snowy heron.

Rare; on the Missouri River, OTOE and RICHARDSON (Aughey 1878).

Green Heron. *Butorides virescens.*
Common names: poke, fly-up-the-creek.
   Apparent status: These little herons were breeding season residents in eastern Nebraska.
   Potential breeder about 1820 in the Engineer Cantonment area, WASHINGTON (Thwaites 1905). On 28 May 1857, Salt Creek, LANCASTER/SAUNDERS (Warren in Baird et al. 1860).

Black-crowned Night-Heron. *Nycticorax nycticorax.*
Common name: American night heron.
   Apparent status: Night-herons probably were more common than the single record indicates. Birds also probably would have nested in the Sand Hills and Rainwater Basin wetland regions.
   Potential breeder about 1820 in the Engineer Cantonment area (Thwaites 1905).

Yellow-crowned Night-Heron. *Nyctanassa violacea.*
   On 10 May 1843, Fort Atkinson area, WASHINGTON (Audubon 1960).

Family Anatidae

Swan.
Tribal names: Omaha—*mi'xaço^n* (white goose); Dakota Sioux—*ma-ġa'-ska, ma-ġa'-taŋ-ka.*
Common name: American white swan.
   Present in the Omaha tribal area, THURSTON (Fletcher and La Flesche 1972). On 27 March 1813, numerous, a few miles west of the confluence of the North Platte and South Platte rivers, and also three shot on same day east of the river confluence, LINCOLN (Stuart 1953). Flying up the Missouri River 9 February 1820 (James 1972, 120). In faunal remains dating to 1822-42 from Fontenelle's post, SARPY (Bozell et al. 1990). On 12 May 1834, central WASHINGTON (Maximilian in Orr and Porter 1983). On 3 October 1843, Little Sioux River, BURT (Audubon 1960).

Trumpeter Swan. *Cygnus buccinator.*
   This large bird is very prominent and would have been obvious when seen on a river and marsh. Many of the records included for

swan in the previous account likely would have been this species. Native Americans were familiar with swans and likely killed them when possible for food. Others also used this bird for food, as indicated by the remains from a historic trading post. This swan bred along the Missouri River flood plain and in the western Sand Hills. Considering these records adds the likelihood that Trumpeter Swans also were present along the Platte. Along the Missouri, birds would have been expected in limited numbers where larger marsh areas occurred, mostly south of the Platte.

The Trumpeter Swan was noted prominently in the early bird history of the Sand Hills. This swan occurred on numerous larger lakes throughout the Sand Hills, and it nested in Cherry County when there were few ranches (Ducey 1988). In the mid-1870s George Grinnell recorded two pairs of adult and young Trumpeter Swans at a lake near the headwaters of the Dismal River in the vicinity of the Cody-North Ranch (Grinnell 1877). Luther North had fed their parents at a lake near where the North Brothers established their ranch. Most ranches were not established in the Sand Hills until about 1880 to 1890. There are other historic records for the period prior to 1900 that indicate nesting in the eastern Sand Hills.

Although this is the species noted by Lewis and Clark (based on editorial interpretations), the specific identification of this swan did not occur until 1832 (American Ornithologists' Union 1983).

Cygnets seen 6 July 1804 by the Lewis and Clark Expedition, HOLT, MO (Burgess 1980). Seen during certain seasons of the year in large flocks throughout the Northwest (Hayden 1863a). Rare in Nebraska (Aughey 1878). Swans on 22 and 24 June 1873, in northwest GRANT and southwest CHERRY (Lindsay 1929, 257). On 6 September 1877; young raised in the summer at the Cody-North Ranch area in headwaters area of the Dismal River, HOOKER (North 1961, 252-254; Grinnell [Yo] 1877).

Goose (Snow Goose or Canada Goose).
Tribal names: Omaha—*m'i-ha;* Pawnee—*ka-to-rūt* and *ka-to-ni-ta-ka* (a
    white goose) (Hayden 1868); Dakota Sioux—*ma-ġa'*.

On 27 March 1813, numbers seen a few miles west of the confluence of the North Platte and South Platte rivers; also shot same day east of the river confluence, LINCOLN (Stuart 1953). On 21 September 1819, along the Missouri River, OTOE (Nichols 1969). Flocks flying up the Missouri River on 9 February 1820 (James 1972). In faunal remains dating to 1820-27 from Fort Atkinson, WASHINGTON (Mundell 1979). Multitudes on 4 March 1835 along the

Platte River near the Grand Pawnee Village, PLATTE (Dunbar 1915, 612). On 1 June 1849, along the Oregon Trail east of Fort Laramie, GOSHEN, WY (Decker 1966, 85).

Snow Goose. *Chen caerulescens.*
Tribal names: Omaha—*kiçnu^n'*; Dakota Sioux—*ma-ġa'-paŋ-paŋ-na* and *ma-ġa'-śe-kśe-ċa-daŋ.*
Common name: white brant.

Apparent status: The Missouri River was an important migratory corridor for this species, and the abundant flocks of birds provided an important seasonal food source. The notation by Prince Maximilian that they nested probably is inaccurate, since these birds nest far to the north of Nebraska. Injured birds may linger into the typical bird breeding season.

Remains from ca. 1775-1845 at the Big Village of the Omaha, DAKOTA (Jackson and Scott 1992). Present in the Omaha tribal area, THURSTON (Fletcher and La Flesche 1972). On 5 October 1819 at Engineer Cantonment (Nichols 1969). Great flocks of brants (geese) passed up the Missouri River in early April 1820 (James 1972). In faunal remains dating to 1822-39 from Cabanne's post, DOUGLAS, and dating to 1822-42 from Fontenelle's post, SARPY (Bozell et al. 1990). On 3 May 1833, at Bellevue, "including a pair of completely white ones with black piniors, (*Anser hyperboreus*) (here called Brant) which are nesting here;" 11 May 1833, northeast KNOX; 9 May 1834, DIXON (Maximilian in Orr and Porter 1983). Observed migrating at several locations in the Dakota Territory and reached Fort Randall in late March or April, TODD, SD (Coues 1874). Abundant during migration; two in April 1865, DAKOTA; two in October 1871 and four in October 1874, LANCASTER (Aughey 1878).

Canada Goose. *Branta canadensis.*
Tribal names: Omaha—*mi'xa to^{n}ga* (big goose); Dakota Sioux—*ma-ġa'-śa-pa.*
Common name: common wild goose.

Many records show this bird was a common nester along the Missouri River. No doubt this goose was abundant elsewhere in the state where suitable habitat occurred, including the Rainwater Basin. Birds probably were especially common in the Sand Hills, even though there was only one record of occurrence. Hunting caused a decrease in the numbers of this goose as the state was settled, and eventually they were exterminated from the state as a breeding species (Ducey 1988).

Present in the Omaha tribal area (Fletcher and La Flesche 1972). Great number of goslings on the banks and in the ponds near the river on 10 July 1804, NE/KS boundary, HOLT, MO; goslings and several others killed on 12 July 1804, eastern RICHARDSON; great numbers of young geese, 19 July 1804, in northeast OTOE; geese killed on 30 July, the Council Bluff area, WASHINGTON; great numbers on 4 August, northeast WASHINGTON; killed on 23 August, northern DIXON; 4 September at Niobrara River and on 6 September, northern BOYD (Lewis and Clark in Swenk 1935). On 5 October 1819, shot by hunters at Engineer Cantonment (Nichols 1969). Potential breeder about 1820 in the Engineer Cantonment area (Thwaites 1905). Great flocks of Canada Geese passed up the Missouri River, early April 1820 (James 1972). In faunal remains dating to 1822-39 from Cabanne's post, DOUGLAS, and dating to 1822-42 from Fontenelle's post, SARPY (Bozell et al. 1990). In 1823 at Keg Island, CASS (Wilhelm 1928). On 25 and 26 April 1833, nesting, DONIPHAN, KS; 29 April 1833, ATCHISON, MO; 29 and 30 April 1833, nesting in Frazer's Island area, OTOE; 3 May 1833, mouth of Platte River, CASS, and Bellevue, SARPY; 4 May 1833, nest with eggs, DOUGLAS; 5 and 6 May 1833, Fort Calhoun area and northeast WASHINGTON; 6 May 1833, east-central BURT; 7 May 1833, nest with eggs at Blackbird Hill, and young at another site; 8 May, young at another site, THURSTON; 8 May 1833, pairs and young, three sites, northeast DAKOTA; 9 May 1833, young, northeast DIXON; 10 May 1833, young, northwest DIXON; 10 May 1834, THURSTON (Maximilian in Orr and Porter 1983). Pair on 10 May 1843, WASHINGTON (Audubon 1960). On 12 May 1843, Blackbird Hill area, THURSTON (Harris in McDermott 1951). Very abundant and bred in Nebraska in the 1860s; young seen on the Missouri River (Aughey in Taylor and Van Vleet 1888b). Broods on several occasions in June 1874 on the Missouri River (Coues 1874). Very abundant; occasionally bred, and young seen along the Missouri River; 2 April 1866, DAKOTA; three on October 1871, October 1872 and three on October 1874, LANCASTER (Aughey 1878). Numerous, 6 September 1877, in the headwaters area of the Dismal River, GRANT/HOOKER (Grinnell [Yo] 1877).

Duck.
Tribal name: Omaha—*mi'xazhi"ga* (little goose). Pawnee—*ki'-i-nuks* and *ki'-sat*. Dakota Sioux—*ću'-kćaŋ* for a kind of duck; *ću-kćaŋ'-pa-ġi* for a duck about the size of a Mallard, with a gray head and white breast; *ću-kćaŋ'-pa-sa-pa* for a species of duck with a black head and neck; *ću-kćaŋ'-taŋ-ka* for the large species of

duck which they call *ću'-kćaŋ; ho'-ta-daŋ* (a small sharp-billed duck); *mc-ġa'-ksi-ća* (duck, ducks, the generic name); *pa-su'-mdc-ś'ka* (a broad-billed duck); *ś'do-ka'* (a kind of spotted duck); *ś'u-pe'-ć'o-wo-ź'u* (a species of duck so called because its entrails are always full).

Remains from ca. 1775-1845 at the Big Village of the Omaha, DAKOTA (Jackson and Scott 1992). On 27 March 1813, numbers a few miles west of the confluence of the North Platte and South Platte rivers, LINCOLN (Stuart 1953). On 22 September 1819, on the Missouri River, OTOE; 5 October 1819, shot by hunters at Engineer Cantonment (Nichols 1969). Flying up the Missouri River, 9 February 1820; great flocks flew northward along the Missouri River, early April 1820 (James 1972). In faunal remains dating to 1820-27 from Fort Atkinson, WASHINGTON (Mundell 1979). In faunal remains dating to 1822-39 from Cabanne's post, DOUGLAS, and dating to 1822-42 from Fontenelle's Post, SARPY (Bozell et al. 1990). Multitudes, 4 March 1835, along the Platte River near the Grand Pawnee Village, PLATTE (Dunbar 1915, 612). On 1 June 1849, along the Oregon Trail east of Fort Laramie, GOSHEN, WY (Decker 1966, 85). On 23 May 1852, shot along the Platte River west of the Loup Fork, [MERRICK?] (Eaton 1974). Shot on 12 June 1871 at two localities north of the Little Blue River, THAYER; the ducks were fried for supper and served with bread, butter and coffee (Green 1954, 202).

Wood Duck. *Aix sponsa.*
Tribal names: Omaha—*mi'xa zhi"ga xage egu^n* (the crying duck); Dakota Sioux—*s'ki-s'ka'.*
Common names: summer duck, bridal duck (from Omaha language), forked duck (Maximilian), summer duck (Hayden).

Apparent status: The flood-plain forest and the many oxbow lakes along the Missouri River historically have provided prime habitat for this duck. Most of the original range for the Wood Duck would have been along the Missouri and the lower reaches of its larger tributaries, and the bird would have occurred where there were large trees suitable for nesting sites westward along the Platte.

Present in the Omaha tribal area, THURSTON (Fletcher and La Flesche 1972). On 15 August 1804 near the old Omaha Indian village near Homer, DAKOTA; 25 August 1804, CEDAR; near the mouth of the Niobrara; 5 September 1806, THURSTON and northern BOYD (Lewis and Clark in Swenk 1935). Potential breeder about 1820 in the Engineer Cantonment area (Thwaites 1905). In faunal remains dating to 1822-39 from Cabanne's post, DOUGLAS, and 1822-42 from

Wood-duck at Engineer Cantonment, by Titian Ramsay Peale

Fontenelle's post, SARPY (Bozell et al. 1990). On 25 and 26 April 1833, numerous pairs, DONIPHAN, KS; 1 May 1833, mated pairs and four specimens collected, Frazer's Island area, OTOE; 2 May 1833, border of CASS and OTOE counties; 3 May 1833, Bellevue; 5 May 1833, numerous pairs, Fort Calhoun area, WASHINGTON; 6 May 1833, numerous pairs, east-central BURT; 8 May 1833, two sites in northeast DAKOTA; 10 May 1834, THURSTON, and Blackbird Hill area, THURSTON; 11 May 1834, southeast BURT; 11 May 1834, northeast WASHINGTON; 12 May 1834, central WASHINGTON (Maximilian in Orr and Porter 1983). On 12 May 1843, BURT; 24 September, Bazile Creek, KNOX; 26 September, Vermillion River, DIXON (Audubon 1960). Adult bird with young about 1846 on a creek [Birdwood Creek?] along the North Platte River, about ten miles west of the Platte Fork, LINCOLN (Ruxton 1951, 86). Two on 7 May 1856, Vermillion River, DIXON; Ioway River [Aowa Creek], DIXON (Warren in Baird et al. 1860). Abundant throughout the West (Hayden 1863a). Rather abundant and breeds; two in May 1865, DIXON; two in June 1865, DAKOTA; two in August 1869, WAYNE; October 1873, SEWARD; two in September 1874, LANCASTER (Aughey 1878).

Green-winged Teal. *Anas crecca.*

Although these birds were considered abundant by Hayden, the few records for the state do not reflect this abundance.

Very abundant throughout the valleys of the Missouri and its larger tributaries (Hayden 1863a). Very abundant during migration; two in September and two in October 1871, SARPY; three in September 1873, CASS; two in October 1873, LANCASTER (Aughey 1878).

American Black Duck. *Anas rubripes.*

Young, 18 July 1859, on North Platte River near Courthouse Rock, MORRILL (Suckley in Beidleman 1956). Occurred sparingly; specimen purchased in October 1874 at Lincoln meat shop, LANCASTER (Aughey 1878). Numerous, 6 September 1877, in headwaters area of the Dismal River, GRANT/HOOKER (Grinnell [Yo] 1877).

Mallard. *Anas platyrhynchos.*
Tribal names: Omaha—*pa'hitu* (green head); Dakota Sioux—*pa-ġoŋ'-ta.*

The breeding range of this duck likely was greater than records indicate. Mallards would have been present at ponds and marshes throughout the state; they would have been common in some places.

Wetlands along the Missouri River and the many lakes and marshes of the Sand Hills would have provided extensive suitable habitat.

Remains from ca. 1775-1845 at the Big Village of the Omaha, DAKOTA (O'Shea and Ludwickson 1992, 234). Present in the Omaha tribal area (Fletcher and La Flesche 1972). Remains in material excavated at the Big Village of the Omaha near Homer, DAKOTA (O'Shea 1982). Potential breeder about 1820 in the Engineer Cantonment area, WASHINGTON (Thwaites 1905). In faunal remains dating to 1822-39 from Cabanne's post, DOUGLAS, and 1822-42 from Fontenelle's post, SARPY (Bozell et al. 1990). On 10 May 1834, Blackbird Hill area, THURSTON (Maximilian in Orr and Porter 1983). On 7 May 1843, NEMAHA/OTOE; 12 May, BURT; 3 October, WASHINGTON (Audubon 1960). Abundant along the Missouri and its tributaries (Hayden 1863a). North Platte River and abundant throughout the Missouri region (Coues 1874). Very abundant during migration; may also breed; two in April 1865, DIXON; three in June 1865, DAKOTA; two in October 1873 and three in October 1874, LANCASTER (Aughey 1878). Numerous 6 September 1877 in headwaters area of the Dismal River, GRANT/HOOKER (Grinnell [Yo] 1877).

Northern Pintail. *Anas acuta.*
Common name: sprigtail.

Apparent status: This duck was more common than records indicate, since the species was known in the Sand Hills from the turn of the century (Ducey 1988).

Sighted in Nebraska (Warren in Baird et al. 1860). Greatly diffused throughout the Northwest (Hayden 1863a). Rather common, especially during migration; two in October 1873 and five in October 1874, SARPY (Aughey 1878).

Blue-winged Teal. *Anas discors.*
Tribal names: Omaha—*a'hi^n hide tu* (blue wing) and *mi'xa wagtho^{n}xe*
(betrayer duck, so called because it betrayed the water monster in the myth of Ha'xegi); Sioux—*ho-pa-wa'-to-to* (blue wings).

Apparent status: This teal probably was one of the most common species of waterfowl throughout Nebraska. Records are available from several regions, including the Missouri River, Rainwater Basin, Platte River, Pine Ridge and Sand Hills.

Present in the Omaha tribal area, northeast Nebraska (Fletcher and La Flesche 1972). Potential breeder about 1820 in the Engineer Cantonment area (Thwaites 1905). On 8 May 1834, opposite the mouth of the Vermillion River, DIXON (Maximilian in Orr and Porter 1983).

On 5 May 1856, Ioway River [Aowa Creek], DIXON; Vermillion River, DIXON (Warren in Baird et al. 1860); 28 July 1856, Pole Creek, [Lodgepole Creek, southern Panhandle of NE]; 10 May 1856, White River, NE (Vaughn in Baird et al. 1860); 7 July 1856, South Platte River (Bryan in Baird et al. 1860). Young, 25 June 1859, on Little Blue River in the Fairbury area, JEFFERSON; on 20 July, west of the Courthouse Rock area, MORRILL (Suckley in Beidleman 1956). Very abundant throughout the valleys of the Missouri and its larger tributaries (Hayden 1863a). Ioway River, DIXON; Vermillion River, southeast SD; very abundant in the Missouri region during migration and doubtless also bred there (Coues 1874). Not as abundant as the Green-winged Teal; October 1867, DIXON (Aughey 1878). Numerous, 6 September 1877, in the headwaters area of the Dismal River, GRANT/HOOKER (Grinnell [Yo] 1877).

Cinnamon Teal. *Anas cyanoptera.*
Common name: red-breasted teal.
   Platte River (Coues 1874).

Northern Shoveler. *Anas clypeata.*
Common name: spoonbill.
   Apparent status: There are surprisingly few records concerning this species. Sightings on only three Missouri River expeditions suggest it was less than common. It could have occurred in greater numbers in the western part of the state, especially in the Sand Hills, where there are nesting records from before 1900 (Ducey 1988).
   In faunal remains dating to 1822-42 from Fontenelle's post, SARPY (Bozell et al. 1990). On 5 May 1856, Aowa Creek, DIXON (Warren in Baird et al. 1860). On 18 July 1859, near the Courthouse Rock area, MORRILL; 20 July, west of the Courthouse Rock area (Suckley in Beidleman 1956). Specimen collected near the mouth of Iowa Creek; very rare (Hayden 1863a). Occasional; May 1865, DIXON (Aughey 1878).

Gadwall. *Anas strepera.*
   Apparent status: This species was a common breeding resident in the Sand Hills, although there is only a single record. There are records of this species, including nesting records, from this region just a few years after 1875 (Bruner 1902; Ducey 1988).
   Numerous, 6 September 1877, in the headwaters area of the Dismal River, GRANT/HOOKER (Grinnell [Yo] 1877).

American Wigeon. *Anas americana.*
Common name: baldpate.
On 11 July 1856, Platte River (Bryan in Baird et al. 1860). Quite rare; specimen taken on the Missouri River near the Bijoux Hills, CHARLES MIX, SD (Hayden 1863a).

Canvasback. *Aythya valisineria.*
Apparent status: This diving duck was present as a breeding bird in larger, deep-water lakes and marshes throughout the western two-thirds of present-day Nebraska.
Found throughout the Missouri region in suitable places; not as common as the Redhead (Coues 1874). Frequently seen in Nebraska (Aughey 1878).

Redhead. *Aythya americana.*
Frequently seen in Nebraska (Aughey 1878).

Lesser Scaup. *Aythya affinis.*
Apparent status: This scaup was a common to abundant migrant in wetland areas.
Numerous, 6 September 1877, in the headwaters area of the Dismal River, GRANT/HOOKER (Grinnell [Yo] 1877).

Common Goldeneye. *Bucephala clangula.*
Tribal name: Dakota Sioux—*na-wa'-te-ska-daŋ*.
Apparent status: These goldeneyes were migrants, seen primarily along the Missouri River and lower Platte River.
In faunal remains dating to 1822-42 from Fontenelle's post, SARPY (Bozell et al. 1990).

Bufflehead. *Bucephala albeola.*
Common names: butter-ball, dipper, spirit duck.
Apparent status: Buffleheads were abundant migrants along the Missouri River.
In faunal remains dating to 1820-27 from Fort Atkinson, WASHINGTON (Mundell 1979). In faunal remains dating to 1822-42 from Fontenelle's post, SARPY (Bozell et al. 1990). Abundant in autumn, winter and spring on the Missouri (Coues 1874). Frequently seen along the Missouri River and its tributaries; two in May 1868, DAKOTA; May 1869, DIXON; May 1875, LANCASTER (Aughey 1878).

Hooded Merganser. *Lophodytes cucullatus.*

Apparent status: This merganser was an uncommon breeding bird in southeast Nebraska, especially along the Big and Little Blue rivers, and in wooded areas along the Platte River.

Young, 25 June 1859, on the Little Blue River in the Fairbury area, JEFFERSON; female birds, 18 July, along the Platte near Courthouse Rock, MORRILL (Suckley in Beidleman 1956). Most abundant of the mergansers in the Missouri region (Coues 1874).

Common Merganser. *Mergus merganser.*
Common name: sheldrake.

In faunal remains dating to 1822-42 from Fontenelle's post, SARPY (Bozell et al. 1990). More or less abundant throughout the upper Missouri country (Hayden 1863a).

Ruddy Duck. *Oxyura jamaicensis.*

Apparent status: The ruddy was a common migrant throughout the state. It regularly bred in areas with suitable wetlands, with greater numbers in the west.

In October 1856, near the mouth of the Platte, CASS (Warren in Baird et al. 1860); 10 October 1857, one hundred miles east of Ft. Laramie, [GARDEN?] (Magraw in Baird et al. 1860); May 1855, White River, NE (Baird et al. 1860). Collected near the mouth of the Platte in 1856; not abundant (Hayden 1863a). October 1858 on the Platte (Baird in Taylor and Van Vleet 1888a). Occurred across the Missouri region in suitable places during migrations and also bred within such limits (Coues 1874). Rather common along the Missouri River during migration; specimen received October 1874, SARPY (Aughey 1878).

Family Cathartidae

Turkey Vulture. *Cathartes aura.*
Tribal name: Omaha—*he'ga.*
Common name: turkey buzzard.

Apparent status: Records indicate it was most commonly seen along the Missouri, but it also would have been expected along the lower Platte and Niobrara. There was one sighting for the western Platte, but these vultures likely were present in canyon areas such as those around Ash Hollow. Nesting would have occurred in each of these areas.

Present in the Omaha tribal area (Fletcher and La Flesche 1972). Potential breeder about 1820 in the Engineer Cantonment area

(Thwaites 1905). Remains of a dead elk were left on 25 April 1811 for the vultures, OTOE (Bradbury in Swenk 1937). On 29 April 1833, ATCHISON, MO; 13 May 1833, northwest KNOX (Maximilian in Orr and Porter 1983). Flock, 23 June 1842, along the Little Blue River, THAYER (Frémont 1956). On 10 May 1843, WASHINGTON; 24 September, Bazile Creek, KNOX (Audubon 1960). Many perched on rocky peaks and outcrops, 8 June 1845, in the Ash Hollow area, GARDEN (Carleton 1983, 228). On 14 May 1856, Cedar Island, Missouri River [Big Cedar Island three miles west of Fort Randall?], TODD/GREGORY, SD (Warren in Baird et al. 1860). Very abundant generally throughout the Northwest (Hayden 1863a). Present ca. 1870, ANTELOPE (Leach 1916). Fort Randall, TODD, SD (Coues 1874).

Family Accipitridae

Osprey. *Pandion haliaetus.*
Common name: fish hawk.

Apparent status: The large Osprey nested at the larger oxbow lakes along the Missouri River. Lakes and rivers with abundant fish and adjacent trees would have been suitable nesting sites. Breeding birds disappeared from the area by 1900.

Potential breeder about 1820 in the Engineer Cantonment area (Thwaites 1905). On 1 May 1833, Frazer's Island area, OTOE (Maximilian in Orr and Porter 1983). On 9 May 1843, at Bellevue, SARPY (Audubon 1960).

American Swallow-tailed Kite. *Elanoides forficatus.*
Tribal name: Omaha—*i^n'be zho^{n}ka* (forked tail).
Common name: white fork-tail (Maximilian in Orr and Porter 1983).

Apparent status: This kite was an uncommon breeder along the Missouri, although it was present in the river's east-central portion and in northeast Nebraska during the breeding season. Eggs were taken in Iowa during the period (Coues 1874, 333).

Present in the Omaha tribal area (Fletcher and La Flesche 1972). Potential breeder about 1820 in the Engineer Cantonment area (Thwaites 1905). On 8 May 1833, northeast DAKOTA; 9 May 1833, northeast DIXON; 7 May 1834, James River and eastern CEDAR; 11 May 1834, pairs, southeast BURT (Maximilian in Orr and Porter 1983). On 10 May 1843, WASHINGTON; 21 May, northwest KNOX; north of the Council Bluff (Audubon 1960; McDermott 1951). In 1859-60 along the Missouri River in Nebraska (Morgan 1959). As far north as CEDAR County and as far west as the meridian of Fort Kearny; in DIXON

County a pair nested four years in succession on Badger Creek; June 1865, DIXON; September 1873, SARPY (Aughey 1878).

Eagle.
Tribal names: Winnebago—*tcaxcep;* Omaha—*xitha';* Pawnee—*lih-ta'-kats;* Dakota Sioux—*ćaŋ-śka'-waŋ-mdi-waŋ* for a species of kite or eagle, *hu-ya'* for the common eagle, *huya ćiŋća* for a young eagle, *waŋ-mdi'* (the royal or war-eagle).
Common name: Omaha-thunderbird.

Remains from ca. 1775-1845 at the Big Village of the Omaha, DAKOTA (Jackson and Scott 1992). Seen in northeast Nebraska on 5 September 1806 (Lewis and Clark in Swenk 1935).

Bald Eagle. *Haliaeetus leucocephalus.*
Tribal names: Omaha—*pacu^n'* (whitish head); Dakota Sioux—*a-nog'-pa-ska.*
Common names: white-headed eagle, gray sea-eagle.

Large trees along the Missouri River and Platte were nesting sites. This eagle was prominent along the Missouri River, where nesting pairs were common. Along the western Platte, it would have been uncommon. One nesting site in a pine at Ash Hollow was well-known to travelers along the wagon trail.

Remains from ca. 1775-1845 at the Big Village of the Omaha, DAKOTA (O'Shea and Ludwickson 1992, 234). Present in the Omaha tribal area (Fletcher and La Flesche 1972). Recorded in remains excavated from the Big Village of the Omaha near Homer, DAKOTA (O'Shea et al. 1982). Potential breeder about 1820 in the Engineer Cantonment area, WASHINGTON (Thwaites 1905). On 25 April 1833, nest on left shore at the mouth of Wolf River [Wolf Creek], DONIPHAN, KS; 10 May 1833, young, northwest DIXON (Maximilian in Orr and Porter 1983). Nest with young, 18 May 1834, in the Ash Hollow area, GARDEN (Townsend 1978, 64). Nesting on 7 May 1843, NEMAHA/OTOE (Audubon 1960). Young, 9 June 1845, in nest west of Ash Hollow, GARDEN (Carleton 1983). Two adults, 14 July 1859, along the Platte River in the Ash Hollow area, GARDEN (Suckley in Beidleman 1956). Captive birds in 1861 at the Yankton Sioux village, Dakota Territory [CLAY, SD] (Ladner 1984). Not infrequently observed and seems generally distributed throughout the Northwest; many specimens were young birds (Hayden 1863a). Occurred frequently in the Missouri region (Coues 1874). Remains in an 1870s Pawnee Sacred Family Bundle from the Loup Fork village (Good 1989, 18). Frequent along the Missouri River (Aughey 1878).

Northern Harrier. *Circus cyaneus.*
Tribal name: Dakota Sioux—*pte-ġo'-pe-ċa.*
Common names: marsh hawk; male sometimes called "blue hawk" (Coues 1874, 331).

Apparent status: Wetland meadows throughout the state would have provided suitable nesting habitat, but the Northern Harrier probably was most abundant in the extensive meadows of the Sand Hills. Fewer numbers would have been present in the Rainwater Basin and at prairie meadows associated with saline wetlands. Birds also may have nested in wet meadows along the Platte.

Potential breeder about 1820 in the Engineer Cantonment area (Thwaites 1905). On 15 October 1856, Cedar Island, GREGORY, SD; 20 October 1856, Running Water, KNOX, MO; Fort Randall, Dakota, TODD, SD (Warren in Baird et al. 1860); three on 7 July 1857, South Platte; Pole Creek [Lodgepole Creek, southern Panhandle of Nebraska] (Bryan in Baird et al. 1860). On 17 May 1843, northwest DIXON; 22 May, Fort Randall Military Reservation, BOYD (Audubon 1960). Very common throughout the Northwest (Hayden 1863a). North Platte River; this was the most common hawk along the Missouri; numerous specimens collected at Fort Randall, TODD, SD (Coues 1874). Three in an 1870s Pawnee Sacred Family Bundle from the Loup Fork village (Good 1989, 18). Occasional to abundant in the northeast; two in October 1869 at Bazile Creek, KNOX; September 1864, OTOE, and two in SARPY; October 1864, DOUGLAS (Aughey 1878).

Sharp-shinned Hawk. *Accipiter striatus.*
Tribal name: Winnebago—*ki'rik'iri'sgera* (pigeon hawk).
Common name: pigeon hawk.

The upland deciduous forests in the east and pine forests in the west provided suitable habitat.

Potential breeder about 1820 in the Engineer Cantonment area (Thwaites 1905). Ranged over the entire Missouri region (Coues 1874).

Cooper's Hawk. *Accipiter cooperii.*
Common name: chicken hawk.

Six birds from Nebraska were dissected (Aughey 1878).

Northern Goshawk. *Accipiter gentilis.*
Common name: American goshawk.

Present but rare on the prairies; August 1867 on the borders of DIXON and CEDAR (Aughey 1878) [This is a very doubtful record considering the summer date.].

Red-shouldered Hawk. *Buteo lineatus.*
Tribal name: Omaha—*gtho^{n}shka'*.
Common name: red-shouldered buzzard.

Apparent status: This hawk was an uncommon breeding bird in the wooded swamps along the Missouri and possibly on a portion of the lower Platte. It occurs in flood-plain forests with standing water and bothersome bugs, so it likely was missed, since this habitat was not hiked very often by explorers or naturalists.

Present in the Omaha tribal area, THURSTON (Fletcher and La Flesche 1972). If the bird ranges throughout the Missouri region, it must be uncommon (Coues 1874).

Broad-winged Hawk. *Buteo platypterus.*
Common name: broad-winged buzzard.

Apparent status: A forest bird, this hawk occasionally nested along the Missouri River and likely occurred to a greater degree than the single record indicates.

Potential breeder about 1820 in the Engineer Cantonment area, WASHINGTON (Thwaites 1905).

Swainson's Hawk. *Buteo swainsoni.*
Common names: Baird's buzzard, Swainson's buzzard.

Hayden said this hawk was confined to the sources of the Missouri River (Hayden 1863a, 152), despite the Loup Fork record. It likely was common in open prairie areas throughout the state and occasionally nested as far east as the Missouri River. It became less common in the savannahs and park land of the eastern prairies, where it was replaced by the Red-tailed Hawk.

In summer of 1857 at Loup Fork of the Platte, PLATTE (Warren 1875). Three in an 1870s Pawnee Sacred Family Bundle from the Loup Fork village (Good 1989, 18). Rather abundant in the vicinity of streams where timber exists; two in August 1867, CEDAR; July 1868, DAKOTA; September 1872, SARPY (Aughey 1878).

Buteo Hawk.
Tribal names: Pawnee—*pi-a'k-i;* Winnebago—*k'eredju'sep.*

Nest, 29 May 1834, on a Sioux ceremonial burial platform near Scott's Bluff, SCOTTS BLUFF (Morgan and Harris 1967, 107). Captive birds in 1861 at the Yankton Sioux village, Dakota Territory [CLAY, SD] (Ladner 1984, 34).

Red-tailed Hawk. *Buteo jamaicensis.*
Tribal name: Omaha—*i"'beçiga* (yellow tail).
Common names: red-tailed buzzard, hen hawk, white-bellied redtail (Krider race).

Mostly prevalent as a breeding bird along the eastern portion of the state, the Red-tailed Hawk would have been replaced by the Swainson's Hawk in the west where few trees occurred.

Present in the Omaha tribal area, northeast Nebraska (Fletcher and La Flesche 1972). Potential breeder about 1820 in the Engineer Cantonment area (Thwaites 1905). In faunal remains dating to 1822-42 from Fontenelle's post, SARPY (Bozell et al. 1990). On 20 October 1856, L'Eau qui Court [Niobrara River]; 11 October 1856, Fort Randall, TODD, SD (Warren in Baird et al. 1860); two on 1 August 1857, along the North Platte (Bryan in Baird et al. 1860). Not uncommon throughout the prairie country of the Northwest (Hayden 1863a). Common, July 1870 at Dakota City, DAKOTA (Aughey 1878).

Ferruginous Hawk. *Buteo regalis.*
Common names: ferruginous buzzard, squirrel hawk.

Apparent status: This magnificent hawk was probably a rare to uncommon breeding bird, although there are no nesting records for the period. There are a few historic nesting records for Nebraska a short while after 1875 (Ducey 1988). This species was not identified until 1844 (American Ornithologists' Union 1983).

On 16 September 1856, Platte River (Wood in Baird et al. 1860). In June 1874 near Ogallala, KEITH (Aughey 1878).

Rough-legged Hawk. *Buteo lagopus.*

The Rough-legged Hawk was a regular visitor during the winter season.

In September 1873 at Beatrice, GAGE (Aughey in Taylor and Van Vleet 1889). Noted at Fort Randall, TODD, SD (Coues 1874). Rare in southern Nebraska; specimen received from Beatrice, GAGE (Aughey 1878).

Golden Eagle. *Aquila chrysaetos.*
Tribal name: Omaha—*xitha' çka* (white eagle).
Common names: war eagle, thunderbird.

The stature that eagles had with the Plains tribes is shown by several tribal names for this bird, but the eagle of most interest to Native Americans was the Golden Eagle. Eagle feathers were an essential part of tribal myth and lore, and the bird's important status is shown by the use of its feathers in the eagle feather headdress. According to Grinnell, two of these birds were worth a horse (a forty to sixty dollar value) among the Sioux (Ludlow 1875).

The Golden Eagle was found all through the country between the Missouri River and the Rocky Mountains, although it was not common. Most common in the western part of Nebraska, it would have had cliff and tree nests on the buttes of the Pine Ridge and in the Wildcat Hills. It nested nearly to the Missouri River in eastern Nebraska, where a mix of prairie and scattered trees provided suitable open country habitat. This species was noted in eastern Nebraska through the early 1880s (Ducey 1988).

Present in the Omaha tribal area, northeast Nebraska (Fletcher and La Flesche 1972). Potential breeder about 1820 in the Engineer Cantonment area (Thwaites 1905). A single eagle was killed by an Arikara scout at Short Pine Buttes, southwest SD (Ludlow 1875). Occasional; seen along the Republican River and Missouri River; September 1876 (Aughey 1878).

Family Falconidae

American Kestrel. *Falco sparverius*.
Tribal name: Omaha—*gthedo^n*.
Common name: sparrow hawk.

Apparent status: This kestrel was present throughout the state where suitable nesting trees were present. This species was especially numerous along the Missouri River, where large cottonwoods provided suitable cavities, but fewer breeding birds lived along the Platte and elsewhere where there were fewer large trees.

Present in the Omaha tribal area (Fletcher and La Flesche 1972). Potential breeder about 1820 in the Engineer Cantonment area (Thwaites 1905). On 8 May 1834, opposite the mouth of the Vermillion River, DIXON (Maximilian in Orr and Porter 1983). On 22 and 24 May 1843, Fort Randall Military Reservation, BOYD, NE and TODD, SD (Audubon 1960). Egg collected in 1843 in Nebraska by Audubon (NMNH specimen 13235). Stuffed skins were a symbol of bravery and were included in the Cau'-i Medicine Bundle of the Pawnee; present ca. 1850 in the Pawnee tribal area on the Loup Fork, PLATTE, and southward in the state (Dunbar 1882). On 31 August 1853, Milk River, NE (Stevens in Baird et al. 1860); 14 July 1856, Platte River; 28 July 1856, Pole Creek [Lodgepole Creek, southern Nebraska Panhandle]; 14 August 1856, North Platte (Bryan in Baird et al. 1860). Very common along the woody bottoms of the

Missouri (Hayden 1863a). Very abundant; breeds; July 1865, DIXON; July 1865, June and July 1866, and August 1867, DAKOTA; August 1867, CEDAR; July 1869, PIERCE; September 1871 and June 1872, SARPY; September 1873, LANCASTER (Aughey 1878).

Merlin. *Falco columbarius.*
Common names: pigeon hawk, American merlin.
Apparent status: The Merlin probably was an uncommon breeding bird here. It usually was seen in woodlands along streams and likely was present in Nebraska's western pine forests, although migrants and wintering individuals were sighted throughout the state.

On 7 May 1843, in the southwest corner of NEMAHA/ RICHARDSON (Audubon 1960). Male and female on 25 October 1856 at the mouth of the Vermillion River, DIXON; 17 October 1856, Fort Randall, TODD, SD (Warren in Baird et al. 1860); 20 August 1857, at North Platte, LINCOLN (Bryan in Baird et al. 1860); abundant in the wooded bottoms of the Missouri region (Hayden in Baird et al. 1860; Hayden 1863a). Common to abundant in the wooded bottoms of the Missouri region (Coues 1874). One in an 1870s Pawnee Sacred Family Bundle from the Loup Fork village (Good 1989, 18). Rather common, breeds; two in August 1869 at Dakota City, DAKOTA (Aughey 1878).

Peregrine Falcon. *Falco peregrinus.*
Common name: duck hawk.
Apparent status: This large falcon probably was more common in the west than the few records indicate. Hayden commented his record was the westernmost known sighting (Hayden 1863a, 152). A Peregrine Falcon was seen chasing a Passenger Pigeon on August 28, 1874, in the Dakota Territory (Ludlow 1875). Birds likely nested in the Black Hills and perhaps on occasion in the Pine Ridge, where there is a reference to possible nesting around 1900 (Ducey 1988).

On 25 October 1856, at the mouth of the Vermillion River, DIXON (Warren in Baird et al. 1860). Seen three times in Nebraska (Aughey 1878).

Prairie Falcon. *Falco mexicanus.*
Common names: American lanier, lanner falcon.
This species was not described scientifically until 1851 (American Ornithologists' Union 1983). Although there are no written records from the Pine Ridge prior to 1875, this falcon probably was a common nester on the buttes there. It was present in the Wildcat Hills,

at Scott's Bluff and elsewhere along the western Platte, where cliffs provided nest sites. Historic records from a decade or two after 1875 note the abundance of this species in these regions (Ducey 1988).

Female, 17 October 1856, at Fort Randall, TODD, SD; male, 20 August 1857, on the North Platte River, NE (Warren in Baird et al 1860). Found at various points along the Missouri and on the Platte, though not abundantly (Hayden 1863a). Occasional; specimen received September 1874 from SARPY (Aughey 1878).

Family Phasianidae

Ruffed Grouse. *Bonasa umbellus.*
Tribal names: Sioux—*wa-zi'-shi-o;* Dakota Sioux—*zi'-ća-ti-hda-bu-daŋ.*
Common names: drumming partridge, mountain grouse, western ruffed grouse.

This grouse historically was limited to habitat along the Missouri River, but it probably never was common. Nesting birds would have been uncommon. Fewer numbers are suggested for later in the period, based on the lack of observations.

Several grouse seen while camped a little below the Council Bluff, 25 July 1804, DOUGLAS (Lewis and Clark in Swenk 1935). Potential breeder about 1820 in the Engineer Cantonment area (Thwaites 1905). Rare, seen only once, RICHARDSON (Aughey 1878).

Sage Grouse. *Centrocercus urophasianus.*
Common names: sage cock, cock of the Plains.

This species was limited to a few areas of sage plains in the western part of the territory.

On 9 September, Loup Fork, PLATTE (Warren in Baird et al. 1860); 12 August 1856, on the North Platte River (Bryan in Baird et al. 1860). On 11 October 1859, Platte River (Trook in Coues 1874); said to be common on the western plains of Nebraska; scarcely found on the Missouri (Coues 1874). Specimens received from North Platte, LINCOLN; Sidney, CHEYENNE, and Pine Bluffs along Lodgepole Creek, LARAMIE, WY (Aughey 1878).

Greater Prairie-Chicken. *Tympanuchus cupido.*
Tribal names: Omaha—*shu* [Omaha tribal names are similar in the two studies that give tribal names for birds (Fletcher and La Flesche 1972; Hayden 1868a).]; Pawnee—*u'-ut, pūks;* Dakota Sioux—*śi'-yo.*

Common names: prairie chicken, pinnated grouse, prairie hen, prairie fowl.

Apparent status: This prairie chicken was common to abundant in eastern Nebraska, where extensive prairie would have provided prime habitat.

Crops planted by the first settlers supplied a new food source that increased bird survival and numbers, so populations increased in areas where farming developed. Small fields were surrounded by wild prairie, and birds readily fed on the crops. Prairie chickens were especially abundant in the latter part of the period from 1750 to 1875. West of Omaha in March 1864, an observer reported thousands near Elkhorn (Martin 1974).

Market-hunting harvested thousands of birds during the early years of the state's history. In 1874 fifty thousand chickens were shipped from six counties in eastern Nebraska. Beck noted that, during a six-week period in 1875, nineteen thousand were shipped by a dealer in Lincoln. Settlers harvested prairie chickens throughout the year by whatever means they could catch the birds. Prairie chicken was on hotel and restaurant menus in Omaha and Nebraska City. The 1877 game law eventually ended hunting from March to July, even though the laws were not enforced well. The first bag limits were seventy-five birds per day. Market-hunting was not prohibited until about 1905.

Hunting and loss of habitat were the primary causes of the species' decline. As prairie converted to towns and farms, grasslands in the eastern part of the state declined. One observer attributed a decline in prairie chickens one year to extensive burning of grassland near Tecumseh (Barnes 1874). It was suggested at the time that settlers should burn the prairie and destroy birds in order to limit bird depredation of crops that were to be planted. An average of four birds and up to six nests per acre were found in burned areas during the breeding season (Beck n.d.).

Present in the Omaha tribal area (Fletcher and La Flesche 1972). Several seen on the prairie on 24 July 1804, eastern SARPY (Lewis and Clark in Moulton 1986). Common as far as the River Jacques [James River, CEDAR], where the Sharp-tailed Grouse start to occur; four on 2 September in CEDAR or across the river in Dakota Territory (Lewis and Clark in Swenk 1935). Prairie grouse shot, 8 May 1811, at Bell Creek, WASHINGTON/BURT, and on 9 May, BURT (Bradbury in Swenk 1937). Several on 27 March 1813, east of the confluence of the North Platte and South Platte rivers, LINCOLN (Stuart 1953, 145). On 22 September 1819, grouse on the Missouri River, OTOE (Nichols 1969). Potential breeder in 1820 in the Engineer Cantonment area (Thwaites 1905). In faunal remains dating to 1820-27 from Fort

Atkinson, WASHINGTON (Mundell 1979). On 11 May 1833, James River area, CEDAR; 11 May 1833, northeast KNOX (Maximilian in Orr and Porter 1983). In May 1834 in the Big Bend area of the central Platte River (Wislizenus 1912). On 19 August 1844, west of the headwaters of the Nemaha River [JEFFERSON?]; 27 May 1845, north of the Little Blue River, ADAMS (Carleton 1983). On 8 May 1849, the coo of prairie hens was heard (perhaps the sound of birds in a lek) along the Oregon Trail near the KS/NE border, JEFFERSON (Decker 1966); 12 May 1849, along the Platte, KEARNEY/PHELPS (Decker 1966, 76). On 23 May 1852, shot along the Platte River west of the Loup Fork [MERRICK?] (Eaton 1974). On 20 October 1856, mouth of the Running Water [Niobrara River], KNOX; two on 7 November 1858, Big Sioux River (Warren in Baird et al. 1860). Big Sioux River, UNION, SD; mouth of the Niobrara River, KNOX; seen up to the Niobrara, with many at Council Bluffs, where large flocks sometimes damaged corn fields; found along the White River, though rarely (Hayden 1863a). Present in the winter of 1861-62, with several shot along the Platte River, in the Columbus area, PLATTE (North 1961, 11 and 136). On 24 March 1864, abundant near the Platte and Elkhorn, DOUGLAS (Martin 1974). Present around 1873 on open prairie along the Platte in central Nebraska, near the Loup (Grinnell [Ornis] 1873). Lack of abundance noted during 1874 hunting season near Tecumseh, JOHNSON, although found in great numbers near Lincoln, LANCASTER (Barnes 1874). Numerous at Fort Randall, TODD, SD (Coues 1874). February, two in May and two in June 1865, and two in July 1866, DAKOTA; two in September 1867 and two in June 1868, DIXON; two in July 1869, WAYNE; two in September and two in October 1874, May and June 1875, and two in September 1876, LANCASTER (Aughey 1878). Young in the area of the Little Blue River, THAYER (Green 1954). Present ca. 1870, ANTELOPE (Leach 1916, 87). Abundant, with 120 bagged in two-hour fall hunt and coveys of fifteen to thirty birds around 1875, historic Jackson Station, PLATTE (Coveter 1876).

Sharp-tailed Grouse. *Tympanuchus phasianellus.*
Tribal name: Sioux—*shi-o'-ći-ka'-la.*

Apparent status: These grouse were most abundant in the western half of Nebraska, with fewest numbers in the eastern third. The records from about 1850 to 1875 limit birds to north of Council Bluffs and west of the Loup Fork.

Grouse [perhaps this species, according to the journal editor] seen on 5 September 1804 near Ponca Creek, northwest KNOX (Lewis and Clark in Moulton 1987). Present starting at the James River; the "pointed tail prairie fowl" are found above the Big Bends (Lewis and Clark in Swenk 1935). Potential breeder about 1820 in the Engineer Cantonment area, WASHINGTON (Thwaites 1905). In faunal remains dating to 1820-27 from Fort Atkinson, WASHINGTON (Mundell 1979). Noted in KNOX in 1823 (Wilhelm 1928). On 20 and 25 October 1856, mouth of the Vermillion River, DIXON (Warren in Baird et al. 1860). Seldom seen below Council Bluffs; from there to the mountains, it was very abundant and often provided travelers with a delicious meal (Hayden 1863a). Present ca. 1870, ANTELOPE (Leach 1916, 87). Present around 1873 on open prairie along the Platte River in central Nebraska, near the Loup (Grinnell [Ornis] 1873). Noted at Fort Randall, with birds at a lek in spring, TODD, SD (Coues 1874). Formerly very abundant, but gradually decreasing in numbers; February, May and July 1865, and August 1866, DAKOTA; August 1867 and June 1868, CEDAR; July 1869, WAYNE; October 1873 and two in October 1874, Fort Kearny, KEARNEY (Aughey 1878).

Wild Turkey. *Meleagris gallopavo.*
Tribal names: Omaha—*çiçi'ka* (spelled *zi-z'i-ka* by Hayden); Dakota Sioux—*wa-gle'-kśuŋ* and *zi'-ća-taŋ-ka.*

Apparent status: Wild Turkeys were present throughout the state where woodland roosts were available, although they were most common along the Missouri, lower Platte, and central and lower Niobrara rivers. Turkeys also occurred in forests and woodlands throughout southeast Nebraska.

Several early Nebraska sources mention the turkey. It was shot during hunts and served at eating places along the Overland Trail. Officers at Fort McPherson hunted these birds along Medicine Creek and the Republican River.

The pressure of hunting reduced the birds in number. Birds at roosts in Frontier County were destroyed by visiting hunters. Turkey meat was not sold, but the feathers were in demand, so many were killed and their carcasses left for vultures (Beck n.d.). Harsh winters also killed birds, especially those with limited shelter.

Fewer records after 1850 indicate turkey numbers were declining, and these birds became rare by the 1870s. Eventually turkeys were extirpated in Nebraska. Reintroduction efforts began in Nebraska during the 1920s and 1930s (Ducey 1988).

The historic range of the Wild Turkey included the Nebraska stretch of the Missouri River, the Platte west to the central part of the state, the lower Niobrara, the Republican as far west as Hitchcock County, and the lower Blue River. Other scattered woodlands, such as those in the Loup and Elkhorn river watersheds, would have provided suitable habitat.

Remains from ca. 1775-1845 at the Big Village of the Omaha, DAKOTA (Jackson and Scott 1992). Present in the Omaha tribal area (Fletcher and La Flesche 1972). On 25 and 26 July 1804, below the town of Council Bluffs, POTTAWATTAMIE, IA; 30 July in the Fort Calhoun area, WASHINGTON; seen and killed on 5 August, BURT/WASHINGTON; killed on 9 August, northeast BURT; 4 September near mouth of the Niobrara River; large flock on 5 September near Ponca Creek, northwest KNOX; 6 September, in northern BOYD or farther north, five of a flock killed; 8 September 1804, western Fort Randall Military Reservation, GREGORY, SD; 2 September 1806, CEDAR; 10 September, NEMAHA/northern RICHARDSON (Lewis and Clark in Moulton 1987; Swenk 1935). Present in May 1811 at Sonora Island, northeast NEMAHA (Brackenridge 1976; Swenk 1937). Present in April and May 1813 in "great plenty" along the Missouri south of the Platte, CASS and other counties (Stuart 1953, 163). Potential breeder about 1820 in the Engineer Cantonment area (Thwaites 1905). Two shot about 1820, likely in southeast Nebraska (Beckwourth 1972, 25). In faunal remains dating to 1820-27 from Fort Atkinson, WASHINGTON (Mundell 1979). In faunal remains dating to 1822-39 from Cabanne's post, DOUGLAS, and 1822-42 from Fontenelle's post, SARPY (Bozell et al. 1990). Noted in northwest Missouri in 1823 (Wilhelm 1928). On 23 April 1833, Cow Island area, PLATTE, MO; 2 May 1833, Frazer's Island area, OTOE; 7 May 1833, THURSTON; 13 May 1834, northeast DOUGLAS; 13 May 1834, southeast CASS; 14 May 1834, southeast CASS; 14 May 1834, northeast OTOE; 15 May 1834, southeast NEMAHA; 16 May 1834, DONIPHAN, KS (Maximilian in Orr and Porter 1983). On 7 May 1843, NEMAHA/RICHARDSON; plentiful on 10 May, WASHINGTON; 12 May, BURT; 13 May at Blackbird Hill, THURSTON; 13 May, DAKOTA; 16 May, northwest DIXON; 24 September, Bazile Creek, KNOX; 28 September, near Elk Point, DIXON; 1 October, hen and young, Big Sioux River, DAKOTA (McDermott 1951; Audubon 1960). Several shot, 13 November 1846, in the vicinity of Fort Vermillion, CLAY, SD (Chittenden and Richardson 1905, 610). A twenty-pound bird killed 19 May 1849, along the Oregon Trail, JEFFERSON area (Gray 1976, 16). First seen on 6 May 1852, a day's journey above the mouth of the Niobrara (Kurz 1970). Present in January 1866 at the Frenchman River fork of the Republican River, HITCHCOCK (Grinnell 1928, 129). Present on 26 September 1869, along the Republican River, HITCHCOCK/RED WILLOW (North 1961, 123). Present occasionally around 1873 on open prairie along the Platte in central Nebraska, near the Loup River (Grinnell [Ornis] 1873). As far up the Missouri as the vicinity of Yankton, YANKTON, SD (Coues 1874). Now rapidly being reduced in numbers and disappearing from localities where a few years ago there were great numbers; August 1865 and 1867, and three in September 1867, DIXON; September 1868, DAKOTA (Aughey 1878). Present ca. 1870, ANTELOPE (Leach 1916, 87). Historic records from before 1875 for DAKOTA, DAWSON, DIXON, FILLMORE, FRANKLIN, FRONTIER, GAGE, KNOX, NEMAHA, NUCKOLLS, OTOE, RED WILLOW and THURSTON (Jones 1959).

Northern Bobwhite. *Colinus virginianus.*
Tribal names: Omaha—*u-she-w'a-the* (one who fools people); Otoe—*to'-shra-eng-a;* Pawnee—*āt-kās* (partridge).
Common names: quail, partridge, bob-white, Virginia partridge.

This quail was most common in the eastern third of the state. Breeding birds were abundant in some areas, especially the southeast part of Nebraska. The nesting range likely did not extend much farther west than the Loup Fork or further north than Fort Randall. Numbers were reduced by hunting throughout the years, but laws enacted in the 1870s caused a slight increase in numbers (Aughey 1878).

Present in the Omaha tribal area (Fletcher and La Flesche 1972). Potential breeder about 1820 in the Engineer Cantonment area (Thwaites 1905). On 17 May 1834, northeast of LEAVENWORTH, KS (Maximilian in Orr and Porter 1983). On 19 August 1844, west of the headwaters of the Nemaha River, JEFFERSON? (Carleton 1983). On 23 April 1856, Iowa Point, DONIPHAN, KS (Warren in Baird et al. 1860). On 17 June 1859, near the headwaters of the south fork of the Nemaha River, NEMAHA, KS; quail were no longer heard after 19 June, north of the Big Blue River in the Fairbury area, JEFFERSON (Suckley in Beidleman 1956). Were not present far up the Missouri; were seldom seen as high up as the White River, but never above that point; around the Council Bluff; quite abundant near Big Sioux, Vermillion and James rivers (Hayden 1863a). Present ca. 1870, ANTELOPE (Leach 1916, 87). Present around 1873 on open prairie along the Platte River in central Nebraska, near the Loup (Grinnell [Ornis] 1873). Quail abundant and hunting excellent in September 1874 near Tecumseh, JOHNSON (Barnes 1874). Abundant along the Missouri up to Fort Randall, TODD, SD; occurred up the Missouri to White River, BRULE, SD, according to Hayden (Coues 1874). Present around 1875, historic Jackson Station, PLATTE (Coveter 1876). Common, but number varies greatly in different years; two in May and three in June 1865, DAKOTA; two in June and September 1867; five in July 1868; eight in October 1874, LANCASTER (Aughey 1878).

Family Rallidae

Black Rail. *Laterallus jamaicensis.*
This species was rare, although it was observed September 1873, RICHARDSON (Aughey 1878).

King Rail. *Rallus elegans.*
Common name: fresh-water marsh hen.
Two in August 1874, HARLAN; two in October 1874, SARPY; two in October 1874 and May 1875, LANCASTER (Aughey 1878).

Virginia Rail. *Rallus limicola.*
Apparent status: This rail was recorded along the Missouri River and probably was present at other wetlands in the region. These rails typically are not seen, but their presence is detected when their song is heard.
On 15 May 1843, northwest DAKOTA (Audubon 1960).

Sora. *Porzana carolina.*
Common names: common rail, Carolina rail, ortolan.
Apparent status: Although this species was noted only a few times, it would have nested in suitable wetland habitat throughout the state.
In 1856 at Yankton Camp, TODD, SD (Warren in Baird et al. 1860). One specimen taken near Durion's Hills; said to be very rare below the Niobrara River (Hayden 1863a). September 1869 near Dakota City (Aughey 1878; Taylor and Van Vleet 1888b).

Common Moorhen. *Gallinula chloropus.*
Specimen received September 1872 from Beatrice, GAGE (Aughey 1878).

American Coot. *Fulica americana.*
Common names: mud hen, *poule d'eau.*
The American Coot probably was more common than records indicate. Coots would have nested in suitable wetlands throughout the state, especially in the Sand Hills and Rainwater Basin wetland regions. Fewer birds nested in the larger marshes along the Missouri.

Potential breeder about 1820 in the Engineer Cantonment area (Thwaites 1905). In faunal remains dating to 1822-42, Fontenelle's post, SARPY (Bozell et al. 1990). On 25 April 1833, DONIPHAN, KS; 5 May 1833, Fort Calhoun area, WASHINGTON (Maximilian in Orr and Porter 1983). On 5 July 1857, Loup Fork of the Platte, PLATTE (Warren in Baird et al. 1860). Not uncommon across the West (Hayden 1863a). Along the North Platte (Coues 1874). Often seen; two in May 1865, DAKOTA; two in June 1866 and September 1867, DIXON; two in September 1871 and two in May 1875, LANCASTER (Aughey 1878).

Family Gruidae

Crane.
Tribal names: Omaha—*pe'to^n*; Dakota Sioux—*pe-haŋ'*.

The Omaha recognized the white crane [possibly the Whooping Crane (*Grus americanus*)], and it played an important role in their medicine (James 1972, 230).

Present in the Omaha tribal area, THURSTON (Fletcher and La Flesche 1972). Great flocks noted moving northward along the Missouri River, early April 1820 (James 1972, 123). In faunal remains dating to 1820-27, Fort Atkinson, WASHINGTON (Mundell 1979). In May 1834 in the Big Bend area of the central Platte (Wislizenus 1912).

Sandhill Crane. *Grus canadensis.*
Tribal name: Dakota Sioux—*pe-haŋ'-ġi-daŋ*.
Common name: brown crane.

Historically these birds were abundant migrants along the Missouri. Changes in the character of the river due to settlement and loss of habitat led to a decline in their numbers along that river after the early historic period. The Platte River also was an important migratory stop for cranes.

The Sand Hills had a population of breeding cranes in suitable meadow wetlands. Hayden sighted the birds during the summer, likely in southwest Cherry County. About 1878 Luther North captured and raised a young crane, whose wing had been broken by a horse, in the western Hooker or eastern Grant County area. The bird lived in the stable during the winter and hunted mice in the ranch house. Eventually it began to wander long distances from the ranch and failed to return (North 1961). A record from 1883 confirms cranes nesting in the eastern Sand Hills of Holt County (Bruner 1902).

Sandhill Cranes were sighted late in the migration season along the Missouri and Platte rivers. There are several May dates, which are after the primary migration. Maximilian noted two cranes along the Missouri in northeast Nebraska. There are three summer dates for this area. Audubon noted cranes in May along the Missouri, south of the Platte. An August 28th date for the lower Platte River, near the Loup Fork, indicates the presence of birds late in the breeding season. John Kirk Townsend recorded Sandhill Cranes along the central Platte during mid-May. These May sightings of "cranes" given in the previous species account, plus another note by Lienhard, could have been non-breeding birds staying in the region during the summer, or they may have been birds that had nested unsuccessfully in the Sand Hills and left to wander elsewhere.

Settlement of the region and the birds' attractiveness as a meal disturbed the nesting of these prominent birds and thus produced a steady decline in their numbers. However, the cranes continued to nest in the Sand Hills after 1875 (Bruner 1902).

Remains from ca. 1775-1845 at the Big Village of the Omaha, DAKOTA (O'Shea and Ludwickson 1992, 234). On 12 April 1820, cranes were heard overhead on the Missouri River flood plain in the vicinity of Boyer Creek, POTTAWATTAMIE, IA (James 1972, 245). In faunal remains dating to 1822-42 from Fontenelle's post, SARPY (Bozell et al. 1990). On 11 May 1833, James River area, CEDAR (Maximilian in Orr and Porter 1983) [The entry says Prince Maximilian noted two cranes, which he thought nested in the area.]. On 18 May 1834, along the central Platte River, likely BUFFALO (Townsend 1978). On 7 May 1843, NEMAHA/OTOE; 3 October, Little Sioux River, BURT (Audubon 1960). Numerous, 28 August 1844, along the Platte south of the Loup Fork, PLATTE (Carleton 1983, 59). On 9 August 1857, Sand Hills [CHERRY?] (Warren in Baird et al. 1860). Not rare, especially in Nebraska's Sand Hills (Hayden 1863a). Rather abundant; August 1867, CEDAR; July 1868, DIXON; June 1875, SEWARD; September 1876, SARPY (Aughey 1878). Summer 1879, young at the Cody-North Ranch, around the headwaters of the Dismal River, HOOKER (North 1961, 269-271).

Whooping Crane. *Grus americana.*
Tribal name: Dakota Sioux—*pe-haŋ'-saŋ*.
Occasional in northern Nebraska (Aughey 1878).

Family Charadriidae

Plover.
On 15 August 1804, plovers recorded at ponds formed by beaver dams on Omaha Creek close to the Omaha village near Homer, DAKOTA (Lewis and Clark in Swenk 1935). On 8 May 1849, along the Oregon Trail near the KS/NE state line, JEFFERSON (Decker 1966, 68); 11 May 1849, on the Oregon Trail along the Little Blue River, THAYER/NUCKOLLS? (Decker 1966, 71).

Black-bellied Plover. *Pluvialis squatarola.*
These birds were sighted occasionally; specimens received September 1874, SARPY (Aughey 1878).

American Golden-Plover. *Pluvialis dominica.*
Common names: golden plover, bull-head.
Apparent status: This plover was a common to abundant migrant on the prairies.
Nebraska (Warren in Baird et al. 1860). Abundant anywhere on the upland prairies of the West, from Fort Pierre to the mountains (Hayden 1863a). Migrates through Dakota Territory in large numbers; noted on the prairies between Fort Randall and Yankton, SD (Coues 1874). Four specimens received October 1873 from Plattsmouth, CASS (Aughey 1878).

Semipalmated Plover. *Charadrius semipalmatus.*
Abundant during spring and fall migrations; two in May 1865, DAKOTA; three in September 1868, WAYNE; four in September 1874, SARPY; two in June 1875, RICHARDSON (Aughey 1878).

Piping Plover. *Charadrius melodus.*
Common names: kildee, ring plover.
The miles-wide, shallow Platte had numerous sandbars (as did other Nebraska rivers), which formed prime nesting habitat. There are surprisingly few records for the Missouri River, considering the extent of sandbar habitat within the historic channel. This plover also would have been likely along the lower Loup and lower Niobrara. The sighting by Lewis and Clark was prior to the 1823 designation of the species (American Ornithologists' Union 1983).
Found as far north as the entrance of the Little Sioux River, HARRISON, IA (Lewis and Clark in Swenk 1935). Five males and females, 8 July 1857, Loup Fork of the Platte, PLATTE (Warren in

Baird et al. 1860). Very abundant on the sandbars in the Platte; seen nowhere else in the West (Hayden 1863a). Common in Nebraska; breeds; two nests in July 1866 along the Missouri River, DIXON; May 1865, DAKOTA; two in July 1868, WAYNE; September 1868, SARPY (Aughey 1878).

Killdeer. *Charadrius vociferus.*
Common name: killdeer plover.

Apparent status: The range of the killdeer was more extensive than the few actual records indicate. Perhaps this bird was seen on such a regular basis that each sighting was not written in journal narratives. Hayden noted it was abundant throughout the Northwest.

Potential breeder about 1820 in the Engineer Cantonment area (Thwaites 1905). In faunal remains dating to 1822-39, Cabanne's post, DOUGLAS (Bozell et al. 1990). Several, 27 May 1845, north of the Little Blue River, ADAMS (Carleton 1983). Two on 30 July 1857, Loup Fork, PLATTE (Warren in Baird et al. 1860); two on 19 July 1856, Platte River (Bryan in Baird et al. 1860). Abundant throughout the country drained by the Missouri River and its tributaries (Hayden 1863a). Abundant throughout the Missouri region (Coues 1874). On 6 September 1877, in the headwaters area of the Dismal River, GRANT/HOOKER (Grinnell [Yo] 1877). Few present; two in May and June 1865, DIXON; June 1865, DAKOTA; two in July 1869, WAYNE; August 1870, PIERCE; two in September 1874, SARPY (Aughey 1878).

Mountain Plover. *Charadrius montanus.*

Apparent status: This plover would have been more common on the High Plains, extending eastward into western Nebraska, although the plains along the Platte and the short grass prairie of western Nebraska also indicate likely historic summer habitat. Warren's Loup Fork sighting was one of Nebraska's first summer bird records. Aughey's many sightings, however, are questionable for the Mountain Plover, which is more typical of the western Plains; he may have seen sandpipers, some of which have a similar profile and the same colors. Aughey's report also says this bird is more abundant in the west, but it does not give any records to support this. Instead Aughey's records are from along the Missouri and Platte rivers, where conditions typically do not produce the short grass areas that provide suitable Mountain Plover nesting sites.

Two, likely summer 1857, at the Loup Fork of the Platte River, PLATTE (Warren in Baird et al. 1860); 10 July 1857, Pole Creek, [Lodgepole Creek, NE]; 12 August 1856, North Platte River (Bryan in Baird et al. 1860). About 120 miles west of Fort Kearny [western

LINCOLN or eastern KEITH?]; breeding in the southwestern portion of Dakota Territory, near the Black Hills, SD (Coues 1874). Abundant, especially in the western part of the state; two in July 1865, September 1866, August 1867 and June 1868, DIXON; September 1872; four in September 1874, SARPY; June 1875, OTOE and RICHARDSON; four in September 1876, BUFFALO (Aughey 1878).

Family Recurvirostridae

American Avocet. *Recurvirostra americana.*
Common name: avocet, avoset.

Records indicate breeding season presence along the Missouri, the Platte and in the Sand Hills. Hayden mentioned the avocet was rare, which suggests these birds may have occurred regularly but not in significant numbers. The Sand Hills historically was prime habitat and supported a large number of breeding birds at the many lakes and wetlands. It was a regular migrant.

A specimen *"recurvirostra"* genus collected 25 April 1811, OTOE (Bradbury in Swenk 1937). On 8 May 1834, opposite the mouth of the Vermillion River, DIXON (Maximilian in Orr and Porter 1983). One bird shot 9 June 1845, along the North Platte, MORRILL (Carleton 1983, 231). Two on 12 August, mid-1850s, Platte River (Magraw in Baird et al. 1860); 6 September 1855, North Platte River below Ft. Laramie (Warren in Baird et al. 1860). Seems to be rare in the West; one specimen killed on the Platte (Hayden 1863a). Fort Randall, TODD, SD (Coues 1874). Abundant in wetlands; September 1873, RICHARDSON; two in September 1874 near Bellevue, SARPY (Aughey 1878). Large flock, 6 September 1877, at the headwaters of the Dismal River, GRANT/HOOKER (Grinnell [Yo] 1877).

Family Scolopacidae

Greater Yellowlegs. *Tringa melanoleuca.*
Common names: greater telltale, greater yellowshanks, tattler, stone snipe.

Apparent status: This big yellowlegs was common to abundant during migration.

On 7 May 1843, NEMAHA/OTOE (Audubon 1960). Platte River (Bryan in Baird et al. 1860). More or less common along the rivers and streams of the West (Hayden 1863a). Occurs wherever there is water in the Missouri region (Coues 1874). Abundant along rivers, creeks and wetlands during migration; three in September 1869, WAYNE; two in August 1870, DAKOTA; September 1873, SEWARD (Aughey 1878).

Lesser Yellowlegs. *Tringa flavipes.*
Common names: lesser telltale, lesser yellowshanks.

Apparent status: This yellowlegs was a common to abundant migrant at a greater number of sites than the records indicate.

No date given, likely mid-1850s on the Platte River (Bryan in Baird et al. 1860); no date given, likely mid-1850s, at the Council Bluff, WASHINGTON (Warren in Baird et al. 1860). Abundant along rivers, creeks and wetlands during migration; five in October 1874, LANCASTER (Aughey 1878).

Solitary Sandpiper. *Tringa solitaria.*
Common names: solitary tattler, wood tattler.

Apparent status: This sandpiper was a regular migrant in some localities, such as the Missouri River wetlands and marshes of the Sand Hills. Fewer numbers were present in western Nebraska.

On 28 April 1856, at Omaha, DOUGLAS; 8 and 10 August 1857, Sand Hills (Warren in Baird et al. 1860); 29 July 1856, Pole [Lodgepole] Creek, NE (Bryan in Baird et al. 1860); 22 July 1856, Little Blue River, northwest Kansas (Magraw in Baird et al. 1860). Abundant along the Missouri and its tributaries (Hayden 1863a). Young seen in August and thought to breed, DAKOTA [Breeding is not likely; this is an incorrect assertion.]; 1873, SEWARD; specimen September 1876 (Aughey 1878).

Spotted Sandpiper. *Actitis macularia.*

Apparent status: Rivers throughout Nebraska were suitable habitat used by migrating and breeding Spotted Sandpipers; fewer birds were present at lakes in the Sand Hills.

On 6 July, likely 1857, Loup Fork, PLATTE (Warren in Baird et al. 1860). Abundant along rivers and streams in the West (Hayden 1863a). North Platte River (Coues 1874). Rather common, especially during migration, but many stopped to breed; six in May 1875, LANCASTER (Aughey 1878).

Upland Sandpiper. *Bartramia longicauda.*
Common names: Bartram's sandpiper, field plover, Bartramian sandpiper or tattler, upland plover, prairie pigeon.

There are a few records of the Upland Sandpiper in the eastern part of the state, with others westward on the Plains. Prairies throughout Nebraska, especially in the east, provided breeding habitat for this common summer species.

Potential breeder about 1820 in the Engineer Cantonment area, WASHINGTON (Thwaites 1905). Noted to be frequent in the low prairies by members of the Long Expedition in summer 1820 while approaching the Loup Fork (James 1972, 285). On 19 August 1844, west of the headwaters of the Nemaha River, JEFFERSON?; 27 May north of the Little Blue River, ADAMS (Carleton 1983). On 5 May 1849, along the Little Nemaha in southeast Nebraska; only a few seen since leaving the Missouri River three days previously (Delano 1936, 8). Three males and females on 7 and 21 July 1856, Loup Fork, PLATTE; two on 7 July, Platte River (Warren in Baird et al. 1860). Nest with eggs, 3 June 1859, northwest of Fort Leavenworth, LEAVENWORTH, KS; common, 17 June on the prairie near the headwaters of the south fork of the Nemaha River, NEMAHA, KS; eggs, 30 June at Fort Kearny, KEARNEY (Suckley in Beidleman 1956). Seen all over the High Plains of the West; rears its young on the upland prairies (Hayden 1863a). Present around 1873 on the open prairie along the Platte River in central Nebraska, near the Loup (Grinnell [Ornis] 1873). Abundant during migration, and many breed; three in May and five in June 1865, DAKOTA; four in August 1867, DIXON; three in September 1869, WAYNE; two in September 1872, three in September 1874 and two in May 1875, LANCASTER (Aughey 1878). Present ca. 1870, ANTELOPE (Leach 1916, 87).

Eskimo Curlew. *Numenius borealis.*
Common name: prairie pigeon.

Apparent status: The Eskimo Curlew was an abundant migrant in limited areas of eastern Nebraska.

Immense flocks once migrated through the Nebraska region. Numbers ranged from twelve, thirty to forty, and fifty to several hundred in a single flock, often with many other flocks of similar numbers of birds. These flocks comprised thousands of birds, most often seen on burnt prairies or an occasional plowed field (Swenk 1915). The largest concentrations of birds—flocks of thousands of birds—occurred from mid-April through mid-May. Hunters from Omaha "slaughtered" birds by the wagonful (Swenk 1915). When especially abundant, they were shot and left in piles to rot on the prairie, while hunters continued killing other birds. Settlers also shot birds when they were numerous, then used them as food.

This species favored burnt prairie habitat and liked plowed fields to a lesser degree. The chief feeding grounds about 1877 were in York,

Fillmore and Hamilton counties (Swenk 1915). Fewer numbers were seen during the 1870s, but small flocks or individual birds were recorded regularly through the 1880s (when the population decline was especially apparent) and into the early 1900s. The last records for Nebraska were in 1911 near Waco, York County, and in 1926 near Hastings, Adams County.

Egg collected 20 June 1860 at Pierre [possibly PIERCE] (NMNH specimen 03811). Flocks in 1869 near West Point, CUMING; abundant in MADISON about 1871; flocks of 30-40 in ANTELOPE during the 1870s; once abundant along the Platte River area, MERRICK; by 1878 birds were seen in small flocks or individually (Swenk 1915). Upper Missouri River; migrated through Missouri region in immense numbers; in May 1873 flocks of 50 to several hundred were noted on prairies along the road between Fort Randall and Yankton, just north of Nebraska (Coues 1874). During migration in early spring; October in northeast Nebraska; specimen received October 1874 from Bellevue, SARPY (Aughey 1878).

Whimbrel. *Numenius phaeopus.*
Common name: Hudsonian curlew.

The whimbrel was rare in Nebraska (Aughey 1878).

Long-billed Curlew. *Numenius americanus.*
Tribal names: Omaha—*ki'kato^{n}ga* (big curlew); Dakota Sioux—*pa-su'-śko-pa* (the prairie curlew).
Common name: sickle-bill.

Apparent status: This curlew was a common to uncommon summer resident throughout the state, with more birds in the west. Audubon's record shows this curlew once reached the eastern border of Nebraska during the breeding season.

Present in the Omaha tribal area (Fletcher and La Flesche 1972). On 6 April 1813, at the "Grand Isle" of the central Platte River, HALL (Stuart 1953, 153). Potential breeder about 1820 in the Engineer Cantonment area (Thwaites 1905). Several noted in the low prairies by members of the Long Expedition in summer 1820 near the Loup Fork, PLATTE (James 1972, 285). On 11 and 12 May 1833, northeast KNOX (Maximilian in Orr and Porter 1983). On 18 May 1834, along the central Platte River, likely BUFFALO (Townsend 1978). On 14 May 1843, at the Big Sioux River, northwest DAKOTA (Audubon 1960). On 19 May 1844, east of the Little Blue River, JEFFERSON; 27 May 1845, north of the Little Blue River, ADAMS (Carleton 1983). Very abundant on the upland prairies of the far west, where it feeds in considerable numbers (Hayden 1863a). Once abundant and still common where not hunted; breeds; two in September 1876, CEDAR; two in June 1868, DIXON; two in August 1869, DAKOTA; two in September 1874, SARPY; two in May 1875, SEWARD (Aughey 1878). Present ca. 1870, ANTELOPE (Leach 1916, 87).

Godwit.
Common name: tell-tale godwit.
On 7 May 1843, NEMAHA/OTOE (Audubon 1960).

Marbled Godwit. *Limosa fedoa.*
Apparent status: Marbled Godwits were regular migrants and rare summer residents. The breeding record for near the Loup is the only historic record of young sighted in Nebraska. There is a hypothetical nesting record from near Norfolk in 1876 (Ducey 1988).

Marbled Godwits and their young were seen in summer 1820 in the low prairies by members of the Long Expedition as they approached the Loup Fork, PLATTE (James 1972, 285). Not very common in the West; specimen taken at Council Bluffs, IA (Hayden 1863a). Common, breeds; two in August 1867, CEDAR; two in September 1869, WAYNE; two in September 1874, LANCASTER (Aughey 1878).

Red Knot. *Calidris canutus.*
Common names: red-breasted sandpiper, robin snipe.
Occasional; specimen received October 1874 from Brownville, NEMAHA (Aughey 1878).

Semipalmated Sandpiper. *Calidris pusilla.*
Apparent status: This sandpiper was an abundant to occasional migrant.

Three on 8 July, likely mid-1850s, Loup Fork of the Platte, PLATTE (Warren in Baird et al. 1860). Collected along the Loup Fork (Hayden 1863a). Abundant bird, occurring throughout the Missouri region (Coues 1874). Occasional during migration; two in July 1869 on Logan Creek, [CEDAR or DIXON] (Aughey 1878).

Least Sandpiper. *Calidris minutilla.*
Apparent status: Least Sandpipers were migrants whose numbers varied in different areas of the state: they were rare along the Platte but abundant in some localities along the Missouri.

On 8 May 1833, northeast DAKOTA (Maximilian in Orr and Porter 1983). 20 August 1856, Scott's Bluff, SCOTTS BLUFF; 20

August 1856, North Platte River (Magraw in Baird et al. 1860). In 1857, Loup Fork of the Platte River, PLATTE (Warren 1875). Observed in the Platte valley; probably rare (Hayden 1863a). Abundant during migration in the Missouri region (Coues 1874). Very abundant; three in September 1867, CEDAR; October 1869, WAYNE; four in October 1874, SARPY (Aughey 1878).

White-rumped Sandpiper. *Calidris fuscicollis.*
This bird was seen only occasionally in Nebraska (Aughey 1878).

Baird's Sandpiper. *Calidris bairdii.*
Apparent status: This sandpiper was a common migrant in some localities, especially along the Missouri River.
Omaha City, DOUGLAS (Warren in Baird et al. 1860). Rather common during migration; two in October 1873, SARPY; three in October 1874, RICHARDSON (Aughey 1878). On 6 September 1877, in headwaters area of the Dismal River, GRANT/HOOKER (Grinnell [Yo] 1877).

Buff-breasted Sandpiper. *Tryngites subruficollis.*
Rare; specimen received September 1874 from Nebraska City, OTOE (Aughey 1878).

Dowitcher.
Could include both the **Short-billed Dowitcher** (*Limnodromus griseus*)
and **Long-billed Dowitcher** (*Limnodromus scolopaceus*).
Common names: red-breasted snipe, gray snipe.
Apparent status: Dowitchers were regular to common migrants, especially in eastern Nebraska's wetlands and river channels.
On 28 April 1856, Omaha City, DOUGLAS (Warren in Baird et al. 1860) [Although it cannot be determined from the historic information exactly which species Warren sighted, it was most similar to the Short-billed Dowitcher, according to current nomenclature.]. Abundant in Dakota Territory during fall migration (Coues 1874). Abundant during migration; two in August 1868, DIXON; September 1869, WAYNE; two in October 1873, NEMAHA; September 1875, SARPY (Aughey 1878).

Long-billed Dowitcher. *Limnodromus scolopaceus.*
Apparent status: The Long-billed Dowitcher was a regular migrant, and large numbers were seen along the Missouri River. The first identification of this species was based on a specimen taken by

Thomas Say during the Long Expedition (ca. 1820) near Boyer Creek, POTTAWATTAMIE, IA (American Ornithologists' Union 1983).

On 28 April 1856, at Omaha City, DOUGLAS (Warren in Baird et al. 1860).

Common Snipe. *Gallinago gallinago.*
Tribal names: Omaha—*toⁿ'iⁿ*; Otoe—*wi-tūh'-e*; Pawnee—*paks-ki'-ra-ruts* (bald-headed bird).
Common names: American snipe, English snipe, Wilson's snipe, solitary snipe.

Wet habitat on the flood plain of the Missouri, in the wooded portion of the eastern Platte, and in the Sand Hills provided suitable nesting areas for Common Snipes. They may have been common in localities, such as Missouri River flood plains and Sand Hills marshes.

Present in the Omaha tribal area (Fletcher and La Flesche 1972). In May 1834 in the Big Bend area of the central Platte River (Wislizenus 1912). On 7 May 1843, NEMAHA/OTOE (Audubon 1960). On 8 May 1849, along the Oregon Trail near the KS/NE state line, JEFFERSON (Decker 1966, 68); 11 May 1849, on the Oregon Trail along the Little Blue River, THAYER/NUCKOLLS? (Decker 1966, 71). On 23 May 1852, twelve were shot along the Platte River west of the Loup Fork [MERRICK?] (Eaton 1974). On 4 May 1854, along the Big Blue River in southeast Nebraska (Martin 1980). Seen quite rarely; a few were killed in low, marshy places near the mouth of the Loup Fork, PLATTE (Hayden 1863a). On 24 April 1856, near Bald Island, NEMAHA (Warren in Coues 1874). Common during migration; two in May 1865, DAKOTA; two in August 1867, CEDAR; two in June 1872, September 1873 and two in October 1874, LANCASTER; two in June 1875, SARPY (Aughey 1878). On 6 September 1877, in the headwaters area of the Dismal River, GRANT/HOOKER (Grinnell [Yo] 1877).

American Woodcock. *Scolopax minor.*
Tribal names: Omaha—*pa'xthega* (freckled head); Otoe—*thka'-ge*; Pawnee—*kau'-pat.*

Flood-plain forest along the Missouri and other large rivers would have been suitable habitat. The Loup Fork probably was near the western limit of its historic range in Nebraska.

Present in the Omaha tribal area, THURSTON (Fletcher and La Flesche 1972). Potential breeder about 1820 in the Engineer Cantonment area, WASHINGTON (Thwaites 1905). On 16 May 1843, young in northwest DIXON (Audubon 1960). On 18 July, likely mid-1850s, Loup Fork of the Platte, PLATTE (Warren in Baird et al. 1860).

Not uncommon near Council Bluffs, IA; specimen obtained near the mouth of the Loup Fork (Hayden 1863a). Occasional; breeds; two in September 1874, SARPY; specimen in September 1876, OTOE (Aughey 1878). Found mid-1870s among willows on the banks of the Missouri River, SARPY area (Phillips 1876).

Wilson's Phalarope. *Phalaropus tricolor.*

Apparent status: This phalarope was an abundant migrant and probably was more common as a breeding bird than records indicate. The only specific record of a likely breeding season occurrence was made by George Grinnell in the Sand Hills.

Three on 28 April, mid-1850s, Council Bluffs, IA, and two at Omaha, DOUGLAS (Warren in Baird et al. 1860). Quite abundant during the spring months along the marshy bottoms and lakes of the lower Missouri (Hayden 1863a). Nesting in Nebraska and Dakota Territory (Coues 1874). Common in eastern Nebraska; two in July 1866, DAKOTA; August 1867 and 1868, DIXON; two in September 1873 and June 1874, SARPY; June 1874, LANCASTER (Aughey 1878). Hundreds on 6 September 1877, in the headwaters area of the Dismal River, GRANT/HOOKER (Grinnell [Yo] 1877).

Family Laridae

Pomarine Jaeger. *Stercorarius pomarinus.*

May 1869 on the Missouri River, DAKOTA; specimen received May 1873 from the Platte River near Fremont, DODGE (Aughey 1878). [These records are not accepted as valid for Nebraska ornithology; see Bray et al. 1986.]

Gull.
Tribal names: Omaha—*ne'tha;* Dakota Sioux—*wi-ća'-taŋ-ktaŋ-ka* and *wi-ća'-taŋ-ktaŋ-ka-daŋ*.

Present in the Omaha tribal area, THURSTON (Fletcher and La Flesche 1972).

Franklin's Gull. *Larus pipixcan.*
Common name: Franklin's rosy gull.

On 9 May 1843, at Bellevue; 11 May, WASHINGTON; 15 May, northwest DAKOTA; 21 May, northwest KNOX (Audubon 1960). On 14 July 1856, Platte River (Bryan in Baird et al. 1860). Nebraska (Coues 1874). Large numbers during spring and fall migration; two in

May 1868, DAKOTA; two in May 1869, WAYNE; three in May 1875, SARPY; three in May 1877, CASS (Aughey 1878).

Ring-billed Gull. *Larus delawarensis.*

Apparent status: The Ring-billed Gull rarely was seen by the first explorations but was noted more commonly about 1875.

Very rare; one specimen taken in the West (Hayden 1863a). Nebraska Territory (Warren in Coues 1874). Rather common; two in May 1867 and May 1868, DAKOTA; June 1868, DIXON; two in May 1873, SARPY (Aughey 1878).

Herring Gull. *Larus argentatus.*

Two specimens received May 1870 from Winnebago Indians, northeast Nebraska (Aughey 1878).

Great Black-backed Gull. *Larus marinus.*

Specimen received in May 1871 from Winnebago Indians who shot it on the Missouri River near Dakota City, DAKOTA (Aughey 1878). [This record is not accepted as valid by Nebraska ornithologists; see Bray et al. 1986.]

Common Tern. *Sterna hirundo.*

On 12 May 1834, southeast WASHINGTON (Maximilian in Orr and Porter 1983).

Arctic Tern. *Sterna paradisaea.*

A few in May 1866, DIXON (Aughey 1878). [This record is not accepted as valid by Nebraska ornithologists; see Bray et al. 1986.]

Forster's Tern. *Sterna forsteri.*

Two specimens received in May 1871 from Winnebago Indians, DAKOTA (Aughey 1878).

Least Tern. *Sterna antillarum.*

Apparent status: This little tern was common to uncommon locally where suitable riverine habitat was available. The historic Missouri River and its numerous open sandbars were used extensively by the Least Tern. It also was noted on the Platte and lower Loup.

Although Lewis and Clark gave a thorough description of this tern, their sighting was not used as the basis for its scientific description. The Least Tern was not described until 1847 (American Ornithologists' Union 1983). Meriwether Lewis indicated its abundance in an entry

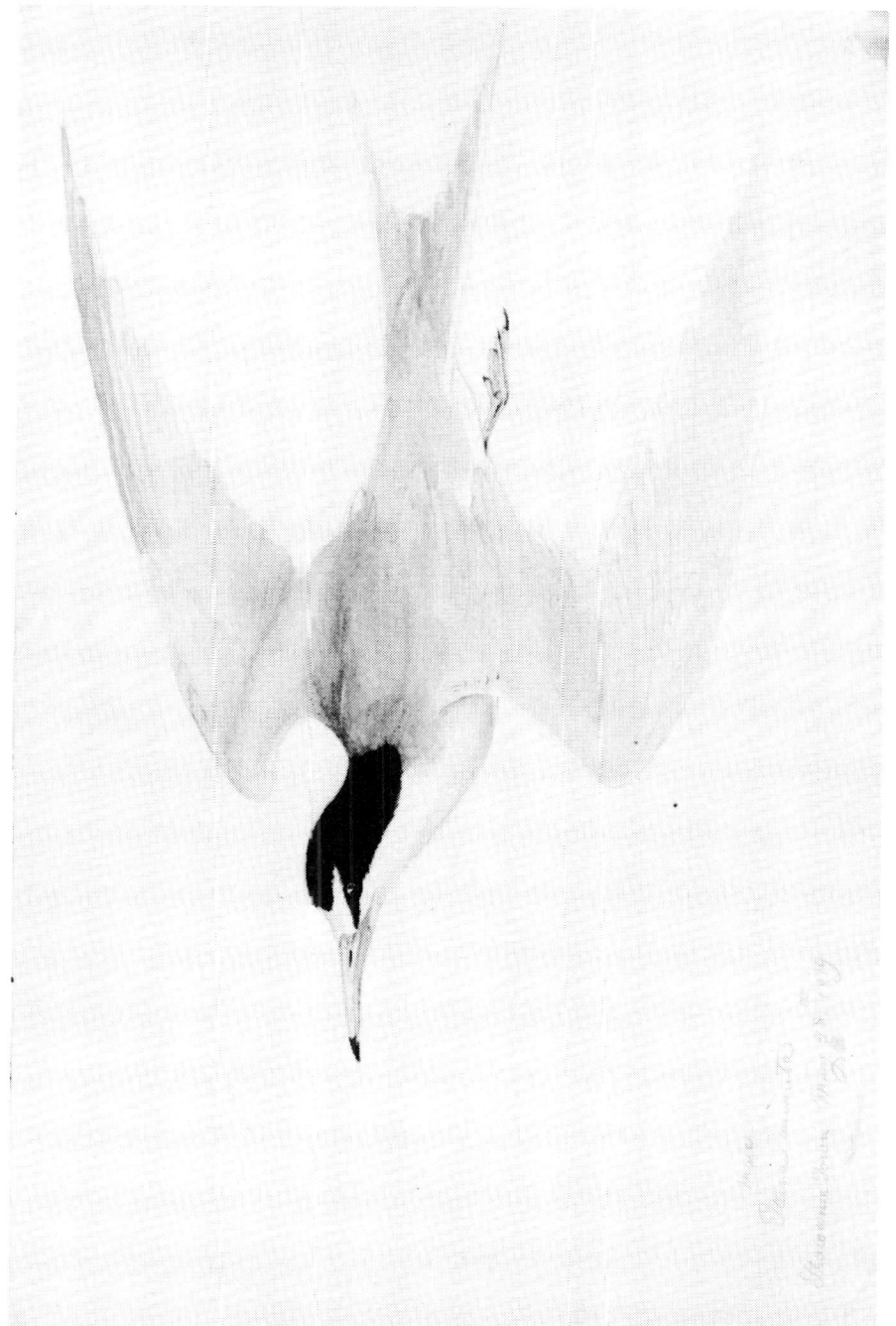

Least Tern, by Titian Ramsay Peale

from early August, while in Burt County, when he wrote:

> I have frequently observed an aquatic bird [*Sterna antillarum*] in the cours of asscending this river but have never been able to procure one before today, this day I was so fortunate as to kill two of them, they are here more plenty than on the river below. they lay their eggs on the sand bars without shelter or nest, and produce their young from the 15th to the last of June, the young ones of which we caught several are covered with down of a yellowish white colour and on the back some small specks of a dark brown. they bear a great resemblance to the young quale of ten days oald, and apear like them to be able to runabout and peck their food as soon as they are hatched—[.] this bird, lives on small fish, worms and bugs which it takes on the virge of the water[.] it is seldom seen to light on trees an[d] qu[i]te as seldom do they lite in the water and swim tho' the foot would indicate that they did[,] it's being webbed. (Moulton 1987, 450)

A complete and thorough description of the bird's features and colors also was included.

Frequently observed, nesting 5 August 1804 on Missouri River sandbars, BURT (Lewis and Clark in Moulton 1987). Potential breeder about 1820 in the Engineer Cantonment area (Thwaites 1905). Birds in 1823 flying about at the mouth of the Platte River, CASS (Wilhelm 1928). On 10 July 1857, Platte River; 1857, Loup Fork, PLATTE (Warren in Baird et al. 1860). One on 15 July 1859, on the North Platte River east of Ash Hollow, KEITH (Suckley in Beidleman 1956). Not abundant, though widely distributed along the Western streams; collected from the Platte (Hayden 1863a). Rather common; must breed here; young in July 1866 on the Missouri River, DIXON; two in August 1867, CEDAR; two in June 1868, DIXON; two in June 1872, SARPY; June 1873 and 1874, LANCASTER (Aughey 1878).

Black Tern. *Chlidonias niger.*
Common name: short-tailed tern.

Apparent status: Marshes along the Missouri, in the Sand Hills and in the Rainwater Basin were used by this bird as breeding habitat, although it was less abundant along the Missouri.

Potential breeder about 1820 in the Engineer Cantonment area (Thwaites 1905). On 15 May, northwest DAKOTA (Audubon 1960). On 8 August 1857, Loup Fork, PLATTE (Warren in Baird et al. 1860). Specimen collected on the Loup Fork (Hayden 1863a). Some years rather common and other years rare; breeds and young seen in July on the Elkhorn River; two in July 1869, PIERCE; two in September 1874, LANCASTER; May 1875, SARPY; September 1876, RICHARDSON (Aughey 1878).

Family Columbidae

Mourning Dove. *Zenaida macroura.*
Tribal name: Omaha—*thitato"ga* (big dove); Dakota Sioux—*tin'-wa-ki-ye-daŋ.*
Common names: turtle dove, Carolina dove, common dove.

Apparent status: This dove was common to abundant across the state, nesting on the ground in the prairies and in trees and shrubs where available. The islands of the Missouri were important nesting sites, since the open forest floor and lack of predators provided prime ground-nesting habitat. Though this was a very common and readily-seen species that provided suitable food, it did not occur in any faunal remains.

Present in the Omaha tribal area, northeast Nebraska (Fletcher and La Flesche 1972). Potential breeder about 1820 in the Engineer Cantonment area, WASHINGTON (Thwaites 1905). On 6 May 1833, east-central BURT; 9 May 1833, northeast DIXON; numerous, 10 May 1833, northeast CEDAR; 11 May 1833, northeast KNOX; numerous and at two sites, 13 May 1833, northwest KNOX; 12 May 1834, northeast DOUGLAS; 13 May 1834, Bellevue area, SARPY; 15 May 1834, northeast RICHARDSON (Maximilian in Orr and Porter 1983). On 29 May 1852, on a branch of Papillion Creek in eastern Nebraska, WASHINGTON/DOUGLAS? (Leach 1916, 26). Mid-1850s at Cedar Island, TODD/GREGORY, SD (Warren in Baird et al. 1860); 7 July 1856, South Platte River (Bryan in Baird et al. 1860). In timber, 17 June 1859, near the headwaters of the south fork of the Nemaha River, NEMAHA, KS; eggs collected in early July at Fort Kearny, KEARNEY; 14 July in the Ash Hollow area, GARDEN; abundant 18 July near Courthouse Rock, MORRILL (Suckley in Beidleman 1956). Quite common throughout the Northwest region; the islands of the Missouri were its favorite breeding places (Hayden 1863a). Abundant; July 1865, DIXON; June 1866, DAKOTA; July 1868, WAYNE; September 1872, SARPY; September 1873 and 1874, LANCASTER (Aughey 1878). Present ca. 1870, ANTELOPE (Leach 1916, 87).

Passenger Pigeon. *Ectopistes migratorius.*
Tribal names: Otoe—*pu-će'-eng-e* (pigeon); Dakota Sioux—*wa-kiŋ'-ye-la* (pigeon, dove).
Common name: wild pigeon.

Apparent status: This extinct pigeon was once present in large flocks, especially among the oak forests of the Missouri River. This large bird was used as food, and many birds were shot for sport from the roaming flocks. Coues' record indicates this species historically may have nested in Nebraska. The Passenger Pigeon became extinct in Nebraska, probably in the 1870s, and throughout its range after 1900.

Present in the woods along the Missouri River at the mouth of the Nodaway River on 18 April 1811, HOLT, MO; 271 were shot (Bradbury in Swenk 1935). Potential breeder about 1820 in the Engineer Cantonment area, WASHINGTON (Thwaites 1905). In faunal remains dating to 1820-27 from Fort Atkinson, WASHINGTON (Mundell 1979). In faunal remains dating to 1822-42 from Fontenelle's post, SARPY (Bozell et al. 1990). On 12 May 1833, near the mouth of the Niobrara River, KNOX (Maximilian in Orr and Porter 1983). On 7 May 1843, southwest corner of NEMAHA/ RICHARDSON (Audubon 1960). While camped on the banks of the Papillion Creek at the end of May 1853, a hunter took several birds; a traveler's entry said that, after a rain, a Mr. Knapp took a rifle and shot four or five wild pigeons (Passenger Pigeons, not Mourning Doves) (Leach 1916, 25-26). Four or five, 29 May 1853, on a branch of Papillion Creek in eastern Nebraska, WASHINGTON/DOUGLAS? (Leach 1916, 25). Two males, 3 May 1856, at the mouth of the Big Sioux, UNION, SD (Warren in Baird et al. 1860). Quite abundant on the lower Missouri (Hayden 1863a). Heard many nesting near Sioux City, WOODBURY, IA (Coues 1874). Abundant in some years, but rarely seen in others; six were bought in September 1874 in a Lincoln butcher shop, LANCASTER (Aughey 1878).

Family Psittacidae

Carolina Parakeet. *Conuropsis carolinensis.*
Common names: Carolina paroquet, Carolina parrot.

Flood-plain forests along the Missouri River were optimum habitat for this bird. Cavities in large cottonwoods were used as shelter and nesting sites. This parakeet was extirpated from Nebraska in the period around 1875, and eventually it became extinct.

The wandering flocks of these birds with their bright colorful plumage made them especially obvious; thus, their plumage proved detrimental. Nesting birds once were present in the cottonwood forests on the river flood plain, but they were gone from the region by the time Nebraska became a state (Swenk 1933). Lewis and Clark noted parakeets were present in this region at a location near Homer during the period from July 11 to August 19, 1804. Say saw the birds at Engineer Cantonment while on Long's Expedition. Prince Maximilian recorded Carolina Parakeets on May 14 at the mouth of the Weeping Water Creek and farther downriver in Otoe and Nemaha counties in 1834; entire skins were suspended as decorations in the hair of the Sioux (James 1972, 111). Audubon listed several observations: on May 7, 1843, they were plentiful opposite Richardson and Nemaha counties; the next three days brought sightings on May 8 opposite Otoe County, on May 9 near Bellevue and on May 10 near the Council Bluff, in Nebraska, where they were still plentiful. Ferdinand V. Hayden and Gouverneur Kemble Warren collected a series of parakeets near Bald Island (i.e., McKissock Island), Nemaha County, on April 24 and 25, 1856. Parakeets also were noted in Dakota Territory. The last records of occurrence probably were related to the observations of the Warren Expedition: of the specimens collected during this expedition, only one (No. 4614) remains in the Smithsonian (McKinley 1965); another specimen is at the Academy of Natural Sciences of Philadelphia; other specimens have been lost. Upriver from Brownville, probably at Bald Island, parakeets nested in the hollows of dead cottonwood trees; young were taken from the nests and sold as pets; one hundred or more were taken in one season (Furnas 1902). Carolina Parakeets were gone from this site by 1866 and eventually became extinct throughout their range. A general overview of this species in the Nebraska region provides additional information on the status of this bright and colorful bird (Swenk 1934a).

Seen as high as the Omaha village, DAKOTA, and seen along the Missouri River up to that point (Lewis and Clark in Swenk 1935). On 22 September 1819, on the Missouri River, OTOE (Nichols 1969). On 14 May 1834, northeast NEMAHA (Maximilian in Orr and Porter 1983). Seen several times from December 1819 to February 1820 at Engineer Cantonment, WASHINGTON (McKinley 1965, 218). "Large flocks" in early October 1833 near the Pawnee village on the Platte River, west of the Loup Fork (Irving 1955, 212). On 7 May 1843, NEMAHA/OTOE; 8 May, OTOE/CASS; 9 May at Bellevue; 10 May, WASHINGTON (Audubon 1960). In August 1844, along the Missouri River in eastern Nebraska (Carleton 1983, 34). Present in the late 1850s or early 1860s along the Missouri River, DAKOTA; some birds caught by settlers and kept in cages (Stephens 1957, 13). Twelve male and female birds, 24 and 25 April 1856, at Bald Island in the Missouri River, OTOE (Warren in Baird et al. 1860). Along the thickly-wooded river bottoms as far up as Fort Leavenworth, possibly as high as the mouth of the Platte, but never seen above that point (Hayden 1863a). Abundant around 1856 to 1866 in the vicinity and breed on an island in the Missouri River about ten miles north of Brownville, NEMAHA (Furnas 1902).

Family Cuculidae

Black-billed Cuckoo. *Coccyzus erythropthalmus.*

Apparent status: This cuckoo was a regular summer resident in shrubby areas along the rivers and in other suitable woods.

Two on 16 May 1856, fifty miles above the mouth of the Platte River, DOUGLAS; 1 July 1857, Fremont, on the Platte, DODGE; 5 August 1857, Loup Fork, PLATTE (Warren in Baird et al. 1860). Quite common along the wooded bottoms of streams in the Northwest (Hayden 1863a). Egg collected 5 June 1874 by W. L. Carpenter at Omaha, DOUGLAS (NMNH specimen 17366). One in September 1876 at Lincoln, LANCASTER (Aughey 1878).

Yellow-billed Cuckoo. *Coccyzus americanus.*

Apparent status: The Yellow-billed Cuckoo was a regular summer resident in shrubby areas along Nebraska's rivers and in other suitable woods.

Mid-1850s on the Elkhorn River; 3 July 1856 and three on 8 July, Loup Fork, Platte River, PLATTE; two on 2 July 1856, fifty miles above the mouth of the Platte River [If these were river miles, then it was the Fort Calhoun area, WASHINGTON.] (Warren in Baird et al. 1860). Quite common along the wooded bottoms of streams in the Northwest (Hayden 1863a). More frequent than the Black-billed Cuckoo; breeds; two in August 1867, CEDAR; two in September 1867, DIXON; September 1874, OTOE and CASS; June 1875, RICHARDSON; two in June 1877, SARPY (Aughey 1878).

Family Tytonidae

Barn Owl. *Tyto alba.*

Occasional; breeds; August 1867, DIXON; July 1868, DAKOTA; June 1872, LANCASTER (Aughey 1878).

Family Strigidae

Owl (likely the Great Horned Owl).

Heard hooting, 10 June 1871, along the Big Blue River, GAGE (Green 1954).

Eastern Screech-Owl. *Otus asio.*

Tribal names: Omaha—*ne' thazhibe;* Dakota Sioux—*po-po'-tka* and *po-po'-tka-daŋ.*

Common names: red owl, mottled owl.

Apparent status: This species was a regular resident in the woody areas of eastern Nebraska. Fewer woodlands in central Nebraska meant fewer birds there.

Present in the Omaha tribal area (Fletcher and La Flesche 1972). Potential breeder about 1820 in the Engineer Cantonment area (Thwaites 1905). Brought to a wagon train camp along the central Platte River by Native Americans in spring 1845 (Hancock 1927, 7). Inhabited wooded tracts of the Missouri region (Coues 1874). Often in wooded areas; breeds; two in September 1867, June 1868, CEDAR; July 1869 and August 1870, DAKOTA; September 1872, SEWARD; September 1874, NEMAHA; June 1875, LANCASTER (Aughey 1878).

Great Horned Owl. *Bubo virginianus.*

Tribal names: Omaha—*pa'nuhu heto^n ego^n* (owl having horns); Dakota Sioux—*hiŋ-haŋ'-he-toŋ-na.*

Apparent status: There are few records for this owl, although it probably was common wherever suitable wooded habitat was present, especially along wooded rivers and upland forests.

Present in the Omaha tribal area (Fletcher and La Flesche 1972). Potential breeder about 1820 in the Engineer Cantonment area (Thwaites 1905). Very common throughout the prairie country of the Northwest (Hayden 1863a). Occurs throughout the Missouri region, chiefly in wooded areas (Coues 1874). One in July 1869, DAKOTA (Aughey 1878).

Snowy Owl. *Nyctea scandiaca.*

Tribal names: Omaha—*i^n'chu^{n}çu^n* (snow white); Dakota Sioux—*hiŋ-haŋ'- śka* (white owl).

Common name: great white owl.

Apparent status: This conspicuous white owl was present on an irregular basis; several likely occurred in some winters.

Present in the Omaha tribal area, THURSTON (Fletcher and La Flesche 1972). Visited the Missouri region in winter; occasionally seen at Fort Randall, TODD, SD (Coues 1874). Frequent in late winter and occasional in late autumn; four in winter 1865; autumn and winter of 1867 and 1870 (Aughey 1878).

Burrowing Owl. *Speotyto cunicularia.*

Tribal name: Sioux—*i-ha'-mi-ko-ti-la* (the owl that lives with the prairie dogs).

Common name: prairie owl.

Apparent status: This little owl was a common summer resident throughout the state. Fewer numbers lived in areas such as the Sand Hills where prairie dog towns were limited mostly to river bottoms. The range of this species was greater than available records indicate. Hayden mentioned that wherever prairie dogs were found, there were burrowing owls.

Type specimens collected in June 1820 on the plains of the Platte, east of the Pawnee Indian village, PLATTE (Swenk 1933). On 13 June 1839, in the vicinity of Scott's Bluff, SCOTTS BLUFF (Wislizenus 1912). Along the central Platte River in June 1843 (Johnson and Winter 1932). On 26 August 1844, along tributaries of the Big Blue River, southeast Nebraska (Carleton 1983). On 11 May 1850, at the east end of the Grand Island, HALL (Muench 1949, 19). Two on the Platte River (Bryan in Baird et al. 1860); 14 August 1857, Running Water, KNOX; two young, 4 August 1857, at the Loup Fork, PLATTE (Warren in Baird et al. 1860); 3 August 1857, thirty-five miles west of Fort Kearny, [DAWSON?] (Magraw in Baird et al. 1860). Eggs found 8 July 1859, along the Platte River west of Fort Kearny, DAWSON (Suckley in Beidleman 1956). In May or June 1864 at a prairie dog town near the confluence of the North and South Platte rivers, LINCOLN (Lienhard 1961, 50). On 2 June 1864, at a prairie dog town west of Kearney, BUFFALO (Dunlap 1969). All prairie dog towns in the Northwest had this owl, including one town ten miles below the mouth of the Niobrara River, KNOX (Hayden 1863a). Characteristic bird, abundant where animal burrows were available throughout the Missouri region (Coues 1874). Abundant in central and western Nebraska and sparingly present almost to the Missouri River; formerly more numerous than at present, but their numbers diminish westward; twelve years ago, quite abundant in the Logan and Elkhorn river valleys, but now seen only occasionally; two in June 1868, WAYNE; three in June 1868, PIERCE; July 1869, WAYNE; June 1875, Sidney, CHEYENNE, and two at Ogallala, KEITH (Aughey 1878).

Barred Owl. *Strix varia.*

Tribal name: Omaha—*wapu'gahahada.*

Apparent status: The Barred Owl was limited to larger forests, mostly cottonwood and adjacent oak forest areas along the Missouri River and lower Platte. Fewer birds existed in forests up to Fort

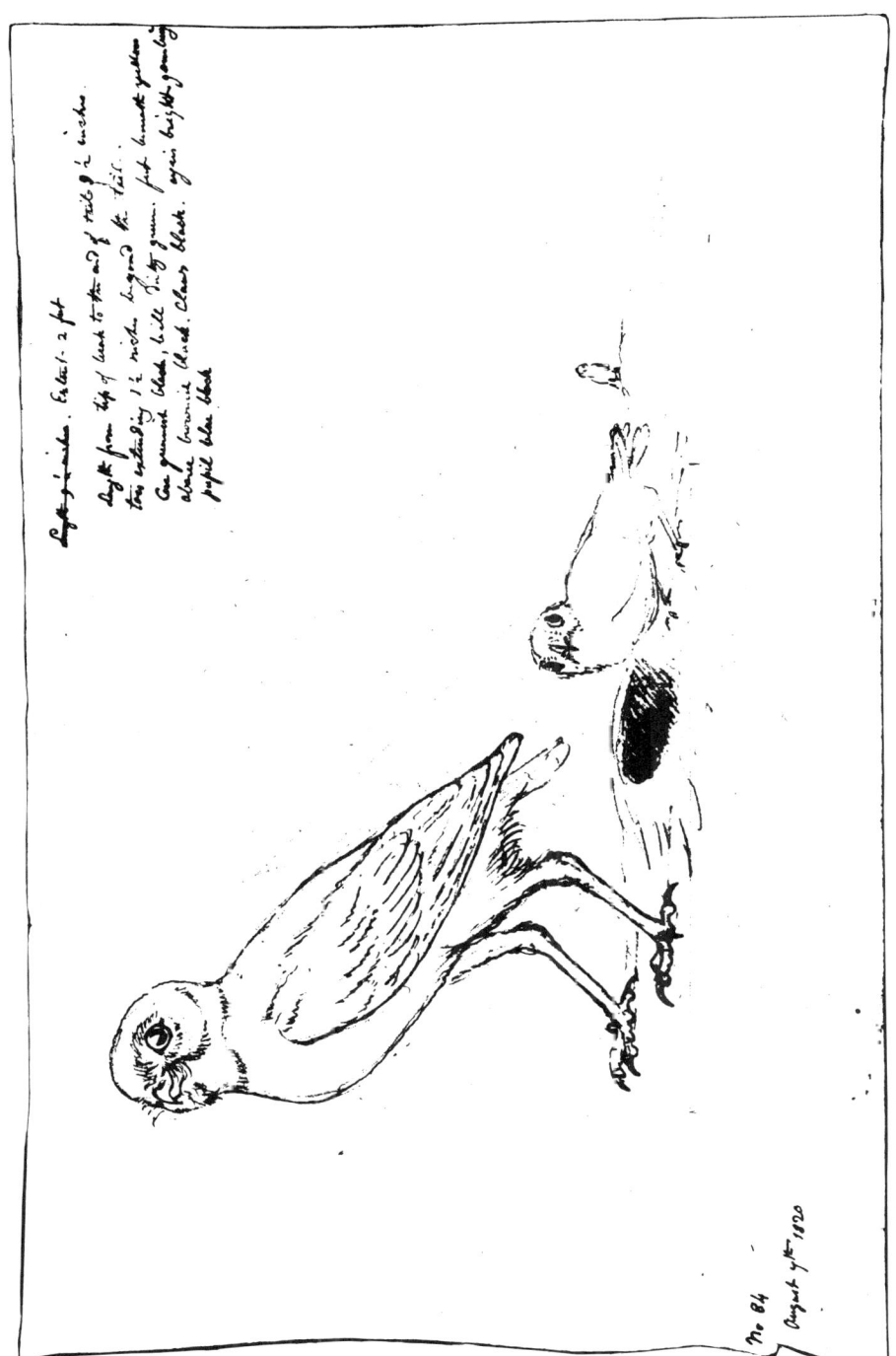

Burrowing Owl, by Titian Ramsay Peale

Randall. The western limit of this bird's range cannot be determined from the available Nebraska records.

Present in the Omaha tribal area (Fletcher and La Flesche 1972). Potential breeder about 1820 in the Engineer Cantonment area, WASHINGTON (Thwaites 1905). On 30 April 1833, singing in the Frazer's Island area, OTOE; 9 May 1834, THURSTON (Maximilian in Orr and Porter 1983). Quite rare in the Northwest (Hayden 1863a). Missouri River; westernmost record of this species at the time (Coues 1874). Very seldom seen; July 1867, DAKOTA (Aughey 1878).

Long-eared Owl. *Asio otus.*

Potential breeder about 1820 in the Engineer Cantonment area (Thwaites 1905). On 28 October 1855, one hundred miles east of Fort Kearny [PLATTE?]; 8 October 1856, White River, NE (Warren in Baird et al. 1860). Not uncommon throughout the Northwest (Hayden 1863a). July 1865, DAKOTA (Aughey 1878).

Short-eared Owl. *Asio flammeus.*

Apparent status: This owl was uncommon in the state, with limited numbers of breeding birds where suitable meadow habitat existed.

Fort Kearny, KEARNEY; 9 October 1855, White River, NE (Warren in Baird et al. 1860); 20 August 1857, north fork of the Platte River (Magraw in Baird et al. 1860). Specimen collected during winter 1872-73 at Fort Randall, TODD, SD (Coues 1874). Frequent on borders of the Missouri River bottoms; nest found in burrow on the side of a bluff, DIXON [This owl nests on the prairie, not in burrows, so this probably is not a valid nesting record.]; September 1868, LANCASTER; July 1870, DAKOTA (Aughey 1878).

Northern Saw-whet Owl. *Aegolius acadicus.*
Common name: Acadian owl (Coues).

Potential breeder about 1820 in the Engineer Cantonment area, WASHINGTON (Thwaites 1905). Specimen collected in January [1870s] at Fort Randall, TODD, SD (Coues 1874).

Family Caprimulgidae

Common Nighthawk. *Chordeiles minor.*
Tribal names: Omaha—*te'ubixo*ⁿ; Dakota Sioux—*pi'-śko.*
Common names: buffalo inflator, bull-bat, pisk, piramidig.

Apparent status: The Common Nighthawk was found throughout the state during the summer breeding season.

Present in the Omaha tribal area (Fletcher and La Flesche 1972). Potential breeder about 1820 in the Engineer Cantonment area (Thwaites 1905). On 22 May 1843, Fort Randall area, TODD, SD; 30 September, Big Sioux River area, DAKOTA (Audubon 1960). On 24 July 1857, at the Loup Fork, PLATTE (Warren in Baird et al. 1860). Nest with eggs, 3 July 1859, in the Fort Kearny area, KEARNEY (Suckley in Beidleman 1956). Very abundant throughout the Northwest (Hayden 1863a). As abundant in most parts of the west as elsewhere (Coues 1874). Common and breeds; two in August 1867 and September 1867, CEDAR; present ca. 1870, ANTELOPE (Leach 1916, 87). August 1874, HARLAN; September 1874, LANCASTER; June 1875, SARPY and OTOE (Aughey 1878).

Common Poorwill. *Phalaenoptilus nuttallii.*
Tribal name: Sioux—*źo'-a-to-pi* (so named from its note).

This bird was a regular on the High Plains of western Nebraska. It was prominent and known to the Sioux tribe, but it is not part of the notes from the historic expeditions from the East. In his description of western birds, Coues commented that

> in places where the birds are numerous the wailing chorus is enough to excite vague apprehensions on the part of the lonely traveler, as he lies down to rest by his camp-fire, or to break his sleep with fitful dreams, in which lost spirits appear to bemoan their fate and implore his intercession. It is not strange that a heated fancy should riot in the circumstances of desolation and imminent peril under which the emigrant or the explorer must often be placed in the western wilderness. Experience comes vividly to mind as I write, of night after night, when I have gradually lost consciousness with a mind peopled with all manner of weird images. Closing my eyes to the stars in the broad expanse above, my only coverlet, and to the ruddy gleam from the embers of the camp-fire, with a thought of home and perhaps a silent aspiration, it might be long before the sense of hearing, unnaturally strained, would desert its post. The monotonous tread of the sentinel would fall heavily on the ear; the horses would seem to champ as never before; the bands of vagrant coyotés would howl with redoubled energy, and all the while the Poor-wills shouted their alarm. (Coues 1874, 261)

Very abundant in most parts of the West (Coues 1874). Rather common in central and western Nebraska in the vicinity of timber; occasional farther east; calling birds, August 1869 along Bow Creek [CEDAR] (Aughey 1878).

Whip-poor-will. *Caprimulgus vociferus.*
Tribal name: Omaha—*ha'kugthi.*
Common names: whipperwhip, night-jar, Nuttall's whippoorwill.

Most records are for the Missouri River, where Whip-poor-will often were common in the extensive flood-plain forest habitat. It also was noted on the lower Niobrara River.

Present in the Omaha tribal area (Fletcher and La Flesche 1972). Potential breeder about 1820 in the Engineer Cantonment area, WASHINGTON (Thwaites 1905). On 26 April 1833, common and heard often, southeast NEMAHA; 3 May 1833, Bellevue, SARPY; 4 and 5 May 1833, DOUGLAS; 7 May 1833, Blackbird Hill, THURSTON; 7 May 1834, these common birds often were heard calling downriver, James River and eastern CEDAR; 8 May 1834, opposite the mouth of the Vermillion River, DIXON; 11 May 1834, northeast WASHINGTON; 13 May 1834, southeast CASS; 15 May 1834, DONIPHAN, KS (Maximilian in Orr and Porter 1983). On 30 September 1843, in the Big Sioux River area, DAKOTA (Audubon 1960). On 19 August 1844, west of the headwaters of the Nemaha River (Carleton 1983). First seen 6 May 1852, one day upriver from the mouth of the Niobrara (Kurz 1970). Heard each spring near the mouth of the Big Sioux River, DAKOTA (Hayden 1863a). One subspecies extends only to the eastern border of the Missouri region (Coues 1874); another subspecies seen on 7 September 1857, in the Black Hills (Warren in Baird et al. 1860). Occasional in eastern Nebraska, where it breeds; two in August 1867 along Bow Creek [CEDAR] (Aughey 1878).

Family Apodidae

Chimney Swift. *Chaetura pelagica.*

As towns were built, these birds would have become more numerous as building chimneys became available and were used as nest sites.

Potential breeder about 1820 in the Engineer Cantonment area (Thwaites 1905). On 7 May 1834, James River and eastern CEDAR (Maximilian in Orr and Porter 1983). Abundant in eastern Nebraska, September 1874 and 1876 (Aughey 1878).

Family Trochilidae

Ruby-throated Hummingbird. *Archilochus colubris.*

Apparent status: This hummingbird probably was limited to forest habitat along the Missouri River, especially south of the Platte.

Present in the Omaha tribal area (Fletcher and La Flesche 1972). Potential breeder about 1820 in the Engineer Cantonment area (Thwaites 1905). On 7 May 1843, the southwest corner of NEMAHA at RICHARDSON (Audubon 1960). One in June 1875 at Lincoln, LANCASTER (Aughey 1878).

Family Alcedinidae

Belted Kingfisher. *Ceryle alcyon.*
Tribal names: Omaha—*noⁿxi'de shkuniⁿ*; Dakota Sioux—*ku-śde'-ća.*

Apparent status: The kingfisher was a regular resident along Nebraska's rivers. The earthen banks of the wild Missouri were excellent locations for nest burrows. This bird also was present elsewhere where habitat was suitable.

Present in the Omaha tribal area (Fletcher and La Flesche 1972). Potential breeder about 1820 in the Engineer Cantonment area, WASHINGTON (Thwaites 1905). Though not common, seen occasionally along all the streams of the Northwest (Hayden 1863a). Present ca. 1870, ANTELOPE (Leach 1916, 87). Frequently seen September 1874 (Aughey 1878).

Family Picidae

Lewis' Woodpecker. *Melanerpes lewis.*
Apparent status: This woodpecker was present occasionally in the pine forests of western Nebraska.

On 17 June 1860, at the Snake River, CHERRY (Coues 1874).

Red-headed Woodpecker. *Melanerpes erythrocephalus.*
Tribal names: Omaha—*tu'cka* and *mu'xpa*; Dakota Sioux—*wa-hnuŋ'-ka.*

Apparent status: Red-headed Woodpeckers lived throughout the year predominantly in the eastern quarter of Nebraska where suitable woodland habitat existed. Numerous tree snags along the Missouri were used by these birds. Elsewhere, where woods were less prevalent, they occurred in fewer numbers.

Present in the Omaha tribal area (Fletcher and La Flesche 1972). Potential breeder about 1820 in the Engineer Cantonment area (Thwaites 1905). On 13 May 1833, BOYD; 15 May 1834, northeast RICHARDSON (Maximilian in Orr and Porter 1983). On 22 May 1843, Fort Randall Military Reservation, TODD, SD (Audubon 1960). On 1 July 1857, Fremont, on the Platte, DODGE; five males and females, 23

April 1856, along the Nemaha River (Warren in Baird et al. 1860); 12 August 1856, along the North Platte River (Bryan in Baird et al. 1860). One of the most abundant birds along the Missouri, many pairs of these birds live in dry trees along the river's wooded bottoms (Hayden 1863a). Common wherever there is enough timber; common; June 1865 and August 1866, DAKOTA; June 1868 and 1869, DIXON; two in September 1874, CASS (Aughey 1878). Present ca. 1870, ANTELOPE (Leach 1916, 87).

Red-bellied Woodpecker. *Melanerpes carolinus.*
Apparent status: This species was limited to the Missouri River area and woodlands on the lower Platte.
Potential breeder about 1820 in the Engineer Cantonment area (Thwaites 1905). On 15 May 1834, northeast RICHARDSON (Maximilian in Orr and Porter 1983). On 23 April 1856, Nemaha Reserve, Nebraska Territory [perhaps the Iowa Indian Reservation at the mouth of the Big Nemaha River, RICHARDSON] (Warren in Baird et al. 1860); two on 26 April 1856, along the Platte River (Bryan in Baird et al. 1860). Quite rare in the Northwest (Hayden 1863a). A rare bird in most portions of the Missouri region (Coues 1874). Rather common in spots in southern Nebraska, but rarely seen north of the Platte; two in September 1874, LANCASTER (Aughey 1878).

Yellow-bellied Sapsucker. *Sphyrapicus varius.*
Common name: yellow-bellied woodpecker.
Apparent status: The Yellow-bellied Sapsucker was common but limited to lowland forests of the Missouri River valley and woodlands on the lower Platte.
On 26 April 1856, mouth of the Platte River, CASS; 29 April 1856, eighty miles above Council Bluffs, IA [If this was river miles, then the site was in THURSTON.]; three, male and female, on 3 May 1856, Big Sioux River, UNION, SD; two on 17 May, above Council Bluffs, IA (Warren in Baird et al. 1860). Very abundant along the wooded bottoms of the Missouri (Hayden 1863a). Common in the wooded bottoms of the Missouri region (Coues 1874). Rather common in the bottoms of the Missouri River and other eastern Nebraska streams; June 1865, DAKOTA; two in June 1868, DIXON; October 1874, CASS; June 1875, LANCASTER (Aughey 1878).

Downy Woodpecker. *Picoides pubescens.*
Apparent status: The Downy Woodpecker lived throughout the state wherever suitable woody habitat was present.

Potential breeder about 1820 in the Engineer Cantonment area (Thwaites 1905). On 12 May 1834, northeast DOUGLAS (Maximilian in Orr and Porter 1983). Two on 26 April 1856, Platte River; Bon Homme Island, KNOX (Warren in Baird et al. 1860). Not uncommon on dry trees of the Northwest river bottoms (Hayden 1863a). Much less abundant than the Hairy Woodpecker, but still frequently seen among the timber of the river bottoms; two in September 1867 and June 1868, DIXON; September 1874, CASS (Aughey 1878). Present ca. 1870, ANTELOPE (Leach 1916, 87).

Hairy Woodpecker. *Picoides villosus.*
Tribal name: Omaha—*zho^n'panini.*

Apparent status: The Hairy Woodpecker was found throughout the state where suitable woody habitat was present. It was more numerous in the Missouri River region than the Downy Woodpecker.

Present in the Omaha tribal area (Fletcher and La Flesche 1972). Potential breeder about 1820 in the Engineer Cantonment area (Thwaites 1905). On 3 May 1856, Big Sioux River, UNION, SD (Warren in Baird et al. 1860). Common in the dry trees of the Northwest river bottoms (Hayden 1863a). Present ca. 1870, ANTELOPE (Leach 1916). The prevailing form in the Missouri region (Coues 1874). Abundant in the woody portions of the Missouri and other river bottoms; two in July 1866, DAKOTA; two in August 1867, CEDAR; September 1874, OTOE; September 1876, CASS (Aughey 1878).

Northern Flicker. *Colaptes auratus.*
Tribal name: Omaha—*tho^n'çiga.*
Common names: golden-winged woodpecker [yellow-shafted subspecies], red-shafted woodpecker, Mexican flicker [red-shafted subspecies].

Apparent status: This species lived throughout the state in wooded areas and was especially abundant in eastern woodlands. Both the red-shafted and yellow-shafted forms historically occurred in Nebraska. Red-shafted flickers were most predominant in areas west of Nebraska. A hybrid of red-shafted and yellow-shafted flickers was noted on September 1, 1857, at Fort Laramie and on the upper Missouri River (Baird et al. 1860; Hayden 1863a).

Present in the Omaha tribal area, northeast Nebraska (Fletcher and La Flesche 1972). Potential breeder about 1820 in the Engineer Cantonment area, WASHINGTON (Thwaites 1905). On 7 May 1834, James River and eastern CEDAR; 15 May 1834, northeast RICHARDSON (Maximilian in Orr and Porter 1983). On 24 May 1843 and 23 September, at Fort Randall Military Reservation, TODD, SD (Audubon 1960; McDermott 1951). On 14 July 1856, Platte River; two on 8 July 1856, South Platte River (Bryan in Baird et al. 1860); two, including young, on 1 July 1857, Fremont on the Platte, DODGE; four, including young, on 27-28 July 1857, Loup Fork, PLATTE; young in summer 1857, fifty miles above the mouth of the Platte [WASHINGTON, if this was river miles]; Little Blue River; three, including young, on 4 July 1856, Squaw Butte, Pine Ridge, NE (Warren in Baird et al. 1860); 31 August 1853, White Earth River (Stevens in Baird et al. 1860); 7 July 1856, Little Blue River (Bryan in Baird et al. 1860); 27 July 1857, Loup Fork; 2 July 1857, on the Missouri River, fifty miles above the mouth of the Platte, WASHINGTON (Warren in Baird et al. 1860). The yellow-shafted form was abundant along the wooded bottoms of the Missouri and its tributaries, while the red-shafted form was abundant in the wooded ravines of the Badlands and westward (Hayden 1863a). Abundant in the wooded portions of Nebraska, breeds; eight in June 1865, DIXON [yellow-shafted form]; occasional; seen on the Niobrara River [KNOX?] and in RICHARDSON; June 1875 from Nebraska City, OTOE (Aughey 1878). Present ca. 1870, ANTELOPE (Leach 1916, 87).

Pileated Woodpecker. *Dryocopus pileatus.*
Tribal name: Omaha—*wazhi^n'gapa* (bird head). The bird head—*wazhi^n'gapa*—was used on the tribal and the Wa'wa^n Pipes.

Available records do not confirm whether this species ever nested in Nebraska, although it possibly did. Suitable habitat existed along the Missouri in southeast Nebraska, where large cottonwood cavities could have been used as nesting sites.

Remains from ca. 1775-1845 at the Big Village of the Omaha, DAKOTA (O'Shea and Ludwickson 1992, 234). Present in the Omaha tribal area (Fletcher and La Flesche 1972). Recorded in material excavated at the site of the Big Village of the Omaha near Homer, DAKOTA (O'Shea et al. 1982). On 7 May 1843, NEMAHA/OTOE; 1 October, Big Sioux River, DAKOTA (Audubon 1960). Since most of the Missouri region is not heavily wooded enough to suit this species, this bird rarely is more than casually present (Coues 1874).

Ivory-billed Woodpecker. *Campephilus principalis.*
The remains of the Ivory-billed Woodpecker were discovered among materials excavated at the Big Village of the Omaha near the present town of Homer (O'Shea et al. 1982). A Pawnee tribe Hako

Ceremony Pipe has the bill of an Ivory-billed Woodpecker on one end (Nebraska State Historical Society collection), which probably was obtained in exchange for other goods from a trader.

Remains from ca. 1775-1845 at the Big Village of the Omaha, DAKOTA (O'Shea and Ludwickson 1992, 234).

Family Tyrannidae

Olive-sided Flycatcher. *Contopus borealis.*
Said to be abundant in the west; July 1869 (Aughey 1878).

Western Wood-Pewee. *Contopus sordidulus.*
Common name: short-legged pewee.
Although there is an 1854 record, this species was not described scientifically until 1859, when a record from Mexico was published (American Ornithologists' Union 1983). The bird was limited to western Nebraska.
Two on 2 June 1854, North Platte River; 24 August 1857, Loup Fork of Platte, PLATTE (Warren in Baird et al. 1860). Frequent in woodland along streams in western Nebraska; two in June 1875 from Wood River, HALL; specimen from Sidney, CHEYENNE (Aughey 1878).

Eastern Wood-Pewee. *Contopus virens.*
Apparent status: This pewee was limited to woodlands in the eastern third of the state.
Potential breeder about 1820 in the Engineer Cantonment area (Thwaites 1905). On 7 May 1843, NEMAHA/OTOE (Audubon 1960). Very few in timber belts along the Missouri; June 1869 at Dakota City, DAKOTA (Aughey 1878).

Yellow-bellied Flycatcher. *Empidonax flaviventris.*
Occurred "sparingly" in eastern Nebraska; bred on the edge of timber belts along the Missouri [This breeding record is not valid; this species never would have nested in Nebraska.]; July 1870 near Dakota City, DAKOTA (Aughey 1878).

Least Flycatcher. *Empidonax minimus.*
Common name: least pewee.
Known to occur along the Missouri and lower Niobrara. This bird was definitely more common as a migrant.
On 17 May 1843, near Vermillion River, northwest DIXON (Audubon 1960). Three on 15 May 1856, L'Eau qui Court [Niobrara

River]; 6 May 1856, Vermillion River, DIXON; 11 May 1856, Nebraska (Warren in Baird et al. 1860). Occasionally seen throughout the Northwest, although not abundant (Hayden 1863a). Rather common; occasionally breeds in northeast Nebraska; 30 May and June 1865, and two in July 1866 at Dakota City, DAKOTA (Aughey 1878).

Eastern Phoebe. *Sayornis phoebe.*
Common names: pewit flycatcher, phoebe-bird, pewee.

Apparent status: This phoebe was limited to the Missouri River valley, the lower portion of the Platte, and elsewhere in southeast Nebraska where suitable habitat was available.

Potential breeder about 1820 in the Engineer Cantonment area (Thwaites 1905). On 7 May 1856, opposite the mouth of the Vermillion, DIXON (Warren in Baird et al. 1860). Quite rare along the Missouri River, although frequently seen on its lower portion (Hayden 1863a). Along the Missouri; June 1866, June 1868 and July 1870 at Dakota City, DAKOTA; two in September 1874, 20 May and June 1875, and June 1877, LANCASTER; September 1876, RICHARDSON (Aughey 1878).

Say's Phoebe. *Sayornis saya.*
Common name: Say's flycatcher.

Apparent status: Say's Phoebe was common in the western part of the state.

On 21 May 1843, mouth of the Niobrara River, KNOX; 24 May, Fort Randall Military Reservation, TODD, SD (Audubon 1960; McDermott 1951). On 15 August 1857, confluence of the Platte rivers, LINCOLN; 14 August 1857, north fork of the Platte (Magraw in Baird et al. 1860). Solitary among the ravines of the Badlands; abundant throughout its range (Coues 1874). Observed only in central and western Nebraska; fall 1876 (Aughey 1878).

Great Crested Flycatcher. *Myiarchus crinitus.*

Apparent status: This flycatcher was prevalent in the lower Missouri valley forests. Fewer lived elsewhere, such as in the state's southeastern and lower Platte River forests. Even fewer occurred as woodland habitat became sparse.

Potential breeder about 1820 in the Engineer Cantonment area (Thwaites 1905). On 15 May 1834, northeast RICHARDSON (Maximilian in Orr and Porter 1983). On 7 May 1843, NEMAHA/OTOE (Audubon 1960). Missouri range restricted to the river's lower portions (Coues 1874). In southeast Nebraska, most abundant in RICHARDSON and NEMAHA; specimen in September 1873 from Brownville, NEMAHA (Aughey 1878).

Western Kingbird. *Tyrannus verticalis.*
Common name: Arkansas flycatcher.
   Apparent status: This species was common throughout the state, but it grew more common towards the west.
   On 21 May, northwest KNOX; 22 and 24 May 1843, Fort Randall Military Reservation, TODD, SD (Audubon 1960; McDermott 1951). On 6 August, and three on 16 August 1856, Loup Fork, PLATTE (Warren in Baird et al. 1860); 28 and 29 July 1856, Pole [Lodgepole] Creek, NE (Bryan in Baird et al. 1860). Not seen until about one hundred miles below Fort Pierre, STANLEY, SD; occurred on the central High Plains (Hayden 1863a). Present ca. 1870, ANTELOPE (Leach 1916, 87). Extensive specimens taken by the Warren Expedition demonstrate the abundance of this species in the upper Missouri and Platte regions (Coues 1874). Egg collected on 13 June 1874 by W. L. Carpenter at Omaha, DOUGLAS (NMNH specimen 17372). Abundant along wooded streams in southwest Nebraska; August 1874 along the Republican River [HARLAN?] (Aughey 1878).

Eastern Kingbird. *Tyrannus tyrannus.*
Tribal name: Omaha—*wati'duka.*
Common names: bee-martin, kingbird.
   Apparent status: This kingbird was present throughout the state, but it was common to abundant in the east.
   Present in the Omaha tribal area (Fletcher and La Flesche 1972). Potential breeder about 1820 in the Engineer Cantonment area (Thwaites 1905). Pairs on 6 May 1833, east-central BURT (Maximilian in Orr and Porter 1983). On 1 July 1857, Fremont on the Platte River, DODGE; May 1855, Cedar Island, TODD/GREGORY, SD (Vaughn in Baird et al. 1860). Very abundant, especially along the lower Missouri; numerous throughout the Northwest (Hayden 1863a). Abundant to the middle of Nebraska; occurred sparingly to Nebraska's western border; June and July 1866, July 1867, September 1869, DAKOTA; two in September 1874, May 1875 and September 1876, LANCASTER (Aughey 1878). Present ca. 1870, ANTELOPE (Leach 1916, 87).

Scissor-tailed Flycatcher. *Tyrannus forficatus.*
   Present ca. 1850 in the tribal area of the Pawnee on the Loup Fork, PLATTE, and to the south in the state (Dunbar 1882). Present

in the Cau'-i Medicine Bundle; "the swallow-tail was a sacred bird, possibly because of its remarkable appearance and rarity in their territory" (Dunbar 1882, 741).

Family Alaudidae

Horned Lark. *Eremophila alpestris.*
Tribal name: Omaha—*ma'çi çka.*
Common names: prairie bird, shore lark, sky lark.

Apparent status: This lark was common to abundant on the open prairies. There were fewer birds in tall grass areas.

Present in the Omaha tribal area (Fletcher and La Flesche 1972). On 25 August 1804, probably the species seen in great numbers around Spirit Mound, CLAY, SD (Lewis and Clark in Swenk 1935). Potential breeder about 1820 in the Engineer Cantonment area, WASHINGTON (Thwaites 1905). Two on 16 July 1856, Platte River; 28 July 1856, Pole [Lodgepole] Creek, NE (Bryan in Baird et al. 1860); 24 October 1857, thirty miles east of Ft. Kearny [HALL/ADAMS?]; 28 July 1856, Pole [Lodgepole] Creek (Magraw in Baird et al. 1860). Large numbers throughout the prairie country of the Northwest, particularly at prairie dog villages, where large numbers occurred (Hayden 1863a). Not present during the winter, but common at Fort Randall after February (Coues 1874). Quite abundant some seasons in eastern Nebraska; early June 1865, DAKOTA; nest on 20 May 1875 and young collected on 16 June, near Lincoln, LANCASTER (Aughey 1878).

Family Hirundinidae

Swallow.
Tribal names: Omaha—*nishku'shku;* Dakota Sioux—*i-ća-pśiŋ-pśiŋ-ća.*

Present in the Omaha tribal area, THURSTON (Fletcher and La Flesche 1972). Potential breeder about 1820 in the Engineer Cantonment area (Thwaites 1905). On 8 May 1834, nesting in hollow trees opposite the mouth of the Vermillion River, DIXON (Maximilian in Orr and Porter 1983). A "great many" nesting on 8 June 1845, in the Ash Hollow area, GARDEN (Carleton 1983, 228). Present ca. 1870, ANTELOPE (Leach 1916, 87).

Purple Martin. *Progne subis.*

Apparent status: The Purple Martin was noted mostly in the Missouri valley, nesting in the hollows of trees along the river, but it likely occurred elsewhere where suitable habitat existed.

On 9 May 1843, at Bellevue, SARPY; breeding in cottonwoods on 22 May, Fort Randall Military Reservation, TODD, SD (Audubon 1960). Five in May 1854 at Cedar Island, GREGORY, SD (Vaughn in Baird et al. 1860); 8 May 1854, Vermillion River, CLAY, SD; 15 May 1854, Nebraska; 23 April, Cedar Island, GREGORY, SD; 23 April, Iowa Point, DONIPHAN, KS (Warren in Baird et al. 1860). Most abundant in the Northwest along the wooded bottoms of streams, where dry trees are favored breeding places (Hayden 1863a). Rather common; breeds; 27 May, 5 and 12 June 1865, and two on 7 June 1868, DAKOTA; 9 June 1867, BURT; 2 June and three on 16 June 1875, LANCASTER (Aughey 1878). Present ca. 1870, ANTELOPE (Leach 1916, 87).

Tree Swallow. *Tachycineta bicolor.*
Common names: green-backed swallow, white-bellied swallow.

Snags along the Missouri River were prime nesting sites for these colonial birds. Fewer numbers existed elsewhere.

On 9 May 1843, at Bellevue, SARPY; 11 May, WASHINGTON (Audubon 1960). Rarer in the Missouri region than other swallows (Coues 1874). Rare in Nebraska (Aughey 1878).

Violet-green Swallow. *Tachycineta thalassina.*

Nested; in August at Pine Bluffs along Lodgepole Creek, LARAMIE, WY (Aughey 1878).

Northern Rough-winged Swallow. *Stelgidopteryx serripennis.*

Apparent status: This swallow was more common than records reveal. The Missouri's earthen banks provided prime nesting habitat. Audubon may have been familiar with it, since its 1838 identification was based on his description (American Ornithologists' Union 1983).

On 9 May 1843, at Bellevue, SARPY (Audubon 1960). Known range includes the Missouri region (Coues 1874). Breeding along the Missouri River bluffs, RICHARDSON (Aughey 1878).

Bank Swallow. *Riparia riparia.*
Common name: sand martin.

Apparent status: Bank Swallows were possibly more prevalent than the previous species, since reports were more numerous. However, some records for this species may have been for other swallows with similar habits. Earthen banks of the Missouri River provided prime habitat for its nest burrows.

On 22 August, a great number of nests along the top of the cliff along the shore, DIXON; 25 August 1804, at Spirit Mound, a large number of "small brown martin" hovered there, catching insects, CLAY, SD (Lewis and Clark in Swenk 1935). Potential breeder about 1820 in the Engineer Cantonment area (Thwaites 1905). Noted in 1823 at the mouth of the Platte River, CASS (Wilhelm 1928). On 12 May 1843, vast numbers flying about holes in the Missouri River bluffs, and 13 May, THURSTON (Audubon 1960; McDermott 1951). On the bluffs on 10 May 1852, great numbers at a spot on the Missouri near the mouth of the Big Sioux, UNION, SD (Kurz 1970, 332). The vertical, earthen banks so conspicuous from the mouth of the Platte to the Niobrara formed nesting places for this bird; frequently associated with the Cliff Swallow, which nests on the rocks below the earthen banks (Hayden 1863a). Travelers along the Missouri in spring 1864 saw thousands of these birds along the river banks, which were, in suitable places, riddled with their nests; in 1872 multitudes of deserted nests were observed higher up the Missouri (Coues 1874). Common in eastern Nebraska; two on 28 May 1865, DIXON; 5 June 1865, DAKOTA; two on 17 June 1875, CASS (Aughey 1878).

Cliff Swallow. *Hirundo pyrrhonota.*
Common name: eave swallow.

Apparent status: The Cliff Swallow was common along the Missouri, Platte and Niobrara rivers, where cliffs provided nesting habitat. In more upland settings, such as the western Niobrara valley, rocky buttes provided a place for nests.

This prominent species was seen by many early explorers. The colony near Blackbird Hill was especially well known. Travelers would stop at the Omaha village and note the swallows' nests on the limestone cliffs along the river. This nesting colony was noted by Lewis and Clark. Maximilian observed the nests at Blackbird Hill, and saw Cliff Swallows at seven additional sites along the Nebraska stretch of the river. Audubon also passed by several bluffs with nesting swallows. Other bird watchers along the Missouri in northeast Nebraska delighted in the swallows' antics as well.

Nests on a rock bluff on 16 July 1804, near Sun [Sonora] Island, northeast NEMAHA (Lewis and Clark in Moulton 1986). Countless birds noted along the Missouri River in 1823, KNOX (Wilhelm 1928). On 2 May 1833, nests on cliffs, Nebraska City area, OTOE; 5 May 1833, Fort Calhoun area, WASHINGTON; 7 May 1833, nests, east-central

Cliff Sparrows [Swallows], by Titian Ramsay Peale

BURT and Blackbird Hill, THURSTON; 8 May 1833, northeast DAKOTA; 9 May 1833, young, northeast DIXON; 12 May 1833, Niobrara River area, KNOX; 13 May 1833, northwest KNOX (Maximilian in Orr and Porter 1983). Colony in 1839 in the Blackbird Hill region, THURSTON (Bray and Bray 1976). Several colony sites on 13 May 1843, at Blackbird Hill; 16 May, a colony of more than two hundred nests, northwest DIXON (Audubon 1960). Colonies with hundreds of nests on 8 June 1845, in the Ash Hollow area, GARDEN (Carleton 1983, 228). In 1850 nests noted along the Missouri near the Niobrara (McDermott 1952). On 4 June 1852, many hundreds nested on the cliffs and flew about, their calls a common sound at Ash Hollow, GARDEN (Eaton 1974, 101-102). Two on 26 July 1856, Pole [Lodgepole] Creek, NE, KIMBALL/CHEYENNE (Bryan in Baird et al. 1860). Breeding on 14 July 1859, in the Ash Hollow area and west along the Platte River, GARDEN (Suckley in Beidleman 1956). Abundant along the Missouri, with nests on the bluffs' vertical sides; near the mouth of the Niobrara, the bluffs and vertical walls sometimes are completely covered with nests; a single shot usually supplies enough specimens (Hayden 1863a). Bluffs near the mouth of the Niobrara in 1873 sometimes were covered completely with their nests (Coues 1874). Occurs in great numbers in eastern Nebraska; 2,100 nests in August along the Niobrara River three miles east of Niobrara, KNOX; 30 May and 5 June 1865, DAKOTA; 9 June 1867, BURT; 1 June and two on 14 June 1875, and two on 16 June 1877, LANCASTER (Aughey 1878).

Barn Swallow. *Hirundo rustica.*
Tribal name: Dakota Sioux—*u-pi'-źa-ta.*

Barn Swallows were common to abundant summer residents. Historically, they nested on rock bluffs, similar to the Cliff Swallow's habitat. An increase in buildings due to settlement may have provided more suitable nesting sites. Fewer numbers were present in areas such as the Sand Hills, where nest sites were limited before ranches were established in the region.

Potential breeder about 1820 in the Engineer Cantonment area (Thwaites 1905). On 22 May 1843, Fort Randall Military Reservation, TODD, SD (Audubon 1960). Builds its nests on the vertical bluffs along the Missouri; countless numbers (Hayden 1863a). Occurs throughout the Missouri region (Coues 1874). Occurs in various localities in eastern Nebraska; breeds; more in OTOE than anywhere else; 1 June and 17 June 1865, DAKOTA; 28 May, 5 June, two on 16 June 1875, and 14 June 1877, LANCASTER (Aughey 1878). Two birds nesting on July 1870 along the western Dismal River, HOOKER (Grinnell in Mitchell 1987).

Family Corvidae

Blue Jay. *Cyanocitta cristata.*
Tribal names: Omaha—*i"cho"g'agiudu"* (fond of mice); Dakota Sioux—*zi-tka'-to* and *te-te'-ni-ća.*

Apparent status: The few records of this obvious species suggest it was uncommon, even in suitable woodland habitat in eastern Nebraska.

Present in the Omaha tribal area (Fletcher and La Flesche 1972). Potential breeder about 1820 in the Engineer Cantonment area (Thwaites 1905). On 7 May 1843, NEMAHA/OTOE (Audubon 1960). Fledged; young on 25 June 1859, in the Fairbury area, JEFFERSON (Suckley in Beidleman 1956). Present ca. 1870, ANTELOPE (Leach 1916, 87). Occurred west to eastern Nebraska (Coues 1874). Comparatively few; breeds; two in September 1874, RICHARDSON; specimen in September 1876 from Nebraska City; abundant in OTOE (Aughey 1878).

Clark's Nutcracker. *Nucifraga columbiana.*
Common names: Clarke's crow, American nutcracker.

Apparent status: The only Nebraska record of this bird in this period was along the Platte River, although it would be expected in the Pine Ridge and Wildcat Hills. These birds were more typical of the area near Fort Laramie, as noted in the Hayden report.

Two on 24 October 1857, thirty miles east of Fort Kearny [HALL?] (Magraw in Baird et al. 1860). First seen in 1857 in the North Platte River valley near Fort Laramie, WY (Hayden 1863a). Found only in the western part of the state; specimen in October 1874 from Sidney, CHEYENNE (Aughey 1878).

Black-billed Magpie. *Pica pica.*
Tribal names: Omaha—*Wazhi"'be çnede* (long-tail bird); Sioux—*ūnk-ći'-ki-ća;* Dakota Sioux—*un-kće'-ki-ha* and *zi-tka'-wa-kaŋ-taŋ-haŋ.*
Common name: American magpie.

Apparent status: This magpie lived along the Missouri River in northern Nebraska. Although it was said not to occur below the Platte River, it was noted in this region by observers during the 1850-65 period. Common in some areas, with large flocks during fall and winter, these birds were easily trapped and kept in camps.

In his journal from the Missouri River from 1803 to 1805, Pierre Tabeau mentioned the problems magpies caused for the Native Americans:

Magpie, by Titian Ramsay Peale

The magpie, the most beautiful bird of the country, is here the plague of the ... [tribes'] horses. These ... [Native Americans] are so clumsy and so careless with their wooden saddles that often the horse's skin and flesh from the neck to the rump are torn away. The voracious bird at the sight of this raw and living flesh buries its claws in it and tears the poor sentient animal. The horse kicks, prances, runs about with all its might, but in vain. The bird, fixed on the sores, loosens its hold only when the horse throws himself upon his back to roll. Yet scarcely does he rise up once more than the enemy seizes again its opportunity. It is observable that among a large number of galled horses, the magpie always chooses that one that it has once tasted, so that the beast finally succumbs, if it be not rescued. Some owners, more through interest than through pity, cover the sores with a piece of leather or with a buffalo paunch sprinkled with ashes. (Abel 1939, 88-90)

Present in the Omaha tribal area, northeast Nebraska (Fletcher and La Flesche 1972). Captive birds on 10 May 1843, at Fort Atkinson, WASHINGTON (Audubon 1960). On 15, 16 and 17 October 1856, at Fort Randall, TODD, SD; 20 October 1856, Running Water [Niobrara], KNOX (Warren in Baird et al. 1860); 5 October 1857, Fort Kearny, KEARNEY; 20 October 1857, thirty miles west of Fort Kearny, in DAWSON (Cooper in Baird et al. 1860); 12 August 1857, North Platte (Bryan in Baird et al. 1860). One of the most common birds in the far West; never observed below Council Bluffs; from there to the Rockies, its numbers increase (Hayden 1863a). Present ca. 1870, ANTELOPE (Leach 1916, 87). The first seen in 1860s or 1870s near Sioux City, WOODBURY, IA (Coues 1874). Occasional in northern and more common in western Nebraska; July 1867, DIXON (Aughey 1878). One of the most familiar birds in eastern Nebraska between 1850 and 1865; some breed in southeast Nebraska in the Peru area, NEMAHA; very numerous in fall and winter (Taylor 1887a).

American Crow. *Corvus brachyrhynchos.*
Tribal names: Omaha—*Ka'xe*; Otoe—*Koth-ah*; Pawnee—*ka-'ka*; Dakota Sioux—*uŋ-ći'-śi-ća-daŋ*.
Common names: common crow, fish crow.

Apparent status: Records for this bird are limited to the Missouri River and other wooded areas along rivers and larger streams. Since this bird is a prominent species, it would have been noted more often in narratives if it were present. The lack of records for the central and western Platte River thus indicates it was uncommon.

Present in the Omaha tribal area (Fletcher and La Flesche 1972). Potential breeder about 1820 near Engineer Cantonment, WASHINGTON (Thwaites 1905). In faunal remains dating to 1822-42 from Fontenelle's post, SARPY (Bozell et al. 1990). Noted in summer 1823 at Keg Island, CASS (Wilhelm 1928). On 27 April 1833, Little Nemaha River area, NEMAHA; 7 May 1833, Blackbird Hill, THURSTON; 7 May 1834, James River and eastern CEDAR (Maximilian in Orr and Porter 1983). On 7 May 1843, NEMAHA/OTOE; 9 May, at Bellevue, SARPY; 10 May, WASHINGTON; 1 October, Big Sioux River, DAKOTA (Audubon 1960). On 25 October 1856, Vermillion River, DIXON (Warren in Baird et al. 1860). Captive birds in 1861 at the Yankton Sioux village, Dakota Territory, CLAY, SD (Ladner 1984, 34). Vermillion River, southeast Dakota, CLAY, SD; very abundant throughout the Northwest (Hayden 1863a). Fort Randall, TODD, SD; present along the whole Missouri River; partial to wooded river bottoms and other water courses (Coues 1874). Large numbers poisoned in 1865, 1866 and 1867 in northern Nebraska, where it was then very abundant (Aughey 1878). Large numbers at winter roost on Hogback Island, north of Peru, NEMAHA, about 1860 and after, at least through 1887 (Taylor 1887b).

Chihuahuan Raven. *Corvus cryptoleucus.*
Common name: white-necked raven.

Noted in summer 1823 along the Missouri River at Keg Island, CASS (Wilhelm 1928) [This is a questionable record, since this species is more typical of western Nebraska.]. One in April 1877 along the Republican River near the western border of the state, DUNDY (Aughey 1878).

Common Raven. *Corvus corax.*
Tribal name: Dakota Sioux—*kaŋ-ġi'*.
Common name: American raven.

Apparent status: Common Ravens were very abundant in some localities; they probably were more common on the prairie than in woodland areas. The large numbers could have been gatherings of migratory birds. During a wolf-hunting excursion in 1858 in which poisoned bait was used, ravens were very numerous in the Elm Creek area of the Platte River. Grinnell noted:

> There were multitudes of ravens everywhere and all of them looking for food. In order to save the wolf bait it was necessary to distribute the small pieces at night after the ravens had gone to roost. Then too the men were obliged to be afoot very early in the morning

in order to begin skinning their wolves before the ravens got about. Otherwise, the hides would be destroyed by the birds. Even as it was, they lost in this way perhaps one hundred hides. Many, many hundreds of ravens were killed by eating the carcasses of the poisoned wolves. (Grinnell 1928, 30)

Remains from ca. 1775-1845 at the Big Village of the Omaha, DAKOTA (O'Shea and Ludwickson 1992, 234). Recorded in material excavated from the Big Village of the Omaha near Homer, DAKOTA (O'Shea et al. 1982). Young in 1820 in the Engineer Cantonment area, WASHINGTON (Thwaites 1905). On 1 May 1833, Frazer's Island area, OTOE; 3 May 1833, CASS; 7 May 1834, James River and eastern CEDAR (Maximilian in Orr and Porter 1983). On 7 May 1843, NEMAHA/OTOE; 15 May, northwest DAKOTA; 17 May, near the Vermillion River, northwest DIXON; 21 May, northwest KNOX; 24 September, Bazile Creek, KNOX (Audubon 1960). On 18 October 1856, Fort Randall, TODD, SD; two on 20 October 1856, L'Eau qui Court [Niobrara River] (Warren in Baird et al. 1860). Very numerous in autumn 1858 in the Elm Creek area, BUFFALO (Grinnell 1928). On 25 June 1859, in the Fairbury area, JEFFERSON (Suckley in Beidleman 1956). Very abundant across the Northwest; always seen near large buffalo herds and follow the hunters for hours; in the Badlands (Hayden 1863a). Formerly frequent, then less common; June 1865 (Aughey 1878). Present ca. 1870, ANTELOPE (Leach 1916, 87).

Family Paridae

Black-capped Chickadee. *Parus atricapillus.*
Tribal name: Dakota Sioux—*wi'-yu-śkiŋ-śkiŋ-na.*
Common name: long-tailed chickadee.

Apparent status: These chickadees were regular and common residents of Nebraska's forest and woodland areas. They formed small flocks during the winter (Coues 1874).

Potential breeder about 1820 in the Engineer Cantonment area (Thwaites 1905). On 2 April 1856, mouth of Big Nemaha River, RICHARDSON (Warren in Baird et al. 1860). Very abundant in the willow bottoms along Northwest rivers (Hayden 1863a). One of the few birds who remain during the winter in the Missouri River region (Coues 1874). Very abundant in eastern Nebraska; two on 1 June, 6 June and 10 June 1865, DAKOTA; two on 8 June and 15 June 1875, 2 June 1876 and 14 June 1877, LANCASTER (Aughey 1878).

Tufted Titmouse. *Parus bicolor.*
Common name: northern titmouse.
 Apparent status: Titmice were limited to the Missouri River from Sarpy County southward.
 On 9 May 1843, SARPY (Audubon 1960). An eastern species that reaches the lower Missouri River in Nebraska; numerous in the Fort Leavenworth, Kansas, area (Coues 1874). Abundant in eastern Nebraska; 30 May, 3 June and 8 June 1865, DAKOTA; 9 June 1866, BURT (Aughey 1878).

Family Sittidae

Red-breasted Nuthatch. *Sitta canadensis.*
Common name: red-bellied nuthatch.
 Apparent status: Few of these nesting birds reached Nebraska along the Missouri River. The birds more likely occurred in higher numbers in the Pine Ridge, Wildcat Hills and westward. Fewer birds were present in pine forests along the central Niobrara valley.
 In 1856, Cedar Island, TODD/GREGORY, SD (Baird et al. 1860). Quite rare in the Northwest; frequent in the Badlands (Hayden 1863a). Occasional in northeastern Nebraska timber; DAKOTA (Aughey 1878).

White-breasted Nuthatch. *Sitta carolinensis.*
Common names: white-bellied nuthatch, slender-billed nuthatch.
 Apparent status: This nuthatch was a regular resident that nested in forest areas along the Missouri, lower Platte and possibly the lower Niobrara.
 Potential breeder about 1820 near Engineer Cantonment (Thwaites 1905). Abundant in wooded regions; occurred along the Missouri River (Coues 1874). Frequent in the timbered areas of eastern Nebraska; 29 May 1865, DIXON; 30 May 1865, DAKOTA; 4 June 1875 and 13 June 1877, LANCASTER (Aughey 1878).

Pygmy Nuthatch. *Sitta pygmaea.*
 This bird was seen in 1875 in the timbered bottoms and bluffs of the Niobrara River (Aughey 1878).

Family Certhiidae

Brown Creeper. *Certhia americana.*
 Apparent status: The Brown Creeper was an uncommon but regular nester along the Missouri River.

Nested in 1865 near Dakota City, DAKOTA (Bruner et al. 1904). Not observed, but said to occur in the Missouri region (Coues 1874). Nest found in June 1865 near Dakota City, DAKOTA (Aughey 1878).

Family Troglodytidae

Wren.
Tribal name: Omaha—*kixaxaja* (laughing bird); Dakota Sioux—*ptegaŋ'-ni-ća-daŋ*.

Wrens were present in the Omaha tribal area (Fletcher and La Flesche 1972).

Rock Wren. *Salpinctes obsoletus.*

Apparent status: Rock Wrens were common in the rocky buttes of western Nebraska, and a few migratory birds were seen elsewhere.

On 25 July 1856, Pole [Lodgepole] Creek (Bryan in Baird et al. 1860); 15 August 1856, Running Water [Niobrara], KNOX (Warren in Baird et al. 1860); three on 13 August 1857, forks of the Platte, LINCOLN (Magraw in Baird et al. 1860). Numerous in the Badlands (Hayden in Coues 1874). Nest on 3 June and feeding young on 10 June 1865 in a slab pile near Dakota City, DAKOTA; nest with young in an old stump in June 1875, LANCASTER (Aughey 1878) [This species nests among rocks, not in stumps, so this is a questionable nesting record.].

Carolina Wren. *Thryothorus ludovicianus.*
Common name: great Carolina wren.

Apparent status: This wren was uncommon.

Potential breeder about 1820 in the Engineer Cantonment area (Thwaites 1905). Adult carrying food on 12 June 1875, RICHARDSON (Aughey 1878).

Bewick's Wren. *Thryomanes bewickii.*

Apparent status: This wren was occasional and a rare breeder in the summer.

Parents feeding young on 12 June 1875, along the Missouri River, OTOE (Aughey 1878).

House Wren. *Troglodytes aedon.*
Common name: Parkman's wren.

Apparent status: The House Wren probably occurred throughout the state where suitable habitat was available. In those locations, it often was common.

On 25 August 1804, Vermillion River area, northwest DIXON (Lewis and Clark in Moulton 1987). On 5 May 1834, Niobrara River area, KNOX; 8 May 1834, at two sites near mouth of the Vermillion River, DIXON; 15 May 1834, southeast NEMAHA (Maximilian in Orr and Porter 1983). On 7 May 1843, NEMAHA/OTOE; 9 May, at Bellevue, SARPY; abundant on 17 May, northwest DIXON; 21 May, abundant, northwest KNOX (Audubon 1960). On 29 April, near Council Bluffs; 25 April 1856, Bald Island, NEMAHA; 3 July 1857, Loup Fork of the Platte River, PLATTE; 26 April 1856, North Platte River (Warren in Baird et al. 1860); 7 July 1856, South Platte (Bryan in Baird et al. 1860). This bird was not rare along the Missouri as far as settlements extend; [Parkman's form] was very abundant throughout the Northwest; a single specimen secured in summer 1857 near the mouth of the Loup Fork (Hayden 1863a). Numerous specimens indicate its abundance in the Northwest (Coues 1874). Abundant in Nebraska (Aughey 1878). Egg collected on 16 June 1874, by W. L. Carpenter at Omaha, DOUGLAS (NMNH specimen 17368).

Winter Wren. *Troglodytes troglodytes.*

[Based on Maximilian's description of the bird and its activities,] on 8 May 1834, opposite the mouth of the Vermillion River, DIXON (Maximilian in Orr and Porter 1983). Expected in the Missouri River region (Coues 1874).

Sedge Wren. *Cistothorus platensis.*
Common name: short-billed marsh wren.

Apparent status: This bird was a regular in wet meadows along the state's larger rivers, especially in limited sites along the Missouri and on the Platte.

On 30 August 1857, Loup Fork, PLATTE (Warren in Baird et al. 1860). Quite rare, although seen occasionally around the Missouri River marshes near the Council Bluff and the Big Sioux River (Hayden 1863a). The specimen taken on the Loup Fork of the Platte was the westernmost record for this species for the United States at that time (Hayden in Coues 1874). Nest in 1867 in a swamp or marsh on the Missouri River bottom, DIXON (Aughey 1878).

Marsh Wren. *Cistothorus palustris.*
Common name: long-billed marsh wren.

Apparent status: Marsh Wrens were present throughout the state where suitable marsh habitat was present. They were abundant in wetland regions, such as the Sand Hills and Rainwater Basin. Fewer numbers occurred along the Missouri River, although birds could have been locally common in marshes of the oxbow lakes.

Potential breeder about 1820 near Engineer Cantonment (Thwaites 1905). On 7 May 1843, NEMAHA/OTOE (Audubon 1960). On 4 May 1856, mouth of Big Sioux; 12 August 1857, western Sand Hills (Warren in Baird et al. 1860). Quite rare, but occasionally seen in marshes on the Missouri River bottoms near the Council Bluff and the Big Sioux River (Hayden 1863a). Occasional in Missouri River marshes; nest with young in June 1875 near Bellevue, SARPY (Aughey 1878).

Family Muscicapidae

Golden-crowned Kinglet. *Regulus satrapa.*

Abundant some years in northern Nebraska; not seen south of the Platte; June 1865 near Dakota City, DAKOTA (Aughey 1878) [This is a late migration date (Sharpe 1993).].

Ruby-crowned Kinglet. *Regulus calendula.*
Common name: ruby-crowned wren.

On 24 April, three on 4 May 1856, mouth of the Big Sioux, UNION, SD; 5 May 1856, mouth of the Vermillion River, CLAY, SD (Warren in Baird et al. 1860). Somewhat rare along the bottoms of the lower Missouri (Hayden 1863a). Occasional in Nebraska; 5 June 1865, DAKOTA (Aughey 1878) [This is a late date for this migratory species (Sharpe 1993).].

Blue-gray Gnatcatcher. *Polioptila caerulea.*
Common name: blue-gray flycatcher.

Apparent status: This gnatcatcher was rare in the Nebraska region.

On 7 May 1843, NEMAHA/OTOE (Audubon 1960). On 25 April 1856, Bald Island, NEMAHA (Warren in Baird et al. 1860). Quite rare (Hayden 1863a). Found sparingly in eastern Nebraska; 2 June 1865, at Dakota City, and 14 June 1875, DAKOTA; 2 June 1875, LANCASTER (Aughey 1878).

Eastern Bluebird. *Sialia sialis.*
Tribal name: Omaha—*wazhi^n'tu.*
Common names: blue bird, red-breasted blue bird.

Extensive transition zones between prairie and woodlands provided a large amount of breeding habitat. No populations of introduced species, like sparrows or starlings, would have been competing for the tree cavities this species used as nest sites.

Present in the Omaha tribal area [likely Eastern Bluebird], THURSTON (Fletcher and La Flesche 1972). Potential breeder about 1820 in the Engineer Cantonment area (Thwaites 1905). On 29 April 1833, singing bird, ATCHISON, MO; 12 May 1834, northeast DOUGLAS (Maximilian in Orr and Porter 1983). On 7 May 1843, NEMAHA/OTOE; 9 May, SARPY; 17 May, northwest DIXON (Audubon 1960). On 24 April 1856, Bald Island, NEMAHA; 11 May 1855, White River, NE (Vaughn in Baird et al. 1860); mid-1850s, five miles above the mouth of the Platte, SARPY; 3 July 1855, near the Loup Fork of the Platte, PLATTE; 8 July 1855, on the Loup Fork of the Platte, PLATTE (Warren in Baird et al. 1860). Not uncommon across the Northwest; also in the Fort Laramie vicinity (Hayden 1863a). Abundant in Nebraska; 29 May and 6 June 1865, DAKOTA; 15 June 1875, LANCASTER (Aughey 1878). Present ca. 1870, ANTELOPE (Leach 1916, 87).

Mountain Bluebird. *Sialia currucoides.*

Apparent status: This bluebird lived predominantly in Pine Ridge forests and along the central Niobrara River. Its status in the Black Hills reflected its lesser numbers in the Pine Ridge.

> This interesting and beautiful bird was very abundant in the Black Hills. I first noticed it near Short Pine Buttes, where I saw a family of full-grown young. Afterward I saw it in the open woodlands near the Belle Fourche, and on French Creek, not far from Harney's Peak. In the latter locality it was especially common, and each little opening in the woods was occupied by a family. In their habits of feeding they closely resemble the eastern blue-bird, (*S. Sialis.*) There is, however, a noticeable difference in their notes; the call of the *arctica* [mountain bluebird] being shorter than, and not nearly so mellow as, that of its eastern congener. (Ludlow 1875, 85)

Snake River; Hayden noted its abundance from Fort Laramie to the Black Hills (Coues 1874).

Townsend's Solitaire. *Myadestes townsendi.*
Common name: Townsend's flycatching thrush.

Accidental in Nebraska; in August along the Niobrara (Aughey 1878).

Thrush.
Tribal names: Omaha—*taçka'çka;* Dakota Sioux—*wa-ġi'-yo-ġi.*
Present in the Omaha tribal area, northeast Nebraska (Fletcher and La Flesche 1972).

Veery. *Catharus fuscescens.*
Common names: Wilson's thrush, tawny thrush.
Apparent status: The Veery was uncommon along the Missouri River south of the Vermillion.
Mouth of the Vermillion River, DIXON (Warren in Baird et al. 1860). Observed along the wooded bottoms of the lower Missouri; not very abundant (Hayden 1863a). Not higher than the mouth of the Vermillion, CLAY, SD (Hayden in Coues 1874). Occasional in Nebraska, especially in the state's southeastern part; 5 June 1875, RICHARDSON (Aughey 1878).

Gray-cheeked Thrush. *Catharus minimus.*
Apparent status: The Gray-cheeked Thrush was a migrant along the Missouri River.
Two on 8 May 1856, mouth of the Vermillion River, CLAY, SD, and Jacques [James] River, YANKTON, SD (Warren in Baird et al. 1860). Not observed above the mouth of the Niobrara River on the Missouri; most abundant along the wooded bottoms of the lower Missouri (Hayden 1863a).

Swainson's Thrush. *Catharus ustulatus.*
Common name: olive-backed thrush.
On 8 May 1856, opposite the mouth of the Vermillion River, DIXON; Jacques [James] River, YANKTON, SD, and the mouth of the Vermillion, CLAY, SD (Warren in Baird et al. 1860). More abundant and more widely distributed than the Wilson's thrush [Veery]; occasionally observed across the Northwest (Hayden 1863a). Abundant in eastern Nebraska; 15 and 17 June 1865, DAKOTA (Aughey 1878).

Hermit Thrush. *Catharus guttatus.*
One on 6 June 1865, DAKOTA (Aughey 1878) [This is a very late date for this migratory species (Sharpe 1993), so it may have been a misidentification of a Veery.].

Wood Thrush. *Hylocichla mustelina.*

Apparent status: Coues described this thrush as common in wooded bottoms of the Missouri, with fewer numbers north of the Platte. It was more abundant along the Missouri south of Nebraska (Coues 1874).

On 7 May 1843, NEMAHA/OTOE; 17 May, northwest DIXON (Audubon 1960). Quite abundant along the Missouri's wooded bottoms to the mountains (Hayden 1863a). Quite numerous along the wooded river bottoms at least as far as Ft. Pierre, STANLEY, SD (Hayden in Coues 1874). Abundant in eastern Nebraska woodlands; 28 May and 10 June 1865, DAKOTA; 15 October 1865, LANCASTER (Aughey 1878).

American Robin. *Turdus migratorius.*
Tribal names: Omaha—*Pa'thi^n wazhi^{n}ga* (Pawnee bird); Dakota Sioux—*śi-śo'-ka.*

Apparent status: Robins were common summer birds with fewer numbers in the winter. They were abundant during migrations (Coues 1874). Nesting took place mostly in wooded areas in southeast Nebraska, the Pine Ridge, and along rivers and large streams.

Present in the Omaha tribal area (Fletcher and La Flesche 1972). Potential breeder about 1820 in the Engineer Cantonment area (Thwaites 1905). On 12 May 1834, northeast DOUGLAS (Maximilian in Orr and Porter 1983). On 10 May 1843, WASHINGTON; 17 May, northwest DIXON (Audubon 1960). On 20 May, Blackbird Hill, THURSTON (Warren in Baird et al. 1860). On 14 July 1859, in the Ash Hollow area, GARDEN (Suckley in Beidleman 1956). Common and widely distributed in different seasons throughout northwest Nebraska (Hayden 1863a). Not abundant in Nebraska, but slowly increasing; 30 May, 4 June and 6 June 1865, DAKOTA; 9 June 1867, BURT; 15 June 1875 and 14 June 1877, LANCASTER (Aughey 1878). Present ca. 1870, ANTELOPE (Leach 1916, 87).

Family Mimidae

Gray Catbird. *Dumetella carolinensis.*

Apparent status: This species was abundant in shrubby habitat, especially along the Missouri and lower Platte rivers. There were fewer numbers elsewhere where suitable habitat existed.

Potential breeder about 1820 in the Engineer Cantonment area (Thwaites 1905). On 14 May 1834, southeast OTOE/northeast NEMAHA (Maximilian in Orr and Porter 1983). Mid-1850s at White

River, northwest Nebraska (Warren in Baird et al. 1860). Nesting about 25 June 1859, along the Little Blue River in the Fort Kearny area, KEARNEY (Suckley in Beidleman 1956). Abundant throughout the Northwest, from the mouth of the Missouri to the mountains (Hayden 1863a). Abundant in woody portions of Nebraska, especially along streams; 4 June and 6 June 1865, DAKOTA; 9 June 1867, BURT; 15 June 1875 and 14 June 1877, LANCASTER (Aughey 1878). Present ca. 1870, ANTELOPE (Leach 1916, 87).

Northern Mockingbird. *Mimus polyglottos.*
Common name: mountain mockingbird.

Potential breeder about 1820 near Engineer Cantonment (Thwaites 1905). On 11 May 1849, "mocking birds" on the Oregon Trail along the Little Blue River, THAYER/NUCKOLLS? (Decker 1966, 71). Rare in southern Nebraska; pair on 12 June 1875, RICHARDSON (Aughey 1878).

Brown Thrasher. *Toxostoma rufum.*
Common names: rust-red thrush, brown thrush, sandy mockingbird, red thrush.

Apparent status: Brown Thrashers were abundant in shrubby habitat, especially along waterways. They possibly occurred in fewer numbers than catbirds, based on information given by Coues.

Potential breeder about 1820 in the Engineer Cantonment area (Thwaites 1905). On 5 May 1834, Niobrara River area, KNOX; 8 May 1834, opposite the mouth of the Vermillion River, DIXON; 10 May 1834, Blackbird Hill area, THURSTON; 11 May 1834, southeast BURT and northeast WASHINGTON (Maximilian in Orr and Porter 1983). May 1856, Running Water [Niobrara], KNOX; two on 6 August 1857, Loup Forks, PLATTE; 8 June 1857, Missouri River (Warren in Baird et al. 1860). Nesting on 25 June 1859, along the Little Blue River, and 26 June, at Thirty-two Mile Creek in the Kearney area, KEARNEY (Suckley in Beidleman 1956). Distributed throughout the Northwest in greater or lesser numbers (Hayden 1863a). Present ca. 1870, ANTELOPE (Leach 1916, 87). At Fort Randall, TODD, SD; noted generally in the Missouri and Niobrara river areas (Coues 1874). Eggs collected on 7, 12 and 16 June 1874 by H. W. Henshaw at Omaha, DOUGLAS (NMNH specimens 17344, 17345 and 17346). Abundant in Nebraska; spring and summer 1875, RICHARDSON and LANCASTER (Aughey 1878).

Family Motacillidae

American Pipit. *Anthus rubescens.*
Common names: tit lark, pipit, wagtail.
    In the 1860s or 1870s at the Snake River, CHERRY (Coues 1874). A few migrate through eastern Nebraska during late April; two on 20 September and 25 September 1874, LANCASTER (Aughey 1878).

Family Bombycillidae

Bohemian Waxwing. *Bombycilla garrulus.*
    Rare in winter; February 1865 (Aughey 1878).

Cedar Waxwing. *Bombycilla cedrorum.*
Common names: cedar bird, cherry bird, wax-wing.
    On 7 May 1843, southwest corner of NEMAHA at RICHARDSON (Audubon 1960). Abundant everywhere in the Northwest (Hayden 1863a). Flocks sighted a few times; breeding in June 1875, near Nebraska City, OTOE (Aughey 1878).

Family Laniidae

Northern Shrike. *Lanius excubitor.*
Common names: great northern shrike, butcher bird.
    Not uncommon from Council Bluffs to Fort Pierre, especially in winter (Hayden 1863a). Common on the upper Missouri in winter; seen several times [in winter 1872-73?] around Fort Randall, TODD, SD (Coues 1874). "Sparingly" in fall; September 1874 along the Nemaha [RICHARDSON?] (Aughey 1878).

Loggerhead Shrike. *Lanius ludovicianus.*
Common names: white-rumped shrike, western shrike.
    Apparent status: This shrike was a regular resident where nesting habitat was available.
    Two on 16 August 1857, Running Water [Niobrara River] (Warren in Baird et al. 1860); 1 August 1857, north fork of the Platte River; 13 August 1857, forks of the Platte, LINCOLN; 26 August 1857, fifteen miles east of Laramie, GOSHEN, WY (Baird et al. 1860). Quite abundant, especially along the Platte to Fort Laramie, the Black Hills and the Badlands (Hayden 1863a). In winter near Fort Randall, TODD, SD (Coues 1874). Rather abundant; young in 1867 along the Missouri, DAKOTA, and 1869, along the Niobrara [KNOX?]; 17 June 1865,

DAKOTA; 28 September 1864, RICHARDSON; 17 June 1875, LANCASTER (Aughey 1878).

Family Vireonidae

White-eyed Vireo. *Vireo griseus*.

Apparent status: This vireo was limited to forests along the Missouri River.

Potential breeder about 1820 in the Engineer Cantonment area (Thwaites 1905). On 7 May 1843, in southwest NEMAHA at RICHARDSON (Audubon 1960). Nest in 1875 along the Missouri in RICHARDSON (Bruner et al. 1904). Occasional in Nebraska; adults feeding young in spring 1875 along the Nemaha River, RICHARDSON (Aughey 1878).

Bell's Vireo. *Vireo bellii*.

Apparent status: This vireo was more common than the few records indicate. Audubon was familiar with this species, since its description is based on specimens he collected along the eastern Missouri River near St. Joseph (American Ornithologists' Union 1983).

On 17 May 1843, near the Vermillion River, northwest DIXON (Audubon 1960; McDermott 1951). Uncommon in Nebraska; breeds along the Missouri and some of its tributaries (Aughey 1878).

Solitary Vireo. *Vireo solitarius*.
Common names: blue-headed vireo, blue-headed flycatcher, lead-colored vireo.

Apparent status: The Solitary Vireo was an uncommon migrant along the Missouri River and likely the lower Platte.

On 5 and 6 May, mid-1850s, at the mouth of the Vermillion River, DIXON (Warren in Baird et al. 1860). Noted with the Warbling Vireo (Hayden 1863a). In the timber belts of eastern Nebraska, but not abundant; June 1865 (Aughey 1878).

Yellow-throated Vireo. *Vireo flavifrons*.

This vireo was somewhat abundant in southeast Nebraska, but was rare north of the Platte; breeds in RICHARDSON (Aughey 1878).

Warbling Vireo. *Vireo gilvus*.
Common name: warbling flycatcher.

Apparent status: This species appeared along the Missouri River and likely on the lower Platte.

On 7 May 1843, southwest corner of NEMAHA at RICHARDSON (Audubon 1960). On 9 May 1857, Missouri River (Warren in Baird et al. 1860). Abundant along the Missouri's wooded bottoms (Hayden 1863a). Abundant in northeast Nebraska, where it breeds; a great many nests among the cottonwoods, May and June 1865, in Dakota City, DAKOTA (Aughey 1878). Egg collected on 14 June 1874 by W. L. Carpenter at Omaha, DOUGLAS (NMNH specimen 17350).

Philadelphia Vireo. *Vireo philadelphicus.*
Common name: brotherly-love vireo.
Common in eastern Nebraska; breeds; 27 May, 5 and 17 June 1865, DAKOTA; 16 June 1877, LANCASTER (Aughey 1878) [These are definite misidentifications; these are atypical occurrence dates, and there are no documented Nebraska nesting records (Sharpe 1993).].

Red-eyed Vireo. *Vireo olivaceus.*
Apparent status: This species was sometimes a common to abundant breeding bird in flood-plain forests along the Missouri, Platte, lower Niobrara and other large river valleys.
Potential breeder about 1820 in the Engineer Cantonment area (Thwaites 1905). In 1857 at Fremont, Platte River, DODGE (Warren in Coues 1874). Common in the timber belts along the Missouri and its tributaries; breeds abundantly; 1865, DAKOTA; 1875, LANCASTER (Aughey 1878).

Family Emberizidae

Blue-winged Warbler. *Vermivora pinus.*
Common name: blue-winged yellow warbler.
Apparent status: This warbler was an uncommon to rare breeding-season resident along the lower Missouri River.
Potential breeder about 1820 in the Engineer Cantonment area (Thwaites 1905). In June 1875 near the mouth of the Nemaha River, RICHARDSON (Aughey 1878).

Golden-winged Warbler. *Vermivora chrysoptera.*
Common name: blue golden-winged warbler.
Occasional in eastern Nebraska (Aughey 1878).

Tennessee Warbler. *Vermivora peregrina.*
In June 1865 in timber south of Dakota City, DAKOTA (Aughey 1878).

Orange-crowned Warbler. *Vermivora celata.*

Apparent status: The Orange-crowned Warbler was a migrant in Nebraska. The species first was identified scientifically from an 1820 specimen taken by Thomas Say of Long's Expedition at Engineer Cantonment near the Council Bluff (American Ornithologists' Union 1983).

On 4 May 1856, mouth of the Big Sioux River, DAKOTA; May mid-1850s at Bon Homme Island, KNOX (Warren in Baird et al. 1860; Hayden 1863a).

Nashville Warbler. *Vermivora ruficapilla.*

Apparent status: This warbler was a migrant in Nebraska's wooded areas. Aughey's nesting record is extremely hypothetical and similar to a reference to breeding made around 1900 in the same region (Ducey 1988).

Range includes the Missouri River region (Coues 1874). Fledged young seen on 10 June 1865, in eastern Nebraska (Aughey 1878) [This is not a valid nesting record. The nearest nesting record for this species comes from Minnesota, and no other Nebraska nesting records exist (Sharpe 1993).].

Northern Parula. *Parula americana.*
Common name: blue yellow-backed warbler.

Apparent status: This species was common to abundant in moist woodlands along the Missouri, especially south of the Platte.

On 27 April 1856, mouth of the Platte River, CASS (Warren in Baird et al. 1860). Very abundant in May and June along the Missouri's wooded bottoms; most abundant on the lower Missouri below Fort Pierre (Hayden 1863a). On the Missouri at least to the Platte (Coues 1874). Reaches Nebraska about late May (Aughey 1878).

Yellow Warbler. *Dendroica petechia.*
Common names: blue-eyed yellow warbler, golden warbler, summer warbler, summer yellow-bird.

Apparent status: The Yellow Warbler was a common Nebraska summer breeding-season resident and was abundant at times. Willows growing near lakes and marshes provided suitable nesting habitat.

Potential breeder about 1820 in the Engineer Cantonment area (Thwaites 1905). On 2 May 1833, Frazer's Island area, OTOE; 9 May 1833, northeast DIXON; 5 May 1834, Niobrara River area; 7 May 1834, James River and eastern CEDAR; 11 May 1834, southeast BURT and northeast WASHINGTON; 12 May 1834, northeast DOUGLAS; 13 May 1834, Bellevue area, SARPY; 14 May 1834, southeast OTOE/northeast

NEMAHA (Maximilian in Orr and Porter 1983). On 10 May 1843, WASHINGTON (Audubon 1960). On 11 and 17 May 1856, Nebraska; 27 April 1856, mouth of the Platte River, CASS; 29 July, likely 1857, Loup Fork, PLATTE (Warren in Baird et al. 1860). Distributed throughout the valleys of the Missouri and its tributaries; very abundant (Hayden 1863a). Egg collected on 12 June 1874 by W. L. Carpenter at Omaha, DOUGLAS (NMNH specimen 17379). Abundant in Nebraska; three on 5 June 1865, DAKOTA; two on 12 June 1875 and two on 14 June 1877, LANCASTER (Aughey 1878).

Chestnut-sided Warbler. *Dendroica pensylvanica.*
On 26 April, mid-1850s, mouth of the Platte River, CASS (Warren in Baird et al. 1860). Rather common in eastern Nebraska during migration; September 1874 (Aughey 1878).

Magnolia Warbler. *Dendroica magnolia.*
Common name: black and yellow warbler.
Apparent status: The Magnolia Warbler appeared as an abundant migrant, especially along the Missouri River.
On 5 May 1856, mouth of the Vermillion River, DIXON (Warren in Baird et al. 1860). Peculiar to the wooded edges of streams and usually very abundant during May and June (Hayden 1863a). Occasional during migration in northeastern Nebraska; May 1865 near Ponca, DIXON (Aughey 1878).

Black-throated Blue Warbler. *Dendroica caerulescens.*
Apparent status: This warbler migrated through the Nebraska area in the spring and fall.
Spring and fall migrant; one in September 1874 near Lincoln, LANCASTER (Aughey 1878).

Yellow-rumped Warbler. *Dendroica coronata.*
Common name: Audubon's warbler.
On 11 May 1843, WASHINGTON (Audubon 1960). Two on 5 May 1856, mouth of the Vermillion River, DIXON; 3 May 1856, mouth of the Big Sioux, UNION, SD; 20 April 1856, mouth of the Platte River, CASS (Warren in Baird et al. 1860). Probably quite rare on the Missouri (Hayden 1863a). Young birds in eastern Nebraska; one on June 1875 (Aughey 1878).

Black-throated Green Warbler. *Dendroica virens.*

On 5 June, and two on 6 June 1865, DAKOTA; two on 14 June 1875, LANCASTER (Aughey 1878) [These are late migratory dates (Sharpe 1993).].

Blackburnian Warbler. *Dendroica fusca.*

On 12 May 1843, BURT (Audubon 1960). Occasional in eastern Nebraska woodlands (Aughey 1878).

Yellow-throated Warbler. *Dendroica dominica.*

One in September 1874 along the Big Nemaha River, RICHARDSON (Aughey 1878).

Pine Warbler. *Dendroica pinus.*

Migrates through eastern Nebraska in spring; April 1865, DAKOTA; April 1875 and 1877, LANCASTER (Aughey 1878).

Prairie Warbler. *Dendroica discolor.*

Apparent status: This warbler was a migrant, although it was noted as common to abundant. The historic records are not accurate in saying this species nested in Nebraska. The accepted status of this species is casual, based on an evaluation of available records (Bray et al. 1986).

Abundant in eastern Nebraska where it breeds; 1 June 1865, young, DAKOTA; nest in a papaw bush near the Big Nemaha River, RICHARDSON; 5 and 20 September 1874, 2 and 14 June 1875, and two on 4 June 1877, LANCASTER (Aughey 1878; Bruner et al. 1904) [These sightings have been considered hypothetical records (Sharpe 1993), but they may be valid, since they occur within the range of migratory dates.].

Palm Warbler. *Dendroica palmarum.*

Abundant early spring migrants in eastern Nebraska; 10 April 1875 and 1 October 1876 (Aughey 1878).

Bay-breasted Warbler. *Dendroica castanea.*

Occasional in eastern Nebraska; September 1874 (Aughey 1878).

Blackpoll Warbler. *Dendroica striata.*

Apparent status: The Blackpoll was common to abundant along the Missouri River and other forest areas in eastern Nebraska.

Four on 11 and 12 May, mid-1850s, Nebraska; 6 May, mid-1850s, mouth of the Vermillion, DIXON; 10 and 12 May, mid-1850s, Cedar Island, GREGORY, SD (Warren in Baird et al. 1860). Abundant on the wooded bottoms and islands of the lower Missouri below Fort Pierre, STANLEY, SD (Hayden 1863a). West to Nebraska (Coues 1874). Rather common in eastern Nebraska during migration; two on 5 June 1865, DAKOTA; 13 and 14 June 1875, LANCASTER (Aughey 1878).

Cerulean Warbler. *Dendroica cerulea.*

Apparent status: This warbler was a regular migrant and nesting bird.

Potential breeder about 1820 near Engineer Cantonment (Thwaites 1905). Not uncommon along the lower Missouri; said to breed abundantly in the Indian Territory (Coues 1874). Abundant in eastern Nebraska along the wooded river bottoms; six nests in plum bushes; nesting in 1865, Pilgrim Hill, DAKOTA (Aughey 1878; Stephens 1957) [The bird in Aughey's nesting record may have been the Black-throated Blue Warbler, since the Cerulean Warbler nests in the treetops (Sharpe 1993).].

Black-and-white Warbler. *Mniotilta varia.*
Common name: black-and-white creeper.

On 5 May and four on 8 May 1857, mouth of the Vermillion, DIXON; 4 May 1856, mouth of the Big Sioux, DAKOTA; 15 May 1856, Nebraska (Warren in Baird et al. 1860). Very abundant in willows along the Missouri bottoms at least as far north as Fort Pierre (Hayden 1863a). In Nebraska woodlands; nest with young in May, and young collected on 5 June 1875, south of Lincoln, LANCASTER (Aughey 1878).

American Redstart. *Setophaga ruticilla.*

Apparent status: Records indicate this species was common along the Missouri River and the lower reaches of its tributaries. It was an abundant breeding-season resident in some areas.

Potential breeder about 1820 in the Engineer Cantonment area, WASHINGTON (Thwaites 1905). On 11 May 1834, southeast BURT; 12 May 1834, northeast DOUGLAS; 14 May 1834, southeast OTOE/ northeast NEMAHA (Maximilian in Orr and Porter 1983). Nebraska; mouth of the Big Sioux River, DAKOTA; 26 April, mid-1850s, mouth of the Platte, CASS; mouth of the Big Sioux, UNION, SD (Warren in Baird et al. 1860). Not uncommon in woods along the Missouri River bottoms and its tributaries, though most abundant on the lower Missouri (Hayden 1863a). Common in the timbered river bottoms;

breeding extensively; 30 May, 3 and 11 June 1865, DAKOTA; 5, 10, 15 and 17 June 1875, LANCASTER (Aughey 1878).

Prothonotary Warbler. *Protonotaria citrea.*

This warbler may have occurred as a breeding bird in the floodplain swamps along the Missouri River in southeast Nebraska, probably mostly south of Nebraska City.

Only reaches the lower Missouri River (Coues 1874). Seen only a few times in southeastern Nebraska; June 1875, RICHARDSON (Aughey 1878).

Worm-eating Warbler. *Helmitheros vermivorus.*

In June 1875 in the southeastern part of the state (Aughey 1878).

Ovenbird. *Seiurus aurocapillus.*
Common names: golden-crowned thrush, orange-crowned accentor.

Apparent status: The Ovenbird was a summer resident in the wooded bottoms of Nebraska's larger rivers. It was especially common along the Missouri, lower Platte and lower Niobrara rivers.

Potential breeder about 1820 near Engineer Cantonment (Thwaites 1905). On 2 May 1833, Frazer's Island area, OTOE (Maximilian in Orr and Porter 1983). Three on 6 and 11 May, mid-1850s, Vermillion River, CLAY, SD; 8 May, mid-1850s, James River, YANKTON, SD; two on 27 April, likely 1856, mouth of the Platte, CASS; 25 April 1856, Bald Island, NEMAHA (Warren in Baird et al. 1860). A common, quiet bird, under thick bushes or trees along the Missouri below Fort Pierre (Hayden 1863a). Once rather abundant in timbered areas of eastern Nebraska, then less frequent; breeds; 20 and 22 April and 3 June 1865, DAKOTA; 13 June 1875, 12 April and 10 June 1877, LANCASTER (Aughey 1878).

Northern Waterthrush. *Seiurus noveboracensis.*
Common name: water thrush.

Apparent status: This was an uncommon species in moist, lowland forests along the Missouri River. If this species nested in Nebraska, it probably was an accidental occurrence.

Potential breeder about 1820 in the Engineer Cantonment area (Thwaites 1905). On 7 May 1843, NEMAHA/OTOE (Audubon 1960). Vermillion River, CLAY, SD; mouth of the Vermillion River, DIXON (Warren in Baird et al. 1860). Less abundant than the Ovenbird, and sighted near the mouth of the Vermillion River (Hayden 1863a).

Occasional in northeast Nebraska; young in June 1865 near Ponca, DIXON (Aughey 1878).

Louisiana Waterthrush. *Seiurus motacilla.*
Seen only in southeast Nebraska; June 1875 along the Big Nemaha River, RICHARDSON (Aughey 1878).

Kentucky Warbler. *Oporornis formosus.*
Rather common in southeast Nebraska, especially in the Missouri River bottoms and along the Nemaha; breeds; June 1875 along the Big Nemaha River, RICHARDSON (Aughey 1878).

Mourning Warbler. *Oporornis philadelphia.*
On 7 May 1843, NEMAHA/RICHARDSON (Audubon 1960). Found in eastern Nebraska; adults feeding young seen in the southeast (Aughey 1878) [This is the only Nebraska record for a species typical of Minnesota (Sharpe 1993).]. Along the Missouri River and in the Fort Laramie area (Coues 1874).

MacGillivray's Warbler. *Oporornis tolmiei.*
One of the nearest records for the region was 31 August 1857, at Fort Laramie (Magraw in Baird et al. 1860). Occurs in the Missouri region (Coues 1874). Seen August 1874 along the "river" in western Nebraska (Aughey 1878).

Common Yellowthroat. *Geothlypis trichas.*
Common name: Maryland yellow-throat.
Apparent status: The yellowthroat probably occurred throughout Nebraska. Wetlands, with their emergent plants, provided habitat for a large number of this species. The willow thickets of the Missouri also provided prime habitat.
On 14 May 1834, northeast OTOE; 14 May 1834, southeast OTOE/northeast NEMAHA; 15 May 1834, southeast NEMAHA; 15 May 1834, northeast RICHARDSON (Maximilian in Orr and Porter 1983). On 12 and 15 May 1857, Nebraska; four on 3 and 6 August, mid-1850s, Loup Fork, PLATTE (Warren in Baird et al. 1860). A very abundant bird, inhabiting the thick willow bottoms of streams along the entire length of the Missouri (Hayden 1863a). Common and breeds; young in June 1875 south of Dakota City, DAKOTA, and near Lincoln, LANCASTER (Aughey 1878).

Hooded Warbler. *Wilsonia citrina.*

Occurs in southeastern Nebraska; September 1874 along the Nemaha River, RICHARDSON (Aughey 1878).

Wilson's Warbler. *Wilsonia pusilla.*

Uncommon in eastern and western Nebraska; August 1874 along the Republican River in southwest Nebraska (Aughey 1878).

Canada Warbler. *Wilsonia canadensis.*

During migration in eastern Nebraska; mid-May 1875 near the Big Nemaha River, RICHARDSON (Aughey 1878).

Yellow-breasted Chat. *Icteria virens.*
Common name: long-tailed chat.

Apparent status: Several records for this species along the Missouri River indicate the availability of the shrub habitat used for breeding. The dynamic habitats along the untamed Missouri provided a large amount of suitable habitat. This bird also could have been expected on the lower reaches of tributary rivers.

Potential breeder about 1820 near Engineer Cantonment (Thwaites 1905). On 11 May 1834, southeast BURT and northeast WASHINGTON; 13 May 1834, northeast DOUGLAS; 13 May 1834, southeast CASS; 14 May 1834, southeast OTOE/northeast NEMAHA; 15 May 1834, southeast NEMAHA; 15 May 1834, northeast RICHARDSON (Maximilian in Orr and Porter 1983). On 21 May 1843, abundant, northwest KNOX (Audubon 1960). On 16 July 1857, Nemaha River, Kansas Territory (Magraw in Baird et al. 1860); 17 May 1856, Nebraska; two on 5 August 1856, Loup Fork, PLATTE; 13 August 1857, forks of the Platte River, LINCOLN (Warren in Baird et al. 1860); 21 August 1856, Platte River (Bryan in Baird et al. 1860). Collected in 1857 along the Nemaha River, RICHARDSON (Swenk 1940). Very abundant among low bushes on the Missouri River bottom (Hayden 1863a). Very abundant in suitable places in most of the Missouri region (Coues 1874). Found in most of Nebraska; breeds in the east; September 1874 and 1876 (Aughey 1878).

Summer Tanager. *Piranga rubra.*
Common name: summer redbird.

Seen only in southeast Nebraska (Aughey 1878).

Scarlet Tanager. *Piranga olivacea.*

Apparent status: This tanager occurred along the Missouri and was most likely a regular breeder from near Fort Atkinson south, where it was more common.

Potential breeder about 1820 in the Engineer Cantonment area (Thwaites 1905). On 6 May 1833, east-central BURT (Maximilian in Orr and Porter 1983). Seen only in southeast Nebraska, in NEMAHA and RICHARDSON; autumn 1874; most abundant along the Nemaha, where it was breeding in 1875 (Aughey 1878).

Western Tanager. *Piranga ludoviciana.*
Common name: Louisiana tanager.

Apparent status: The Western Tanager was present in the pine forests along the central Niobrara and in the Pine Ridge and Wildcat Hills. The record by Hayden was the easternmost known record at the time (Coues 1874).

On 18 June 1860, at the Snake River, CHERRY (Hayden in Coues 1874).

Northern Cardinal. *Cardinalis cardinalis.*
Common names: red bird, cardinal grosbeak, Virginian redbird.

Apparent status: Cardinals appeared mostly in woodlands along the Missouri River below the Platte and regularly nested from the mouth of the Platte River to a short distance northward. Birds also were found along the lower Platte and other woodland areas in southeast Nebraska. They were present occasionally along the Missouri north of Nebraska.

Potential breeder about 1820 near Engineer Cantonment (Thwaites 1905). On 15 May 1834, northeast RICHARDSON (Maximilian in Orr and Porter 1983). On 23 April 1856, Iowa Point, DONIPHAN, KS; does not occur above Fort Pierre, SD, on the Missouri (Hayden 1863a). Abundant in southeast Nebraska, where it breeds; August 1874, HARLAN; three in September 1874, RICHARDSON (Aughey 1878).

Rose-breasted Grosbeak. *Pheucticus ludovicianus.*
Common name: red-breasted grosbeak.

Apparent status: This grosbeak nested along the Missouri, lower Platte and Niobrara rivers. It was most abundant along the Missouri, especially in the more extensive woodlands south of the Platte.

Potential breeder about 1820 in the Engineer Cantonment area (Thwaites 1905). On 13 May 1834, northeast DOUGLAS; 13 May 1834, Bellevue area; 14 May 1834, northeast OTOE (Maximilian in Orr and

Porter 1983). On 9 May 1843, SARPY (Audubon 1960). On 8 September 1856, Vermillion River; 10 May 1856, Ponca Island, KNOX; 12 May 1856, Running Water [Niobrara River] (Warren in Baird et al. 1860). Abundant along the wooded bottoms of the Missouri (Hayden 1863a). Rather abundant in northern Nebraska; two in June 1865 (Aughey 1878).

Black-headed Grosbeak. *Pheucticus melanocephalus.*

Along the Republican River in southwest Nebraska; two specimens in June 1875 from Kearney Junction, BUFFALO (Aughey 1878).

Blue Grosbeak. *Guiraca caerulea.*

Apparent status: This bird was uncommon in eastern Nebraska.

On 24 May 1843, Fort Randall Military Reservation, TODD, SD (Audubon 1960). Three on 4 and 5 August 1857, Loup Fork of the Platte River, PLATTE (Warren in Baird et al. 1860). Only seen at the Loup Fork of the Platte (Hayden 1863a). Occasional; specimen in September 1873 from Grand Island, HALL (Aughey 1878).

Lazuli Bunting. *Passerina amoena.*
Common name: lazuli finch.

Apparent status: This bird was a common to abundant summer resident where suitable woody habitat was available in the West.

On 24 May 1843, Fort Randall Military Reservation, TODD, SD (Harris in McDermott 1951). Quite abundant in wooded areas of the western Missouri River region (Hayden 1863a).

Indigo Bunting. *Passerina cyanea.*
Common name: indigo-bird.

Apparent status: This species was limited to the state's Missouri valley area.

On 7 May 1843, NEMAHA/OTOE (Audubon 1960). Ranged along the lower Missouri River (Coues 1874). Rare; specimen in June 1875 from Beatrice, GAGE; specimen in 1875 from Columbus, PLATTE (Aughey 1878).

Dickcissel. *Spiza americana.*
Common name: black-throated bunting.

Apparent status: The Dickcissel probably occurred to some extent throughout Nebraska prior to 1875, where it was common to abundant. Records from several localities indicate its range was mostly eastern Nebraska.

Potential breeder about 1820 near Engineer Cantonment (Thwaites 1905). Nine on 1, 3, 10, 24 and 29 July and 3 and 30 August, likely 1856, Loup Fork of the Platte, PLATTE; four on 30 June, likely 1856, Elkhorn River; 1 July, mid-1850s, Fremont on the Platte, DODGE (Warren in Baird et al. 1860); 19 July, mid-1850s, Platte River (Bryan in Baird et al. 1860). Common on 17 June 1859, near the headwaters of the south fork of the Nemaha River, NEMAHA, KS; common and nesting on northwestern Kansas prairies (Suckley in Beidleman 1956). Very abundant along the Missouri River and its tributaries (Hayden 1863a). Egg collected on 13 June 1874 by W. L. Carpenter at Omaha, DOUGLAS (NMNH specimen 17338). Common in eastern Nebraska; found west to the state line; two in September 1874, in both HARLAN and RICHARDSON; September 1875, LANCASTER (Aughey 1878).

Rufous-sided Towhee. *Pipilo erythrophthalmus.*
Common names: ground robin, marsh robin, towhee bunting, chewink, Arctic spotted towhee.

Apparent status: This towhee occurred predominantly in the wooded areas of large rivers and was abundant in some localities.

Potential breeder about 1820 in the Engineer Cantonment area (Thwaites 1905). On 28 April 1833, Good Sun [Sonora] Island area, northeast NEMAHA; 1 and 2 May 1833, common, Frazer's Island area, OTOE; 5 May 1834, Niobrara River area, KNOX; 7 May 1834, James River and eastern CEDAR; 10 May 1834, Blackbird Hill area; 11 May 1834, northeast WASHINGTON; 12 May 1834, northeast DOUGLAS; 13 May 1834, Bellevue area (Maximilian in Orr and Porter 1983). On 20 May 1843, near Vermillion River, northwest DIXON; 21 May, abundant, northwest KNOX (Audubon 1960). Present in May 1843, northwest CEDAR (Harris in McDermott 1951). Five on 24 and 25 April 1856, Bald Island, Missouri River, NEMAHA; 23 April 1856, Iowa Point, DONIPHAN, KS; four on 9 May, likely 1856, Bon Homme Island, KNOX; 11 May, likely 1856, the Tower, BOYD (Warren in Baird et al. 1860). Nest with eggs and one collected on 12 June 1859, twenty-two miles northwest of Fort Leavenworth, ATCHISON, KS (Suckley in Beidleman 1956). Quite abundant on the wooded bottoms of the Missouri until about latitude $43°$; near the mouth of the Niobrara, the arctic towhee begins to be seen in great numbers (Hayden 1863a). Abundant migrant; a few breed; four specimens in May and June 1865 (Aughey 1878). Egg collected on 4 June 1874 by W. L. Carpenter at Omaha, DOUGLAS (NMNH specimen 17378).

American Tree Sparrow. *Spizella arborea.*
Common name: Canadian sparrow.
   Apparent status: This sparrow was an abundant species in the winter.
   Not rare along the Missouri or other areas of the West (Hayden 1863a). On 15 October 1856, Cedar Island, GREGORY, SD (Warren in Baird et al. 1860); 2 August 1856, Pole Creek, Kansas Territory [Lodgepole Creek, NE] (Bryan in Baird et al. 1860). Abundant in river-bottom undergrowth at Fort Randall in October; they remain during the winter, TODD, SD (Coues 1874). Abundant; a few breed here in summer; June 1877 near Lincoln, LANCASTER (Aughey 1878) [This species has never nested within hundreds of miles of Nebraska (Ducey 1988).].

Chipping Sparrow. *Spizella passerina.*
Common name: western chippy.
   Apparent status: The Chipping Sparrow was a regular summer nesting bird where suitable habitat was present, and it was prevalent in the western pine forests.
   Potential breeder about 1820 near Engineer Cantonment (Thwaites 1905). On 10 May 1843, WASHINGTON (Audubon 1960). On 25 April 1856, Bald Island, NEMAHA (Warren in Baird et al. 1860); August 1856, Pole Creek, Kansas Territory [Lodgepole Creek, NE] (Bryan in Baird et al. 1860). Quite common throughout the Northwest (Hayden 1863a). Very abundant in portions of Nebraska; sighted in 1866, DAKOTA (Aughey 1878).

Clay-colored Sparrow. *Spizella pallida.*
Common name: clay-colored bunting.
   Apparent status: This sparrow was uncommon on the state's prairies.
   On 9 May 1843, at Bellevue, SARPY; 17 and 18 May, near the Vermillion River, northwest DIXON (Audubon 1960). Not rare throughout the northwestern prairies (Hayden 1863a). On 14 May 1857, Nebraska (Warren in Baird et al. 1860); 1 August 1856, Pole Creek, Kansas Territory [Lodgepole Creek, NE] (Bryan in Baird et al. 1860). Abundant in parts of Nebraska, spring and fall; two on 27

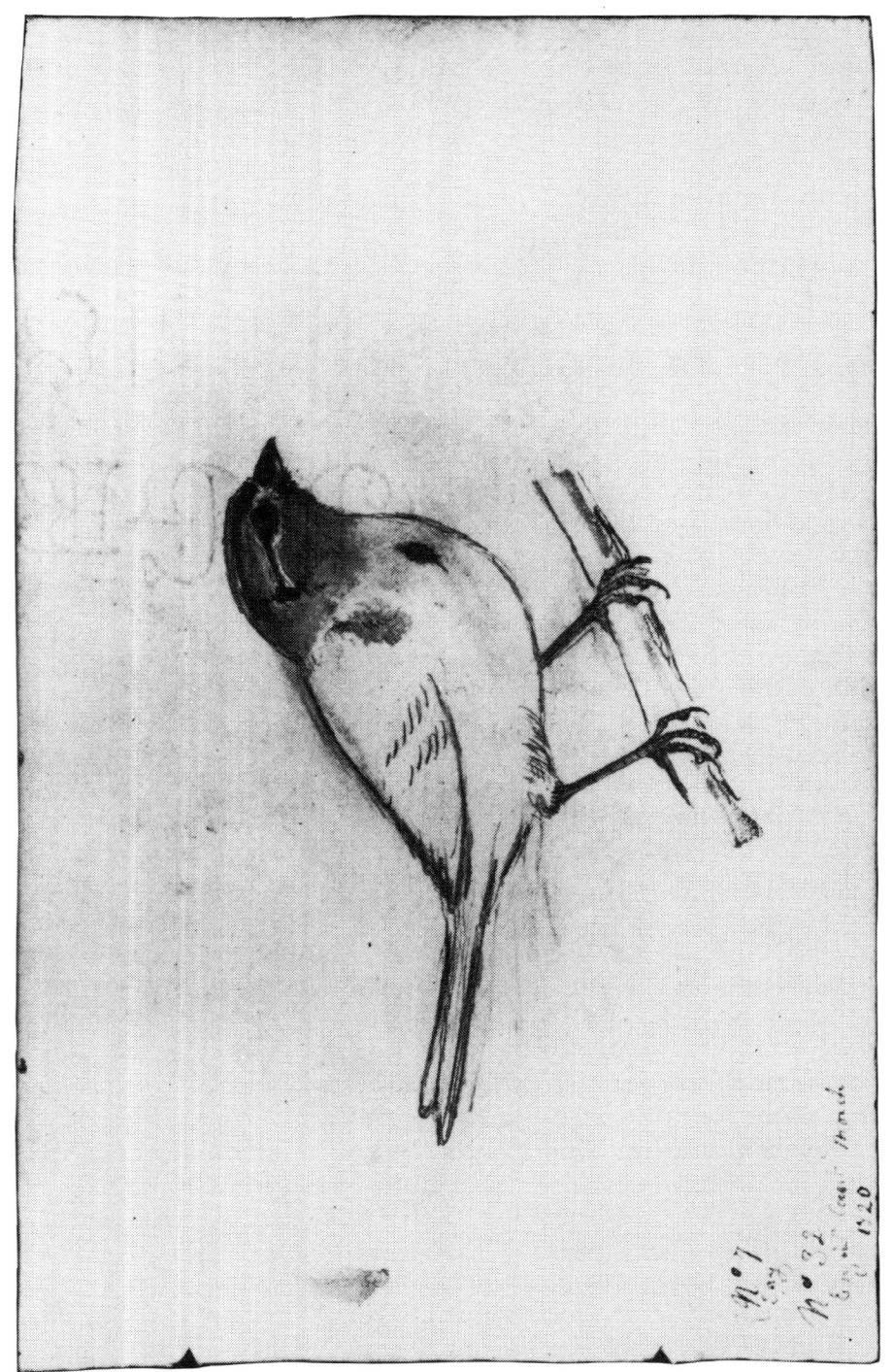

Sparrow at Engineer Cantonment, by Titian Ramsay Peale

May 1865, DAKOTA; 12 October 1874, RICHARDSON; 20 May 1875, 16 May 1877, LANCASTER (Aughey 1878).

Field Sparrow. *Spizella pusilla.*

Apparent status: This species was more common than the few records indicate, based on the status given by Hayden.

On 10 May 1843, WASHINGTON (Audubon 1960). On 3 and 24 May 1856, Big Sioux River, UNION, SD (Warren in Baird et al. 1860). Quite common throughout the Northwest (Hayden 1863a).

Vesper Sparrow. *Pooecetes gramineus.*
Common names: bay-winged bunting, grass finch.

Apparent status: The Vesper Sparrow was an abundant nesting species on the state's prairie lands.

Two on 4 August 1856, Pole Creek, Kansas Territory [Lodgepole Creek, NE] (Bryan in Baird et al. 1860); three on 29 July 1857; Loup Fork of the Platte, PLATTE; 17 June 1860, Snake River, CHERRY (Warren in Baird et al. 1860). Abundant on 15 July 1859, along the North Platte River east of Ash Hollow, GARDEN or KEITH (Suckley in Beidleman 1956). Abundant on the broad upland prairies of far western Nebraska (Hayden 1863a). Abundant in the Missouri River region (Coues 1874). Abundant in certain localities; two on August 1874, HARLAN; September 1874, 1 and 13 June 1875, LANCASTER (Aughey 1878).

Lark Sparrow. *Chondestes grammacus.*
Common name: lark finch.

Apparent status: The Lark Sparrow was an abundant nesting species on the state's grasslands.

On 23 and 24 May 1843, Fort Randall Military Reservation, TODD, SD (Audubon 1960; McDermott 1951). On 14 May, mid-1850s, Big Sioux River, UNION, SD; 1 July, mid-1850s, Fremont on the Platte, DODGE; 27 and 28 July, nine on 30 July, 4 and 5 August 1857, Loup Fork, PLATTE; 19 August 1857, western Sand Hills [CHERRY?] (Warren in Baird et al. 1860); 19 July 1856, Platte River (Bryan in Baird et al. 1860). Occurs in great numbers throughout the Northwest prairie country (Hayden 1863a). One of the most abundant characteristic birds of the prairie regions of the West (Coues 1874). Abundant in northeast Nebraska, where it breeds; 25 May and two on 1 June 1865, DAKOTA; two on September 1874 and September 1876, LANCASTER (Aughey 1878). Eggs collected on 12 and 22 June 1874 by W. L. Carpenter at Omaha, DOUGLAS (NMNH specimen 28417).

Lark Bunting. *Calamospiza melanocorys.*
Tribal name: Dakota Sioux—*wa'-mdo-ska.*
Common names: white-winged blackbird, prairie lark finch.

Apparent status: This bunting was prevalent on the open prairies of western Nebraska and was abundant in some places. The first identification of this species is based on specimens taken near the forks of the Platte River in 1834 by John Kirk Townsend (American Ornithologists' Union 1983).

On 25 August 1804, possibly the species seen at Spirit Mound, CLAY, SD (Lewis and Clark in Swenk 1935). Present on the plains of the Platte; ca. 18 May 1834, in the Ash Hollow area, GARDEN (Townsend 1837). On 13 May 1843, Blackbird Hill, THURSTON; 17 May, the Vermillion River area, northwest DIXON (Audubon 1960; McDermott 1951). Two on 19 July, mid-1850s, Platte River; 19 July, mid-1850s, south fork of the Platte River; 25 July, Pole Creek [Lodgepole Creek, NE] (Bryan in Baird et al. 1860); three on 1, 6 and 17 August, mid-1850s, Loup Fork of Platte River, PLATTE (Warren in Baird et al. 1860); 13 August 1857, at the Loup Fork of the Platte River, LINCOLN; 20 August 1857, north fork of the Platte (Magraw in Baird et al. 1860). Peculiar to the western Plains; quite abundant in the Northwest (Hayden 1863a). Rather abundant in southern Nebraska, where it breeds; June 1875 (Aughey 1878).

Savannah Sparrow. *Passerculus sandwichensis.*

Apparent status: This sparrow was an abundant migrant in the region.

On 9 May 1843, at Bellevue, SARPY (Audubon 1960). On 3 May 1856, mouth of Big Sioux River, DAKOTA; 8 May 1856, Vermillion River, DIXON; Loup Fork of the Platte, PLATTE (Warren in Baird et al. 1860); 19 August 1857, north fork of the Platte (Magraw in Baird et al. 1860). Very abundant on the western prairies (Hayden 1863a). Extremely abundant in the Missouri region, especially during migration; breeds in the northern portions of the territory (Coues 1874).

Grasshopper Sparrow. *Ammodramus savannarum.*
Common name: yellow-winged sparrow.

Apparent status: This little sparrow was a common dweller on the prairies of historic Nebraska. It was more abundant where grass cover was available for nesting; areas heavily grazed by bison or with little grass growth provided less nest cover.

Eleven on 3, 21, 24, 27 and 28 July 1857, 3 August, Loup Fork, PLATTE (Warren in Baird et al. 1860). Nesting on 25 June 1859, on the ground among grass along Little Blue River in southeast Nebraska,

*Grasshopper Sparrow,
by John James Audubon*

JEFFERSON? (Suckley in Beidleman 1956). Abundant along the Platte River valley; twelve specimens taken along the Loup Fork (Hayden 1863a). Very abundant along the Platte, based on specimens collected by Hayden (Coues 1874). Abundant and breeds; June 1875 and 1877 (Aughey 1878).

Henslow's Sparrow. *Ammodramus henslowii.*
Common name: Henslow's bunting.
  Hayden considered the species rare (Hayden 1863a). The Loup Fork record was the westernmost known record at the time (Coues 1874).
  On 9 May 1843, at Bellevue, SARPY; 17 May, northwest DIXON (Audubon 1960). On 10 June 1857, Loup Fork of the Platte, PLATTE (Warren in Baird et al. 1860). One specimen obtained in 1857 in the Platte valley (Hayden 1863a). Specimen received in September 1874 from Kearney Junction, BUFFALO (Aughey 1878).

Fox Sparrow. *Passerella iliaca.*
  Specimen taken on the Platte River (Coues 1874).

Song Sparrow. *Melospiza melodia.*
  Apparent status: This sparrow was a less common, although regular, summer resident.
  Potential breeder about 1820 near Engineer Cantonment (Thwaites 1905). On 10 May 1834, Blackbird Hill area, THURSTON (Maximilian in Orr and Porter 1983). On 25 April 1856, Bald Island, OTOE; 11 September 1857, Loup Fork of the Platte, PLATTE (Warren in Baird et al. 1860). Not abundant in the Northwest (Hayden 1863a). Common in certain localities; two in June 1865 at Dakota City, DAKOTA (Aughey 1878). Present ca. 1870, ANTELOPE (Leach 1916, 87).

Lincoln's Sparrow. *Melospiza lincolnii.*
Common name: Lincoln's finch.
  Apparent status: This species was an abundant migrant. Audubon named this species in 1834 and was especially familiar with it (American Ornithologists' Union 1983).
  On 13 May 1843, Blackbird Hill, THURSTON; 17 May, near the Vermillion River, northwest DIXON (Audubon 1960). On 25 April 1856, Bald Island, NEMAHA; 26 April 1856, Platte River; 5 April 1856, Big Sioux River, UNION, SD; four on 8 April, 6 and 8 May, likely 1856, Vermillion River, CLAY, SD (Warren in Baird et al. 1860). Abundant throughout the Northwest (Hayden 1863a). Numerous during migrations

in Dakota Territory, arriving in September; common in spring and fall in Iowa (Coues 1874). Abundant spring and fall migrant; most seen in late September and October; September 1874, LANCASTER (Aughey 1878).

Swamp Sparrow. *Melospiza georgiana.*

Seen, likely in 1856, at the Vermillion River, CLAY, SD (Warren in Baird et al. 1860). Quite rare; probably confined to the lower Missouri (Hayden 1863a).

White-throated Sparrow. *Zonotrichia albicollis.*

Apparent status: This sparrow was an abundant seasonal migrant.

On 7 May 1834 [based on the description of the bird seen], James River and eastern CEDAR (Maximilian in Orr and Porter 1983). Two on 23 April 1856, Big Nemaha River, RICHARDSON; 1 May 1856, Wood's Bluff, BURT?; two on 2 May 1856, Blackbird Hill, THURSTON; 3 May 1856, Big Sioux River, DAKOTA; five on 8 May 1856, Vermillion River and Big Sioux River; 14 October, Cedar Island, GREGORY, SD; 6 September 1856, White Earth River [White River] (Warren in Baird et al. 1860). Very abundant throughout the Northwest (Hayden 1863a). The specimen collected by Hayden represented the westernmost known limit of its range (Coues 1874). Abundant in spring and fall during migration; two on 27 May 1865, DAKOTA; 12 October 1874, RICHARDSON; 20 May 1875 and 16 May 1877, LANCASTER (Aughey 1878).

White-crowned Sparrow. *Zonotrichia leucophrys.*
Common names: Ridgway's sparrow, white-crowned finch.

Apparent status: The White-crowned Sparrow was an abundant seasonal migrant.

On 10 May 1834 [white-crowned finch], Blackbird Hill area, THURSTON (Maximilian in Orr and Porter 1983). On 8 May 1856, Vermillion River, CLAY, SD; 28 July 1856, Pole Creek [Lodgepole Creek, NE]; 20 September 1856, Republican River, NE (Bryan in Baird et al. 1860). Very abundant throughout the prairies of the Northwest (Hayden 1863a). Occasional; young in June 1875 along the Missouri River, DIXON; breeding rare; specimen in September 1874 from Blair, WASHINGTON (Aughey 1878) [This species does not and never has nested in Nebraska (Ducey 1988).].

Harris' Sparrow. *Zonotrichia querula.*
Common name: Harris' finch.

Apparent status: This sparrow was a common seasonal migrant and winter visitor.

On 7 May 1843, NEMAHA/OTOE; 8 May, OTOE/CASS; 10 May, WASHINGTON; 16 and 17 May, near the Vermillion River, northwest DIXON; 7 October, near the Nishnabotna River, RICHARDSON (Audubon 1960; McDermott 1951). On 24 April 1856, Bald Island, NEMAHA (Warren in Baird et al. 1860). Not as abundant as the White-crowned Sparrow; confined to the borders of the lower Missouri (Hayden 1863a). A characteristic bird of the Missouri River basin; numerous in October at Fort Randall; a few remain during the winter (Coues 1874). Common along the Missouri River; young in northeastern Nebraska; September 1874 (Aughey 1878) [This species nests on the Arctic tundra, not in Nebraska (Ducey 1988).].

Dark-eyed Junco. *Junco hyemalis.*
Tribal name: Sioux—*pa-ća-shi'-wa-ta* (short bill).
Common names: eastern snow-bird, snow bird, white-winged snowbird.

Apparent status: The junco possibly nested in the western forests of the Pine Ridge and less often, if not just occasionally, along the Missouri, where it was a migrant.

On 8 May 1834, opposite the mouth of the Vermillion River, DIXON [The entry also claimed birds nested, though that is hypothetical.] (Maximilian in Orr and Porter 1983). On 6 May 1856, Vermillion River, CLAY, SD (Baird et al. 1860). Not uncommon throughout the Northwest (Hayden 1863a). Mostly in spring migrations; a few during the whole year; February and May 1875 (Aughey 1878).

McCown's Longspur. *Calcarius mccownii.*
Common names: Maccown's bunting, chestnut-shouldered longspur.

Apparent status: As a nesting bird, it would have been uncommon to occasional on the western Plains, but migrants were seen elsewhere in the state.

On 19 October 1857, forty miles west of Fort Kearny, DAWSON? (Magraw in Baird et al. 1860). Noted near Fort Laramie (Coues 1874). A few in Nebraska; August 1874 near Orleans along the Republican River, HARLAN (Aughey 1878). Four specimens collected on 18 September 1878, by George Grinnell at the Dismal River, likely HOOKER/GRANT (CABM specimens B555, B556, B557 and B558).

Lapland Longspur. *Calcarius lapponicus.*
 On 5 November 1874 (Aughey 1878).

Chestnut-collared Longspur. *Calcarius ornatus.*
Common names: chestnut-collared bunting, black-bellied longspur, chestnut-collared lark or ground-finch, black-shouldered longspur, chestnut-collared lark bunting.
 Apparent status: As nesting birds, they would have been common to occasional, with nesting reaching the eastern half of the state. The first identification of this species is based on specimens taken near the forks of the Platte River in 1834 by John Kirk Townsend (American Ornithologists' Union 1983).
 Not uncommon on the prairies along the Platte; mid-May 1834 near the forks of the Platte, LINCOLN (Townsend 1837). On 16 May 1843, northwest DIXON (Audubon 1960). On 14 April 1857, Running Water [Niobrara River] (Baird et al. 1860). Peculiar to the prairies of the upper Missouri, where it is quite abundant (Hayden 1863a). Breeds abundantly in Dakota Territory; abundant and characteristic of the Missouri area (Coues 1874). Abundant and breeds; young in June, July and August; 27 May 1865, DIXON; two on 30 May and 10 June 1865, and two on 14 June 1875, DAKOTA (Aughey 1878).

Snow Bunting. *Plectrophenax nivalis.*
Common name: snowflake.
 Apparent status: This bunting was an abundant winter visitor in some areas of Nebraska and extremely abundant at some Missouri River localities.
 Reached Fort Randall, TODD, SD, on 15 November [1872] and were abundant until leaving early in March, although a few birds remained through April [1873] (Coues 1874). Common and abundant in winter; three in February 1865, DAKOTA and DIXON; November 1874, February 1875 and February 1877, LANCASTER (Aughey 1878).

Blackbird.
Tribal names: Omaha—*mo^{n}gthi'xta;* Pawnee—*li-kū't-ska-ti;* Dakota Sioux—*wa-hpa'-ho-ta, wa-hpa'-taŋ-ka* and *zi-tka'-taŋ-ka.*
 Present in the Omaha tribal area (Fletcher and La Flesche 1972). On 8 May 1849, along the Oregon Trail near the KS/NE state line, JEFFERSON (Decker 1966); 11 May 1849, on the Oregon Trail along the Little Blue River, THAYER/NUCKOLLS? (Decker 1966, 71); 28 May 1849, about twenty-five miles east of Chimney Rock, MORRILL (Decker 1966, 82).

*Chestnut-collared Lark-Bunting [Longspur]
(second from top), by John James Audubon*

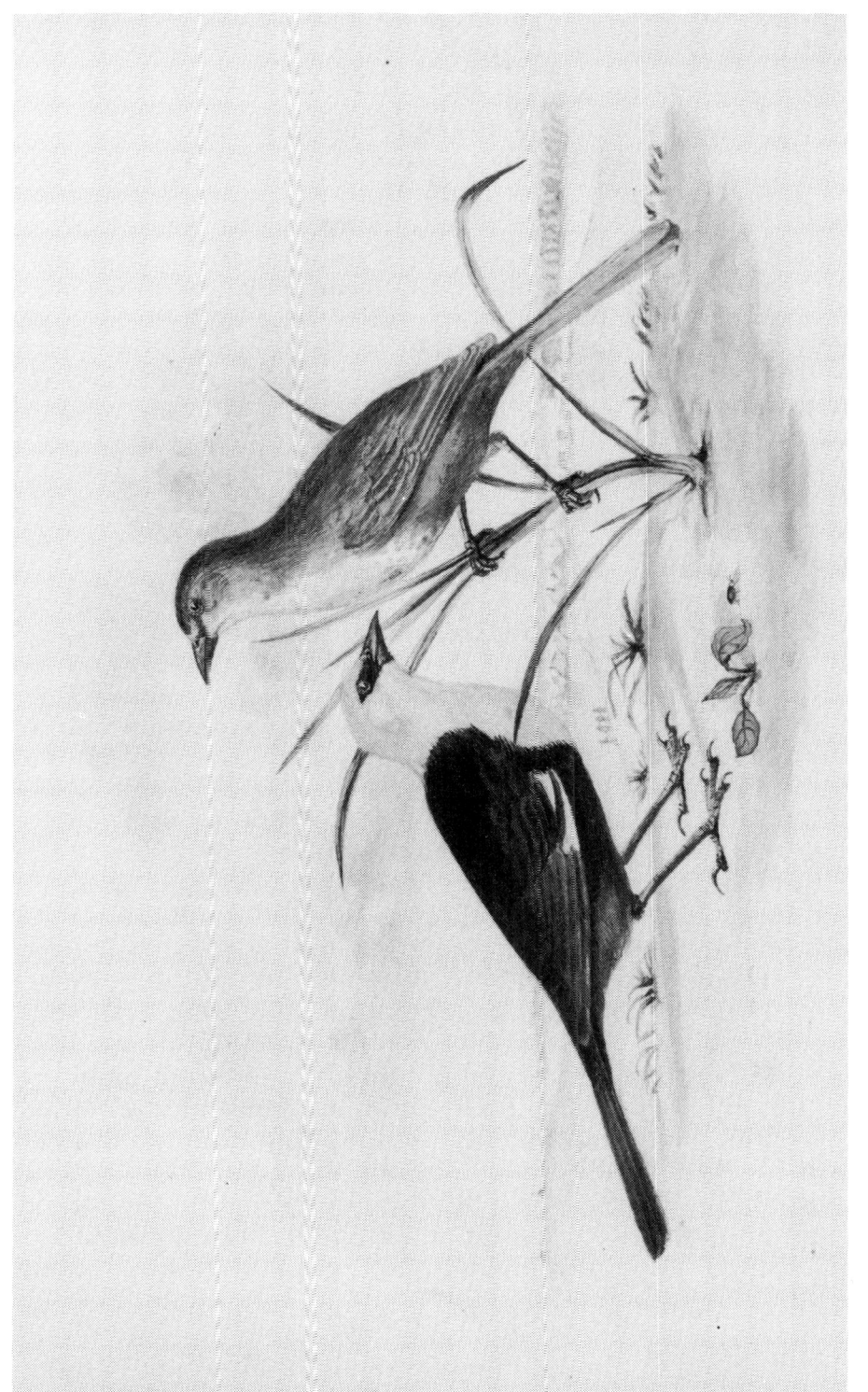

Blackbird, by Titian Ramsay Peale

Bobolink. *Dolichonyx oryzivorus.*
Common names: reed-bird, rice-bird.

Apparent status: The Bobolink was an abundant to common summer resident in wetland meadows along the Missouri, Platte and other Nebraska rivers. The Sand Hills and other locations also provided extensive breeding habitat. Large flocks occurred during migration.

Potential breeder about 1820 near Engineer Cantonment (Thwaites 1905). On 11 and 20 July 1857, Loup Fork of the Platte, PLATTE (Warren in Baird et al. 1860); on 20 August 1856, fifty miles east of Ft. Laramie [SCOTTS BLUFF?] (Magraw in Baird et al. 1860). Large flocks of birds in breeding areas (Coues 1874). Very abundant, breeds; 30 May, 5 and 15 June 1866, DAKOTA; 30 May and two on 12 June 1875, LANCASTER (Aughey 1878). Present ca. 1870, ANTELOPE (Leach 1916, 87).

Red-winged Blackbird. *Agelaius phoeniceus.*
Tribal name: Dakota Sioux—*wa'-mdo-śa.*
Common names: red-shouldered troupial, swamp blackbird, red-winged starling.

Apparent status: This blackbird was a common summer resident in marshy areas across Nebraska. Large flocks were observed during migration and at winter roosts.

On 25 August 1804, Vermillion River area, northwest DIXON (Lewis and Clark in Moulton 1987). Potential breeder about 1820 in the Engineer Cantonment area (Thwaites 1905). On 27 April 1833, Good Sun [Bon Homme or Sonora?] Island area, northeast NEMAHA; 8 May 1834, opposite the mouth of the Vermillion River, DIXON (Maximilian in Orr and Porter 1983). On 9 May 1843, at Bellevue, SARPY; 10 May, WASHINGTON (Audubon 1960). On 1 July 1856, at Fremont, DODGE; 1 and two on 10 August 1856, Sand Hills on the Platte; 23 April 1856, Big Nemaha River, RICHARDSON; 1 and 3 July, likely 1856, Loup Fork of the Platte, PLATTE (Warren in Baird et al. 1860); 14 July 1856, Platte River (Bryan in Baird et al. 1860); 25 October 1857, one hundred miles east of Fort Kearny, PLATTE? (Magraw in Baird et al. 1860). Common throughout the Northwest (Hayden 1863a). Common in suitable places throughout the Missouri River area (Coues 1874). Present ca. 1870, ANTELOPE (Leach 1916, 87). Common along watercourses; spring 1875, west of Lincoln, LANCASTER (Aughey 1878).

Meadowlark.
Tribal names: Omaha—*ta'tithi"ge;* Dakota Sioux—*śdo'-śdo-daŋ.*
Common name: field-lark.

While traveling up the Missouri River in Knox County in 1834, Maximilian wrote of the Meadowlark: "The great yellow-breasted lark (*Sturnella*) was scattered individually everywhere in the prairie. Its short thrush-like luring call and then a short, to be sure, but pleasantly whistling stanza could be heard" (Orr and Porter 1983, 404).

Present in the Omaha tribal area (Fletcher and La Flesche 1972). On 6 April 1813, at the "Grand Isle" of the central Platte River, HALL (Stuart 1953, 153). In faunal remains dating to 1822-42 from Fontenelle's post, SARPY (Bozell et al. 1990). On 11 May 1833, scattered everywhere on the prairie, northeast KNOX; 7 May 1834, James River and eastern CEDAR (Maximilian in Orr and Porter 1983). In May 1834, in the Big Bend area of the central Platte River (Wislizenus 1912). Very abundant on the prairies; 10 and 20 May 1865, 15 June 1865 and June 1866, DAKOTA; two on 27 May 1875 and three on 27 June 1875, LANCASTER (Aughey 1878). Present ca. 1870, ANTELOPE (Leach 1916, 87).

Eastern Meadowlark. *Sturnella magna.*
Common names: old field lark, meadow lark.

Apparent status: The Eastern Meadowlark was a common species in wet meadows throughout the state, especially along the Missouri and the Platte and in the Sand Hills. It might have been uncommon in the few wet meadow areas of the lower Niobrara.

Three in July and three on 13 August, likely 1856, Loup Fork, PLATTE (Warren in Baird et al. 1860). Probably does not extend above latitude 43° on the Missouri, where it is replaced by the Western Meadowlark (Hayden 1863a).

Western Meadowlark. *Sturnella neglecta.*
Common names: prairie lark, western lark, old field lark, Missouri meadow lark.

Apparent status: Western Meadowlarks were common to abundant summer residents across the Nebraska prairies. They were much more common than Eastern Meadowlarks.

The Western Meadowlark first was named by John James Audubon when he heard its song in northeast Nebraska and collected specimens along the Missouri River during his 1843 expedition. His was the first mention of what eventually became recognized as a new species. The actual species identification, however, is based on

*Meadow Lark,
by John James Audubon*

specimens from along the Missouri River near old Fort Union in North Dakota (American Ornithologists' Union 1983). Sightings prior to this date are included in distribution records for this species, since it was the most common lark of the open plains.

Prairie larks included in supper on 25 August 1804, near the Vermillion River; undoubtedly the species on the plains around Spirit Mound, northeast? DIXON (Lewis and Clark in Moulton 1987). First noted on 6 April 1813, in the area of the Grand Island, HALL (Stuart 1935). Potential breeder about 1820 near Engineer Cantonment, WASHINGTON (Thwaites 1905). On 22, 23 and 24 May 1843, south of Fort Randall, BOYD, and at Fort Randall, TODD, SD (Audubon 1960). On 11 May, mid-1850s, at the Tower, BOYD; 15 May 1856, Nebraska; fifty miles above the mouth of the Platte [If these are river miles, then the location was in WASHINGTON.]; nine males and females seen 3, 11 and 22 July, 3 August, and 13 July 1857, Loup Fork, PLATTE (Warren in Baird et al. 1860); 12 July 1856, Platte River; 18 July 1856, Pole Creek [Lodgepole Creek, NE] (Bryan in Baird et al. 1860). Nesting, 25 June 1859, along the Little Blue River near Kearney, WEBSTER; nesting, 30 June, in the Fort Kearny area, KEARNEY; nesting, 16 July, along the Platte River west of Ash Hollow, GARDEN (Suckley in Beidleman 1956). One of the most abundant birds on the prairie in the Northwest (Hayden 1863a). Present everywhere, June 1864 along the Platte River Road (Keller 1982). Perhaps the most abundant of all prairie species (Coues 1874).

Yellow-headed Blackbird. *Xanthocephalus xanthocephalus.*
Common name: yellow-headed troupial.

Apparent status: This notable blackbird was a common summer resident in larger cattail marshes and lakes in the state. Records from along the Missouri River and near Fort Laramie indicate this blackbird was present across Nebraska. The most suitable habitat was located in the Sand Hills and Rainwater Basin. This species first was identified from a specimen taken by Charles Lucien Bonaparte in 1820 at the Pawnee villages on the Loup Fork west of Fullerton, in Nance County (American Ornithologists' Union 1983).

Potential breeder about 1820 in the Engineer Cantonment area (Thwaites 1905). Specimens collected and birds in great numbers on 20 April 1820 along the Platte River near the Pawnee village, PLATTE/ MERRICK (Swenk 1933). On 27 April 1833, Good Sun [Sonora?] Island area, northeast NEMAHA; 7 May 1834, James River and eastern CEDAR (Maximilian in Orr and Porter 1983). On 9 May 1843, abundant near Fort Atkinson, WASHINGTON; 12 May, considerable numbers in the Blackbird Hill area, THURSTON; 16 May, in the Vermillion River area, northwest DIXON (Audubon 1960; McDermott 1951). On 8 May 1849, along the Oregon Trail near the KS/NE state line, JEFFERSON (Decker 1966, 68). On 4 May 1854, along the Big Blue River in southeast Nebraska (Martin 1980). On 15 July 1856, forks of the Platte River, LINCOLN; 25 August 1857, South Platte River (Bryan in Baird et al. 1860); 20 August 1857, north fork of the Platte; 26 August 1857, fifteen miles east of Fort Laramie (Magraw in Baird et al. 1860). Quite common across the Northwest; found around marshy lakes on the prairies (Hayden 1863a). Very abundant and breeds; two on 10 May, two on 20 May and June 1865, May 1866, three in June 1867, May 1868, two in June 1869, DAKOTA; May and June 1872, 8 May 1875, two in June 1875, two in June 1877, LANCASTER (Aughey 1878).

Rusty Blackbird. *Euphagus carolinus.*
Common name: rusty grackle.

Apparent status: Most records for this species are from eastern Nebraska, where it was occasionally abundant.

On 28 October, in the 1850s, twenty miles below Sioux City, IA, in DAKOTA (Warren in Baird et al. 1860). Near Sioux City, IA, about 1870 (Coues 1874). Abundant in early spring and late September and October; a number of specimens examined in October 1874, RICHARDSON and LANCASTER (Aughey 1878). George Grinnell collected two specimens, 15 September 1878, at the Dismal River, HOOKER/GRANT (CABM specimens B254, B255).

Brewer's Blackbird. *Euphagus cyanocephalus.*
Common name: blue-headed blackbird.

Aughey wrote in his notes pertaining to the economic ornithology of the Rocky Mountain Locust:

> During my early years in Nebraska, countless numbers of these birds, along with the crow blackbird [Common Grackle], were destroyed by the early settlers. The blackbirds visited the corn-fields in September, and stripped the ends of the ears to get at a grub that infested the corn. If abundant rains followed, a portion of the exposed corn was damaged. The impression became general that the blackbirds were destroying the corn. The farmers soaked corn in strychnine and sowed it around their corn-fields for the birds to eat. I have seen dead blackbirds and other birds that were destroyed in this way piled up in heaps three and four feet high. And yet the birds were comparatively innocent. (Aughey 1878, 35)

The birds mostly had eaten locusts.

On 23 April 1856, mouth of the Big Nemaha, RICHARDSON; 18 October 1856, Fort Randall, on the Missouri River, TODD, SD (Warren in Baird et al. 1860); 22 July 1856, Platte River (Bryan in Baird et al. 1860). Not uncommon along the Missouri and its tributaries (Hayden 1863a). Flocks following wagon trains on the Platte River Road in central Nebraska, eating waste grain, in 1864 (Keller 1982) [Although the journal editor designated these Brewer's Blackbirds, the entry only said "noisy blackbirds," which does not sufficiently identify the species.]. Common at Fort Randall, TODD, SD (Coues 1874). Once very abundant; a number examined in September 1866, Dakota City, DAKOTA; twelve in September 1874, LANCASTER (Aughey 1878).

Common Grackle. *Quiscalus quiscula.*
Common names: purple grackle, crow blackbird.

Apparent status: Common Grackles were regular residents of the state, but they were more abundant in the east.

Potential breeder about 1820 near Engineer Cantonment (Thwaites 1905). On 27 April 1833, Good Sun [Sonora?] Island area, northeast NEMAHA; 11 May 1833, northeast KNOX (Maximilian in Orr and Porter 1983). On 23 April 1856, Big Nemaha, RICHARDSON; five males and females, 25 April 1856, Bald Island, NEMAHA (Warren in Baird et al. 1860). Not rare along the Missouri (Hayden 1863a). Abundant in the eastern Missouri region (Coues 1874). Rather abundant in eastern Nebraska (Aughey 1878). Grinnell collected one specimen, 15 September 1878, at the Dismal River, HOOKER/GRANT (CABM specimen B264).

Brown-headed Cowbird. *Molothrus ater.*
Tribal name: Dakota Sioux—*wa-hpa'-ho-ta.*
Common names: cow bird, cowpen-bird, cow blackbird, cow bunting, buffalo-bird.

Apparent status: Despite the few records, which come from the eastern and southern parts of the state, this species probably was common throughout Nebraska prior to 1875. According to one observer,

> Cow-birds appear to be particularly abundant in the West; more so, perhaps, than they really are, for the numbers that in the East spread equally over large areas are here drawn within small compass, owing to lack of attractions abroad. Every wagon-train passing over the prairies in summer is attended by flocks of the birds; every camp and stock-corral, permanent or temporary, is besieged by the busy birds, eager to glean subsistence from the wasted forage. Their familiarity under these circumstances is surprising. Perpetually wandering about the feet of the draught-animals, or perching upon

their backs, they become so accustomed to man's presence that they will hardly get out of the way. I have even known a young bird to suffer itself to be taken in hand, and it is no uncommon thing to have the birds fluttering within a few feet of one's head. The animals appear to rather like the birds, and suffer them to perch in a row upon their back-bones, doubtless finding the scratching of their feet a comfortable sensation, to say nothing of the riddance from insect parasites. (Coues 1874, 185-186)

Potential breeder about 1820 in the Engineer Cantonment area (Thwaites 1905). On 9 May 1843, at Bellevue, SARPY; 10 May, WASHINGTON (Audubon 1960). Two on 16 July 1856, Platte River; Pole Creek [Lodgepole Creek, NE] (Bryan in Baird et al. 1860); three on 1 and 3 August 1857, Loup Fork, PLATTE (Warren in Baird et al. 1860). Abundant everywhere in the Northwest; thousands visit camp mules and horses (Hayden 1863a). Particularly abundant in the West—common in association with wagon trains (Coues 1874). Abundant; eggs in the nests of other birds in June (Aughey 1878).

Orchard Oriole. *Icterus spurius.*
Common name: chestnut hangnest.

Apparent status: The Orchard Oriole was present in open woodlands and was more abundant in eastern Nebraska.

Potential breeder about 1820 near Engineer Cantonment (Thwaites 1905). On 7 May 1843, NEMAHA/OTOE (Audubon 1960). On 5 August 1857, Loup Fork, PLATTE (Warren in Baird et al. 1860). Very abundant across the Northwest, especially along wooded Missouri River bottoms (Hayden 1863a). Abundant in eastern portions of the Missouri River region (Coues 1874). Common but not abundant; breeds; specimen, June 1865 near Dakota City, DAKOTA; June 1875 near Lincoln, LANCASTER (Aughey 1878).

Northern Oriole. *Icterus galbula.*
Common names: golden robin, firebird, hangnest, Baltimore oriole, Bullock's oriole.

Apparent status: This eastern oriole was prevalent in forest areas in the state. It was common to abundant in eastern Nebraska.

Potential breeder about 1820 in the Engineer Cantonment area (Thwaites 1905). On 9 May 1833, young, northeast DIXON; 10 May 1834, Blackbird Hill area; 11 May 1834, northeast WASHINGTON; 12 May 1834, northeast DOUGLAS; 13 May 1834, southeast CASS; 15 May 1834, northeast RICHARDSON (Maximilian in Orr and Porter 1983). On 10 May 1843, WASHINGTON (Audubon 1960). On 30 June 1857, Elkhorn River; 25 July 1857, Loup Fork of the Platte, PLATTE

(Warren in Baird et al. 1860). Abundant throughout wooded portions of the Missouri country [Baltimore form]; quite rare but occasionally occurs along the lower Missouri [Bullock's form] (Hayden 1863a). Common in woodlands and orchards in eastern Nebraska; adults feeding young, 1865, near Dakota City, DAKOTA; June 1865, DIXON [Bullock's form]; in 1873 at Lincoln, LANCASTER [Baltimore form]; frequently seen; August 1874 on the Republican River, HARLAN? (Aughey 1878). Present ca. 1870, ANTELOPE (Leach 1916, 87).

Family Fringillidae

Gray-crowned Rosy-Finch. *Leucosticte tephrocotis.*
Common name: gray-crowned finch.
    Apparent status: This finch appeared as a winter visitor.
    Frequently seen in winter, but rare in summer; June 1865 and February 1875 (Aughey 1878) [Aughey's June 1865 record is a misidentification, since this species would not be present in the summer.].

Pine Grosbeak. *Pinicola enucleator.*
    Apparent status: Pine Grosbeaks were winter visitors.
    Occurs in small numbers in winter in southeast Nebraska; December 1874, two in January 1875, February and November 1876, LANCASTER (Aughey 1878).

Purple Finch. *Carpodacus purpureus.*
    Purple Finches were rare in this area, according to Hayden (Hayden 1863a).
    On 8 May 1856, Vermillion River, DIXON (Warren in Baird et al. 1860). Found as far north as Fort Randall, where small flocks were seen in October, TODD, SD (Coues 1874). In October 1876 (Aughey 1878).

Cassin's Finch. *Carpodacus cassinii.*
Common name: Cassin's purple finch.
    Snake River, CHERRY (Coues 1874).

Common Redpoll. *Carduelis flammea.*
Common name: redpoll linnet.
    Irregular, with some large flocks in winter; 4 and 10 February 1865, DAKOTA; two in February 1875, LANCASTER (Aughey 1878).

American Goldfinch. *Carduelis tristis.*
Common names: thistle bird, yellow bird.

Apparent status: The goldfinch was a common to abundant summer nester and winter visitor in some areas of the state.

Potential breeder about 1820 near Engineer Cantonment (Thwaites 1905). On 7 May 1843, NEMAHA/OTOE (Audubon 1960). On 14 and 16 May 1856, Running Water [Niobrara River], KNOX (Warren in Baird et al. 1860). On 14 July 1859, in the Ash Hollow area, GARDEN (Suckley in Beidleman 1956). Very abundant in the Northwest (Hayden 1863a). Common in northern Nebraska; three in June 1865 (Aughey 1878).

Evening Grosbeak. *Coccothraustes vespertinus.*

Occasional birds, seen only in Nebraska; October 1874, LANCASTER (Aughey 1878).

CONCLUSION

Birds always were present on the Plains, but today the dim trails of history only suggest the diverse bird life present in Nebraska between 1750 and 1875.

Nebraska's first people intimately knew the birds and other animals with which they lived on the wild plains of the past. Birds were an essential part of Native American tribal life: birds served as food and enriched their cultures in many ways. The tribes that lived in this area watched and knew well the wonderful Golden Eagle, a vivid bird of the air, and a Thunderbird dream was a great honor and strong "medicine" to be shared with the tribe; the Pawnee Hako Ceremony reveals the importance of birds in tribal celebrations of the renewal and awakening of the earth in spring; Native American languages of the Northern Plains were rich with words relating to birds and their habits. Bird parts were essential equipment for brave warriors, and mystic art with a bird motif often graced a shield. Feathers might no longer have provided flight, but they certainly blew in the wind with a horse racing across the prairie. A hill swarming with swallows came to be a prominent Missouri River landmark for the Omaha people.

Changing times brought great changes in the history of birds in Nebraska. The first non-native explorers in our region were looking for natural resources, but concentrated only on those with the greatest economic return. Trappers knew birds, but they had more important things to note and record during their first journeys.

As the United States expanded to the west, written records and the scientific study of birds along the Missouri followed a similar progression. In 1804 Lewis and Clark noted scene after scene, one bird after another, as their expedition moved up the Missouri River. Prince Maximilian and Karl Bodmer visited the Missouri valley and made vivid visual records of this wild country. As prominent bird watcher John James Audubon traveled the region, he excitedly observed a Yellow-headed Blackbird and the Western Meadowlark, now Nebraska's official state bird. Bright and colorful Carolina Parakeets, which later became extinct as heavy settlement wrought changes upon the land and its people, often were seen as flocks fed in the trees along the river. But these events and many more have all become a part of the bird lore of the historic Missouri River region between 1750 and 1875.

Western Nebraska was discovered and explored decades later than land in the east, which was accessible due to Missouri River steamboat travel. There were no such rivers in the west, so for years longer its open country remained a vast, unknown territory to nearly everyone but the region's Native Americans. Eventually the wide, shallow Platte provided a path to the mountains, and wagon trains replaced steamboats. As thousands of pioneers headed west on the Oregon Trail, their personal diaries record many informative bird sightings and events, such as enjoying a duck-and-biscuit dinner on the open plains. These pioneer observations form yet another small part of the state's bird lore.

The remote Sand Hills were the state's last frontier. This open land of prairie and marsh was too untraveled to provide significant bird information before 1875. Its harsh and steady winds, shifting sands and unmarked land made travel unpleasant and settlement unlikely. Many believed the area's dunes of sand indicated desert-like conditions, which further added to its undeserved poor reputation. Still, a few explorers took notes that provide a brief glimpse of the birds then present in Nebraska's Sand Hills. We read of the waterbirds in this land of sand, grass and marsh, especially the Sandhill Crane, which raised its young each summer in the wet meadows that formed in the valleys between the dunes. Although these birds no longer nest in the Sand Hills, the current generation of Nebraska bird watchers still can enjoy their spectacular migration.

As Nebraska Territory changed from a wild and open land, its prairies and plains became range for herds of cattle. As the range became settled, twisted barbed wire enclosed pastures and fields. The land became property, controlled and dominated by individuals intent on eking a living from the land. As the land was altered, the changes nearly always dramatically affected its migratory and resident birds.

This history of Nebraska's birdlife describes the prominent role birds have played in the lives of generations of people who lived in the present-day state of Nebraska before 1875. Although today's bird watcher listening to Western Grebes calling on a Sand Hills lake may only record a note of the bird being seen, the entire scene—a slight breeze, a sky filled with fluffy clouds and the flocks upon the water—gives that observer quite a thrill. As the days pass, information collected today will be written into the future history of birds in Nebraska. Although these important studies give us but a static view of birdlife in Nebraska, through them we may gain a knowledge of the wonderful life of the "winged ones."

BIBLIOGRAPHY

Abel, Annie Heloise, ed. *Tabeau's Narrative of Loisel's Expedition to the Upper Missouri.* Translated by Rose Abel Wright. Norman, Oklahoma: University of Oklahoma Press, 1939.

Adams, Alexander B. *Sunlight and Storm: The Great American Plains.* New York, New York: G. P. Putnam's Sons, 1977.

Aeschbacher, William D. "Development of the Sandhill Lake Country." *Nebraska History* 27 (1946): 205-221.

Allis, Samuel. "Forty Years among the Indians and on the Eastern Border of Nebraska." *Transactions and Reports of the Nebraska State Historical Society* 2 (1887): 133-166.

———. "Letters concerning the Presbyterian Mission in the Pawnee Country near Bellevue." *Kansas Historical Collections* 14 (1918): 690-741.

American Ornithologists' Union. *Checklist of North American Birds: The Species of Birds of North America from the Arctic through Panama, including the West Indies and Hawaiian Islands.* 6th ed. Lawrence, Kansas: Allen Press, 1983.

———. "Thirty-eighth Supplement to the American Ornithologists' Union Check-list of North American Birds." *The Auk* 108 (1991): 750-754.

———. "Thirty-fifth Supplement to the American Ornithologists' Union Check-list of North American Birds." *The Auk* 102 (1985): 680-686.

———. "Thirty-seventh Supplement to the American Ornithologists' Union Check-list of North American Birds." *The Auk* 106 (1989): 532-538.

———. "Thirty-sixth Supplement to the American Ornithologists' Union Check-list of North American Birds." *The Auk* 104 (1987): 591-596.

Audubon, Marie R., ed. *Audubon and his Journals.* New York, New York: Dover Publications, Inc., 1960.

Aughey, Samuel. *Notes on the Nature of the Food of the Birds of Nebraska.* First Annual Report of the United States Entomological Commission for the Year 1877 Relating to the Rocky Mountain Locust. Washington, D.C.: U.S. Entomological Commission, 1878.

Baird, Spencer Fullerton. *Review of American Birds, in the Museum of the Smithsonian Institution.* Smithsonian Miscellaneous Collections, vol. 12. Washington, D.C.: Smithsonian Institution, 1874.

Baird, Spencer Fullerton, Thomas M. Brewer, and Robert Ridgway. *A History of North American Birds: Land Birds.* 3 vols. Boston, Massachusetts: Little, Brown and Company, 1874.

Baird, Spencer Fullerton, John Cassin, and George Newbold Lawrence. *The Birds of North America: The Descriptions of Species Based Chiefly on the Collections in the Museum of the Smithsonian Institution.* In Vol. 9, Part 2 of *Reports of Explorations and Surveys, to Ascertain the Most Practicable and Economical Route for a Railroad from the Mississippi*

River to the Pacific Ocean. Philadelphia, Pennsylvania: J. B. Lippincott & Co., 1860.

Barnes, E. R. "Nebraska" [Note on the abundance of prairie chickens near Tecumseh]. *Forest and Stream* 3 (1874): 140.

Beck, John V. "The History, the Family, the Range, the Hunting, the Life of the Greater Prairie Chicken in Nebraska: Yesterday, Today, Tomorrow," n.d. MS. 3546, Box 5. Nebraska State Historical Society, Lincoln, Nebraska.

Beckwourth, James Pierson. *The Life and Adventures of James P. Beckwourth as told to Thomas D. Bonner.* Lincoln, Nebraska: University of Nebraska Press, 1972.

Beidleman, Richard G., ed. "The 1859 Overland Journal of Naturalist George Suckley." *Annals of Wyoming* 28 (1956): 68-79.

Benson, Maxine, ed. *From Pittsburgh to the Rocky Mountains: Major Stephen Long's Expedition, 1819-1820.* Golden, Colorado: Fulcrum, Inc., 1988.

Boller, Henry A. *Among the Indians: Four Years on the Upper Missouri, 1858-1862.* Lincoln, Nebraska: University of Nebraska Press, 1972.

Bowers, Alfred W. *Hidatsa Social and Ceremonial Organization.* Bureau of American Ethnology, Bulletin 194. Washington, D.C.: Smithsonian Institution, 1965.

Bozell, John R., Steven Donnelly, Mary Rogers, and Stephanie Zink. *Animal Procurement and Utilization at the Bellevue Trading Post and Indian Agency: 1822-1842.* Lincoln, Nebraska: Nebraska State Historical Society, 1990.

Bozell, John R., Lynn M. Snyder, and Carl R. Falk. *Descriptive Analysis of Unmodified Vertebrate Remains Recovered from the Schuyler Site (25CX1), Colfax County, Nebraska.* Department of Anthropology, Division of Archeological Research, Technical Report 82-06. Lincoln, Nebraska: University of Nebraska, 1982.

Brackenridge, Henry Marie. *Journal of a Voyage up the River Missouri Performed in 1811.* Millwood, New York: Kraus Reprint Co., 1976.

Brandon, William. *Quivira: Europeans in the Region of the Sante Fe Trail, 1540-1820.* Athens, Ohio: Ohio University Press, 1990.

Bray, Edmund C., and Martha Coleman Bray, eds. and trans. *Joseph N. Nicollet on the Plains and Prairies: The Expeditions of 1838-39.* St. Paul, Minnesota: Minnesota Historical Society Press, 1976.

Bray, Tanya E., Barbara K. Padelford, and W. Ross Silcock. *The Birds of Nebraska: A Critically Evaluated List.* Bellevue, Nebraska: By authors, 1986.

Brewer, Thomas Mayo. *North American Oology; Being an Account of the Habits and Geographical Distribution of the Birds of North America . . . .* Smithsonian Contributions to Knowledge, Vol. 11. Washington, D.C.: Smithsonian Institution, 1857.

Bruner, Lawrence. "Birds that Nest in Nebraska." *Proceedings of the Nebraska Ornithologists' Union* 2 (1901): 48-61.

———. "A Comparison of the Bird-life Found in the Sand Hill Region of Holt County in 1883-84 and in 1901." *Proceedings of the Nebraska Ornithologists' Union* 3 (1902): 58-63.

———. *Some Notes on Nebraska Birds: A List of the Species and Subspecies Found in the State, with Notes on their Distribution, Food Habits, etc.* Reprint from the Report of the Nebraska State Horticultural Society, 1896. Lincoln, Nebraska: Nebraska State Horticultural Society, 1896.

Bruner, Lawrence, Robert H. Wolcott, and Myron H. Swenk. *A Preliminary Review of the Birds of Nebraska.* Omaha, Nebraska: Klopp and Bartlett Co., 1904.

Burgess, Harold. "Trumpeter Swans Were Common Lewis and Clark Birds." *Bluebird* 47 (1980): 28-29.

Carleton, James H. *The Prairie Logbooks.* Lincoln, Nebraska: University of Nebraska Press, 1983.

Carriker, Melbourne Armstrong, Jr. "Notes on the Nesting of Some Sioux County Birds." *Proceedings of the Nebraska Ornithologists' Union* 3 (1902): 75-89.

Cary, Merritt. "Some General Remarks upon the Distribution of Life in Northwest Nebraska." *Proceedings of the Nebraska Ornithologists' Union* 3 (1902): 63-75.

Catlin, George. *Letters and Notes on the Manners, Customs, and Condition of the North American Indians.* 2 vols. Minneapolis, Minnesota: Ross & Haines, Inc., 1965.

Chamberlain, Von Del. *When Stars Came Down to Earth: Cosmology of the Skidi Pawnee Indians of North America.* Los Altos, California: Ballena Press, 1982.

Chapman, Berlin Basil. *The Otoes and Missourias.* Oklahoma City, Oklahoma: Times Journal Publishing Company, 1965.

Chittenden, Hiram M. *The American Fur Trade of the Far West.* 2 vols. Lincoln, Nebraska: University of Nebraska Press, 1986.

Chittenden, Hiram Martin, and Alfred Talbot Richardson, eds. *Life, Letters and Travels of Father Pierre-Jean DeSmet, S.J., 1801-1873: Missionary Labors and Adventures among the Wild Tribes of North American Indians.* 4 vols. New York, New York: Francis P. Harper, 1905.

Clark, Thomas D., ed. *Gold Rush Diary: Being the Journal of Elisha Douglass Perkins on the Overland Trail in the Spring and Summer of 1849.* Lexington, Kentucky: University of Kentucky Press, 1967.

Clark, William Philo. *The Indian Sign Language, with Brief Explanatory Notes of the Gestures Taught Deaf-mutes in our Institutions.* Philadelphia, Pennsylvania: L. R. Hammersly & Co., 1885.

Cole, Gilbert L. "Along the Overland Trail in Nebraska in 1852." *Proceedings and Collections of the Nebraska State Historical Society* 10 (1902): 172-181.

Connecticut Audubon Birdcraft Museum [CABM]. "Catalogue of the Bird Collection." Manuscript compiled by Dennis Varza, c. 1970. Fairfield, Connecticut.

Coues, Elliott. *Birds of the Northwest: A Hand-book of the Ornithology of the Region Drained by the Missouri River and its Tributaries.* U.S. Geological Survey Miscellaneous Publications, No. 3. Washington, D.C.: U.S. Geological Survey, 1874.

Coveter, R. G. "Shooting Notes from Nebraska." *Forest and Stream* 7 (1876): 27.

Cross, Major Osborne. *March of the Regiment of Mounted Riflemen to Oregon in 1849.* Fairfield, Washington: Galleon Press, 1967.

Culin, Stewart. *Games of the North American Indians.* Twenty-fourth Annual Report of the Bureau of American Ethnology, 1902-1903. Washington, D.C.: Smithsonian Institution, 1907.

DeBenedictis, Paul A. "The Thirty-ninth Supplement to the American Ornithologists' Union Check-list of North American Birds." *American Birds* 47, no. 3 (1993): 384-386.

Decker, Peter. *The Diaries of Peter Decker: Overland to California in 1849 and Life in the Mines, 1850-1851.* Edited by Helen S. Giffen. Georgetown, California: Talisman Press, 1966.

Delano, Alonzo. *Across the Plains and Among the Diggings.* New York, New York: Wilson-Erickson, Inc., 1936.

Densmore, Frances. *Mandan and Hidatsa Music.* Bureau of American Ethnology, Bulletin 80. Washington, D.C.: Smithsonian Institution, 1923.

———. *Teton Sioux Music.* Da Capo Press Music Reprint Series. Reprint of Bureau of American Ethnology, Bulletin 61 (1918). New York, New York: Da Capo Press, 1972.

Dodge, Richard Irving. *The Plains of North America and Their Inhabitants.* Edited by Wayne R. Kim. Newark, Delaware: University of Delaware Press, 1989.

Dorsey, George A. *The Pawnee: Mythology.* Part 1. Washington, D.C.: Carnegie Institute of Washington, 1906.

Ducey, James E. "Bird Items and their Use in Some Omaha Indian Artifacts." *Nebraska Bird Review* 60 (1992): 154-163.

———. "Men's Friendship Led to Collection." *Sunday World-Herald Magazine of the Midlands* (28 September 1986): 6-7.

———. *Nebraska Birds: Breeding Status and Distribution.* Omaha, Nebraska: Simmons-Boardman Books, 1988.

Dumont, Philip A. "Notes on Nebraska Flickers Contained in the Talbot Collection." *Nebraska Bird Review* 1 (1933): 32.

Dunbar, John Brown. "Letters Concerning the Presbyterian Mission in the Pawnee Country, near Bellevue, Neb., 1831-1849." *Collections of the Kansas State Historical Society* 14 (1915): 570-784.

———. "The Pawnee Indians: Their History and Ethnology." *Magazine of American History* 4 (1880)[1880a]: 241-281.

———. "The Pawnee Indians: Their Habits and Customs." *Magazine of American History* 5 (1880)[1880b]: 321-345.

———. "The Pawnee Indians: Their Habits and Customs." *Magazine of American History* 8 (1882): 734-756.

Dunlap, Kate. *The Montana Gold Rush Diary of Kate Dunlap*. Edited and annotated by J. Lyman Tyler. Annals of the West, Vol. 1. Denver, Colorado: F. A. Rosenstock Old West Publishing Company, 1969.

Eaton, Herbert. *The Overland Trail to California in 1852*. New York, New York: G. P. Putnam's Sons, 1974.

Edmunds, Russell David. *The Otoe-Missouria People*. Phoenix, Arizona: Indian Tribal Series, 1976.

Ewers, John C., Marsha V. Gallagher, David C. Hunt, and Joseph C. Porter. *Views of a Vanishing Frontier*. Omaha, Nebraska: Joslyn Art Museum Center for Western Studies, 1984.

Ewers, John Canfield. *Indian Life on the Upper Missouri*. Norman, Oklahoma: University of Oklahoma Press, 1968.

Falk, Carl R., and Carole A. Angus. "A Descriptive Summary of Vertebrate Remains Recovered from the Archeological Investigation of the Walker Gilmore Site (25CC28)." In Daniel R. Haas, *Walker Gilmore: A Stratified Woodland Period Occupation in Eastern Nebraska*. Department of Anthropology Laboratory, Notebook No. 6. Lincoln, Nebraska: University of Nebraska, 1983.

Feder, Norman. "Bird Quillwork." *American Indian Art Magazine* 12 (No. 3, Summer 1987): 46-57.

———. "European Influences on Plains Indian Art." In *The Arts of the North American Indian: Native Traditions in Evolution*, edited by E. L. Wade. New York, New York: Hudson Hills Press, 1986.

Fletcher, Alice C., and Francis La Flesche. *The Omaha Tribe*. 2 vols. Reprint of the Twenty-seventh Annual Report of the Bureau of American Ethnology, 1905-1906. Lincoln, Nebraska: University of Nebraska Press, 1972.

Fletcher, Alice Cunningham. "The Hako: A Pawnee Ceremony." In the Twenty-second Annual Report of the Bureau of American Ethnology, 1900-1901, pt. 2. Washington, D.C.: Smithsonian Institution, 1904.

Ford, Lemuel. *March of the First Dragoons to the Rocky Mountains in 1835: The Diaries and Maps of Lemuel Ford*. Edited by Nolie Mumey. Denver, Colorado: Eames Brothers Press, 1957.

Franzwa, Gregory M. *Maps of the Oregon Trail*. Gerald, Missouri: The Patrice Press, 1982.

Frémont, John Charles. *Narratives of Exploration and Adventure*. Edited by Allan Nevins. New York, New York: Longmans, Green and Company, 1956.

Furnas, Robert W. "The Carolina Paroquet." *Proceedings of the Nebraska Ornithologists' Union* 3 (1902): 107.

Galatowitsch, S. M. "Using the Original Land Survey Notes to Reconstruct Presettlement Landscapes in the American West." *Great Basin Naturalist* 50 (1990): 181-191.

Ghent, William James. *The Road to Oregon: A Chronicle of the Great Emigrant Trail.* New York, New York: Longmans, Green and Co., 1929.

Gibbs, P. "Duke Paul Wilhelm Collection." *American Indian Art Magazine* 7 (No. 3, Summer 1982): 52-61.

Gilmore, Melvin Randolph. *Prairie Smoke.* New York, New York: Columbia University Press, 1929.

Good, Diane L. *Birds, Beads and Bells: Remote Sensing of a Pawnee Sacred Bundle.* Anthropological Series No. 15. Lawrence, Kansas: Kansas State Historical Society, 1989.

Gray, Charles Glass. *Off at Sunrise: The Overland Journal of Charles Glass Gray.* Edited by Thomas D. Clark. San Marino, California: Huntington Library, 1976.

Green, A. L. "The Otoe Indians." *Publications of the Nebraska State Historical Society* 21 (1930): 175-209.

Green, Thomas L., ed. "Notes on a Buffalo Hunt: The Diary of Mordecai Bartram." *Nebraska History* 35 (1954): 193-222.

Grinnell, George Bird. *The Cheyenne Indians, their History and Ways of Life.* 2 vols. New Haven, Connecticut: Yale University Press, 1923 [1923a].

——— [Ornis, pseud.]. "Elk Hunting in Nebraska." *Forest and Stream* 1 (1873): 116.

——— [Yo, pseud.]. "Nebraska Notes." *Forest and Stream* 9 (1877): 152.

———. "An Old-time Bone Hunt." *Natural History* 23 (1923) [1923b]: 329-336.

———. *Two Great Scouts and their Pawnee Battalion: The Experiences of Frank J. North and Luther H. North.* Cleveland, Ohio: Arthur H. Clark Co., 1928.

———. "The Young Dog's Dance." *Journal of American Folklore* 4 (1891): 307-313.

Haas, Daniel R. *Walker Gilmore: A Stratified Woodland Period Occupation in Eastern Nebraska.* Department of Anthropology, Division of Archeological Research, Notebook No. 6. Lincoln, Nebraska: University of Nebraska, 1983.

Haecker, F. W., and R. Allyn Moser. "Present Day Bird Life along the Missouri River Compared with Say's and Audubon's Findings." *Nebraska Bird Review* 9 (1941): 31-35.

Hafen, LeRoy Reuben, and Ann Woodbury Hafen. *Handcarts to Zion: The Story of a Unique Western Migration, 1856-1860.* Far West and the Rockies Historical Series, 1820-1875, vol. 14. Glendale, California: Arthur H. Clark Co., 1960.

———, eds. *To the Rockies and Oregon, 1839-1842*. Far West and the Rockies Historical Series, 1820-1875, vol. 3. Glendale, California: Arthur H. Clark Co., 1955.

Hancock, Samuel. *The Narrative of Samuel Hancock, 1845-1860*. The Argonaut Series, vol. 1. New York, New York: Robert M. McBride & Company, 1927.

Hanson, Charles, Jr. "The Swanskin." *Nebraska Bird Review* 45 (1977): 45-50.

Hayden, Ferdinand Vandeveer. "Brief Notes on the Pawnee, Winnebago and Omaha Languages." *Proceedings of the American Philosophical Society* 10 (1868): 389-421.

———. "On the Enthnography and Philology of the Indian Tribes of the Missouri Valley." *Transactions of the American Philosophical Society* 12 (1863) [1863b]: 231-461.

———. "On the Geology and Natural History of the Upper Missouri." *Transactions of the American Philosophical Society* 12 (1863) [1863a]: 1-218.

Hewitt, Randall Henry. *Across the Plains and Over the Divide: A Mule Train Journey from East to West in 1862*. New York, New York: Broadway Publishing Co., 1906.

Hoover, Herbert T. *The Yankton Sioux*. Indians of North America. New York, New York: Chelsea House Publishers, 1988.

Howard, James Henri. *The Ponca Tribe*. Bureau of American Ethnology, Bulletin 195. Washington, D.C.: Smithsonian Institution, 1965.

Hume, Edgar Erskine. *Ornithologists of the United States Army Medical Corps*. Publications of the Institute of the History of Medicine, 1st series, Vol. 1. Baltimore, Maryland: The John Hopkins Press, 1942.

Irving, John Treat, Jr. *Indian Sketches Taken during an Expedition to the Pawnee Tribes, 1833*. Edited and annotated by John Francis McDermott. The American Exploration and Travel Series, No. 18. New ed. Norman, Oklahoma: University of Oklahoma Press, 1955.

Jackson, H. Edwin, and Susan L. Scott. "Vertebrate Remains from Big Village." In *Archaeology and Ethnohistory of the Omaha Indians: The Big Village Site*. Edited by John M. O'Shea and John Ludwickson. Lincoln, Nebraska: University of Nebraska Press, 1992.

James, Edwin. *Account of an Expedition from Pittsburgh to the Rocky Mountains, under the Command of Major Stephen H. Long*. Barre, Massachusetts: Imprint Society, 1972.

Johnson, Overton, and William H. Winter. *Route across the Rocky Mountains: Narratives of the Trans-Mississippi Frontier*. Princeton, New Jersey: Princeton University Press, 1932.

Jones, J. Knox, Jr. "Some Early Records of the Wild Turkey in Nebraska." *Nebraska Bird Review* 27 (1959): 42.

Karol, Joseph S., and Stephen L. Rozman. *Everyday Lakota: An English-Sioux Dictionary for Beginners.* Rev. ed. St. Francis, South Dakota: The Rosebud Educational Society, 1974.

Kaul, Robert B., and Stephen B. Rolfsmeier. *Native Vegetation of Nebraska.* University of Nebraska Conservation and Survey Division. Lincoln, Nebraska: University of Nebraska, 1993.

Kay, J. "Wisconsin Indian Hunting Patterns, 1634-1836." *Annals of the Association of American Geographers* 69 (1979): 402-418.

Keller, Robert H., Jr. "The 1864 Overland Trail: Five Letters from Jonathan Blanchard." *Nebraska History* 63 (1982): 71-86.

Kline, H. A. "Notes from Nebraska." *Ornithologist* 8 (1883): 18-19.

Kurz, Rudolph Friederich. *Journal of Rudolph Friederich Kurz.* Edited by John Napoleon Brinton Hewitt. Lincoln, Nebraska: University of Nebraska Press, 1970.

———. *Journal of Rudolph Friedrich Kurz: An Account of his Experiences among Fur Traders and American Indians on the Mississippi and the Upper Missouri Rivers during the Years 1846 to 1852.* Edited by John Napoleon Brinton Hewitt. Bureau of American Ethnology, Bulletin 115. Washington, D.C.: Smithsonian Institution, 1937.

Ladner, Mildred D. *William de la Montagne Cary: Artist on the Missouri River.* The Gilcrease-Oklahoma Series on Western Art and Artists, vol. 3. Norman, Oklahoma: University of Oklahoma Press, 1984.

Leach, A. J. *Early Day Stories: The Overland Trails.* Norfolk, Nebraska: Huse Publishing Company, 1916.

Lewis, Meriwether, and William Clark. *Original Journals of the Lewis and Clark Expedition, 1804-1806.* Edited by Reuben Gold Thwaites. Vol. 1. New York, New York: Antiquarian Press Ltd., 1959.

Lienhard, Johann Heinrich. *From St. Louis to Sutter's Fort, 1846.* Edited and translated by Erwin G. Gudde and Elisabeth K. Gudde. The American Exploration and Travel Series, no. 33. Norman, Oklahoma: University of Oklahoma Press, 1961.

Lindsay, Charles, ed. "The Diary of Dr. Thomas G. Maghee." *Nebraska History Magazine* 12 (1929): 247-304.

Lowie, Robert H. *Myths and Traditions of the Crow Indians.* Anthropological Papers of the American Museum of Natural History, Vol. 25, Pt. 1. New York, New York: American Museum of Natural History, 1918.

———. *The Religion of the Crow Indians.* Anthropological Papers of the American Museum of Natural History, Vol. 25, Pt. 2. New York, New York: American Museum of Natural History, 1922.

Lowie, Robert Harry. *Indians of the Plains.* Lincoln, Nebraska: University of Nebraska Press, 1982.

Ludlow, William. *Report of a Reconnaissance of the Black Hills of Dakota Made in the Summer of 1874.* Washington, D.C.: U.S. Army Engineer Department, 1875.

Ludwickson, John, D. Blakeslee, and J. O'Shea. *Missouri National Recreation River: Native American Cultural Resources.* Wichita State University Publications in Anthropology, No. 3. Wichita, Kansas: Wichita State University, 1987.

McDermott, Edith Swain. *The Pioneer History of Greeley County, Nebraska.* Greeley, Nebraska: Citizen Printing Company, 1939.

McDermott, John Francis, ed. *Journal of an Expedition to the Mauvaises Terres and the Upper Missouri in 1850,* by Thaddeus Ainsworth Culbertson. Bureau of American Ethnology, Bulletin 147. Washington, D.C.: Smithsonian Institution, 1952.

———, ed. *Up the Missouri with Audubon: The Journal of Edward Harris.* American Exploration and Travel Series, no. 15. Norman, Oklahoma: University of Oklahoma Press, 1951.

McIntosh, C. Barron. "The Route of a Sand Hills Bone Hunt: The Yale College Expedition of 1870." *Nebraska History* 69, no. 2 (Summer 1988): 84-94.

McKinley, Daniel. "The Carolina Parakeet in the Upper Missouri and Mississippi River Valleys." *The Auk* 82 (1965): 215-226.

———. "The Carolina Parakeet in the West: Additional References.' *Nebraska Bird Review* 46 (1978): 3-7.

Martin, Charles W. "The Diary of William H. Woodhams, 1852-1854: The Great Deserts or Around and Across." *Nebraska History* 61 (1980): 1-101.

———. "Joseph Warren Arnold's Journal of his Trip to and from Montana, 1864-66." *Nebraska History* 55 (1974): 463-552.

Missouri River Commission. *Map of the Missouri River From its Mouth to Three Forks, Montana.* Washington, D.C., 1895.

Mitchell, John G. "A Man Called Bird." *Audubon Magazine* 89, no. 2 (1987): 81-104.

Moore, John H. "The Ornithology of Cheyenne Religionists." *Plains Anthropologist* 31 (1986): 177-192.

Morgan, Dale L., and Eleanor T. Harris, eds. *The Rocky Mountain Journals of William Marshall Anderson.* San Marino, California: The Huntington Library, 1967.

Morgan, Dale Lowell. *Overland in 1846: Diaries and Letters of the California-Oregon Trail.* 2 vols. Georgetown, California: Talisman Press, 1963.

Morgan, Lewis Henry. *The Indian Journals, 1859-62.* Edited by Leslie A. White. Ann Arbor, Michigan: University of Michigan, 1959.

Morton, Julius Sterling. *Illustrated History of Nebraska.* 3 vols. Lincoln, Nebraska: Jacob North & Company, 1907.

Moulton, Gary E., ed. *The Journals of the Lewis and Clark Expedition.* Vol. 2: *August 30, 1803-August 24, 1804,* by Meriwether Lewis and William Clark. Lincoln, Nebraska: University of Nebraska Press, 1986.

———, ed. *The Journals of the Lewis and Clark Expedition.* Vol. 3: *August 25, 1804-April 6, 1805,* by Meriwether Lewis and William Clark. Lincoln, Nebraska: University of Nebraska Press, 1987.

Muench, Joyce R., ed. *The Kilgore Journey to California in the Year 1850,* by William H. Kilgore. New York, New York: Hasting House, 1949.

Mundell, R. L. "Descriptive Analysis of Vertebrate Remains from Fort Atkinson: The Military Period." In *Archeological Investigations at Fort Atkinson (25WN9); Washington County, Nebraska 1956-1971,* by G. F. Carlson. Publications in Anthropology, No. 8. Lincoln, Nebraska: Nebraska State Historical Society, 1979.

Murie, James R. *Ceremonies of the Pawnee.* Part I: *The Skidi* and Part II: *The South Bands.* Edited by Douglas R. Parks. Smithsonian Contributions to Anthropology, No. 27. Washington, D.C.: Smithsonian Institution, 1981.

Nasatir, Abraham Phineas, ed. *Before Lewis and Clark: Documents Illustrating the History of the Missouri, 1785-1804.* St. Louis, Missouri: St. Louis Historical Documents Foundation, 1952.

National Museum of Natural History [NMNH]. "Specimen Catalogue of the Division of Birds," n.d. Manuscript. Smithsonian Institution, Washington, D.C.

Nichols, Roger L., ed. *The Missouri Expedition, 1818-20: The Journal of Surgeon John Gale, with Related Documents.* The American Exploration and Travel Series, no. 56. Norman, Oklahoma: University of Oklahoma Press, 1969.

North, Luther Hedden. *Man of the Plains: Recollections of Luther North, 1856-1882.* Edited by Donald F. Danker. Pioneer Heritage Series, vol. 4. Lincoln, Nebraska: University of Nebraska Press, 1961.

O'Brien, Patricia J., and Diane M. Post. "Speculations about Bobwhite Quail and Pawnee Religion." *Plains Anthropologist* 33, No. 122 (1988): 489-504.

Orchard, William C. *The Technique of Porcupine Quill Decoration among the Indians of North America.* Ogden, Utah: Eagles View Publishing, 1984.

Orr, William J., and Joseph C. Porter, eds. "A Journey through the Nebraska Region in 1833 and 1834 from the Diaries of Prince Maximilian of Wied." *Nebraska History* 64 (1983): 325-453.

O'Shea, John M., and John Ludwickson. *Archaeology and Ethnohistory of the Omaha Indians.* Lincoln, Nebraska: University of Nebraska Press, 1992.

O'Shea, John M., George D. Shrimper, and John Ludwickson. "Ivory-billed Woodpeckers at the Big Village of the Omaha." *Plains Anthropologist* 27, No. 97 (1982): 245-248.

Parmalee, Paul W. "The Avifauna from Prehistoric Arikara Sites in South Dakota." *Plains Anthropologist* 22, No. 77 (1977): 189-222.

———. "Inferred Arikara Subsistence Patterns Based on Selected Faunal Assemblage from the Mobridge Site, South Dakota." *The Kiva* 44 (1979): 191-218.

Perkey, Elton A. *Perkey's Nebraska Place Names*. Lincoln, Nebraska: Nebraska State Historical Society, 1982.

Phillips, C. H. "The Fauna of Nebraska." *Forest and Stream* 6 (1876): 284.

Phillips, Paul Chrisler. *The Fur Trade*. Norman, Oklahoma: University of Oklahoma Press, 1961.

Purcell, Emerson R. *Pioneer Stories of Custer County, Nebraska*. Broken Bow, Nebraska: Custer County Chief, 1936.

Radin, Paul. *The Winnebago Tribe*. Lincoln, Nebraska: University of Nebraska Press, 1990.

Riggs, Stephen Return. *A Dakota-English Dictionary*. Minneapolis, Minnesota: Ross & Haines, Inc., 1968.

Roper, Donna. "A Note on the Quail and the Pawnee." *Plains Anthropologist* 39 (1994): 73-76.

Rothenberger, S. J. "Extent of Woody Vegetation on the Prairie in Eastern Nebraska, 1855-57." In *Proceedings of the Eleventh North America Prairie Conference*, edited by Thomas B. Bragg and James Stubbendieck. Lincoln, Nebraska: University of Nebraska, 1989.

Ruxton, George Frederick Augustus. *Life in the Far West*. Edited by LeRoy R. Hafen. Norman, Oklahoma: University of Oklahoma Press, 1951.

Rydjord, John. *Indian Place Names: Their Origin, Evolution, and Meanings*. Norman, Oklahoma: University of Oklahoma Press, 1968.

Sanford, Mollie Dorsey. *Mollie: The Journal of Mollie Dorsey Sanford in Nebraska and Colorado Territories, 1857-1866*. Lincoln, Nebraska: University of Nebraska Press, 1959.

Sclater, Philip Lutley. *Catalogue of a Collection of American Birds*. London N. Trubner and Co., 1862.

Sharpe, Roger S. "Samuel Aughey's List of Nebraska Birds (1878): A Critical Evaluation." *Nebraska Bird Review* 61 (1993): 3-10.

Skinner, Shirley M., ed. *Pioneer Stories of Brown, Keya Paha and Rock Counties, in Nebraska*. Ainsworth, Nebraska: Star-Journal, Inc., 1980.

Snyder, Lynn M., and John R. Bozell. *Identifications and Analysis of Vertebrate Faunal Remains Recovered from the Logan Creek Site (25BT3), Burt County, Nebraska*. Department of Anthropology, Division of Archeological Research. Technical Report No. 83-03. Lincoln, Nebraska: University of Nebraska, 1983.

Spring, Agnes Wright. *Caspar Collins: The Life and Exploits of an Indian Fighter of the Sixties*. New York, New York: Columbia University Press, 1927.

Stephens, T. C. *The Birds of Dakota County, Nebraska*. Nebraska Ornithologists' Union Occasional Papers, No. 3. Lincoln, Nebraska: Nebraska Ornithologists' Union, 1957.

Stuart, Robert. *The Discovery of the Oregon Trail: Robert Stuart's Narratives.* Edited by Phillip Ashton Rollins. New York, New York: Charles Scribner's Sons, 1935.

———. *On the Oregon Trail: Robert Stuart's Journey of Discovery.* Edited by Kenneth A. Spaulding. Norman, Oklahoma: University of Oklahoma Press, 1953.

Swenk, Myron Harmon. "Distribution and Migration of the Chat in Nebraska and other Missouri Valley States." *Nebraska Bird Review* 8 (1940): 33-44.

———. "The Eskimo Curlew and its Disappearance." *Proceedings of the Nebraska Ornithologists' Union* 6 (1915): 25-44.

———. "The Exact Type Localities of the Birds Discovered in Nebraska by Thomas Say on the Long Expedition." *Nebraska Bird Review* 1 (1933): 33-35.

———. "A History of Nebraska Ornithology. I: The Ancient Period (continued)." *Nebraska Bird Review* 2 (1934) [1934b]: 137-143.

———. "A History of Nebraska Ornithology. II: Period of Explorations of the Early Century (1804-1854)." *Nebraska Bird Review* 3 (1935): 115-125.

———. "A History of Nebraska Ornithology. III: Period of Explorations of the Early Nineteenth Century (1804-1854)." *Nebraska Bird Review* 5 (1937): 51-57.

———. "The Interior Carolina Parakeet as a Nebraska Bird." *Nebraska Bird Review* 2 (1934) [1934a]: 55-59.

Taylor, W. E. "The Migration of the American Magpie to Eastern Nebraska, 25 Years Ago." *American Naturalist* 21 (1887) [1887a]: 1122-1123.

———. "Missouri River Crow Roosts." *American Naturalist* 21 (1887) [1887b]: 1123-1124.

Taylor, W. E., and A. H. Van Vleet. "Notes on Nebraska Birds." *Ornithologist and Oologist* 13 (1888) [1888a]: 49-51.

———. "Notes on Nebraska Birds." *Ornithologist and Oologist* 13 (1888) [1888b]: 169-172.

———. "Notes on Nebraska Birds." *Ornithologist and Oologist* 14 (1889): 163-165.

Thwaites, Reuben Gold, ed. *James's Account of S. H. Long's Expedition, 1819-1820,* by Edwin James. Vols. 14 and 15 of *Early Western Travels.* . . . Cleveland, Ohio: The Arthur H. Clarke Company, 1905.

Tomkins, William. *Indian Sign Language.* New York, New York: Dover Publications, 1969.

Townsend, John K. *Across the Rockies to the Columbia.* Lincoln, Nebraska: University of Nebraska Press, 1978.

———. "Description of Twelve New Species of Birds, Chiefly from the Vicinity of the Columbia River." *Journal of the Academy of Natural Sciences of Philadelphia* 7 (1837): 187-193.

———. "List of the Birds Inhabiting the Region of the Rocky Mountains, the Territory of the Oregon, and the Northwest Coast of America."

Journal of the Academy of Natural Sciences of Philadelphia 8 (1839): 151-158.

Twedt, Curtis M., and Carl W. Wolfe. "Botanical Pioneers of the Nebraska Sandhills." In *Proceedings of the Fifth Midwest Prairie Conference*. Ames, Iowa: Iowa State University, 1976.

Ubelaker, Douglas H., and Walter R. Wedel. "Bird Bones, Burials and Bundles in Plains Archeology." *Plains Anthropologist* 40 (1975): 444-452.

Walker, James R. *Lakota Myth*. Edited by E. A. Jahner. Lincoln, Nebraska: University of Nebraska Press, 1983.

Warren, Gouverneur Kemble. *Preliminary Report of Explorations in Nebraska and Dakota, in the Years 1855-'56-'57*. Washington, D.C.: U.S. Army Corps of Topographical Engineers, 1875.

Welsch, Roger L. *Omaha Tribal Myths and Trickster Tales*. Chicago, Illinois: Swallow Press, 1981.

Weltfish, Gene. *The Lost Universe: Pawnee Life and Culture*. Lincoln, Nebraska: University of Nebraska, 1977.

Wildschut, William. *Crow Indian Medicine Bundles*. Edited by John C. Ewers. Contributions from the Museum of the American Indian, Vol. 17. 2nd ed.; New York, New York: Museum of the American Indian, 1975.

Wilhelm, Paul, Duke of Wurttemberg. *First Journey to North America in the Years 1822 to 1824*. Translated by William G. Bek. South Dakota Historical Collections, Vol. 19. Pierre, South Dakota: South Dakota State Historical Society, 1928.

Williams, Jacqueline B. *Wagon Wheel Kitchens: Food on the Oregon Trail*. Lawrence, Kansas: University Press of Kansas, 1993.

Willman, Lillian M. "The History of Fort Kearny." *Publications of the Nebraska State Historical Society* 21 (1930): 211-318.

Wilson, Gilbert Livingstone. *Hidatsa Eagle Trapping*. Anthropological Papers of the American Museum of Natural History, Vol. 30, Pt. 4. New York, New York: American Museum of Natural History, 1928.

Wislizenus, Frederick Adolf. *A Journey to the Rocky Mountains in the Year 1839*. Translated by Frederick A. Wislizenus, Esq. St. Louis, Missouri: Missouri Historical Society, 1912.

Wissler, Clark. *Ceremonial Bundles of the Blackfeet Indians*. Anthropological Papers of the American Museum of Natural History, Vol. 7, Pt. 2. New York, New York: American Museum of Natural History, 1912.

———. *Societies of the Plains Indians*. Anthropological Papers of the American Museum of Natural History, Vol. 11. New York, New York: American Museum of Natural History, 1916.

Wolcott, Robert H. "Record of Nebraska Ornithology." *Proceedings of the Nebraska Ornithologists' Union* 3 (1902): 93-105.

INDEX

Note: In Chapter Five, only bird families, bird species, bird varieties and counties have been indexed.

Allis, Samuel, 79
American Fur Company, 59, 68, 139
Anderson, William Marshall, 79
Anderson Lake, 124
Anhinga, 131
Arapaho tribe, 7
Arikara tribe, 34
Arkansas River, 50, 139
Art, 7, 47-48, 60, 63, 72-73, 76, 78, 88, 267
Ash Hollow, 78, 89, 91-92, 95, 135, 140, 142, 144, 147
Astor, John Jacob, 68, 139
Astor Party, 68
Atkinson, Col. Henry, 61
Atlantic Ocean, 82
Audubon, John James, 3, 60, 62, 81-83, 85-87, 100, 129, 131-132, 135, 140-141, 146, 267
Aughey, Samuel, 105, 130-131, 133-135, 142-143
Avocet, American, 90, 185

Badlands, 26, 91, 126, 137
Baird, Spencer Fullerton, 99-100, 102, 130, 132, 142
Bald Island, 100, 117, 141
Bazile Creek, 24
Bellevue, Nebraska, 10, 77-78, 83, 119-120, 139, 152-153
Bell, John R., 82, 85-86
Big Alkali Lake, 124
Big Buckboard Lake, 124
Big Blue River, 26, 81, 91
Big Nemaha River, 10, 99, 117
Big Sioux River, 10, 84-85, 119
Big Village of the Omaha, 10, 17
Bird family, 156-266

Accipitridae, 130-131, 170-175
Alaudidae, 216
Alcedinidae, 131, 209
Alcidae, 131
Anatidae, 130-131, 159-169
Anhingidae, 131
Apodidae, 131, 208
Ardeidae, 157-159
Bombycillidae, 131, 234
Caprimulgidae, 206-208
Cathartidae, 169-170
Certhiidae, 131, 226-227
Charadriidae, 130, 186-188
Ciconiidae, 131
Cinclidae, 131
Columbidae, 199-200
Corvidae, 131, 221-225
Cuculidae, 131, 202
Emberizidae, 130, 136, 236-265
Falconidae, 175-177
Fringillidae, 265-266
Gaviidae, 131, 156
Gruidae, 184-185
Hirundinidae, 131, 216-220
Laniidae, 234-235
Laridae, 130, 195-198
Mimidae, 232-233
Motacillidae, 131, 234
Muscicapidae, 130, 229-232
Paridae, 225-226
Pelecanidae, 156-157
Phalacrocoracidae, 131, 157
Phasianidae, 177-183

283

Picidae, 209-213
Podicipedidae, 131, 156
Psittacidae, 200-202
Ptilogonatidae, 131
Rallidae, 183-184
Recurvirostridae, 188
Scolopacidae, 130, 188-195
Sittidae, 226
Strigidae, 130-131, 202-206
Threskiornithidae, 131
Trochilidae, 208-209
Troglodytidae, 227-229
Tyrannidae, 130-131, 213-216
Tytonidae, 130-131, 202
Vireonidae, 235-236
Bird list, 32, 119, 130, 135-136, 140-142
Bird parts, 1, 7, 9, 13, 16-23, 25-36, 38-39, 41-48, 50, 52-57, 59-61, 63, 82, 88, 90, 100, 102, 105, 136-137, 140-141, 150, 267
Bird symbolism, 1, 7, 13, 16, 18-20, 22, 38-39, 41-45
Birdwood Creek, 103, 123
Bison, 9, 12-13, 15-17, 23, 28, 32, 35-36, 40, 43, 59, 68, 71, 76, 81, 91-92, 95, 106, 108, 114, 128
Bittern, American, 14, 49, 54, 67, 149, 157-158
Black Hills, 12, 26, 28, 31, 55, 97, 99-100, 106, 137, 150
Blackbird
    Brewer's, 136, 146, 262-263
    Red-winged, 49, 67, 77, 132, 145, 148-149, 258
    Rusty, 109, 149, 262
    Yellow-headed, 71, 83, 93, 135, 139, 145, 261-262, 267
Blackbird Hill, 74-77, 114, 116

Blair, Nebraska, 119
Blanchard, Jonathan, 96
Blue River, 62, 81, 88-89, 127, 142
Bluebird
    Eastern, 49, 132, 145, 148, 229-230
    Mountain, 150, 230
    Western, 105
Bobolink, 111, 147-149, 258
Bobwhite, Northern, 15, 36-37, 49, 54, 92, 106, 109, 132, 145, 147, 151, 182-183
Bodmer, Karl, 3, 73, 75-76, 78, 267
Bon Homme Island, 117
Bow Creek, 10
Brackenridge, Henry Marie, 68, 114, 139
Bradbury, John, 68
Brant, 25, 69, 111
Breeding, 1, 9, 41, 89, 93, 108, 129, 133-135, 137, 139-140, 143, 146-147, 149
Bridger's Pass, 100
Brownville, Nebraska, 119
Bryan, Lieutenant F. T., 100
Buffalo. *See* Bison
Bufflehead, 142, 152-153, 168
Bundle, 13, 37-38, 45-46
Bunting
    Indigo, 245
    Lark, 49, 55, 78, 132, 135, 140, 147-148, 250
    Lazuli, 146, 245
    Snow, 142, 146, 255
Burial, 27, 79, 103, 136, 144
Burlington Northern Railroad, 126
Butterfly, Monarch, 74

Cabanne's post, 22, 74, 152-153
California, 91, 93
Calumet Bluffs, 76
Cantonment Leavenworth, 72

Cantonment Misscuri, 61
Cardinal, Northern, 140, 244
Carleton, Maj. Gen. James Henry, 62, 88-90, 121-122
Carriker, Melbourne Armstrong, Jr., 125
Cary, William de la Montagne, 26
Cassin, John, 100
Catbird, Gray, 102, 142, 232-233
Catlin, George, 61, 72, 116
Cedar Canyon, 111
Ceremonial objects, 13-14, 16-23, 25, 28, 31, 34, 39, 42-46, 88, 136-137
Ceremony, 1, 7, 9, 13-14, 16-23, 25, 27, 29, 31, 34-35, 38-46, 88, 267
Chat, Yellow-breasted, 77, 132, 135, 140, 148, 243
Cheyenne tribe, 7
Chickadee, Black-capped, 29, 49, 55, 225
Chief Blackbird, 76
Chief Cheyenne, 38, 44
Chief Little Bow, 10
Chief Pipe-Chief, 44
Chief Pitalesharu, 34
Chief Red Cloud, 30-31
Chimney Rock, 90
Chrisman, Berna Hunter, 111-112
Clan, 7, 13, 15-16, 25, 41
Clark, John Hawkins, 95
Clark, Lt. William, 64, 67, 87, 113, 267
Claw Hammer Lake, 124
Clear Lake, 124
Clothing, 1, 7, 28, 34, 44, 76, 90
Cody, William "Buffalo Bill," 108, 123
Cody-North Ranch, 106, 108
Cody Lake. *See* Jefford Lake
Collins, Col. Caspar Wever, 102
Columbus, Ohio, 93
Columbia River, 68

Columbus California Industrial, Company, 93
Connecticut Audubon Society, 109
Continental Divide, 80
Cook, James, 30-31
Cooper, James Graham, 100
Coot, American, 147, 152, 183-184
Cormorant, Double-crested, 49, 55, 157
Cosmology, 34-35, 38-39, 45-46
Coues, Elliott, 104-105, 119, 130-133, 135, 142-143, 146
Council Bluff, 67, 69, 71, 74, 89, 113, 116, 135
Council Bluffs, Iowa, 92, 119
Cow Island, 114
Cowbird, Brown-headed, 49, 80, 83, 132, 148, 263-264
Crane
    Sandhill, 49, 55, 67, 71, 78, 82, 88, 108, 144, 146, 149, 152, 184-185, 268
    Whooping, 16, 49, 55, 185
Creeper, Brown, 135, 226-227
Crescent Lake National Wildlife Refuge, 124
Crow tribe, 48, 55
Crow, American, 132, 152, 223-224
Cuckoo
    Black-billed, 148, 202
    Yellow-billed, 202
Culbertson, Thaddeus Ainsworth, 96
Curlew
    Eskimo, 109, 134, 144, 146, 190-191
    Long-billed, 14, 49, 76, 78, 89, 132, 134, 139, 147-148, 151, 191-192
Custer, Gen. George Armstrong, 150

Dad's Lake, 124

Dakota tribe, 48-55
Dakota Territory, 97, 106, 119
Dance, 13, 22, 25, 27-31, 38, 41, 74
Decatur, Nebraska, 117
Decker, Peter, 93
Denver, Colorado, 101
Department of Dakota, 106
DeSmet, Fr. Pierre-Jean, S.J., 90-91
De Villasur, Lt. Col. Pedro, 60
Diamond Bar Lake, 103
Dickcissel, 148, 245-246
Dismal River, 27, 97, 103, 108-109, 122-123
Dove, Mourning, 50, 76, 102, 132, 140, 147, 151, 199
Dowitcher
    Long-billed, 135, 193-194
    Short-billed, 193
Dreidoppel, David, 73, 76-77
Drum, 37, 44
Duck
    American Black, 108, 149, 165
    Canvasback, 96, 102-103, 168
    Ring-necked, 152
    Ruddy, 169
    Wood, 14, 50, 67, 71, 77, 102, 132, 138, 140, 145, 151-152, 163-165
Dunbar, John Brown, 32, 34, 79
Dunlap, Kate, 96

Eagle
    Bald, 1, 19, 25, 36, 38-39, 50, 56-57, 63, 73, 83, 90, 132-133, 136, 139-140, 142, 145, 147, 171
    Golden, 18, 20-23, 25, 29, 31, 37, 42, 44, 50, 56-57, 137-138, 174-175, 267

Egret
    Great, 67, 158
    Snowy, 158-159
Elk, 15, 59, 81, 85, 106, 128
Elkhorn River, 10, 61, 71, 89, 97, 122
Ender's Lake, 124
Engineer Cantonment, 2, 26, 71, 114, 129-132, 135, 139
England, 82
Euro-Americans, 1, 2, 7, 10, 26, 60, 62-63, 110, 120, 128-129
Eustis, Captain, 90
Expedition, 1-2, 15, 22, 26-27, 48, 59-65, 67-69, 71-74, 76-78, 80-82, 85-90, 96-97, 99-100, 104, 106, 114, 116-117, 120, 122-123, 125, 129, 131-132, 134, 138-142, 146-150
Expedition list, 3, 96
Extinction, 4, 78, 145

Fairbury, Nebraska, 81
Falcon
    Peregrine, 133, 176
    Prairie, 133, 146, 150, 176-177
Finch
    Cassin's, 136, 142, 265
    Purple, 265
    Savannah, 83
Flicker, Northern, 25, 50, 132, 140, 145, 148, 150, 211-212
Flycatcher
    Great Crested, 140, 214-215
    Least, 135, 213-214
    Olive-sided, 213
    Scissor-tailed, 215-216
    Yellow-bellied, 213
    Willow, 105
Fontenelle's post, 152

Food, 1, 7, 9-10, 16, 23, 34, 36, 41, 69, 83, 88, 92-93, 95, 102-103, 105, 111-112, 142, 151-152
Fort Atkinson (Nebraska), 71, 83, 153
Fort Benton (Montana), 91
Fort Berthold (North Dakota), 47
Fort Calhoun, Nebraska, 71
Fort Clark (North Dakota), 76
Fort Davy Crockett (Colorado), 80
Fort Kearny (Nebraska), 78, 81, 91-93, 95, 97, 100-101, 120-121
Fort Laramie (Wyoming), 31, 79, 90-91, 97, 99, 102
Fort Lisa (Nebraska), 71
Fort Lookout (South Dakota), 99
Fort Leavenworth (Kansas), 69, 88-89, 96-97, 102
Fort McPherson (Nebraska), 103-104
Fort Pierre (South Dakota), 97, 99
Fort Randall (South Dakota), 86, 99, 104, 146
Fort Randall Military Reservation (South Dakota), 67, 86, 104, 146
Fort Riley (Kansas), 100
Fort Union (North Dakota), 81, 87, 96-97, 99
Fort Vermillion (South Dakota), 91
Frazier Lake, 124
Frémont, Lt. John Charles, 81, 87, 120
French, 12, 59-61, 63-64, 76, 80
Frenchman's Creek, 37
Fullerton, Nebraska, 135
Fur trader, 1, 2, 59-60, 62-63, 68, 79, 267

Gadwall, 149, 167
Gale, John, 61
Garden Creek, 146
Game laws, 112
Games, 23-24
Gentes. *See* Clan
German, 61-62, 71, 73-74, 96
Gilmore, Nebraska 109
Gnatcatcher, Blue-gray, 229
Godwit, Marbled, 147, 192
Goldeneye
    American, 152
    Common, 50-51, 55, 168
Goldfinch, American, 266
Goose
    Canada, 51, 54, 74, 86, 132, 140, 145, 149, 151-153, 160-162
    Snow, 51, 146, 151-153, 160-161
Goose Creek, 123
Gordon Creek, 60
Goshawk, Northern, 172
Grackle, Common, 109, 263
Grand Island, 93-95, 120
Grand Isle, 69
Grand Pawnee Village, 12, 32, 62, 79, 88, 121, 147
Great American Desert, 71, 149
Grebe
    Eared, 150, 156
    Western, 268
Green Bay, Wisconsin, 12
Green River, 80
Grinnell, George Bird, 103, 106, 108, 123, 130, 132, 144, 147, 149-150
Grosbeak
    Black-headed, 143, 245
    Blue, 146, 148, 245
    Evening, 150, 266
    Pine, 265
    Rose-breasted, 111, 244-245
Grouse
    Blue, 103
    Ruffed, 51, 137, 145, 150, 177
    Sage, 102, 147-148, 177

Sharp-tailed, 51, 91, 102,
  105-106, 111, 137,
  144, 146-147, 150,
  179-180
Gulf Coast, 82
Gull
  Franklin's, 141, 195-196
  Great Black-backed, 105,
    143, 196
  Herring, 143, 196
  Ring-billed, 196

Hackberry Lake, 124
Hair, 16, 27, 37
Hammond, W. A., 100
Hancock, Samuel, 92
Harrier, Northern, 38, 51, 133,
  147, 172
Harris, Edward, 62, 82-83, 85-87,
  129, 131-132, 140-141, 146
Hat Creek, 125
Hawk
  Broad-winged, 173
  Buteo, 173
  Cooper's, 51, 172
  Ferruginous, 133, 174
  Pigeon, 13, 51
  Fish, 83
  Red-shouldered, 51, 54,
    173
  Red-tailed, 51, 133, 138,
    152, 174
  Rough-legged, 133, 174
  Sharp-shinned, 51, 172
  Swainson's, 38, 133, 147,
    173
Hayden, Ferdinand Vandeveer, 2,
  15, 32, 48, 55, 97, 100,
  104, 117, 119-123, 126,
  130-131, 133, 135, 141,
  143, 147-149
Headdress, 22-23, 30-31, 33, 61,
  74, 88
Heron
  Black-crowned Night, 159
  Blue, 83

  Great Blue, 51, 55, 93,
    132, 158
  Green, 159
  Yellow-crowned Night,
    141, 159
Hidatsa tribe, 25
Horse River, 91
Homer, Nebraska, 10, 17, 136
Hudson's Bay Company, 59-60
Hummingbird, Ruby-throated,
  208-209

Independence, Missouri, 78-79
Indian agency, 10
Iowa (counties)
  Harrison, 186
  Pottawattamie, 181, 185,
    194
  Woodbury, 200, 223
Iowa tribe, 10, 73, 83,
Irving, John Treat, 26
Isle à Beau Soleil. *See* Sonora
  Island and Sun Island
Isle of Cedar, 64

Jackson Station, 109, 144
Jaeger, Pomarine, 105, 143, 195
James, Edwin, 26, 61
James River, 12, 77, 117, 119
Jay
  Blue, 14, 36, 51, 111, 137,
    142-143, 221
  Gray, 150
  Pinyon, 51, 55, 137
Jefferson, Thomas, 64
Jefford Lake, 103
Journal, 1-4, 12, 34, 48, 55, 60-64,
  67-69, 71-74, 76-83, 85-93,
  95-97, 99-103, 105-106,
  108-111, 113-114, 116-117,
  119-123, 125-126, 129-135,
  138-144, 146
Junco, Dark-eyed, 51, 55, 137,
  150, 254

Kansas, 36, 60, 69, 81, 100, 138-139
Kansas (counties)
    Atchison, 246
    Doniphan, 162, 165, 171, 181-182, 184, 208, 217, 244, 246
    Leavenworth, 182, 190
    Nemaha, 182, 190, 199, 246
Kansas Territory, 99
Kaskopa Creek. *See* Goose Creek
Kearny, Col. Stephen Watts, 89
Kestrel, American, 51, 132-133, 146, 175-176
Kilgore, William H., 95
Killdeer, 89, 108, 132, 134, 143, 147, 149, 152, 187
Kingbird
    Eastern, 51, 74, 132, 145, 215
    Western, 148, 150, 215
Kingfisher, Belted, 36, 39, 51, 54, 119, 131, 209
Kinglet
    Golden-crowned, 229
    Ruby-crowned, 229
Kiowa tribe, 7
Kite, American Swallow-tailed, 53-54, 63, 77, 133, 145, 170-171
Knot, Red, 192
Kurz, Rudolph Friederich, 62, 96, 120

Lahontan, Louis Armand de Lom d'Arce, Baron de, 59
Lake Cody, 123
Lake Dora, 124
Lake McConaughy, 69
Lakota tribe, 12, 26-29, 55
Language, 13-16, 18, 20, 25, 32, 39, 42, 44, 48-58
Laramie Peak, 102

Lark, Horned, 51, 105, 132, 150-151, 216
Lawrence, George Newbold, 100
Leach, A. J., 110-111
Legend, 1, 7, 9, 12-15, 19-21, 23, 26-29, 34-41, 110, 129, 136-138
Lewis, Capt. Meriwether, 64, 67, 87, 267
Lewis and Clark Expedition, 2, 10, 15, 61, 64-65, 67, 71, 87, 132, 138, 267
Lienhard, Johann Heinrich, 93
Lincoln, Nebraska, 126-127, 143-144
Lisa, Manuel, 68
Little Blue River, 89, 102, 120-121
Little Nemaha River, 93, 95
Little Salt Creek, 126
Little Sioux River, 10
Lodgepole Creek, 100
Lone Tree Prairie, 117
Loisel, Regis, 63-64
Long, Maj. Stephen Harriman, 61, 69-71, 87, 139
Longspur
    Chestnut-collared, 78-79, 135, 140, 255-256
    Lapland, 255
    McCown's, 109, 136, 149, 254
Loon, Common, 51, 55, 131, 136, 156
Louisiana Purchase, 2, 61-64
Loup Fork, 12, 34, 38, 60, 79, 81, 88, 97, 99-100, 109, 121-123, 147
Loup River, 12, 32, 45, 61, 88-89, 99, 104, 135, 139, 147
Ludlow, William, 106, 150

Mackay, James, 60, 63, 122
McKissock Island, 117
Maghee, Thomas G., 104, 123, 125

Magpie, Black-billed, 52, 71, 221-223
Magraw, W. M. F., 100
Mallard, 14, 18, 20, 52, 87, 102-103, 108, 132, 136, 149, 151-153, 165-166
Mallet, Paul, 60, 63
Mallet, Pierre, 60, 63
Mandan tribe, 17, 25, 34, 76
Marsh, Othniel Charles, 103-104, 148
Martin, Purple, 77, 89, 150, 217
Maximilian, Prince of Wied, 3, 10, 22, 61, 73-74, 76-78, 87, 96, 114, 116, 130-132, 135, 139-140, 267
Meadowlark
    Eastern, 86-87, 129, 143, 147-148, 259
    Western, 3, 62, 86-87, 102, 129, 132, 135, 141-143, 146-148, 259-261
Medicine Bow, 99
Merganser
    Common, 52, 152, 169
    Hooded, 142, 169
Merlin, 38, 147, 176
Middle Creek, 126
Middle Loup River, 99
Middle Marsh Lake, 124
Migration, 1, 4, 9, 25, 71, 77, 92, 133-135, 139, 142-143
Military equipment, 7, 17, 31, 35, 46, 60-61
Missionary, 79, 90-91
Mississippi River, 12, 59, 63, 82, 85
Missouri (counties)
    Atchison, 170, 230
    Holt, 160, 162, 200
    Platte, 181
Missouri River, 1-2, 4, 9-11, 14, 17, 22-26, 29, 37, 54, 59-65, 67-69, 71-74, 76-78, 80-83, 85, 87, 89-93, 96-97, 99-100, 104-105, 109-110, 113-119, 125, 127, 129, 132-135, 138-142, 144-146, 151-152, 267-268
Missouri River Commission, 104, 146
Missouria tribe, 26
Mitchell, John G., 103
Mockingbird, Northern, 233
Moon Lake, 124
Moorhen, Common, 183
Montana, 99
Moran Lake, 124
Mormon Trail, 92, 95
Mounds, 13, 15, 113
Mounted riflemen, 93
Mud Lake, 123

Nebraska City, Nebraska, 100, 141
Nebraska (counties)
    Adams, 179, 187, 190-191, 216
    Antelope, 110, 170, 179-180, 182, 190-192, 199, 207, 209-212, 215-217, 221, 223, 225, 230, 232-233, 252, 258-259, 265
    Boyd, 162-163, 172, 175, 181, 209, 246, 261
    Brown, 124
    Buffalo, 158, 185, 188, 191, 204, 225, 245, 252
    Burt, 10, 67, 156-157, 159, 165-166, 170, 178, 181, 185, 198-199, 215, 217, 220, 226, 232-233, 237, 239-240, 243-244, 253
    Cass, 157, 162, 165, 169, 181, 186, 196, 198, 201-202, 208, 210-211, 218, 224-225,

237-238, 240-241,
243, 254, 264
Cedar, 15, 157-158, 163,
170, 172-173, 176,
178-181, 185, 192-
194, 198-199, 203,
207-208, 211, 224-
225, 237, 246, 253,
259, 261
Cherry, 60, 99, 104, 125,
156, 160, 184-185,
209, 234, 244, 249,
265
Cheyenne, 177, 204, 213,
220-221
Clay, 121
Cuming, 191
Custer, 111-112
Dakota, 60, 63, 143, 156-
158, 161-163, 165-
166, 168, 170-171,
173-174, 176, 179-
187, 189-192, 194-
196, 198-199, 201-
203, 206-208, 210-
218, 220, 224-227,
229-242, 247, 249-
250, 252-253, 255,
258-259, 262-265
Dawson, 182, 204, 223,
254
Dixon, 85, 143, 157-158,
161-162, 165-168,
170-172, 175-176,
179-182, 184-185,
187-188, 190, 192-
196, 198-199, 202,
206, 208, 210-214,
216, 218, 220, 223-
226, 228, 230-233,
235, 237-238, 240-
242, 246-247, 250,
252-255, 258, 261-
262, 264-265

Dodge, 195, 202, 209, 212,
215, 236, 246, 249,
258
Douglas, 161-163, 166,
172, 177, 179, 181,
187, 189, 193-195,
199-200, 202, 208,
211, 215, 228, 230,
232-233, 236-238,
240, 243-244, 246-
247, 249, 264
Dundy, 224
Fillmore, 182
Franklin, 158, 182
Frontier, 182
Gage, 174, 182-183, 202,
245
Garden, 169-171, 199, 216,
220, 232, 249-250,
261, 266
Garfield, 110
Grant, 104, 108, 123, 124,
160, 162, 165-168,
184, 187-188, 193-
195, 254, 262-263
Hall, 158, 191, 204, 213,
216, 221, 245, 259,
261
Harlan, 183, 207, 215,
244, 246, 249, 254,
265
Hitchcock, 181
Holt, 184
Hooker, 108, 160, 162,
165-168, 184-185,
187-188, 193-195,
220, 254, 262-263
Jefferson, 88, 102, 167,
169, 179, 181-182,
186, 190-191, 194,
221, 225, 252, 255,
262
Johnson, 179, 182
Kearney, 179-180, 190,
199, 206-207, 223,
233, 261

Keith, 174, 188, 198, 204, 249
Kimball, 220
Knox, 72, 157, 161, 165, 170, 172, 179-182, 191, 195, 199-200, 204, 211-212, 214-215, 218, 220, 223, 225, 227-228, 233-234, 237, 243, 245-246, 259, 263, 266
Lancaster, 157, 159, 161-162, 165-166, 168, 176, 179, 183-184, 189-190, 192, 194-195, 198-200, 202-203, 206-207, 209-210, 214-217, 220, 225-227, 229-230, 232-236, 238-242, 246-247, 249, 253, 255, 258-259, 262-266
Lincoln, 120, 157, 159-160, 163, 165, 176-178, 188, 204, 214, 227, 234, 243, 250, 255, 262
Loup, 10
McPherson, 104, 124
Madison, 191
Merrick, 163, 179, 191, 194, 261
Morrill, 165, 167, 169, 188, 199, 255
Nance, 261
Nemaha, 68, 77-78, 157, 166, 171, 176, 181-182, 185, 188, 192-194, 200-203, 208-209, 212-215, 218, 221, 223-225, 228-230, 232, 234-236, 238, 240-247, 252, 254, 258, 261, 263-264, 266

Nuckolls, 121, 182, 186, 194, 233, 255
Otoe, 113, 117, 156-157, 159-160, 162-163, 165-166, 170-172, 178, 181-182, 185, 188, 192-195, 201-202, 206-207, 211-214, 218, 220-221, 224-225, 227-230, 232, 234, 237, 240-246, 252, 254, 264, 266
Phelps, 179
Pierce, 176, 187, 191, 198, 204
Platte, 109, 156, 161, 163, 173, 175, 177, 179, 182, 184-187, 189-194, 198, 202, 204, 206-207, 212-213, 215, 228, 230, 233, 238, 242-243, 245-246, 249-250, 252, 258-259, 261, 264
Red Willow, 181-182
Richardson, 113, 117, 140, 158-159, 162, 176-177, 181, 183, 186, 188, 193, 198-202, 209-212, 214-215, 217, 221, 225, 227, 231, 233-236, 239, 241-244, 246, 249, 253-254, 258, 262-264
Sarpy, 67, 109, 156-159, 161-163, 165-174, 176-178, 181, 183-188, 191-196, 198-199, 200, 202, 207-208, 217, 224, 226, 229-230, 237, 245, 247, 259, 264
Saunders, 39, 159

Scotts Bluff, 173, 192, 204, 258
Seward, 165, 185, 189, 192, 203
Sheridan, 99
Thayer, 163, 170, 179, 186, 194, 233, 255
Thurston, 114, 116, 156-159, 161-163, 165-166, 173, 181-182, 184, 194-195, 203, 206, 208, 210, 216, 218, 220, 224, 230, 232-233, 250, 252-253, 262
Washington, 71, 157-160, 162-163, 165-166, 168, 170-171, 173, 178-181, 184, 189-190, 194-196, 199-202, 206, 208-209, 211-212, 216-218, 223-225, 232-233, 237-238, 240, 243, 246-247, 249, 253-254, 258, 261, 264
Wayne, 165, 179-180, 186-187, 189-190, 192-193, 196, 199, 204
Webster, 261
Wheeler, 110
York, 191
Negro Lake, 124
Nemaha River, 26, 64, 88-89, 93, 101, 113, 127
Nest, 13, 25, 36, 41, 64, 73, 79, 89-90, 102-103, 108, 112
Nesting, 1-2, 4, 9, 25, 41, 74, 89, 92, 95-96, 102, 106, 108, 119, 133-135, 137, 140, 142-143, 147
New York, 82, 100
Nicollet, Joseph Nicolas, 10, 80
Nighthawk, Common, 14, 25, 52, 102, 132, 146, 148, 150, 206-207

Niobrara River, 10, 12, 24-26, 30, 60-61, 71-72, 76, 96-97, 99-100, 104, 117, 119, 123-125, 127, 137-138, 150-151
Nishnabotna River, 96
Nodaway Island, 64, 66, 73
Nodaway River, 68
North, Luther Hedden, 40, 108, 149
North Dakota, 99
North Marsh Lake, 124
North Platte, Nebraska, 103-104, 108
North Platte River, 69, 89-91, 93, 100, 102, 121, 123, 125, 142, 147, 150
Northwest Company, 59
Nutcracker, Clark's, 221
Nuthatch
    Pygmy, 143, 226
    Red-breasted, 226
    White-breasted, 226
Nuttall, Thomas, 68

Oak Creek, 126
Oglala tribe, 31, 33
Omaha, Nebraska, 2, 91, 103, 109, 144, 152
Omaha Creek, 10
Omaha tribe, 1, 7, 10, 12, 14-24, 32, 48-54, 59, 61, 67, 76-77, 114, 129, 131-132, 134, 136, 151, 267
Oregon Territory, 81, 92-93
Oregon Trail, 1, 62, 78, 92-93, 95, 101, 120-121, 146, 268
Oriole
    Baltimore, 77, 111, 264-265
    Bullock's, 264-265
    Northern, 140, 148, 264-265
    Orchard, 111, 148, 264
Osage River, 138
Osprey, 133, 170

Otoe tribe, 7, 10, 17, 26, 48, 50-54, 61
Otter Lake, 124
Ovenbird, 135, 241
Owl
    Barn, 130-131, 143, 202
    Barred, 20, 52, 54, 132, 204, 206
    Burrowing, 52, 76, 80, 88, 91, 96, 102, 132-133, 137, 139, 146-148, 204-205
    Eastern Screech-, 53, 133, 203
    Great Horned, 17, 20, 52, 133, 202-203
    Long-eared, 133, 143, 150, 206
    Northern Saw-whet, 139, 206
    Short-eared, 133, 206
    Snowy, 52, 133, 143, 146, 203

Pacific Fur Company, 68
Pahuk Hill, 36, 39-40
Papillion Creek, 10, 89
Parakeet, Carolina, 1, 27, 77-78, 83, 139, 141, 145, 200-202, 267
Parula, Northern, 135, 237
Pawnee tribe, 1, 7, 10, 12, 18-19, 21, 27, 32, 34-46, 48-55, 59-61, 63, 88, 121-122, 135, 137, 139, 147, 267
Peale, Titian Ramsay, 71
Pelican, American White, 14, 52, 54, 156-157
Perkins, Elisha Douglass, 92
Peru, Nebraska, 110, 117
Pewee
    Eastern Wood-, 213
    Western Wood-, 135, 148, 150, 213
Phalarope, Wilson's, 134, 149, 195
Pheasant, Ring-necked, 91
Philadelphia Academy of Sciences, 78
Philadelphia, Pennsylvania, 100
Phoebe
    Eastern, 214
    Say's, 214
Pigeon, Passenger, 52, 68, 76, 78, 132, 145, 152-153, 199-200
Pine Ridge, 26, 30, 106, 125-126, 137, 150
Pintail, Northern, 166
Pipe, 1, 17-20, 27, 31-32, 34, 36, 39, 43-45, 47, 56, 136-137
Pipit
    American, 142, 150, 234
    Sprague's, 141
Platte River, 2, 10, 12, 26, 32, 36, 39, 45, 54, 59-60, 62, 68-69, 72, 74, 78-81, 88-93, 95-97, 99-100, 102, 104, 106, 109, 113-115, 117, 119-122, 127-128, 132-135, 138-140, 144, 146-147, 268
Platte River Road, 81, 91, 120, 142, 146
Plover
    American Golden, 138, 146, 186
    Black-bellied, 186
    Mountain, 134, 147-148, 187-188
    Piping, 138, 141, 147, 186-187
    Semipalmated, 186
    Upland, 89, 106, 144
Pole Creek. *See* Lodgepole Creek
Ponca tribe, 7, 11-12, 24-25, 151
Ponca Creek, 29, 76, 117
Pony Lake, 124
Poorwill, Common, 52, 55, 135, 137, 207
Prairie-Chicken, Greater, 15, 32, 52, 54, 67, 76, 105-106, 112, 132, 138, 144-145, 147, 151, 177-179

Prairie wolf, 15, 81, 95

Rail
    Black, 183
    King, 183
    Virginia, 85, 141, 183
Rainwater Basin, 121, 157, 159, 161, 166, 172, 183, 198, 228, 261
Raven
    Chihuahuan, 224
    Common, 52, 132, 136, 146, 224-225
Red Deer Lake, 124
Redhead, 135, 143, 168
Redpoll, Common, 265
Redstart, American, 77, 135, 240-241
Reports. *See* Journal
Reservations, 1, 7, 26. *See also specific reservations*
Riggs, Stephen Return, 48
Robin, American, 52, 55, 77, 132, 147, 151, 232
Rocky Mountains, 68, 79-80, 82, 89, 100, 109, 139-140, 150
Rosy-Finch, Gray-crowned, 52, 55, 137, 143, 265
Round Lake, 124

St. Joseph, Missouri, 82, 93
St. Louis, Missouri, 17, 64, 67-68, 71, 80-82, 91, 96-97, 99, 141
Salt Basin, 126
Salt Creek, 34, 126
Sand Hills, 1, 12, 26, 59-60, 63, 97, 103-104, 106, 108, 122-124, 127-128, 133-134, 144, 148-150, 268
Sand Hills Bone Expedition, 27, 103, 148
Sandpiper
    Baird's, 108, 149, 193
    Buff-breasted, 193
    Least, 108, 147, 192-193
    Semipalmated, 108, 147, 192
    Solitary, 143, 149, 189
    Spotted, 134, 147, 189
    Upland, 76, 134, 146-147, 189-190
    White-rumped, 193
Sanford, Mary E. "Mollie" Dorsey, 100-101
Santee tribe, 1, 7, 12, 26, 29, 47-48, 117
Sapsucker, Yellow-bellied, 143, 210
Say, Thomas, 61, 69, 130, 139
Scaup, Lesser, 108, 149, 152, 168
Schick Lake, 103, 123
Scotts Bluff, 79-80, 100, 150
Shoveler, Northern, 152, 167
Shrike
    Loggerhead, 150, 234-235
    Northern, 146, 234
Sign language, 9, 48, 55-58
Sioux City, Iowa, 119
Sioux Nation, 7, 26-27, 30-31, 37, 48-55, 59, 80, 90, 103, 137, 150
Skidi tribe, 38, 40, 44-46
Smith, E. Willard, 80-81
Smithsonian Institution, 96, 100, 102, 142
Snake River, 60, 68, 97, 150
Snipe, Common, 14, 53-54, 109, 134, 147, 149, 151, 194
Snipe Lake, 124
Social status, 7, 17, 19
Societies, 9, 28
Society of Jesus, 90
Solitaire, Townsend's, 230
Song, 27-28, 40-41, 43-44, 74
    Bird, 27-28, 40, 74, 81, 86-88, 101, 141, 143
Sonora Island, 68, 114
Sora, 183
South Dakota, 86
South Dakota (counties)

Brule, 182
Charles Mix, 168
Clay, 171, 173, 181, 216-218, 224, 229, 231, 241, 250, 252-254
Gregory, 104, 172, 181, 199, 215, 217, 226, 240, 247, 253
Stanley, 215, 232, 240
Todd, 104, 161, 170, 172, 174-177, 179-180, 182-183, 188, 199, 203, 206-207, 209, 212, 215, 217, 220, 223-226, 233-234, 245, 247, 249, 255, 261, 263, 265
Union, 179, 200, 210-211, 218, 229, 240, 249, 252
Yankton, 182, 231, 241
South Loup River, 103, 123
South Marsh Lake, 124
South Pass, 89
South Platte River, 69, 80, 93, 95, 99-100, 121
Spanish, 60
Sparrow
American Tree, 105, 143, 146, 247
Baird's, 141
Chipping, 247
Clay-colored, 136, 141, 247, 249
Field, 249
Fox, 142, 252
Grasshopper, 146, 148, 250-252
Harris', 83, 135-136, 143, 146, 254
Henslow's, 99, 148, 252
Lark, 132, 141, 146, 148-149, 249
Lincoln's, 252-253
Savannah, 148, 250
Song, 111, 148, 252
Swamp, 253
Vesper, 147-148, 249
White-crowned, 143, 253
White-throated, 253
Species list, 2, 64, 71, 78, 87, 99, 131-136, 140-142
Specimen, 2, 68, 73, 77, 109, 119, 129, 139, 141-142
Steamboat
Antelope, 80
El Paso, 96
Genoa, 97
Omega, 82, 116
Yellowstone, 73
Sterns Creek, 151
Stilt, Black-necked, 53
Stuart, Robert, 68-69, 139
Sublette, William L., 79
Suckley, George, 102, 130, 132, 134, 142
Sun Island. *See* Sonora Island
Swallow
Bank, 67, 138, 145, 217-218
Barn, 53, 55, 86, 103, 144, 149, 220
Cliff, 64, 80, 89, 95-96, 119, 132, 145, 147, 150, 218-220
Green-backed, 83
Northern Rough-winged, 67, 83, 86, 119, 217
Tree, 217
Violet-green, 143, 150, 217
Swan, Trumpeter, 1, 60, 104, 108, 141, 144, 149, 159-160
Swenk, Myron Harmon, 110
Swift
Chimney, 143, 208
White-throated, 135

Tabeau, Pierre Antoine, 2, 61, 63-64, 138
Tanager
Scarlet, 71, 74, 244

Summer, 143, 243
Western, 150, 244
Teal
Blue-winged, 14, 53, 102, 108, 132, 137, 142, 149, 151, 166-167
Cinnamon, 142, 167
Green-winged, 102, 165
Tern
Arctic, 143, 196
Black, 143, 148, 198
Common, 140, 196
Forster's, 143, 196
Least, 67, 72, 141-142, 147-148, 196-198
Teton tribe. *See* Lakota
Thrasher, Brown, 102, 142, 148, 233
Thrush
Gray-cheeked, 136, 231
Hermit, 143, 231
Swainson's, 231
Wood, 111, 232
Thunderbird, 13, 25, 27-29, 31, 37
Titmouse, Tufted, 105, 226
Tobacco, 38
Tool, 17, 130, 152
Tower, 119, 146
Towhee, Rufous-sided, 53, 55, 73, 77, 132, 137, 141, 142, 246-247
Townsend, John Kirk, 78, 82, 140
Trade, 17, 19-20, 32, 34, 59, 64, 91, 137
Trout Lake, 124
Turkey, Wild, 15, 53, 57, 68, 76, 78, 81, 83, 87, 91-92, 111, 132, 138, 145, 147, 151-153, 180-182

Union Pacific Railroad, 109
United States Army, 79, 100, 129, 146
United States Army Engineer Department, 106
United States Army Medical Corps, 102
United States Army Topographic Engineers, 69, 100, 104, 119
United States Entomological Commission, 105
United States War Department, 100
University of Nebraska-Lincoln, 142, 144

Valentine National Wildlife Refuge, 124
Valentine, Nebraska, 104
Veery, 231
Vermillion River, 12, 67, 86, 96, 100, 116, 119
Victoria Creek, 111
Village, 1, 10, 19, 26, 32, 35, 38, 60, 63, 67, 77, 90, 114, 122, 135-136, 139, 151
Vireo
Bell's, 85, 141, 235
Philadelphia, 236
Red-eyed, 236
Solitary, 150, 235
Warbling, 104, 235-236
White-eyed, 235
Yellow-throated, 235
Vision quest, 25
Vulture, Turkey, 53, 74, 89, 132-133, 139, 146, 169-170

Walker Gilmore Site, 151
War decorations, 21-22
Warbler
Bay-breasted, 239
Black-and-white, 240
Black-throated Blue, 238
Black-throated Green, 239
Blackburnian, 239
Blackpoll, 135, 239-240
Blue-winged, 139, 145, 236
Canada, 243

Cerulean, 240
Chestnut-sided, 238
Golden-winged, 236
Hooded, 243
Kentucky, 242
MacGillivray's, 136, 242
Magnolia, 135, 238
Mourning, 143, 242
Nashville, 142-143, 237
Orange-crowned, 135, 237
Palm, 239
Philadelphia, 143
Pine, 239
Prairie, 143, 239
Prothonotary, 135, 142, 241
Tennessee, 236
Virginia's, 105, 143
Wilson's, 243
Worm-eating, 241
Yellow, 53, 77, 135, 145, 148, 237-238
Yellow-rumped, 135, 238
Yellow-throated, 239
Warren Expedition, 48, 99-100, 104, 116, 120, 125, 130, 132, 141, 146-148, 150
Warren, Maj. Gen. Gouverneur Kemble, 12, 97, 100, 117, 122, 131, 149
Waterthrush
Louisiana, 242
Northern, 135, 145, 241-242
Watt's Lake, 124
Waxwing
Bohemian, 143, 234
Cedar, 141, 234
Weeping Water Bottom, 117
Weeping Water Creek, 74
Weston, Missouri, 81
Whimbrel, 191
Whip-poor-will, 14, 53, 74, 76-77, 88, 132, 138, 208
Whistle, 19, 25, 27-28, 31, 47-48, 57, 137

White Bear Bluffs, 76
Whitewater Lake, 124
Wigeon, American, 168
Wildcat Hills, 125-126, 150
Wilhelm, Paul, Duke of Wurttemberg, 17, 35, 48, 61, 71-72
Williams, Rev. Joseph, 81
Willman, William, 120
Winnebago tribe, 7, 10-11, 13-14, 49-51, 53
Wislizenus, Frederick Adolph, 80
Wolf Lake, 124
Woodcock, American, 14, 53, 109, 134, 147, 151, 194
Woodhams, William H., 96
Woodpecker
Downy, 111, 210-211
Hairy, 54, 105, 111, 211
Ivory-billed, 17, 63, 136, 212-213
Lewis', 150, 209
Pileated, 17, 20, 27, 54, 136, 212
Red-bellied, 132, 140, 210
Red-headed, 32, 36, 54, 111, 132, 140, 209-210
Wood-Pewee. *See* Pewee
Wren
Bewick's, 227
Carolina, 227
House, 67, 77, 83, 132, 140, 148, 227-228
Marsh, 149, 228-229
Rock, 55, 143, 227
Sedge, 147-148, 228
Winter, 140, 228
Wyoming (counties)
Goshen, 161, 163, 234
Laramie, 177, 217

Yale University, 103-104
Yankton, South Dakota, 119
Yankton tribe, 12, 26, 47

Yellowlegs
 Greater, 188-189
 Lesser, 189
Yellowstone River, 81
Yellowthroat, Common, 135, 140, 148, 242

James E. "Jim" Ducey is a fifth generation Nebraskan. He earned his B.S. from the University of Nebraska-Lincoln in 1979 and his Masters in Biology from the University of Nebraska at Omaha in 1984. Ducey served as president of the Audubon Society of Omaha and as chairman of the Nebraska Audubon Council. His field research currently focuses on bird distribution in the Nebraska Sand Hills, as well as wetlands and land conservation. He remains a strong advocate for conservation and preservation of Nebraska's wetlands and environmental heritage.

Jim has written *Nebraska Birds: Breeding Status and Distribution* (1988) and numerous articles that have appeared in publications such as the *Magazine of the Midlands*, *Nebraskaland* and the *Nebraska Bird Review*. He actively has sought opportunities to share his research through the development of an online database focusing on the historical heritage of the Sand Hills. He also has created an internet site that contains resources on ancient avifaunas and bird records of North America from 40,000 B.C. to A.D. 1750. It is sponsored by the Birdnet site maintained at the Smithsonian Institute.

Biography by M.E. Ducey
Photograph by Diane Gonzolas

MAIL ORDER FORM

Please send the following to the address below (**PRINT CLEARLY**):
Name _____
Street/Box _____
City _____ State _____ Zip Code _____

QUANTITY	TITLE	TOTAL
_____	Robert E. Adwers, ***Rudder, Stick and Throttle: Research and Reminiscences on Flying in Nebraska*** (458 pp; ISBN 0-9631699-4-7) $25.00	_____
_____	Jerry E. Clark, ***Anson to Zuber: Iowa Boys in the Major Leagues*** (234 pp; ISBN 0-9631699-1-2) $20.00	_____
_____	Jerry E. Clark and Martha E. Webb, ***Alexander the Great: The Story of Grover Cleveland Alexander*** (60 pp; ISBN 0-9631699-2-0) $11.00	_____
_____	James E. Ducey, ***Birds of the Untamed West: The History of Birdlife in Nebraska, 1750 to 1875*** (311 pp; ISBN 0-9631699-5-5) $25.00	_____
_____	Joyce M. Lierley, ***Affectionately Yours: Three English Immigrants, the American Civil War, and a Michigan Family Saga*** (419 pp; ISBN 0-9631699-8-X) $22.50	_____
_____	Allen Shepherd, *et al.* (eds.), ***Man of Many Frontiers: The Diaries of "Billy the Bear" Iaeger*** (553 pp; ISBN 0-9631699-3-9) $25.00	_____
_____	Martha E. Webb, ***How to Clean, Repair, Store and Display Your Heirloom Papers and Photographs*** (70 pp; ISBN 0-9631699-9-8) $14.00	_____

SUBTOTAL $ _____

NE residents add 6.5% **SALES TAX** _____
(unless providing tax number)
Add $3.00 **SHIPPING** for your first copy
and $1.75 each additional copy _____

TOTAL BALANCE enclosed (U.S. funds only) $ _____

--OVER--

Mail order and check or money order (payable: *Making History*) to:
Making History, 2415 N. 56th Street, Omaha, Nebraska 68104.

Wholesale discounts available; call 402-551-0747 for information.